# The English Constitution

Manchester University Press

# About the author

W. Elliot Bulmer was educated at the Universities of Edinburgh and Glasgow. His career has included service as a Logistics Officer in the Royal Navy, Research Director of the Scottish Constitutional Commission, and Lecturer in Politics at the University of Dundee. He has spent many years working as a constitutional advisor for the International Institute for Democracy and Electoral Assistance, a non-partisan intergovernmental pro-democracy organisation.

All views expressed in this book are the author's opinions and do not necessarily reflect the views of any organisation with which he is affiliated.

# The English Constitution

## Refoundation, restoration, and reform

## W. Elliot Bulmer

MANCHESTER UNIVERSITY PRESS

The right of W. Elliot Bulmer to be identified as the author of this work has been
asserted in accordance with the Copyright, Designs and Patents Act 1988.

Published by Manchester University Press
Oxford Road, Manchester, M13 9PL

www.manchesteruniversitypress.co.uk

British Library Cataloguing-in-Publication Data
A catalogue record for this book is available from the British Library


ISBN    978 1 5261 9003 1    hardback
ISBN    978 1 5261 9002 4    paperback

First published 2025

The publisher has no responsibility for the persistence or accuracy of URLs for
any external or third-party internet websites referred to in this book, and does not
guarantee that any content on such websites is, or will remain, accurate or appropriate.

EU authorised representative for GPSR:
Easy Access System Europe, Mustamäe tee 50, 10621 Tallinn, Estonia
gpsr.requests@easproject.com

Typeset in Garamond
by R. J. Footring Ltd, Derby, UK

# Contents

Then said I unto them, Ye see the distress that we are in, how Jerusalem lieth waste, and the gates thereof are burned with fire: come, and let us build up the wall of Jerusalem, that we be no more a reproach.

(Nehemiah 2: 17)

Parliaments in former Times esteem'd it as their most incumbent temporal Duty, to oversee, recognize, and restrain, within the Bounds of Law, the Commands and Acts of Kings; and to take care that that great and honourable Trust reposed in the Hands of the Prince, for the Good of the People, might be rightly and duly administered, and not perverted or abused to the Invasion of their Rights, or the Subversion of the Constitution.

(*Lex Parliamentaria*, 1690)

# Foreword

## Alexandra Hall Hall

The United Kingdom is one of only a handful of countries in the world without a written constitution. In many ways, it is understandable why the British have never felt the need for one. Our history has largely been one of stability, peaceful adaptation, and growth. We have prided ourselves on avoiding the extremes of fascism or communism or, indeed, most '–isms' that have roiled other countries. We 'won' the war and played a constructive role in establishing the major post-war international institutions.

Unlike some colonial powers, we, the British, largely, gracefully accepted the end of our Empire. We have helped other countries rebuild after coups or violent insurrections, but have been spared such extreme turbulence at home. The significant exception in living memory – the conflict in Northern Ireland – was resolved peacefully through the Good Friday Agreement – affording us even more grounds for the belief that our system has served us well.

The great institutions of state – the monarchy, Houses of Parliament, courts of law, professional Civil Service – have been capable of moderate adaptations over time. We have been able to devolve some powers to Scotland, Northern Ireland, and Wales, while preserving our overall union. We have been able to introduce major new institutions – such as the National Health Service – and adopt many enlightened laws, even on sensitive matters such as abortion, gay rights, and equality, without major controversy. We have avoided the extreme culture wars that have polarised societies in other countries. We have prided ourselves on being citizens of a country founded on decency, integrity, toleration, moderation, and common sense, leavened with the famous British senses of 'fair play' and humour. Given this record, why would we feel any need for change?

But pride can become exceptionalism. Exceptionalism can become complacency. Complacency can become apathy. Apathy can become neglect. And neglect can become corrosion. That something has worked well in the past is no guarantee that it will continue to work well into the future.

I believe there is now a yawning gap between our fondly held image of ourselves and the actual reality. The United Kingdom is in a state of decay. The institutions which once worked for us are no longer fit for purpose. The compact of trust between leaders and citizens has broken down. Our economy is struggling, our infrastructure is crumbling, our public services are threadbare.

Our very Union is under strain. The core values which once underpinned our society are no longer respected. The unwritten conventions which once guided our leaders are no longer observed. Our unwritten constitution, once regarded as a source of our strength, has now been exposed as a weakness.

I draw on my experience as a diplomat to reach this conclusion. For most of my career, beyond the essential services of visa and consular work, the core strategic objectives of the Foreign Office were defined as being to promote security, prosperity and good governance. The last was often derided, with many arguing we should not be wasting our time on such a nebulous, 'airy-fairy' concept, at the expense of the more tangible goals of security and prosperity. Yet we always understood that good governance was the foundation on which the other objectives were built.

Good governance was not a distraction from achieving economic growth, or enhancing our security, but a necessary precondition. A country which was 'badly' governed was more likely to be corrupt, and, for instance, to award business contracts on the basis not of merit, but of cronyism and paybacks; it was more likely to turn a blind eye to abuses by government officials, to mistreatment of minorities, or to neglect of certain communities, exacerbating inequality and instability; it was more likely to pursue grandiose or wasteful schemes to glorify its leaders, to enrich its privileged elites, or to distract from other pressing problems; it was more likely to base policy decisions on flawed information or bad advice; it was more likely to have difficulty sustaining good relations or resolving disputes peacefully with neighbouring states.

Unfortunately, many of the examples of bad governance and features of failing societies which I have witnessed overseas I now see in evidence at home. The United Kingdom remains a democracy, but is no longer a well governed one.

\* \* \* \* \*

For constitutional experts like Dr Bulmer, the flaws in our system have been apparent for a long time. He rues the 'constitutional vandalism' of successive Conservative-led governments, and the 'constitutional complacency' of successive Labour governments. For me, while I was always aware that our system was not perfect, the penny fully dropped only during Brexit. It was not that I thought Brexit was illegal or immoral, though I certainly thought it was unwise. It was the *way* in which Brexit was delivered which set off my alarm bells. Brexit was launched purely as a way for the ruling Conservative Party to manage its internal divisions, without regard for the greater good. It was driven forward without its backers ever fully understanding or honestly explaining its implications. There was no attempt to forge any national consensus on what kind of Brexit we should aim for, or an agreed plan on how to deliver it. Opponents were derided as 'enemies of the people', their concerns swept aside. Even now, the government remains in denial about the costs of Brexit, and looks for scapegoats to blame.

Brexit exposed the extent to which our political system was failing. It exposed that our system has no checks and balances against an over-reaching executive. It exposed that our parliamentary conventions can be breached with impunity. It exposed that governments can lie to the public and suppress inconvenient analysis or scrutiny of its actions. It exposed that governments can concentrate vast legislative powers in themselves, exploiting so-called 'Henry VIII' powers. It exposed that our government, relying on a skewed parliamentary majority, can ride roughshod over the views of a significant minority, on a matter of huge political and economic significance, and blatantly ignore the express will of the devolved nations. With Brexit, the lingering façade of good governance in the United Kingdom was destroyed. All governments tend to run out of steam after years in office. Many governments make honest mistakes. But what the years before and after the Brexit referendum demonstrated is that we have no proper guardrails to protect us against a government which is determined *wilfully* to abuse its powers and exceed its authority. The 'good chap' theory of British government, if it ever truly existed, is definitely dead now.

As a former diplomat, the contrast between the ideals our politicians have promoted overseas and their behaviour at home has simply become too extreme to ignore. As Dr Bulmer writes, 'In terms of politics and government, we look more and more like the countries we used to laugh at'.

The United Kingdom urgently needs the same form of constitutional renewal that we have encouraged abroad. It will not be enough merely to change the government, or the people who lead it. We should not have to rely purely upon the honour and integrity of individual politicians, or their willingness to act with self-restraint, for a high quality of government. Further piecemeal reforms will not be sufficient to address the problems. We have to put stronger guardrails in place. We need a proper constitution.

\* \* \* \* \*

This is why Dr Bulmer's book resonates so strongly with me. In it, he brilliantly sets out how we came to this pass, argues the case for why a written constitution is essential for our democratic renewal, and explains the process by which one might be constructed.

What distinguishes Dr Bulmer from other constitutional experts is his novel suggestion that the United Kingdom's new settlement should be based on a restructuring of the very Union itself. He notes that while Scotland and Wales have a very clearly defined sense of their national identities, English identity has been largely subsumed within a broader British identity, and that English nationalism has frequently been regarded as something rather shameful and embarrassing – typified by the caricature of the xenophobic, narrow-minded 'little Englander'. England's large size relative to Scotland, Ireland, and Wales creates a fundamental imbalance. As he writes, the inherent problem of the Union is that Scotland – and large parts of Wales too – 'will accept no master, while England will accept no equal'.

Dr Bulmer believes that rather than trying forever to suppress English nationhood, it is time to set it free, by letting Scotland and Wales have as much autonomy as they want and giving England its own constitution. A 'willingness to *let go* ... is vital to the cultural, as well as to the political and economic, health of England'. Though I have always felt a strong attachment to the Union, I found myself nodding in agreement, and feeling an exciting sense of possibility in his novel approach.

The final genius of his book is that it does not just explain *why* a written constitution has become essential, or the *how* – the procedural mechanisms by which a constitution might be drawn up and adopted – or the *'who'* – for the English – but also the *'what'* – exactly what an actual English constitution might look like. This is not to be prescriptive, but to help ground abstract concepts in a tangible form to which the 'constitutionally illiterate' English can relate. The aim is to avoid the mistake that was made with Brexit – launching a grand scheme, but with no concrete vision of where we might land.

Yet, despite his bold ideas, Dr Bulmer is no radical. He writes as someone who appreciates and admires many aspects of our unwritten constitution and heritage, with all its quirks and eccentricities. His recommendations are for a constitution which both conservatives and progressives, traditionalists and modernisers, should be able to embrace, drawing on the old, but embracing the new. This is a book written not out of rejection or distaste for England, but out of deep affection for it.

* * * * *

A constitution along the lines which Dr Bulmer proposes is nothing to be afraid of. It is an opportunity for renewal and growth. The very process of discussing and drafting a constitution should enable a healthy national debate about what kind of country we wish to be, what values we espouse, and in what direction we wish to head. It will allow us to reflect on what elements of our tradition, history, and institutions we wish to preserve, and which elements have become outdated, or no longer fit for purpose. The process is almost as important as the final result. Nor does a new constitution need to involve a wholesale rejection of our past. It is about equipping us better to face the future. It encourages us to drop our sense of English exceptionalism, and accept we may have some things to learn from other countries. Rather than resting on the laurels of what we once were, it encourages us to consider how we might become better.

Dr Bulmer elegantly compares the advantages of a written constitution to an unwritten one by using the analogy of a bowl and a colander: both get wet, but only one holds any water. While reading his book, another analogy sprang to my mind. The political arrangement we have now is like a much loved, but old sweater, with threadbare elbows and fraying edges, which has become shapeless and baggy, and no longer fits. It has reached the end of its useful life. Patching it up is no longer sufficient. If we pull on just one loose strand of wool, the sweater will unravel further.

Yet, it is hard to throw away such a cherished item. Instead, we can try to reknit it, to produce a better-fitting, longer-lasting, stronger design, by incorporating some new material into the strongest strands of the original wool. A good constitution, like a good sweater, should feel familiar and comfortable, be sufficiently resilient to withstand ordinary wear and tear, but also sufficiently flexible to be able to accommodate changing times and needs.

Dr Bulmer brilliantly and eloquently sets out in this book why it is time for the United Kingdom to reknit its own constitutional sweater. It is beautifully written, highly readable, and extremely persuasive. I strongly commend it to all who care about the future of our country.

## Note

Alexandra Hall Hall is the former UK ambassador to the Republic of Georgia and former lead envoy for Brexit at the British embassy in Washington, DC. She is now a writer at *Byline Times* and a member of the Commission on Political Power, looking at constitutional reform in the UK.

The comments made in this Foreword do not imply agreement with every point or argument made in the book.

# Acknowledgements

I particularly wish to thank:

- John Drummond, Sumit Bisarya, Prof. Tom Ginsburg, and Dr Asanga Welikala for their many years of encouragement, mentoring, professional advice, and friendship;
- Alexandra Hall Hall for writing the most excellent Foreword;
- Robert Byron of Manchester University Press for quickly seeing the merit of this work and supporting its publication;
- Dr Mark Sammut Sassi for his editing of early drafts;
- Ralph Footring for meticulous copy-editing;
- B. Thomas Hall, retired procedural clerk of the House of Commons of Canada, for many invaluable small revisions to the text;
- Prof. Peter Edge, Dr Benjamin Lewis, Dr John Stanton, Timothy Kingston-Hepner, Dr Peter Reid, Dr John Ritzema, Revd. Laurence Price, and several other people who have given helpful feedback;
- Above all, my wife Eva Dominguez, for keeping the home fires burning and allowing me time to write when I should have been doing all the things.

The planning and research for this book were undertaken in 2020–2021, during which time I was Lecturer in Politics at the University of Dundee. It was written while I was working as a constitutional advisor for the International Institute for Democracy and Electoral Assistance, first in Sudan (2021–2022) and then in the Netherlands (2023–2024). I am grateful to both institutions, and to my colleagues.

All quotations from copyrighted works are believed to fall under 'fair dealing'.

# Introduction

## (a) The constitution and the English question

England is in many ways a fine country. There is still much about it to love and admire. England has, however, been let down by decades of corrupt, incompetent, short-sighted, and careless government. The symptoms of mis-government can be seen in England's economic record, its social problems, its crumbling infrastructure, and overstretched public services. The inability of the state to act in the interests of ordinary people, or to shield and protect strug-gling families at a time of severe economic crisis, is causing pain and suffering in millions of households. Nearly one child in three is living in poverty.[1] More than two million people have relied upon foodbanks.[2] Untreated sewage is being poured into the rivers and onto the beaches.[3] Unsustainably high energy prices – caused largely by privatisation, deregulation, and a lack of public invest-ment in energy generation, storage, and network capacity – place an unbearable burden upon the economy.[4] For the majority of people, quality of life has declined since the financial crisis of 2008.[5] Outside the Customs Union and the Single Market, England is isolated from its European neighbours, under a self-imposed economic blockade that continues to cripple trade.[6] The country is not living up to its potential.

Moreover, England is not at peace with itself. We have witnessed the populist polarisation of politics, the collapse of standards of conduct in public life, and the explosion of high-level corruption. To contain this powder keg of fear and anger, arising in response to a system that has let people down, draconian measures were enacted to prevent protest. Human rights, the judiciary, and the rule of law came under sustained attack, not only from the right-wing tabloid press, but also from Cabinet ministers. In terms of politics and government, we look more and more like the countries we used to laugh at. As one commentator put it in the summer of 2022, Italians seemed to be getting out the popcorn, finding our political chaos more gripping and dramatic than their own. Any reprieve offered by the Labour Party's electoral victory in 2024 was very short-lived.

Every country is only as good as its government. The world is full of countries boasting of great histories, vibrant cultures, fine cuisines, beautiful landscapes, and charming people, but which are reduced to poverty, squalor, violence, and misery by bad government. The health, prosperity, and well-being of ordinary people are determined not by the natural advantages or resources of their country, but by the extent to which the state governing them is willing and able to serve the common good. Where the common good prevails – where, that is, a robust democratic state enables public interests to be inclusively discerned and responsibly applied – the people flourish. Where public interests are choked by concentrations of private power, or distorted by corruption, injustice, tyranny, incompetence, or any other form of misrule, the people suffer.

If there seems to be one reliable rule in the field of democracy and development, it is that improvements in the quality of democracy reliably improve just about every measure of social and economic well-being. That rule holds true at just about every level of economic development. The point is not necessarily that democracy promotes growth, but that it is more effective than authoritarianism at turning wealth into well-being. High-income countries that are strongly democratic perform better across a range of quality-of-life indicators than high-income countries that are weakly democratic, or not democratic at all. Low-income countries that are functioning democracies do better, in terms of their development, service delivery, and outcomes, than low-income countries under authoritarian rule. Autocracies fare much worse than democracies on policy coordination, efficient use of resources, and anti-corruption policies.[7] The problem is not only that governments become 'dumber' (that is, less able to make wise policy choices in the public interest) as the quality of democracy declines; it is also a matter of purposeful intent, since undemocratic regimes 'are not there to govern a country well, they are there to milk a country'.[8]

The failure of England – as a nation, an economy, and a society – to live up to its potential should therefore spur us to consider the weakness of English democracy. As currently established, the state often fails – sometimes spectacularly fails – to serve the common good. Restoring England's hope for the future, its prosperity, and its quality of life must begin, then, with the improvement of English democracy.

Democracy must not be understood in theoretically absolute terms, as the people actually *ruling*. That would be impossible: how can millions of people collectively decide every little aspect of policy? Neither should it merely be reduced to having an elected government, which can be a cloak for authoritarian populism and 'elective dictatorship'. Rather, democracy is a complex institutional structure which establishes a form of representative, responsible, and rule-bound 'public government'. The people do not rule directly, but public institutions are required to be responsive, and responsible, to the public. Defined in this way, 'democracy' is really just a convenient term for what the fifteenth-century Florentine political theorist, historian, and statesman Francesco Guicciardini called a 'governo largo' – a wide, open, broad-based government, in which power is broadly shared and publicly accountable, so that public life is centred upon public needs.[9] It is system of government not only *by* and *of* the people, but also *for* the people. This can be contrasted with what Guicciardini called a 'governo stretto' – a narrow, restricted, closed, private, self-seeking, public-ignoring state.

The chronic institutional dysfunction of Westminster and Whitehall is exhaustively described works such as *The Blunders of Our Governments* by Anthony King and Ivor Crewe,[10] Ian Dunt's *How Westminster Works ... and Why It Doesn't*,[11] and Rory Stewart's first-hand account of high office, *Politics on the Edge*.[12] These show that the British state was badly governed for a long time before Brexit and Boris, and has suffered from much the same maladies under Labour as under the Conservatives. After the Brexit referendum, however, things went from bad to worse. We witnessed a divided ruling party, an embarrassingly rapid turnover of Prime Ministers, crapshoot decision-making, a breakdown in relations between Whitehall and the devolved nations, and – under Boris Johnson in particular – an ethical collapse at the highest levels, and corruption, incompetence, misgovernment, and misbehaviour on an unprecedented – perhaps previously unimaginable – scale. The state of public life had not looked so bad since the days of 'Old Corruption'.[13]

If it were only a matter of specific individuals, or of one party, the problem could easily be fixed by means of a resignation or a general election. Many Labour supporters thought that all would be put to rights after the Tories lost the 2024 general election. But the country has been let down not only by this Government or that Government, by this party or that Prime Minister. It is the *system of government*, the *stretto* constitutional order as a whole, that has failed us. It has become obvious, in a way that it was not so discernible before, that we live in an ill-constituted, or rather un-constituted, state. There is no foundation of 'common right, freedom and safety' (to quote from the 1649 'Agreement of the People')[14] on which to base the exercise of public power. Everything looks and feels unsettled, shaky, and fragile – as if it is held together, if it all, only by cobwebs, bluster, and desperation.

On the other side of politics, many read the laments on the condition of England in the popular right-wing press, and imagine it to be all the fault of town planners, European Commissioners, London media lovies, left-wing Labour councillors, and the so-called 'Blob'. They, too, are mistaken. The problem lies in the nature of the British state itself, and specifically in a constitutional arrangement that has failed to secure government in the public interest.

It is difficult to see how, even under good leadership, we can recover from the current crisis without structural and cultural change to the constitutional and political system whose breakdown has brought us to this place. See it or not, constitutional renovation has become a precondition for the restoration of the legitimacy, credibility, authority, and moral integrity of the state, as well as for the health, well-being, and prosperity of the people. The words of the eighteenth-century democrat Thomas Paine are more relevant now than they have ever been:

> For want of a constitution in England to restrain and regulate the wild impulse of power, many of the laws are irrational and tyrannical, and the administration of them vague and problematical.[15]

To achieve that constitutional renovation, it is necessary to bring together two conversations. The first is a conversation about the British constitution – its long decline and precipitous disintegration, and the prospects for its restoration and reform. The second is a conversation about the condition of England, English national identity, and the revival of English nationalism in healthy, civic, and democratic – and therefore constitutional – ways.

These two conversations cannot take place in isolation from one another. The renewal and restoration of England, as a place and as an idea, is inseparable from the constitutional renewal and restoration of the English state. The inability of the British political class to answer the 'English question' has hindered attempts to find a coherent and credible settlement to overcome the United Kingdom's constitutional malaise.

Meanwhile, that constitutional malaise is itself a cause of many of England's economic, political, social, and cultural woes. There can be no solution to the constitutional question which does not also resolve the English question, and there can be no solution to the English question which does not also resolve the constitutional question.

In response to that need, this book proposes both a constitutional solution to the English question and an English solution to the constitutional question. It offers a solution to England's profound and persistent crisis of politics and governance that puts constitutional refoundation at its heart.[16] It also offers a solution to the United Kingdom's constitutional problems that starts by taking seriously England's status as a nation. The book demonstrates, in practical terms, how such a solution might be expressed in a written constitution for a renewed England in a very different type of United Kingdom, one which fills the 'English gap' left by the Blair reforms of the 1990s.

In doing so, it seeks to address two audiences, in the hope of building some common ground between them. The first group are those in England who want to reform the British constitution, but who do not acknowledge, or have much sympathy for, England's claims as a political nation – or who are still committed to the maintenance of the United Kingdom at all costs. The second group are those interested in an English revival, but who do not understand, or perhaps very much care about, constitutional reform. The first group tend to be on the centre-left, and the second group tend to be on the right. Yet, neither side can get what they want without the other: England can flourish only if it is well constituted, and a well constituted state must recognise England's claim to national and political existence.

### (b) The constitution

The starting point is that a proper written constitution is no longer an optional extra; it has now become a necessity. The British constitution has exhausted itself. It offers little or no protection against the perilous political storms assailing us. The overall picture of corruption, incompetence, and carelessness is familiar to all who have observed British politics in recent years. Institutional decay and economic plundering have combined into a maelstrom of misrule. Decisions harmful to the lives and livelihoods of millions of people have been made on the fly, shamelessly unmoored from any moral principle, often with an eye only to what will dominate the current news cycle and distract attention from some even worse decision. We have witnessed a shameless cannibalisation of the country from the top: from David Cameron's austerity and privatisation programme, which seemed to destroy what was left of the public sphere, through the recklessness of Brexit-without-a-plan, Liz Truss's unfunded tax cuts, sewage in rivers, dodgy PPE contracts, and Downing Street parties during the Covid-19 lockdown, to uncollected rubbish on the streets of Birmingham. One is reminded of John of Gaunt's deathbed speech in William Shakespeare's *Richard II*: 'That England that was wont to conquer others hath made a shameful conquest of itself'.[17]

Inevitably, amidst all this devastation and decay, one feels like a Roman of the Late Republic, wailing 'o tempora, o mores'.[18] However, merely calling for a return to moral decency cannot save us, because the problem is not limited to specific individuals of bad character. It is systemic and institutional. The institutions that should check misrule, corruption, and the abuse of power have been corroded. The unwritten rules are frayed to breaking point. Almost everything – Parliament, political parties, the media, the Civil Service, the schools – has failed us. If healthy democracy and good government are to be restored, the whole political system, and the constitutional order that underpins it, needs to be renewed, renovated, rebuilt, repaired, refounded.

All honest citizens have a stake in that endeavour; everyone has a common interest in 'getting the constitution done'. That applies to the centre-right as well as to the left. While recognising that the main impetus for change comes from the centre-left, constitution-building cannot be confined to those infamously tagged by Suella Braverman, then Home Secretary, as '*Guardian*-reading, tofu-eating wokerati'.[19]

Moderate Conservatives, who would previously have defended the 'unwritten constitution',[20] but are now dismayed by what has become of it, should be keener than ever to engage with constitutional refoundation. Indeed, that shift is happening. There is already growing support for a written constitution, even from some previously unlikely quarters. Of course, this is not entirely new. As far back as 2004, Tim Renton, a Tory peer and former Chief Whip to Margaret Thatcher, said that 'Change must come, change that will lead to better legislation and to Westminster again becoming the focus of interest, respect and even of good government'.[21]

Thoughtful people from across the political spectrum are beginning to recognise that the absence of clear, legitimate, and enforceable constitutional rules is a problem. 'Small-c' conservative establishment figures, who would previously have defended the subtle wisdom and flexible genius of the unwritten constitution, now stand aghast at how easily its conventions and norms have been torn apart, and how exposed and undefended it leaves us.

An interesting contribution to this debate comes from Sir Thomas Legg, Lord Green of Hurstpierpoint, and Sir Martin Donnelly. One could hardly imagine a trio of more solidly small-c conservative names: a King's Counsel, a Conservative member of the House of Lords who also happens to be an Anglican priest, and a former Permanent Secretary. Nevertheless, they came to the logical conclusion that the unwritten system is unsalvageable and that the only solution now lies in the adoption of a proper written, codified, entrenched, supreme-and-fundamental-law, constitution.[22]

Academics, commentators, and op-ed writers are increasingly recognising that our social and economic woes stem, in large measure, from a problem of governance, and that the problem of governance stems from constitutional dysfunction.[23] Although such views are not yet universal, they are certainly much less rare than they were. To accept that the unwritten constitution is fundamentally broken, and that something must be done about it if our democracy and prosperity are to be restored, is no longer a fringe position.

### (c) The English question

Many who seek constitutional reform naturally assume that it should take place in the context of a British state. Indeed, one of the main impulses for support for a written constitution among the Unionist centre-left is a desire to 'hold the Union together' and to reassert a constitutional 'Britishness'.[24] To those people, the message is that it is time to let the Union go (at least in the form we know it, with a single, sovereign British Parliament).

For three centuries, 'English' and 'British' were – at least to the English, if not to the Scottish and the Welsh, and later the Irish – practically synonymous. Any distinction between them was easily glossed over. That is no longer the case. As Gavin Esler writes, England used to be the 'last bastion of the survival of Union Jack flag-waving Britishness', but with the emergence of an English identity 'that bastion has now fallen'.[25] People are sorting into 'English identifiers' and 'British identifiers'. By 2016, the year of the Brexit referendum, 37% of English people still considered themselves to be 'equally English and British'. However, more than half (53%) of the population came down on one side or the other: 33% emphasised their English identity over a British identity, and 20% emphasised their British identity over an English identity.[26]

Another difficulty is that these differences of national identity have become politicised. In the 2019 general election, which the Conservatives fought on a promise to 'Get Brexit done', Labour won most votes among those in England who identified as 'more British than English', while the Conservatives won most votes among those in England who identified as 'more English than British' or 'equally British and English'.[27] That is to say, Britishness generally leans left and pro-European, while Englishness leans right and Eurosceptic. Those in England who identify solely or primarily as British are more likely to favour closer relations and reintegration with the European Union, while those who emphasise their English identity tend to be more supportive of Brexit and less comfortable with the idea that England is a European nation. This feeds into an unhelpfully divisive narrative where the left can dismiss those interested in the English question as 'little Englanders', while the right can dismiss constitutional reformers as 'liberal Remainers', whose supposed concern for human rights, judicial independence, the integrity of elections, the rights of the opposition, and so on, is little more than a thinly veiled, garlic-scented, Blob plot to reverse Brexit.

It is important to get beyond such polarisation. It is not to be expected that centre-left British progressives, English civic nationalists, and moderate conservatives will agree on everything. These groups will naturally differ in their tastes, policy preferences, and perhaps fundamental values. Nevertheless, the solution they must stumble towards is the same: a renewed constitutional settlement, expressed in a decent and robust written constitution, that re-establishes a normal, healthy, well governed, democratic England – with or without the rest of the United Kingdom.

Despite Labour winning a majority of the seats in England, Scotland, and Wales in 2024, the United Kingdom as it currently exists remains broken, perhaps beyond repair. About half of the Scottish electorate still want independence, even if they are more divided than in recent years on how and when to get it.[28] Although Wales, along with England, voted narrowly for Brexit in 2016, the Welsh, too, are increasingly chafing under the constraints of the United Kingdom. Support for Welsh independence – while still below reported levels of support for Scottish independence and for Irish reunification – rose steadily from 2016 to 2024.[29]

If thorough reform had been undertaken in the early twentieth century, when 'Home Rule all round' was briefly on the political agenda, or after 1945, when post-war Britain was reconstructed, or even in 1997, when New Labour came into office promising devolution, it might have been a different story. As it stands, however, clinging to the current form of the United Kingdom is not only likely fail in the long turn, but also to poison relationships. The more the United Kingdom tries to block a democratic route to Scottish independence, the more resentment will swell and the more difficult it will be to find a solution that works for all. As discussed in Chapter 3, there is still much that we might want to preserve in the Union, or salvage from it – shared history, cultural proximity, and common interests – but all that could be squandered if the British Government tries to hold on to it too tightly.

Respectable opinion-formers within England, mostly of the metropolitan centre-left, have long tended to view Englishness with distain, as a 'racist, backward-looking, imperialistic and xenophobic' force.[30] These are the sort of people who have been most prominent in the debates over constitutional reform, and they have kept England well out of it. Yet if we are to reform the state in ways that hold the Union together more loosely, the English need to drop the fear and suspicion of Englishness and to become more comfortable with their own national identity. Middlebrow disdain for Englishness confuses cause and effect. If England has so far failed to move beyond ethnic tribalism, and to develop an inclusive, democratic, civic form of nationalism, it is chiefly because England lacks the state, constitution, and institutions of its own in which this type of civic nationalism could flourish.

The anti-Englishness of the centre-left parties also ignores English radical movements like the Levellers and Lollards, and folk-heroes of English resistance to social injustice, from the Peasants' Revolt to the Tolpuddle Martyrs. Names like John Ball, Wat Tyler, John Milton, Algernon Sydney, James Harrington, Henry Neville, John Lilburne, Richard Overton, and Henry Ireton all bear witness to a progressive and democratic English radical tradition that has never quite been destroyed. The Liberal Democrats are the natural heirs of that tradition, as well as to the Whig tradition, which always defended English liberty, and it is a shame that they have largely abandoned it. There is nothing liberal or democratic about denying Scotland and Wales the right to become independent. There is nothing liberal or democratic in denying England's right to become a modern democracy, for the sake of propping up the United Kingdom in its current, unreformed, top-down, imperialist form.[31]

The Labour Party, being a product of imperial British nationalism and of the Union, is mostly sceptical of these older English progressive traditions, and remains staunchly British in its constitutional outlook. There is a certain type of socialist (still around, if rarer than they used to be) who has a deep distrust of other, non-Marxian, radical traditions derived from the pre-industrial era, especially when those radical traditions use biblical allusions in making their case for a more democratic state and a more just socio-economic order, or when they appeal to the nation or the common folk, rather than the 'proletariat', as the proper object of their transformative political zeal. Even so, some voices within or associated with the Labour Party, such as the former Labour MP John Denham, do at least take England's national existence seriously. A few, such as the scholar and activist Stuart White, have even begun to imagine England a normal democratic nation-state, freed from old imperial burdens.[32]

It is in such a state that a normal and healthy English democracy – shorn of its desire to rule over Scotland, Wales, and Northern Ireland – could take shape. A normal England would be undergirded by a written constitution – one firmly in the tradition of the Westminster Model, but incorporating the Charter 88 agenda,[33] for which constitutional reformers have campaigned since the tercentenary of the Glorious Revolution. It would be sustained by an inclusive and civic national identity, and oriented not towards imperial power but towards serving the common good of its citizens. That is the kind of constitution to which this book points.

To those who *do* see the need for England to have its own political space and identity, the core message is that the constitution matters. With the left and centre-left excluding themselves from active interest in England and political Englishness, it is little wonder that those speaking for England, insofar as they have broached constitutional issues at all, have done so mainly in arch-conservative or even reactionary terms. That approach is not good enough. In reimagining England, the constitution deserves better – more thoughtful, more critical, more creative – attention.

Peter Hitchens, for example, writing in favour of English independence in the *Daily Mail*, assumes that the English constitutional order is essentially unbroken, still adequately grounded upon Magna Carta, the 1689 Bill of Rights, the Church of England, the English Crown, and the English Parliament at Westminster.[34] That position, though it may once have been valid, has become untenable. The values, principles, moderation, and self-restraint upon which it was built have fallen away. The world in which it made sense has changed. To restore what has been lost, we have to renovate – that means reforming as well as repairing.

A common theme of right-wing English (and Anglo-centric British) constitutional thought is a desire to roll back the New Labour reforms and to return to a simpler *status quo ante,* in which the sovereignty of the Westminster Parliament was unchallenged by devolved institutions, by the European Union, or by a Supreme Court. This reactionary agenda made some headway during the tenure of Boris Johnson, and is supported by most factions of the Conservative Party. Sadly, it plays directly into the hands of unscrupulous authoritarian populists. It is a Rogues' Charter for those who would destroy, not conserve, England's hard-won heritage of freedom. An English national revival cannot be complete without, at the very heart of the state- and nation-building project, a written constitution: a new Magna Carta. Such a constitution would empower the people through democratic institutions and would protect them against corruption, abuse of power, and the erosion of their rights and liberties.

As well as inviting the centre-right to engage with the constitutional question, this book also invites those on the left to reconsider the English question. It recognises that England is a nation in its own right. Although England's national life has long been overshadowed by the imperial necessities of Britishness, it has retained the essential marks of nationhood, which may provide a foundation for a post-imperial English democratic constitutional rebirth.

This book therefore rejects the standard left-wing notion that England and Englishness are to be scorned, as if they were inherently backward or exclusionary concepts. It challenges the assumption – still common among British progressives – that England, as a political entity, does not matter, and that constitutional reform must be pursued only on a United Kingdom-wide basis. It specifically repudiates the idea that 'preserving the Union', at least in its current form, is one of the primary functions of a new constitution. Indeed, it could well be that one of the primary functions of a constitution is to end the Union, or else to recast it in a very different form.

That is not necessarily to say that this book is a work of English nationalism. It recognises and embraces English nationhood, but it is more accurately described as a work of post-Unionism. It sees the Union in its current guise as spent, unnecessary, and unhelpful, and so looks beyond it. Coming to terms with this might, one day, be forced upon England by political developments in Scotland, Wales, and Northern Ireland. Attempts to stop Scottish independence, by limiting the ability of the Scottish Government and Parliament to lay the foundations for a transition to statehood, or by being much more heavy-handed in the use of reserve powers, threatens to try the patience of the Scots and risks turning what has until now been an entirely peaceful and lawful independence movement into something much uglier. A better, more courageous, course is for England to anticipate the demand for greater autonomy, and to respond generously and proactively, in a way that builds friendship and not enmity. Voluntary withdrawal from 'Outer Britain', and with it the rediscovery and rehabilitation of English nationhood, is doubly beneficial; it not only lays the foundation for a more democratic, fairer, and better-governed England, but also sets us on the path to a more equal, harmonious, and mature relationship among all the nations of these islands.

## (d) Structure and argument of the book

The book is divided into eight chapters. After this introductory chapter, Chapter 1 discusses the constitutional crisis afflicting the United Kingdom, tracing its long slow collapse from the 'majoritarian heyday' of the mid-twentieth century, through a period of incoherent reform, to its present disintegration. In so doing, it explains what a (written) constitution is, what a constitution does, and why a written constitution is now so urgently needed.

Chapter 2 discusses the long-term pressures on the Union, arguing that the constitution is difficult to reform in ways that will meet the reasonable demands of all countries in the Union. The best – neatest, easiest – solution would be for England, Scotland, Wales, and all of Ireland gracefully, in an orderly and democratic way, to dissolve the Union and look to a friendly association of independent, cooperating, post-Union states. It also recognises, however, that public opinion is not in that place. There are plenty of people in England, Scotland, Wales, and Northern Ireland who wish for a Union to continue in some form or other.

Instead of recommending the total dissolution of the Union, therefore, Chapter 2 recommends its transformation, from an *incorporating* Union, in which legal sovereignty rests in the Westminster Parliament, to an *unincorporating* Union, which presents itself as one state to the outside world – that is, for the purposes of foreign affairs, defence, and citizenship – but otherwise functions as an intergovernmental union between freely cooperating autonomous states.

Chapter 3 considers English national identity. It argues that, in the absence of a political nation-state, English identity has become merely cultural. However, it would be possible, with the restoration of English institutions, to rediscover, under the layers of the British imperial past, a healthy, democratic, and inclusive English national identity. It posits a view of England as a nation comfortable in its own skin, that no longer feels a need dominate others within these islands or overseas, nor to deny its European nature.

Chapter 4 considers the outline and parameters of a viable and acceptable constitution. It proposes a moderate constitutional settlement, firmly in the tradition of the Westminster Model, drawing not from continental revolutionary ideas, but from the familiar and practical constitutional experiences of Commonwealth countries. This would reconcile the need for major institutional reform with a desire to conserve the best aspects of England's constitutional heritage.

Chapter 5 then examines, in some detail, the content of the draft Constitution, explaining the design choices made and the reasons for these choices.

Chapter 6 considers the process of getting from here to there – that is, how constitution-making might work in an English and Union-wide context.

Finally, Chapter 7 sounds the note of warning against placing too much hope in constitutions. The constitution is necessary, but not sufficient. There is still a need for public ethics and civic virtue if the country is to flourish.

The Annex presents a draft Constitution with English statehood at its centre, which fleshes out the design choices discussed in the book. This draft is intended to be a practical guide and a point of reference – for wider public audiences and policy-makers, as well as legal and political academics – in their discussions on the constitution. As Sir Roger Scruton said, 'Just to criticise institutions, and never to say what you are wishing to put in their place, is a very unhelpful thing'.[35] Well, this draft is an attempt to be helpful.

Despite increased public and political support for a written constitution in principle, much misunderstanding about constitutions remains. Those in favour of a written constitution sometimes present it as if it were a panacea, or a golden treasure chest of policy solutions. They make the mistake of thinking that a constitution can fix everything. Those against a written constitution see it as a Pandora's box, containing all their fears. They make the mistake of thinking that a written constitution is either useless or pernicious.

Those two extremes are equally misguided. Both stem from ignorance about what constitutions actually are and do. Few people, on any side of the constitutional debate, have read a modern written constitution, or have much idea what a written constitution is, does, or might contain. In a country like England, which has no experience of life under a written constitution, and lacks even a common lexicon on which to draw, it is necessary to provide a 'worked example'. This will encourage a more realistic and less abstract discussion, engaging with the detailed, often mundane, practicalities of constitutional design. The most effective way to do that is to present a draft Constitution that 'grounds' the conversation by showing people what a written constitution might look like in an English context. It enables the arguments to be made in a more concrete and tangible way. With a draft Constitution on the table, one can argue for or against this or that provision, and conduct the debate on a genuinely constitutional level, in terms of sections and subsections.

It is argued that a suitable constitution for England would be a comprehensive restatement, with some necessary reforms and adaptations to context, of the institutional rules and basic principles of the Westminster Model's parliamentary democracy – the *quod semper, quod ubique, quod ab omnibus*[36] – of the constitutional order to which we are all heirs, and on which we should broadly agree. The constitution would not try to settle every issue of controversy, but it would provide a consensual foundation and a fair basis for democratic politics. Getting the constitution right will not fix everything, but without it nothing can be fixed.

The draft Constitution proposed in this book is not the first – there have been several such attempts over the years.[37] In particular, three earlier drafts are worthy of attention. The first was that published in 1991 by the Institute for Public Policy Research (IPPR).[38] The second was written by Richard Gordon KC and published as *Repairing British Politics: A Blueprint for Constitutional Change* in 2010.[39] The third draft is that produced by the House of Commons' Political and Constitutional Reform Committee in 2014, shortly before the eight hundredth anniversary of Magna Carta.[40]

There is no desire to take anything away from these texts. The IPPR draft embodies all the usual demands of the constitutional reform agenda – proportional representation to the House of Commons, a reformed upper house, a justiciable

Bill of Rights, the codification and limitation of the prerogative powers of the Crown, regional devolution, and so forth. It is a solid, technically sound, constitution. We could have done far worse than to adopt it as soon as Tony Blair came to power in 1997 – if we had, so much of our recent discontent and present misery might have been avoided, but sadly that moment was never seized.

The Political and Constitutional Reform Committee's draft is also a comprehensive and technically sound text. It seems to have benefited from skilful drafting. However, it makes some strange design choices – no doubt driven by the political dynamics of the Committee at the time. For example, it would retain first-past-the-post system for elections to the Commons, but establish a new upper house in which elected senators would serve for fifteen-year terms. Such proposals would be hard to accept and hard to justify to supporters of constitutional reform.

Richard Gordon's draft contains some interesting and novel proposals. Foremost is the creation of a new 'Citizens' Branch',[41] similar to proposals advanced by neo-Machiavellian political theorists such as John McCormick.[42] However, in terms of its technical drafting it is the weakest of the three. The text is, in parts, rather vague and often reads more like 'heads of proposals' for a drafting committee than the finished work of a constitution. There are obvious gaps which courts would have to fill. If one is concerned about the extent of judicial power under a written constitution, the solution is to be more, not less, precise about the institutional mechanics.

Crucially, none of these previous drafts takes England seriously. They are all based on an Anglo-centric Unionism that gives some recognition to Scotland, Wales, and Northern Ireland, but leaves England out of the picture. The IPPR draft would divide England into regions to make it fit more easily into the United Kingdom. The Political and Constitutional Reform Committee's draft would continue, in broad outline, the current devolved structure in which all of England is directly governed by the Government in Westminster, but it would reverse the basis of devolution from that adopted in 1999 to that proposed in 1979: in other words, every policy area not expressly devolved would be reserved. That would be totally unacceptable in Scotland, and probably in Wales and Northern Ireland too. Gordon's draft barely mentions devolution, and would leave it all to be sorted out by ordinary legislation. All propose to prop up the Union in its existing form by denying any place for a distinct English national politics. That is something the draft Constitution presented in this book seeks to remedy.

For readers who like to have a general idea of the direction of travel before the journey starts, a summary of the main provisions and principles of the proposed draft Constitution is set out at the beginning of the annex, before the main text of the draft Constitution.

The draft Constitution does not claim to be the only or last word in what a written constitution *should* look like. It is intended only to educate the reader, and to encourage more focused and informed public debate, by providing a worked example of what a moderate and technically sound constitution for England *could* look like.

Nevertheless, an attempt has been made to present a viable and acceptable draft: an example constitution which is complete, technically sound, and which incorporates the best practice of other Westminster Model constitutions, but is not far-fetched, outlandish, or excessively radical. Its design choices are based upon a search for the middle ground and the common ground: a sensible compromise between moderate reformers and moderate conservatives.

The aim is to push the public conversation, on both the English question and the constitutional question, forward. By showing a constitution in 'chapter and verse' (or section and subsection), it tries to get beyond generalities and to focus on the important details that other scholars, policy advocates, and political pundits tend to overlook. This attention to detail demonstrates the practicality, viability, and acceptability of a written constitution in an English context. It makes the idea of a written constitution – which for some people is still an abstract, alien, and unconvincing novelty – into something more imaginable, intelligible, tangible, familiar, and attainable, and therefore more desirable.

Some chapters build upon arguments developed in my previous book, *Westminster and the World: Commonwealth and Comparative Insights for Constitutional Reform*.[43] Readers seeking a more detailed constitutional history of the United Kingdom, a more taxonomic analysis of the Westminster Model, a defence of written constitutions against common counter-arguments, or a more comparative survey of constitutional design options, are directed to that work. Given the severity of the situation, the aim of this book is to keep things focused on practical solutions rather than to get too bogged down in matters of history or theory.

### (e) Facing the future

Political events continue to move fast. At the time of going to press, the Labour Party had just marked a year in office, following the 2024 general election in which it won almost two-thirds of the seats in the House of Commons. That result might be interpreted as a partial reprieve for the constitutional status quo. Labour – perhaps the most sincerely (if not the most ardently) British Unionist party – won a majority of the seats in England, Scotland, and Wales. The Scottish National Party (SNP) lost the majority in Scotland it had held since its 2015 surge, and was reduced to a rump of just nine MPs. Independence looks far away, and the Union seems more secure that it has been for some time. In the same way, some people who have been outspoken critics of British institutions under Conservative Governments might be mollified by Labour rule, especially if – initially, at least – it is more competent and less corrupt.

Without descending into punditry, one can of course point out the fragility of Labour's achievement. The party's impressive seat count belies the shallowness of its support: in terms of vote share, Labour performed less well than in 2017, when Jeremy Corbyn led the party to defeat. Many of those were tactical votes, lent to Labour to kick the Tories out. The challenges facing the Labour Government are immense. It will be hard for it to reverse chronic economic decline, restore public services, take back the political narrative from the far right, and undo the damage of Brexit, before public patience runs out and the political pendulum starts to swing the other way. Implicit trust in the unwritten constitution might not be revived, especially under such an overwhelming majority. In Scotland and Wales, patience for the Union might begin once again to waver. In England, the danger of further far-right populist reaction, involving more constitutional destruction, is very real, as Reform UK continues to surge in opinion polls.

This book is not built, however, on such shifting sands. Beneath the political froth, the election results, the headlines, and the opinion polls, the longer-term trends are more stable. The underlying structural and constitutional problems of the United Kingdom are not going away. Unless fixed, these problems will – soon enough – show themselves to be just as unresolved and crippling under Labour as under the Conservatives.

The constitutional conversation might be taking place in whispers in the wings rather than on centre stage, but it nevertheless continues, and cannot be silenced. The SNP is in turmoil, and its electoral spell over Scotland is, for the time being, broken, but the campaign for Scottish independence is bigger than the SNP, and is by no means dead. The Scottish Government has already thrown down the gauntlet to the unreformed British state, in the form of detailed proposals for a written constitution for an independent Scotland.[44]

Meanwhile in Wales, the Independent Commission on the Constitutional Future of Wales has published its interim report, backed by Labour, with Welsh independence as one of the options under consideration.[45] While the willingness of the Labour Government at Westminster to hand over power to Wales is doubtful, the debate in Wales, within and beyond Labour, shows signs of progress.

Before the 2024 general election, Labour had announced an interesting, if limited, package of constitutional reforms.[46] These proposals, drawn up by former Prime Minister Gordon Brown, did not appear in the Labour manifesto and are unlikely to be taken up by the Labour Government, but the report nevertheless shows an encouraging advance in Labour's constitutional thinking – recognising, for the first time, both the importance of constitutional entrenchment and the connection between constitutional forms and socio-economic outcomes.[47]

Even with these rumbling conversations on reform of the constitution, and underlying pressures of the future of the Union, it is recognised that much of what is proposed in this book might seem far-fetched now, within the limited horizons and bleak expectations of today's politics. Yet this book is written not only for today, but for the future, when all are forced to admit that the existing British state and its constitution are broken, that what we have now cannot hold, and that we cannot go back to how things were before. It is at that point, when people are searching for clear, practical suggestions for how to rebuild a democratic constitution from the ruins of a crumpled and corrupted British imperial state, that this book might be most helpful.

# Notes

1 D. Hirsh (2023) *The Cost of Child Poverty in 2023* (Child Poverty Action Group).

2 B. Francis-Devine (2024) *Food Banks in the UK* (House of Commons Research Briefing 8585) (House of Commons Library).

3 Rivers Trust (2024) *State of Our Rivers 2024 Report*, https://theriverstrust.org/key-issues/state-of-our-rivers, accessed 7 September 2024.

4 A. Cooban (2022) 'Why UK energy prices are rising much faster than in Europe', *CNN Business*, 19 August, https://edition.cnn.com/2022/08/19/energy/energy-prices-uk-europe-explainer/index.html, accessed 7 September 2024.

5 N. Ferris (2022) 'The UK is facing two lost decades for living standards', *New Statesman*, 24 March.

6 C. Giles (2022) 'Brexit and the economy: the hit has been "substantially negative"', *Financial Times*, 30 November.

7 Bertelsmann Stiftung (2024) 'Transformation Index 2024', https://atlas.bti-project.org, accessed 12 June 2024.

8 Bertelsmann Stiftung (2024) 'Less democratic, less successful: the nexus between authoritarian trends and deteriorating governance performance, presentation given to the International Institute for Democracy and Electoral Assistance, 12 June.

9 A. Brown (trans. and ed.) (1994) *Guicciardini: Dialogue on the Government of Florence* (Cambridge Texts in the History of Political Thought) (Cambridge University Press).

10 A. King and I. Crewe (2014) *The Blunders of Our Governments* (2nd edn) (Oneworld Publications).

11 I. Dunt (2023) *How Westminster Works ... and Why It Doesn't* (Weidenfeld and Nicolson).

12 R. Stewart (2023) *Politics on the Edge* (Jonathan Cape).

13 'Old Corruption' was the term used by Victorian reformers to refer to the eighteenth-century system of oligarchic politics: rotten and pocket boroughs, the 'widespread use of pensions, sinecures and gratuitous emoluments granted to persons whom the British government ... wished to bribe, reward or buy', and the whole 'parasitical system through which the elite fed its insatiable appetite for power and money at the people's expense' – W. D. Rubinstein (1983) 'The end of Old Corruption in Britain, 1780–1860', *Past & Present*, No. 101, pp. 55–86; see also P. Harling (1995) 'Rethinking Old Corruption', *Past & Present*, No. 147, pp. 127–158).

14 'An Agreement of the People of England, and the places therewith incorporated, for a secure and present peace, upon grounds of common right, freedom and safety' – Leveller petition, presented to Parliament, 1649, https://oll.libertyfund.org/page/1648-9-the-agreement-of-the-people, accessed 18 June 2023.

15 T. Paine (1791) *The Rights of Man*, ch. IV, https://www.gutenberg.org/files/3742/3742-h/3742-h.htm, accessed 25 October 2022.

16 In passing, it is worth noting that there is no such crisis in Scotland or Wales, except insofar as their membership of the United Kingdom results in England's crisis being imposed upon them. The reforms incorporated into the structure of Scottish and Welsh devolved institutions, including proportional representation, have for the most part worked well, and even as English governance is in turmoil, the Scottish and Welsh governments have mostly remained focused on the delivery of public services to the extent possible within the constraints imposed by the Union.

17 Act II, Scene 1, 722–749.

18 'O [what wicked] times! O [what corrupt] manners!' – Cicero, *Against Catiline*, 1.1.2.

19 B. Davis (2019) 'Suella Braverman blames "*Guardian*-reading, tofu-eating wokerati" for disruptive protests', *Evening Standard*, 19 October.

20 Some may quibble about the term 'unwritten constitution', insisting that the constitution is largely 'written', it is just not codified. It is true that Acts of Parliament, Orders-in-Council, parliamentary Standing Orders, judicial decisions, canonical learned commentaries, the Ministerial Code, the Cabinet Manual, and other documents exist in written form. What is less clear is whether these add up in any useful sense to a

constitution, since they do not act as supreme and fundamental laws. Such debates quickly dissolve into semantics. However, the term 'written constitution' is generally understood, and I stick by it as the most widely accepted term. For greater definitional precision, one may interpret 'written constitution' throughout this book simply as a convenient shorthand for 'written, codified, entrenched, supreme, and fundamental law', and 'unwritten constitution' for a system of government that lacks a written, codified, entrenched, supreme, and fundamental law.

21 T. Renton (2004) *Chief Whip: People, Power and Patronage in Westminster* (Politico's), p. 339

22 T. Legg, S. Green, and M. Donnelly (2021) 'Constitutional reform: sustaining a viable United Kingdom through the 21st century' (Policy Reform Group), https://consoc.org.uk/wp-content/uploads/2021/01/Const.-Reform-1-final.pdf, accessed 15 April 2025.

23 See, for example, M. Dawson (2022) 'Britain's political meltdown and its constitutional dimension', Verfassungsblog, https://verfassungsblog.de/britains-political-meltdown-and-its-constitutional-dimension, accessed 25 October 2022.

24 G. Witte (2015) 'After 800 years, Britain finally asks: do we need a written constitution?', *Washington Post*, 7 June, https://www.washingtonpost.com/world/europe/after-800-years-britain-finally-asks-do-we-need-a-written-constitution/2015/06/07/6097b50c-e908-11e4-8581-633c536add4b_story.html, accessed 25 October 2022.

25 G. Esler (2021) *How Britain Ends: English Nationalism and the Rebirth of Four Nations* (Apollo), p. 78.

26 A. Henderson and R. Wyn Jones (2021) *Englishness: The Political Force Transforming Britain* (Oxford University Press), p. 55.

27 J. Denham (2021) 'Who speaks for England? How the people of England view England, Britain and the Union' (22 April), https://j-denham.medium.com/who-speaks-for-england-d087abde142e, accessed 25 October 2022.

28 Politics.co.uk (2024), 'Scottish independence poll: the result of an IndyRef today – 11 March 2024', https://www.politics.co.uk/reference/scottish-independence-polls, accessed 15 April 2025.

29 W. Hayward (2022) 'Support for Welsh independence is growing – people are fed up with being forgotten', *The Guardian* (30 August), https://www.theguardian.com/commentisfree/2022/aug/30/support-welsh-independence-growing-scotland-uk, accessed 21 November 2022.

30 J. Denham (2019) 'Nationalism in England is not just a rightwing nostalgia trip', *The Guardian* (13 August), https://www.theguardian.com/commentisfree/2019/aug/13/english-nationalism-brexit-remain-and-reform, accessed 25 October 2022.

31 The word 'imperialist' needs qualification. It has become, at least on the progressive left, a word of repudiation, and to describe the British state as 'imperial' is therefore to damn it. It is not my intention to use the word in that coded, ideologically laden way. In describing the United Kingdom as an imperial state, my aim is simply to recognise that the Union was founded by and for empire, and that that state retains the deep impression of the assumptions of imperial rule upon its institutions.

32 S. White (2021) 'A new kind of dreaming: democratic English patriotism', in J. Jeffrey (ed.), *Belonging, Place and the Nation* (Compass), https://www.compassonline.org.uk/wp-content/uploads/2021/02/Belonging-Place-and-the-Nation.pdf, accessed 25 October 2022.

33 Charter 88 was a campaigning organisation, formed in 1988, to achieve a written and reformed constitution.

34 P. Hitchens (2022) 'Why England should leave the UK instead of persuading the others to stay and embrace a golden future', *Daily Mail*, 18 May.

35 R. Scruton (2017) Address to the Oxford Union (21 December), https://www.youtube.com/watch?v=KUbfMQ91Mps, accessed 25 October 2022.

36 St Vincent of Lerins, *Commonitorium*, 'What always, what everywhere, what by all' – in other words, those things that are universally accepted as the essence of Westminster Model democracy.

37 A. Blick (2015) *Beyond Magna Carta: A Constitution for the United Kingdom* (Bloomsbury), pp. 212–221.

38 Institute for Public Policy Research (1991) *The Constitution of the United Kingdom*, https://www.ippr.org/files/images/media/files/publication/2014/01/the-constitution-of-the-united-kingdom_1991-2014_1420.pdf, accessed 25 October 2022.

39 R. Gordon (2010) *Repairing British Politics: A Blueprint for Constitutional Change* (Hart Publishing).

40 House of Commons Political and Constitutional Reform Committee (2014) 'A new Magna Carta?', https://publications.parliament.uk/pa/cm201415/cmselect/cmpolcon/463/46321.htm, accessed 25 October 2022.

41 Gordon, *Repairing British Politic*, p. 150.

42 J. P. McCormick (2011) *Machiavellian Democracy* (Cambridge University Press).

43 W. E. Bulmer (2020) *Westminster and the World: Commonwealth and Comparative Insights for Constitutional Reform* (Bristol University Press).

44 Scottish Government (2023) *Creating a Modern Constitution for an Independent Scotland* (Building a New Scotland, Paper 4.).

45 Welsh Government (2022) *Interim Report of the Independent Commission on the Constitutional Future of Wales*.

46 Labour Party (2022) *A New Britain: Renewing Our Democracy and Rebuilding Our Economy* (Report of the Commission on the UK's Future).

47 Ibid., pp. 53–54.

# The collapse of the unwritten constitution

## (a) Development of the English constitution

On 11 September 2022, three days after Queen Elizabeth II's death, the Privy Council met at St James's Palace and solemnly proclaimed King Charles III as our new monarch. Behind all the theatre of monarchy – the pomp and ceremony, the marching red coats, and the liveried trumpeters – what took place was a swift passage through one of the most difficult moments in the life of any country: the transfer of authority from one head of state to another.

Unlike in many other countries at such moments, there was no coup, no assassination, no violence, no fratricide, no uprising, no turmoil. Instead, we saw Penny Mordaunt, who had been appointed as Lord President of the Council a few days earlier, reading out draft Orders-in-Council, and the new King, in the presence of his Privy Council, calmly saying 'Approved'. The mechanism at the very heart of the British state was, in a rare moment, naked to the public view. This is, for the most part, how we are governed, not only at these pivotal times of transition, but day to day: by the monarch's formal intonement of 'Approved' to measures drafted by officials and put forward by ministers. The person of the monarch changes, but the government must be carried on; the state machinery built by the Tudors keeps on turning.

The evening before the Accession Council, Charles had already made his first public address as King. In it, he promised to 'uphold the constitutional principles at the heart of our nation' and to 'respect the precious traditions, freedoms and responsibilities of our system of parliamentary government'. He praised both an 'abiding love of tradition' and a 'fearless embrace of progress', and he acknowledged the 'sovereign's particular relationship with and responsibility towards the Church of England', while also undertaking to treat everyone with 'loyalty, respect and love', regardless of background or belief.[1] The next day, meeting with both Houses of Parliament at Westminster Hall, he recognised Parliament as 'the living and breathing instrument of our democracy' and rededicated himself to the 'precious principles of constitutional government'.[2]

There were other nods to the contractual nature of the monarchy in the first few days of Charles's reign. In his first public address, the King recognised Wales as a country: not a mere region, but a country in its own right. In the Accession Council, the King was required by law to make a declaration recognising the 1689 Scottish Claim of Right and the liberties of the Scottish kirk.

This is all *constitutional* stuff. Crown and Parliament, Government and People, Church and State, tradition and modernity, England and the Union – these are the cardinal posts on which the 'constitution' hangs. On three occasions – first to the people by televised address, then to the Privy Councillors in the Accession Council, and then to Parliament at Westminster Hall – the King symbolically and ceremoniously bound himself to the great institutions of state and to the constitutional order by which he, like the rest of us, would be governed. For all the gilt and trimmings, for all the display and pageantry, we were reminded – by the King himself – that the monarchy is entirely dependent upon Parliament, and ultimately upon the people, and that the whole is bound up in an ineffable and venerable constitutional order that is archaic, but not entirely without merit, nor without its charms.

The deep origins of the English constitution lie in the Middle Ages. A conventional starting point is 1066, the year of the Norman Conquest, which destroyed the Anglo-Saxon state and laid new institutions of governance, taxation, military control, and ownership, over the native English. This altered, but did not destroy, the underlying bedrock of English law. William the Conqueror swore at his coronation to uphold the existing Anglo-Saxon laws. From this practical concession gradually emerged the synthesis of Anglo-Saxon laws and Norman laws, which became the common law.[3] Other important early constitutional milestones include the signing of Magna Carta in 1215, as well as the first recorded summoning of a recognisable Parliament, including representatives of the Commons, in 1265.[4]

By Tudor times, a recognisably organised, centralised state had been constructed. The Henrician and Elizabethan Reformations, and the accompanying social and economic changes, further augmented the power of the Crown and strengthened the central administrative state in England. At the same time, conversely, the Tudor age embedded that state power more securely in a proto-constitutional structure of the Privy Council, the Courts of Law, and Parliament.[5]

The constitutional system that came to define the English and, later, British state was built upon those medieval and Tudor foundations. However, it was transformed by a period of bloody and painful state formation lasting from about 1603 (the accession of James VI of Scotland to the English throne) to 1746 (the final Hanoverian victory over the Jacobites at the Battle of Culloden). During that nearly a century and a half, these islands were embroiled in civil wars, revolutions, foreign invasions, and repeated lapses into either tyranny or anarchy.

The Glorious Revolution of 1688 was the pivotal moment of that difficult time. It put an end, in the words of the 1689 Bill of Rights, to 'popery and arbitrary power', and created a proto-parliamentary state. Power, both public and private, national and local, was in the hands of a loosely bounded ruling class, consisting of the aristocracy, the gentry, the solid yeomanry, the 'monied interest' and the City of London, and the commercial and professional upper middle classes.

This was a remarkably open and inclusive political order, compared with most other prominent European societies at the time. It was oligarchic rather than democratic, but – at least until the agricultural and industrial revolutions shifted the basis of wealth – it did more or less actually reflect the prevailing social order. The post-1689 settlement established a recognisably *political* and *public* life – with parties, elections, newspapers, pamphlets, campaigns, and lobbying. It also achieved a degree of personal and civil liberty that was rare elsewhere. Many of the laws were harsh and fell heavily upon the poor, but there was a rule of law, a reliable protection of private rights against the state, a functioning and essentially independent judiciary, and a right to due process and trial by jury.

This state rested, constitutionally, upon three three-legged stools: a trinity of trinities. The first stool was composed of the King, Lords, and Commons, who jointly possessed the legislative power. The second consisted of the Bill of Rights Act, the Act of Union, and the Act of Settlement, which together set the institutional and legal framework for the exercise of public power. These Acts defined the state. They regulated the relationship between the King, the Lords, and Commons, as well as between England and Scotland, almost in the manner of an (uncodified and unentrenched) proto-constitution. The third stool was the religious balance of power: Anglicans privileged in England, Wales, and Ireland; Scots Presbyterians in second place, along with tolerated English Protestant Dissenters; and the Roman Catholics – there is no avoiding this brute fact – oppressed and excluded.

This Hanoverian settlement laid the institutional and normative foundations for the next two centuries of imperial grandeur. However, while stable, it did not remain static. The settlement was gradually expanded to include sections and classes of the population that had previously been excluded from it. The Reform Acts of 1832, 1867, and 1884 expanded the right to vote. Legal restrictions on Roman Catholics, Jews, and other minorities were removed.

In parallel to these statutory changes, the nineteenth century also saw the consolidation of 'constitutional conventions', unwritten rules that constrained the power of the monarch and made the House of Commons the real power in the land. These conventions were described in canonical works such as John Stuart Mill's *Considerations on Representative Government* (1861), Walter Bagehot's *The English Constitution* (1867), and – most influential and enduring of all – A. V. Dicey's *Introduction to the Study of the Law of the Constitution* (1885). With the power of the Lords clipped by the Parliament Act 1911, and with universal suffrage finally achieved in 1928, the long transformation of an English eighteenth-century oligarchic limited monarchy into a British twentieth-century parliamentary democracy was completed.

### (b) The British constitution in its prime

There was something quite splendid about the British system in its prime. It had grown up through the ages, without any master plan or grand design, but with a rooted, organic complexity that embodied pragmatic compromise and inherited wisdom. It was (and still is) full of quaintness, colour, and obscure interest. Where else are vital decisions about who runs the country made by MPs going to the tearoom and writing letters to the 1922 Committee? Where else – outside of a nineteenth-century Ruritanian romance, perhaps – could one find a House of Lords, a Court of Arches, a Privy Council, a Lord Privy Seal, a Shadow Lord Chancellor, a Crown Steward and Bailiff of the Manor of Northstead, a Gentleman Usher of the Black Rod, an Earl Marshal, Lascelles Principles, Short Money, Early Day Motions – which have nothing to do with the health of the bowel – the Salisbury Convention, or the Ponsonby Rule? As one wit observed, it is missing only wizards and dragons.

Beneath the gothic relics was hidden a simple yet devastatingly effective system of government. Seen through the eyes of mid-twentieth-century scholars, it had a lot to commend it.[6] Despite its bizarre quirks and theoretical absurdities, Britain's unwritten constitution performed, in practice, rather better than tolerably well. It delivered strong and stable government that was both responsive and responsible. It excelled in comparison with the weakness of democracy in other European countries at the time. Democracy in the inter-war years of the twentieth century collapsed across much of continental Europe, and its post-war restoration in countries such as Italy and France remained chronically unstable.[7] Meanwhile, British democracy sailed steadily on, with a record for stability and dependability, balanced by the ability to adapt to circumstances and to make rapid, radical shifts in policy when required.

According to Bagehot, the 'efficient secret' of the Westminster parliamentary system is the fusion of executive and legislative powers under the leadership of a Cabinet headed by a Prime Minister.[8] The Cabinet, made up of the ministers responsible for the principal Government departments, is an 'executive committee' of Parliament, consisting of people in whom the parliamentary majority have, for the time being, placed their trust.[9]

In contrast to the inefficiencies and frustrations of American presidential democracy, Cabinet government ensured efficient and coherent administration. Laws were made under the leadership of those who would have to implement them. Legislative and executive policy could be brought into harmony, with the Prime Minister at the apex. Instead of deadlock, delay, and dithering, there would be unity, decisiveness, and democratic responsibility.

The sovereignty of Parliament was unchallenged constitutional orthodoxy.[10] In theory, it gave absolute power – the power to make and unmake any law – to any Government with a working majority in the House of Commons. However, that power was in practice used cautiously and responsibly. The absolute sovereignty of Parliament was hemmed in by ill-defined and amorphous, but nevertheless real and genuinely constraining, expectations about what was, and was not, morally and politically acceptable. Some quite draconian restrictions on civil liberties were enforced in wartime – even general elections were postponed – but these measures rested upon public consent, were applied with restraint, and were lifted as soon as it became possible to do so. The 'liberties of the subject' – freedom of speech, freedom of assembly, freedom of religion, freedom from arbitrary arrest, search or seizure, freedom from torture, the right to due process of law and a fair trial, and the rest of the established liberal canon of basic civil rights – were not declared or guaranteed by a written constitution, but were in practice (for the most part) protected by the common law, a tradition of liberty rooted in the legacy of Magna Carta and a political hatred of anything that hinted at arbitrary power.[11]

The relationships between the Crown, the Prime Minister and Cabinet, between the two Houses of Parliament, and between the Government and the Opposition were regulated by conventions. Although these unwritten rules of parliamentary government were not enforceable in the courts, they were understood and accepted as legitimate by all political actors, and were sustained through an informal but effective process of self-regulation.[12] The conventions hung together, in a logically coherent way, around the unifying principle that a Government could gain and hold office only by virtue of having the confidence of the House of Commons. The Government was responsible to the House of Commons, and through the House of Commons to the people, such that the people – as 'the true political sovereign' – could ultimately exercise control over the actions of both Government and Parliament.[13]

This arrangement gave the Prime Minister tremendous power. As long as a Prime Minister could win general elections and hold together a disciplined majority in the House of Commons, he or she could dominate the whole political process. The Prime Minister was head of the Cabinet, the chief advisor to the Crown, the leader of the majority party, the source of nearly all public patronage, the visible face of the Government, and the person with the mandate to carry out the party's manifesto promises. The Prime Minister, with a large corps of professional civil servants on hand, was able to take the initiative and to carry out policies in a vigorous and energetic way.

At the same time, however, Prime Ministers at the high point of the British constitution's reputation were not despotic rulers. They were subject to the law, which was applied by independent judges. They always had to carry their colleagues and parliamentary party with them, to justify their decisions in vigorous parliamentary debates, to respond to criticism and scrutiny from their own backbenchers as well as the Opposition, and ultimately to answer to the people at the next general election.

A core conventional doctrine was 'collective responsibility': ministers had to govern together, as a team; important policy questions had ultimately to be brought to the Cabinet for decision, and the decision of the Cabinet would then bind all members of the Government. One consequence of collective responsibility was that, because the Government had to be unified, the Prime Minister, as the head of the Government, was not a president or a commander-in-chief. He or she was, in some essential if ineffable sense, only a 'first among equals'. Some Prime Ministers were more forceful, more hands-on, and more concerned with details of government than others, but, crucially, no Prime Minister could ever govern alone. They always had to govern with and through the Cabinet, and with the backing of their parliamentary party. Even Winston Churchill, at the height of his wartime dominance, explained to Franklin Roosevelt that he continuously had to consult and have the support of the Cabinet.[14] In the same way, Margaret Thatcher – one of the most autocratic of Prime Ministers – was ultimately brought down when the Foreign Secretary,

Douglas Hurd, resigned from the Cabinet, thereby precipitating a loss of party confidence in her leadership.

Even rank-and-file Members of Parliament, despite strong party discipline and the influence of the party whips, were never entirely subordinate to the Prime Minister. Labour Prime Ministers always had to balance the ideological wings of a party that spanned from near-Bolshevism on the left to moderate social democracy on the right, while internal party structures like the National Executive Committee meant the leader's control over the party was never absolute. Conservative Prime Ministers generally had a freer hand, but a disgruntled chair of the party's 1922 Committee, representing Tory backbenchers, could create trouble if the 'Squires of the Shires' felt that things were not going their way.

The Civil Service, despite 'Yes, Minister' jokes of administering for administration's sake, was respected for its impartiality, capability, and professionalism. Judicial independence was firmly established.[15] Other public and semi-public institutions, including the BBC, the Church of England, local authorities, and the great universities, were recognised as having autonomous spheres of action, in which they could contribute to the common good according to their distinct natures and purposes, while remaining largely free from Government control.

The strongest check on prime ministerial power was democracy itself. Thanks to free, fair, and regular elections, the Government's great powers were held under an even greater responsibility to the people. The Opposition was able not only to criticise the Government, but also to serve as an alternative 'Government in waiting', ready to take power in a general election. The first-past-the-post electoral system was (and is) crudely majoritarian and unfair to minor parties. Occasionally (as in 1951 and 1974) it produced anomalous or inconclusive results. Nevertheless, in terms of ensuring democratic responsibility, it could be brutally effective.

The genius of parliamentary democracy is not that the people rule, but that those who rule must always be representative of and responsible to the people. Prime Ministers can lead their party, Parliament and the country – but only as far, only for as long, and only in the general direction, that their party, Parliament, and the country are willing to be led. The people – either directly or through Parliament – have the power to 'kick the rascals out', and the rascals have tended not to forget this.

A collapse of parliamentary confidence swiftly and peacefully removed Neville Chamberlain from power in 1940, and replaced him with Winston Churchill. Just as easily, the people at the ballot box removed Churchill from power in 1945 and replaced him with Clement Attlee, and the vast machinery of the British state, previously devoted to defeating the Nazis, was turned on a sixpence towards building the National Health Service. To quote Hastings Lees-Smith, acting Leader of the Labour Party in May 1940:

> I do not believe that there is any other form of government which could have carried through so great a change so smoothly and in so short a space of time. It convinces me that our form of parliamentary government is the most civilised in peace and is the most formidable weapon of control in war.[16]

Moreover, British democracy was embedded in a healthy civic culture, in which a plurality of interests and opinions, dissent, and opposition were respected. In legislation and policy-making, the Government might get its way, but the Opposition, minor parties, and the various interest groups in society could all have their say. Various advisory councils, boards, and committees, established by Government departments or by Acts of Parliament, meant that public policy was widely debated, at least among those directly affected by or with experience of the matter at hand. Policy-making followed processes and procedures, not fleeting whims. So constrained, both officially and unofficially, prime ministerial power never collapsed into arbitrary or capricious rule. The Cabinet, the Civil Service, the Courts, Parliament, and the people would never have allowed it.

## (c) Decline of the British constitution

Although the reputation of the British system of government was riding high in the post-war decades, by the late 1960s signs of dissatisfaction were starting to appear. By-election victories by Plaid Cymru (1966: Carmarthen) and the Scottish National Party (1967: Hamilton), as well as the outbreak of 'The Troubles' in Northern Ireland in 1969, showed that the British constitutional order, while still unchallenged in England, was not universally accepted across the United Kingdom. The state was not as firmly established or well constituted as had been thought. As Jason Cowley put it, 'Britain never completely acquired the crucial marks of modern statehood, such as having a written constitution'.[17] The Union, and with it the entire British constitutional order, was based on deals between elites; never had there been a time when the peoples of the four nations had come together to hammer out agreed terms.[18]

With the end of Empire came a nagging fear that Britain was in precipitous, perhaps terminal, decline. Some of the blame fell on institutions perceived as old, stuffy, and out of touch. The continued presence of hereditary peers in the House of Lords – despite declared intentions to do away with them in the Parliament Act 1911 and a light leavening of Life Peers after 1958 – was just symptom of a much deeper problem: a system of government whose ossified class system, old-school-tie networks, and imperialistic attitudes could not keep pace, after The Beatles and the Pill, with modern society in a changing world.

Early attempts at reform, in the form of the devolution referendums in Scotland and Wales in 1979, came to nought. In the 1980s, however, there was a lively debate about reform of the British constitution. The Alliance – a union of the remnants of the old Liberal Party with the newly formed Social Democratic Party – included a broad agenda for constitutional change in its 1983 general election manifesto.[19] Campaigning organisations such as Charter 88, the Electoral Reform Society, and the Institute for Public Policy Research promoted a coherent, comprehensive package of reforms, including (but not limited to) devolution, reform of the House of Lords, proportional representation, a Supreme Court, and a justiciable Bill of Rights. These reforms would have transformed the United Kingdom from a 'majoritarian democracy', with power concentrated in the hands of the Prime Minister at the head of the majority party in the House of Commons, into a so-called 'consensus democracy', where power is dispersed both geographically and institutionally.[20]

This transformed constitutional settlement would have produced a 'kinder, gentler democracy', more inclusive and better able to accommodate a range of previously marginalised needs and interests.[21] It would have moderated policy and hindered the unchecked ideological imposition of Thatcherism. The Thatcherite opposition to reform was not, therefore, inspired by conservative values such as caution, traditionalism, prudence, or moderation. Indeed, Thatcher repudiated those values, and supported unreformed British institutions only to the extent that she could use them in the service of her radical ideological goals.

Such use of traditional institutions for neoliberal ends was an unsustainable contradiction. The principles, values, and ethos on which the British system of government had been built since Victorian times were insidiously undermined by the all-pervading economic logic of neoliberalism. After all, if we are 'work hard, play hard' rational utility-maximisers, seeking our own advantage and material gain while reciting the Thatcherite mantra that 'greed is good', then we can no longer be held back by unwritten rules, ethical norms, self-restraint, unspoken understandings, or gentlemanly reserve.

Tony Blair's New Labour won a landslide majority in the 1997 general election with a mandate for constitutional reform but went on to enact it only partially, in a piecemeal, incoherent, *ad hoc* way. Reform was presented merely as a 'modernisation' of governance arrangements, while neglecting the redistribution of power, transparency, and accountability, and ignoring the role constitutions play in expressing values, setting norms, and conveying a sense of identity.

Labour has always been a constitutionally cautious, even conservative, party.[22] The Labour Government of 1945 had an impressive social, economic, and industrial agenda, but it took the constitution for granted and never saw any need to re-establish the state, of which it was now the master, on a renewed democratic constitutional foundation. In some ways, this was a good thing. It preserved the tradition of parliamentary government, which some on the far left would have torn up. It gave England socialism without The Party, without the Stasi, without Gulags. As Cowley notes:

> This was a very British revolution, and a pragmatic experiment with socialism. The state was powerful but not all-powerful. It was not a vindictive exercise in destruction but one of creation: about a new social contract between the state and the individual to enhance the common good. The monarchy, the landowning families and the ancient public schools were untouched. Individual freedom and the great British institutions were cherished.[23]

This 'softly-gently' approach might have been understandable, even wise, in 1945, when the British constitution was working well and when its reputation, both globally and domestically, was unsullied. However, it left a deeply conservative impression on Labour's constitutional thought, which was woefully inadequate for the changed situation of 1997.

The result of the New Labour reforms was an unbalanced and unstable constitutional order, incorporating elements of consensus democracy at the periphery – in Scotland, Wales, and Northern Ireland – while maintaining (and even strengthening) centralised, majoritarian power at the Anglo-British core.[24] This made the constitutional situation, in England anyway, even worse than before. The old system had a certain logic and coherence about it, a shared set of expectations and conventions which, at least in their own terms, worked well together. The reforms went far enough to break that old settlement, but not far enough to put a new settlement in its place. They left a legacy of contradiction, confusion, disarray, and uncertainty. There is a lesson from this experience: sometimes a little change can be more dangerous, more unsettling, than a bigger but more coherent change. Tinkering at the edges may be more risky than refoundation. New Labour bodged the constitution when it should have rebuilt it.[25]

Territorial governance, in particular, was a mess. Devolved institutions in Scotland, Wales, and Northern Ireland were designed to meet specific needs in those countries, but there was no attempt to pursue corresponding developments in England. Some token efforts were made towards the creation of English regional assemblies, but the Government's heart was never in it, and neither was that of the public. The pilot scheme proposed for the North East amounted to little more than a local government reform and was soundly rejected in a 2004 referendum.[26] England as a whole, as a nation, was never fitted into the scheme. There was never a solution to the so-called West Lothian Question: why should an MP for West Lothian in Scotland have responsibility for voting on English matters in the House of Commons, but not on Scottish matters, which are devolved?

The Conservatives, then under David Cameron, eventually offered 'English votes for English laws' (EVEL) as the solution. This was a parliamentary procedure requiring English-only legislation to be passed by a majority of MPs from English constituencies. However, it was unsatisfactory and later repealed. There is still no English Parliament distinct from the British Parliament, and no English Government distinct from the British Government. England has continued to be the neglected core of the United Kingdom.

These half-reformed institutions made the British system of government extremely vulnerable when it was hit by the Brexit vote in 2016, which at once polarised the population and paralysed the leadership of the major parties. The problem, on the constitutional level, was not just that institutions needed reform to make them work better. It was, more worryingly, that they were in danger of not working at all. The unwritten constitution had crumbled, finally succumbing to the slow but inexorable process of erosion that began under Margaret Thatcher and John Major, worsened under Tony Blair, was not addressed by Gordon Brown, reached a point of crisis under David Cameron and Theresa May, and was ruthlessly exploited by Boris Johnson.

The same timid conservatism animates the constitutional proposals Labour set out in 2022 in *A New Britain: Renewing Our Democracy and Rebuilding Our Economy*.[27] Although its specific proposals are 'small beer', the report, to give it its due, does have three encouraging elements. The first is the recognition that the broken, over-centralised constitutional structure of the state has a bearing on socio-economic performance. That realisation might have been a 'light bulb moment' for Labour: constitutional issues are not irrelevant to the everyday concerns of ordinary people; rather, the functioning of the state and its institutions, the distribution of power, and the protection of rights, can have powerful effects on the quality of governance, the shaping of policy, and ultimately on political and economic outcomes.

The second interesting element is a recognition that the constitution is more than just a system of government; it is also foundational to identity, belonging, and civic integration. It is an expression of the 'social contract'. So, constitutional matters are not just about *how* we are governed, but about *who* we are. In an increasingly diverse and multicultural society, the constitution can be an important means of political integration, setting the framework and common ground for living together. It is not just a charter of government, but a unifying covenant.[28]

The third, and perhaps most encouraging, feature of *A New Britain* is the recognition of the need for constitutional entrenchment: some way of protecting the foundations from being undermined by the Government of the day. The proposal is to achieve entrenchment through what are technically known as 'manner and form' provisions. Parliament would still be theoretically 'sovereign', but a specified list of 'constitutionally protected statutes' could be enacted, amended, or repealed only by a special parliamentary procedure. This procedure would give a stronger veto (although perhaps not an absolute veto – the paper is unclear on the details) to a reformed second chamber. This second chamber, known as the 'Assembly of Nations and Regions', would have a responsibility to protect constitutional fundamentals in general and the devolution settlement in particular. This is genuine constitutionalism, albeit in an embryonic stage.[29]

These reform proposals are better than nothing, but fall a long way short of the comprehensive and coherent constitutional refoundation needed. *A New Britain* is stuck in the rut of New Labour's incremental, piecemeal, tinkering, minimalist approach, exhibiting a lack of joined-up, comprehensive thinking. This is evident, for example, in the lack of any commitment to proportional representation for the Commons, without which there can be no real transformation of politics at the centre.

The crux of the whole scheme is the reformed second chamber, which would form the link between devolution to 'nations and regions', on the one hand, and the constitutional entrenchment of fundamentals, on the other. Prime Minister Sir Keir Starmer has, however, announced that this will not be a priority for the first term of the Labour Government elected in 2024,[30] which shows the current leadership's lack of attention to constitutional issues.

Even if there were a commitment to an Assembly of Nations and Regions, it is not easy to agree a formula. Giving Scotland, Wales, and Northern Ireland a share of seats in proportion to their populations will do nothing to protect their respective interests, because of England's numerical dominance. Giving them substantial over-representation – so that, combined, Scotland, Wales, and

Northern Ireland can outvote England – would be a blatant, open challenge to the Anglo-centricity of the Union. This betrays the main driver behind these proposals: a desire to prop up the Union. Even on its own terms it fails, because it ignores England. There is some vague reference to devolution within England, but no proposal for an English Parliament, and no recognition that England is a nation desperately in need of the revitalising power of a national political life of its own.[31]

### (d) Disintegration of the British constitution

The period of Conservative rule from the Brexit vote in 2016 to the 2024 general election was characterised by the reckless abuse of constitutional norms and conventions, chronic instability, high turnover in ministerial office, a decline in public ethics and institutional integrity, attempts to politicise the Civil Service, a lack of respect for the rights of the Opposition and of Parliament, the salami-slicing of devolution, and efforts to undermine the Supreme Court, the rule of law, and the principles of the legal system. It also saw an erosion of basic democratic civility, with opponents to the Brexit agenda being branded as enemies and traitors. Our goodly heritage of parliamentary democracy was threatened by these abuses. Some of them were, in isolation, relatively minor, such as breaking pairing arrangements.[32] Others were more troubling, such as when Boris Johnson unilaterally changed the Ministerial Code to remove the rule that ministers found to have deliberately misled the House of Commons are expected to resign. Great or small, these abuses piled on top of each other, with cumulatively fatal results.

The unwritten constitution was held together by what has been described as the 'Good Chaps' theory. In the words of Andrew Rawnsley, there was 'an underlying assumption that everyone can be trusted to behave in the proper way'.[33] A perceptive Irish scholar, writing in the 1930s, noted that, in England, 'the stability of its government lay in the fact that a people aristocratic in tendency and republican by temperament turned at the right historic moment to the democratic form of state and the ideal became that everyone should be a gentleman'.[34] However, that gentlemanly way, whatever it once might have been, no longer applies; at least, it no longer acts as a guide to public service, and endures only in a debased form, as dilettantism. As Andrew Blick and Peter Hennessy argue in *Good Chaps No More*, the moral consensus, shared values, and sense of constitutional propriety on which the 'British constitution' once rested have disintegrated.[35] Those in power no longer regard themselves as bound by previously accepted norms of proper behaviour. The most basic conventions have been strained. The unwritten rules, at crucial moments, have been unenforced, even unrecognised. Public life has become a something of a free for all, without self-restraint, moral responsibility, or ethical principles.[36]

'The British constitution under Liz Truss' would almost be worth a book in its own right. So much happened in such a short time to reveal the weaknesses of the constitutional and governance system, and the effects of these weaknesses on the ability of the state to serve the public. Within a few weeks of Truss's appointment as Prime Minister, the Chancellor of the Exchequer, Kwasi Kwarteng, announced a 'mini-budget', which proposed using borrowing to fund tax cuts for those making more than £150,000 a year. Financial institutions from the Bank of England to the International Monetary Fund – hardly known for their left-wing radicalism – denounced the move.[37] The pound fell to near parity with the US dollar. Mortgage interest rates rose. Middle-class home-owners in Tory constituencies got worried. The Tory backbenchers who represented them got worried too. Many soon regretted the change of leadership, perhaps concluding that more damage would be done by the misdirected zeal of Hayek-filled ideologues than was ever done by wayward and lackadaisical amateurs.

The 2022 mini-budget showed how constitutional failure begets governance failure, which begets poor policy choices, which in turn begets bad outcomes for ordinary people. Following public outcry and strongly voiced concern from backbench Tory MPs, the policy of unfunded tax cuts for the rich was quickly reversed. This was an embarrassing U-turn for the Government and a personal humiliation for the Chancellor of the Exchequer. Once again, however, the damage – in terms of public trust and market confidence – was already done. Truss publicly distanced herself from her Chancellor, straining the principle of collective ministerial responsibility; the tax-cut policy, according to Truss, had not even been discussed or agreed in Cabinet.[38] In other words, the conventionally established policy-making processes, which are supposed to ensure that policies are properly considered and coordinated, had broken down. Policies were made and unmade on the fly. Ministers changed tack when it suited them. There was no careful consideration of evidence, negotiation, scrutiny, and debate, just rash action and hasty reaction. That is no way to run a Government. It is no way to run a country.

In response to the ensuing economic turmoil, more than 200,000 people signed a petition calling for an early general election. With her party trailing far behind Labour in the opinion polls, Truss faced the threat of electoral wipe-out. Some polls predicted that the Conservatives would be pushed into third place, leaving the Scottish National Party as the official opposition. To avoid such a rout, the Conservative backbench 1922 Committee swung into action, and Truss was forced to resign.

Faced with the prospect of a widely unpopular Government, and another Conservative leadership election, some people began to wonder whether the newly acceded King could step in, at his own initiative, to dissolve Parliament, call a general election, and put everyone – except for most Tory MPs – out of their misery. The short answer is 'Almost certainly not'. The residual reserve power of the monarch to dismiss a Prime Minister, last used in 1834, is like a bee's sting: painful to the stung, fatal to the stinger. In the end, such fantastic scenarios were avoided by the Conservative Party's keen instinct for self-preservation. With Boris Johnson's return to power thwarted, and Penny Mordaunt pulling out of the party's internal leadership contest, the Tory MPs quickly selected Rishi Sunak as leader, and therefore as Prime Minister, without going to a divisive vote of the party membership. Nevertheless, the fact that such an exceptional royal intervention was being even hypothetically discussed shows the extent to which former constitutional certainties had unravelled.

This was just one in a long list of incidents, great and small, which all point to the same trend. In 2019, for instance, the question of whether the Queen could refuse assent to Bills passed by Parliament – a question we all thought had been settled in the negative for three centuries – was being earnestly debated.[39] The unwritten constitution has come adrift from its moorings. That which was once safely settled, secure, and accepted has become dangerously unsettled, frail, and contested.

The removal from office first of Boris Johnson and then of Liz Truss does – at the most basic level – show that the parliamentary system creeks along. Likewise, we can see the swift, peaceful, and efficient handover of power from Rishi Sunak to Sir Keir Starmer – swapping places on the front benches, the Leader of the Opposition becoming Prime Minister, and the Prime Minister becoming Leader of the Opposition – as evidence that democracy is not dead. Yet this does not negate the conclusion that the unwritten British constitution has reached its breaking point. The ability to remove a wayward leader from office is a very low threshold of success for a democratic constitutional system.[40] There was just about enough resilience in the parliamentary system – or, rather, in the 1922 Committee, which in the middle of 2022 became the real power in the land – to oust Johnson and Truss.[41] There is not, however, enough resilience to stop such people getting into power in the first place. If the guardians and gatekeepers fail to protect the public interest by keeping the obviously unfit out of office, the system has a structural vulnerability that needs to be addressed.

We should not allow the results of the 2024 general election to distract us from the reality of the deep, serious, and long-term constitutional crisis that the United Kingdom faces. The alarming constitutional trends continue. Starmer's victory might have brought an end to chaos and instability. It does not, however, mean that constitutional problems have gone away. He may revive hopes for, in his own words, 'a government of service', but his landslide was achieved with just one-third of the votes, many of them cast tactically. Labour has inherited an unconstituted state with, on the one hand, no legitimate or unifying foundation, and, on the other, few, if any, checks and balances to guard against the temptations of power. This state is ill-equipped to ensure good government in the public interest.

Meanwhile, from the Opposition benches and the right-wing press, Tory rhetoric continues to focus on rolling back as many of the New Labour reforms as possible. In tune with certain reactionary legal academics, they seem to regard fundamental human rights and judicial restraint upon government action as somehow alien and illegitimate. There is a dedicated constitutional reactionary movement on the right that seeks to restore the hard power of the pre-1997 majoritarian state, without the soft restraints that mitigated the abuse of that power. If this vast unrestrained power, real and potential, were to fall into the hands of an authoritarian populist leader, it could be swiftly fatal to democracy.

The need for constitutional refoundation – to reform democratic institutions and to restore eroded institutional norms and trust – is therefore more urgent than it has ever been. Blue or red, the Prime Minister rules over a desolate and disordered constitutional landscape. A lack of constitutional foundations continues to cause institutional fragility and the precarity of civil liberties. The 'soft guardrails' of democracy (the conventions, practices, and norms which should promote proper conduct and restrain improper conduct, and which are essential to decent democratic public life) have already been removed.[42] There is nothing solid behind them to stop us falling into the abyss.

Unless authority can be institutionalised rather than personalised – unless it can be made to flow again, as it once did, through established public institutions, such as the Civil Service, the Cabinet, and Parliament, within known limits – then policy will keep on bouncing around, without any certainty, substance, coherence, rationale, or restraint. Unless rights and rules of governance can be secured and protected by a written constitution, political expediency will continue to overrule our once most sacred fundamental principles. If England is to be well governed, it must have a good constitution.

### (e) What is a constitution?

A constitution may be defined as a 'supreme and fundamental law'. It is a law that is supreme in status (it is superior to other laws and capable of being changed only by means of a special amendment process) and fundamental in scope (it declares the basic principles of the state, it establishes and regulates governing institutions, and it defines and protects the fundamental rights of citizens). In the words of Thomas Paine, a constitution is characterised as follows:

> A constitution is not a thing in name only, but in fact. It has not an ideal, but a real existence; and wherever it cannot be produced in a visible form, there is none. [...] It is the body of elements to which you can refer and quote article by article; and which contains the principles upon which the government shall be established, the manner in which it shall be organized, the powers it shall have, the mode of elections, the duration of Parliaments, or by what other name such bodies may be called; the powers which the executive part of the Government shall have; and, in fine, everything that relates to the complete organization of a civil government, and the principles upon which it shall act, and by which it shall be bound.[43]

Democratic constitutions proclaim the foundational values of the state, providing guiding and grounding principles, and a shared civic basis for national identity. They organise and regulate public institutions, legitimise the exercise of public power, and make the relationship between these institutions more stable and predictable. They establish democratic mechanisms of representation to ensure inclusion in decision-making. They also enforce the accountability and responsibility of the governors to the governed – providing not only ways to get rid of a Government, but also to challenge and scrutinise its actions.

Constitutions separate the partisan policy-making functions of the Government from the permanent, non-partisan structures of the state. They protect the neutrality and independence of institutions like the Civil Service, the judiciary, the Electoral Commission, the Boundaries Commission, the Auditor-General, and so forth. Many constitutions also distribute power and resources territorially, typically between national, regional, and local levels of government.

Another important function of constitutions is to protect fundamental rights and to provide guarantees for particular persons or groups who might not be adequately protected by simple majoritarian politics.

Constitutions can even try to promote public ethics and to orientate the state to particular public-regarding policy goals, so that Governments are constrained in various ways to abstain from corruption and to focus their efforts on promoting the common good.

A constitution must be above other laws and protected against changes made by ordinary parliamentary majorities. That combination of *supremacy* and *entrenchment* is how the constitution defends enduring fundamentals against surrender to expediency. Otherwise, everything would depend on the pleasure of the Prime Minister or the ruling majority; all rights and institutions would be thrown, as they are now, into precarity and confusion.

The United Kingdom notoriously lacks such a constitution. Instead, it has only a messy accumulation of statutes, charters, conventions, precedents, and traditions. This 'unwritten constitution' might more properly be called no constitution at all, because it does not adequately serve any of the functions or purposes of a constitution.

Not being codified, supreme, or entrenched, Britain's unwritten constitution is woefully deficient at performing the tasks constitutions are supposed to perform. It cannot prevent attacks on human rights, because all rights depend upon the sovereignty of Parliament, which can take them away at will. An unwritten constitution does not establish and define institutions, nor regulate and restrain the exercise of public power. It cannot protect the independence of the judiciary or of the Electoral Commission, nor resist attempts to politicise the Civil Service. It cannot stop the undermining of devolution, nor end the disregard for the key conventions of parliamentarism on which the whole edifice is built. It cannot even provide an authoritative statement of the basic principles on which the state is founded, or the overarching purposes to which the state is orientated (for example, to uphold justice and promote the common good). In short, an unwritten constitution is to a written constitution as a colander is to a bowl: it can get wet, but it does not hold any water.

Any attempt to pin down the unwritten constitution is a bit like trying to define the rules of Mornington Crescent – the parlour game in which the whole point is for players to demonstrate humour in the adept application of non-existent rules. As the then Cabinet Secretary and Head of the Civil Service Robin Butler expressed it, 'We make it up as we go along, and call it flexible'.[44] That is fine larks for a parlour game, but not for the serious business of governing a country. Without clear and binding constitutional rules, nothing can ever be safe, stable, settled, or predictable.

A proper written constitution – declaring principles, protecting rights, and defining the roles and powers of major governing institutions – while by no means a 'magic bullet', would certainly help. It would make the rules known, make them more enforceable, and clarify expectations. Reforms that broaden, balance, and restrain power would be beneficial, too: proportional representation, a stronger second chamber, devolution, and independent 'fourth branch' commissions such as the Electoral Commission, the Judicial Appointments Commission, and the Honours Commission. All these things would moderate and restrain the exercise of power. They would filter out malfeasance and dampen the swings of excess. They would make it harder to bend rules to partisan or personal advantage. Above all, they would encourage Governments to think before they act, to build consensus, to reach agreement, and to justify their decisions. That would lead, over time, to better governance processes, better policy decisions, and better socio-economic development outcomes.

### (f) Public government and constitutional refoundation

The state, in a well constituted polity, is a public entity, belonging to the public, in which public office is a public trust to be used for publicly discerned public purposes, and where citizens in public life are faithful stewards of the public good, for which they are responsible to the public.

Our recent experience has been the opposite of that vision. We have seen public power perverted for private purposes. Private individuals, holding no public office – being neither ministers of the Crown nor civil servants – have been seconded to 10 Downing Street by private think tanks. Friends of Prime Ministers have been appointed to high office, or have received lucrative public contracts, under dubious circumstances. For too long, a party that called itself Conservative proved to be incapable of conserving anything good, worthy, or honourable. The state became riddled with corruption, shamelessness, and duplicity. Good government, public service, and truth itself were all abandoned, while the Spirit of Corruption rampaged unchecked through all our public institutions. That way lies certain ruin. No democracy can survive, no country can flourish, in such conditions.

The British state, once a globally respected bastion of good government, has degenerated beyond recognition. The former Conservative MP Rory Stewart – a moderate Tory hounded out by the hard right – noted that 'our government and Parliament, which once had a reasonable claim to be the best in the world, is now in a shameful state'.[45] Mark Thomas, founder of the 99% Organisation, has described it as a 'plunder state', which exists only to extract resources from the country and transfer them to a rich few.[46]

As noted by Stephen Bush, political editor of the *New Statesman*, the United Kingdom has become 'a state that lacks relevant expertise, has been poorly led at an official level as well as a ministerial one, and lacks the basic capacity to fulfil its aims'.[47] He was writing that about the evacuation of Afghanistan, but it is true across the board, in every policy area, from Brexit to the Covid response and to cancelled projects like the HS2 railway. The public interest comes last, if at all.

Do not say, 'But it was ever thus!' It was not. During the period of its greatness – once the reforming zeal of the nineteenth century had put an end to 'Old Corruption' – English governance acquired a well deserved reputation for propriety, rectitude, and public service. There might have been ideological differences about how to serve the public, but the idea of service, rather than plunder, was ingrained. This ethos of public service was sustained by informal but strong norms among the governing class. They enforced it, and reinforced it, even among themselves. George Orwell wrote in 1941 that 'Public life in England has never been openly scandalous. It has not reached the pitch of disintegration at which humbug can be dropped'.[48] In other words, there were scandals, but there was also a culture of self-regulation that kept them in check. Those who acted against the expected norms of public service were disgraced.

That has long gone. Since Brexit, we have seen, more so than ever, corruption and abuse of office openly indulged; the use of public office for private advantage has been laughed off, without shame, remorse, or consequence. Although the House of Commons Privileges Committee found that Boris Johnson had lied to Parliament,[49] he evaded serious punishment by resigning his seat – and then landed a weekly full-page column in the *Daily Mail*.[50] Meanwhile, Conservative MPs, many of whom had been given knighthoods at his hand, jumped to his defence, some threatening revenge against the Privileges Committee, or against those MPs voting to endorse its findings.[51] This is not how leaders in serious, sensible countries should behave. The people who run businesses, care for the elderly, teach children, repair drains, fight fires, drive vans, stack shelves, or perform heart surgery would be out on their ear if they behaved in that way.

There needs to be a great repentance for all this. In allowing our public life to descend into this disarray, so many institutions – the Government, Parliament, the political parties, the press, the BBC, the schools that supposedly train our leaders – have done things which they ought not to have done, and have not done those things which they ought to have done. England's descent into public misery will not be reversed unless it humbles itself and turns from these things.

We might reasonably expect the Labour Government which came to power in 2024 to set a better record, in terms of public ethics, than its immediate predecessors. Still, it is folly to entrust the well-being of the state to the character of particular persons. While we undoubtedly need leaders with passion, courage, vision, and integrity, we also need to *institutionalise* good governance. Good government relies upon rules, norms, systems, and institutions, not only upon individuals, even the best of whom are prone to all human failings. It has been said already, but bears reiteration: in the absence of constitutional renewal, Starmer – or, indeed, any subsequent Prime Minister, left or right – will rule over the same unconstituted state, with the same lack of checks and balances, the same unconstrained yet unchanneled power, the same procedural confusion, and the same vulnerability to corruption, manipulation, and abuse of office. Even if this is a tolerable risk under favourable circumstances, it could be fatal in the hands of a Government with authoritarian tendencies.

The decay of the unwritten constitution means that it is no longer possible to speak of mere constitutional *reform*, if reform is understood as selective changes to particular laws, institutions, or practices, designed to address specific issues of governance. It is too late for that. In the 1980s or 1990s, constitutional reformers wanted to change a system that, although in need of improvement, was still basically working and intact. Now the existing political system can no longer be defended even on its own terms, because nobody knows anymore what those terms are supposed to be. The tear in our constitutional fabric is too big to be patched up just by proportional representation, or House of Lords reform, or any isolated institutional tinkering of that nature. The limits of 'making do and muddling through' have been reached. Trying to fix it through isolated, uncoordinated reforms will only deepen the confusion.

Instead, we must speak of constitutional *refoundation* – a process of negotiating a new constitutional settlement that includes *restoration* as well as *reform*. 'Refoundation' has a subtle double meaning: it means to 'found again', that is, to re-establish; it also means to renew from the foundations – to replace the exhausted unwritten constitution, based upon the twin pillars of parliamentary sovereignty and conventions, with a new written constitution. Only such a constitution, a supreme and fundamental law, established above the power of this or that Government, can provide a secure basis for a stable and effective democratic state.

The questions we must now ask ourselves are constitutional in nature. Who are we? How should we govern ourselves? What is our common ground? What do we stand for? What will we not stand for? What rights and duties will we owe to one another? These questions have not been asked in England for a very long time, and never in a democratic context. Other countries have wrestled with these questions more recently, as their states have had to be rebuilt from the rubble of war or revolution. England, thanks to the British Empire, avoided that. The answers, implied in the unwritten constitution that reached its maturity in the imperial age, were self-evident to everyone who mattered. They had all been settled and put to rest. However, the stability of the British state from the mid-eighteenth to the late twentieth century was achieved by firm adherence to shared norms, tolerance, forbearance, and a willingness not to push limits to breaking point.[52] All that has gone. These questions have been dug up and disturbed from their resting places. They are now unsettled and unsettling questions. We cannot, even if we wanted to, put them back in the ground.

## (g) Objections answered

There are some good theoretical arguments – and many more bad ones – against written constitutions.[53] Most of these come down to some version of the following: that, on democratic grounds, the current Government and the parliamentary majority, with a mandate from the people, should be unduly constrained neither by the choices of past generations nor by the decisions of unelected judges. That argument is, however, based upon an understanding of democracy that is both false and misleading.

It is false because democracy cannot be reduced to majority rule. Democracy is a complex political system that combines representative and responsible government with civil liberties and the rule of law, checks and balances, impartial administration, decentralised authority, and the means of participatory engagement in public decision-making. To give absolute power to a Government backed by an ordinary parliamentary majority is not democracy, but a grotesque caricature of it.

Parliamentary sovereignty allows the current majority to kick over all the barriers that restrain abuses of power and that provide guarantees for the continuity of democracy. Attempts by any party to weaken the judiciary, politicise the Civil Service, sideline the Opposition, infringe the liberties and established civil rights of the people, centralise power, restrict public participation, capture of the Electoral Commission, evade accountability, or change the rules to suit themselves must therefore be seen as attacks on democracy. The function of the constitution is not to restrict democracy, but to protect it – its institutions, rules, processes, and values – from such attacks.

Perhaps some on the anti-constitutional populist left are sincere, if misguided, in their opposition to restraints on what they see as the power of the people's representatives. In other hands, however, the anti-constitutionalist argument only *pretends* to care about democracy, even in its most crudely majoritarian sense. What reactionary parliamentary sovereigntists loathe above all is not restrictions on power as such, but only restrictions that apply to them and their ilk. They are, after all, quite happy to impose restrictions on the Scottish Parliament or the Supreme Court. For those who feel they have an in-born right to rule, and who claim the Palace of Westminster as their natural habitat, written constitutions are irksome because they limit the power of their caste, which has always 'instinctively scorned constraints', to rule as they please.[54]

A common criticism of written constitutions is to note that authoritarian regimes, like the Soviet Union, have had written constitutions, which have served only as elaborate window-dressing for despotism. That is no argument, however, against a written constitution; it is only an argument against an authoritarian constitution. A constitution of that sort is not under consideration. This book proposes a liberal-democratic constitution of Westminster provenance. If we wish to make international comparisons, it should be to places like Australia, Canada, and Ireland, not to the former Soviet bloc.

It must be admitted that a written constitution is not a fool-proof guarantee. Many decent constitutions, sincerely democratic in intent, have been overthrown, suspended, or whittled away by acts of deliberate constitutional vandalism. The infamous example is that of the Weimar Republic in inter-war Germany, whose constitution was manipulated and then overthrown by Hitler. Some post-colonial constitutions in Africa were also of that type: democratic at the moment of independence, but swept away by military coups, or salami-sliced into irrelevance by populist dictators with no respect for them. The risk of that is perhaps less in England than in some other places; the tradition of the rule of law probably still runs deep enough that a constitution is likely to be respected and obeyed, especially if the process of adopting it is seen as legitimate. Yet this should serve as a warning. The fact that the Weimar Republic's constitution failed does not mean that written constitutions are worthless, but that they must be well designed; the Germans applied that lesson in the current constitution of the Federal Republic, which corrects the faults of its inter-war predecessor.[55]

In any case, that is not how written constitutions work. Mere 'parchment barriers' and 'paper constitutions' have no magical power. They do not make authoritarian backsliding, the erosion of human rights, systemic corruption, or other abuses of power impossible. They do, however, make these things much harder. They protect against casual, accidental, thoughtless violations. They interpose the courts as another forum in which Governments can be caused to pause, to think again, to justify themselves against a higher law and deeper principles. Since amending the constitution would need more than an ordinary parliamentary majority, opposition parties, exercising their power of veto, would be able, in most foreseeable circumstances, to stop constitutional vandalism before it is too late.

A written constitution provides a clear line in the sand. It marks out what is – and what is not – within the bounds of acceptability. That raises the stakes of anti-democratic measures. If a Government were to attempt to go beyond the constitution, it would have to do so openly and deliberately. This carries the risk of undermining that Government's own authority and uniting the public against its unconstitutional actions. After all, as the legitimacy of the Government depends upon the constitution, to attack the constitution is to saw through the branch on which its power rests.

Besides, to indulge the theoretical arguments against a written constitution is a luxury we can no longer afford. They assume there is an alternative – that a decent political system can be maintained in the absence of a written constitution, by well respected conventions, by a settled consensus about what is 'done' and 'not done', by unspoken agreement about the nature of the political system, and by a sense of self-restraint that prevents misgovernment and the abuse of office. Those assumptions, even if perhaps once valid, no longer apply.

There is a distinction between 'specific' support and 'diffuse' support for public authority. Specific support refers to support for particular policies. This ebbs and flows. Prime Ministers come and go. There are some policies we like and some we dislike. Such fluctuations in specific support can cause the Government to fall or to lose an election, but do not cause regimes to collapse. Diffuse support, on the other hand, is a generalised support for the political system as a whole – the perceived public legitimacy the state and its institutions. If diffuse support is lost – if people come to the see system itself as deficient, unfair, corrupt, rigged against them – then catastrophic system failure may result.[56] We are not, perhaps, quite there yet – but we are perilously close.

So, a written constitution is not one option among a range of other acceptable options. It has become an urgent necessity. To protect civil liberties, safeguard parliamentary democracy, promote good government, restore public confidence, and stabilise the foundations of the state, a new constitution is needed. Things simply cannot go on as they have before. The ground rules and basic principles must be agreed, written down in an enforceable supreme and fundamental law, made hard enough to change that the Government cannot just bend, break, or waive the rules for its own convenience, and then shared and taught so that everyone knows exactly where they stand.

## Notes

1 ITV News (2022) 'King Charles III: read the King's inaugural address following the death of the Queen in full' (9 September), https://www.itv.com/news/2022-09-09/king-charles-iii-delivers-first-speech-to-the-nation-read-his-address-in-full, accessed 21 November 2022.

2 Associated Press (2022) 'Read King Charles III's full first address to the UK Parliament', PBS News website (12 September), https://www.pbs.org/newshour/world/read-king-charles-iiis-full-first-address-to-the-uk-parliament, accessed 21 November 2022.

3 S. D. Sargent (1976) *An Examination of the Laws of William the Conqueror* (MA thesis, University of Massachusetts), https://scholarworks.umass.edu/cgi/viewcontent.cgi?article=3071&context=theses, accessed 21 October 2022.

4 K. Mackenzie (1951) *The English Parliament* (Pelican), pp. 14–17.

5 D. Hay (1966) *Europe in the Fourteenth and Fifteenth Centuries* (Longman), pp. 88–92, 110.

6 W. I. Jennings (1959) *Cabinet Government* (3rd edn) (Cambridge University Press); W. I. Jennings (1965) *The Queen's Government* (Revised edn) (Penguin Books); A. Birch (1969) *The British System of Government* (2nd edn) (George Allen and Unwin); J. Harvey and L. Bather (1966) *The British Constitution* (Macmillan).

7 J. C. Adams and P. Barile (1966) *The Government of Republican Italy* (2nd edn) (Houghton Mifflin); P. Williams (1958) *Politics in Post-war France* (2nd edn) (Longmans, Green and Co.).

8 W. Bagehot (1873) *The English Constitution* (2nd edition), https://historyofeconomicthought.mcmaster.ca/bagehot/constitution.pdf, accessed 1 November 2022.

9 Ibid.

10 A. V. Dicey (1915) *Introduction to the Study of the Law of the Constitution* (8th edn) (Macmillan).

11 W. I. Jennings (1965) *The Queen's Government* (revised edn) (Penguin Books).

12 These core conventions, according to Dicey, *Introduction to the Study of the Law*, included the following. (1) The party which for the time being command a majority in the House of Commons, has (in general) a right to have its leaders placed in office. (2) The most influential of these leaders ought (generally speaking) to be the Premier, or head of the Cabinet. (3) A Ministry which is outvoted in the House of Commons is in many cases bound to retire from office. (4) A Cabinet, when outvoted on any vital question, may appeal once to the country by means of a dissolution. (5) If an appeal to the electors goes against the Ministry, it is bound to retire from office, and has no right to dissolve Parliament a second time. (6) The Cabinet is responsible to Parliament as a body, for the general conduct of affairs. (7) The action of any Ministry would be highly unconstitutional if it should involve the proclamation of war, or the making of peace, in defiance of the wishes of the House. (8) If there is a difference of opinion between the House of Lords and the House of Commons, the House of Lords ought, at some point, not definitely fixed, to give way. (9) Parliament ought to be summoned for the despatch of business at least once in every year. (10) If a sudden emergency arises, such as through the outbreak

of an insurrection, or an invasion by a foreign power, the Ministry ought, if it requires additional authority, at once to have Parliament convened and obtain any powers which it may need for the protection of the country.

13 Dicey, ibid.

14 A. M. Schlesinger (1994) 'Leave the constitution alone', in A. Lijphart (ed.), *Parliamentary Versus Presidential Government* (Oxford University Press), p. 91.

15 This was more in practice than in theory, given the absence of a transparent judicial appointment process and the anomalous position of the Lord Chancellor before these defects were partially remedied by the Constitution Reform Act 2005.

16 *Hansard*, House of Commons, 13 May 1940, col. 1505.

17 J. Cowley (2022) *Who Are We Now? Stories of Modern England* (Picador), p. 246.

18 J. Hawes (2021) *The Shortest History of England* (Old Street Publishing).

19 Liberal–SDP Alliance (1983) Election manifesto, https://www.libdems.co.uk/manifestos/1983/1983-liberal-manifesto.shtml, accessed 1 November 2022.

20 A. Lijphart (1999) *Patterns of Democracy* (Yale University Press).

21 Ibid.

22 E. Dorey (2008) *The Labour Party and Constitutional Reform: A History of Constitutional Conservatism* (Palgrave Macmillan).

23 Cowley, *Who Are We Now?*, p. 145.

24 M. Flinders (2009) 'Constitutional anomie: patterns of democracy and "tThe governance of Britain"', *Government and Opposition*, Vol. 44, No. 4., pp. 385–411.

25 It is worth noting that under Gordon Brown (whose position on the constitution, while not well informed, was always both more principled and more radical than that of Tony Blair), Labour's 2010 manifesto called not only for referendums on voting reform and an elected second chamber, but also for 'An all-party commission to chart a course to a written constitution'. Labour's defeat in the general election of that year meant that the sincerity of that call – and the party's ability to implement a proper constitution-building process – was never tested. See 'A future fair for all', Labour Party manifesto 2010.

26 K. Knock (2006) 'The North East referendum: lessons learnt?', *Parliamentary Affairs*, Vol. 59, No. 4, pp. 682–693.

27 Labour Party (2022) *A New Britain: Renewing Our Democracy and Rebuilding Our Economy* (Report of the Commission on the UK's Future) (Labour Party).

28 For more on the concept of covenant in relation to the role and purpose of constitutions, see W. E. Bulmer (2015) *A Constitution for the Common Good: Strengthening Scottish Democracy After the Independence Referendum* (2nd edn) (Luath Press).

29 It would not be the first 'manner and form' provision to operate in the United Kingdom: there are some provisions of the Scotland Act, relating to the electoral system, that are entrenched by requiring a two-thirds majority in the Scottish Parliament. However, except for the provision in the Parliament Act giving the House of Lords a veto over legislation to extend the life of Parliament, it would be the first to apply to Westminster, rather than to a devolved legislature.

30 N. Gutteridge (2023) 'Keir Starmer to place Lords reform on hold', *Telegraph*, 15 October.

31 The same stale Unionism and lack of constitutional imagination was evident when Nicola Sturgeon, then First Minister of Scotland, attempted to launch a second Scottish independence referendum campaign in June 2022. Labour's David Lammy MP, at the time Shadow Foreign Secretary, immediately denounced it, saying that Labour was a Unionist party and would categorically rule out a referendum on Scottish independence. There was no attempt to consider how acceptance of Scottish independence could be part of a wider movement to dismantle the reliquary of the British imperial state and to rebuild England's own democratic institutions.

32 A pairing arrangement is an agreement of honour, reached between the Government and Opposition whips, to enable Members to absent themselves (because of illness, compassionate reasons, or urgent business) from the House for important votes, by making sure that the absence of a Member from one side is balanced by the absence of a Member from the other. The breakdown of pairing arrangements at a crucial point of the Brexit

process was just one example of the ways in which the normal, unwritten, informal rules were strained.

33  A. Rawnsley (2019) 'Mr Johnson's plot to subvert democracy is more dangerous than Brexit itself', *The Guardian*, 11 August.

34  W. Starkie (1935) *Raggle-Taggle: Adventures with a Fiddle in Hungary and Roumania* (E. P. Dutton and Co.), p. 107.

35  A. Blick and P. Hennessy (2019) *Good Chaps No More? Safeguarding the Constitution in Stressful Times* (Constitution Society), https://consoc.org.uk/wp-content/uploads/2019/11/FINAL-Blick-Hennessy-Good-Chaps-No-More.pdf, accessed 20 November 2022.

36  As discussed later, there has been a partial return to political normality since the 2024 election, but the damage has nevertheless been done. Rules once held sacred, having been broken when convenient, can be more easily broken again.

37  Trickle-down theory has been thoroughly debunked. Cutting taxes on high incomes to stimulate growth might have been defensible policy in the 1970s, but after forty years of such policies, the deep social damage of Cameron's austerity, and the economic catastrophe of Brexit, a different approach is called for – an approach that the current British state is constitutionally incapable of delivering.

38  E. Piper and A. MacAskill (2022) 'Cabinet was not informed of plans to scrap top rate of tax, Truss says', Reuters, 2 October, https://www.reuters.com/world/uk/uk-pm-truss-says-cabinet-was-not-informed-plans-scrap-top-rate-tax-2022-10-02, accessed 11 April 2023.

39  The draft Constitution in the Annex solves this problem. Bills having been passed by both Houses are certified by the Speaker of the House of Commons and the Lord Speaker, and then presented to the monarch for Royal Assent, which must be given within thirty days; if it does not receive Royal Assent during that time, the House may resolve that Royal Assent shall nevertheless be deemed to have been given, and the Bill shall thereupon be enacted.

40  J.-W. Müller (2021) *Democracy Rules* (Penguin Books), p. 46.

41  P. Norton (2023) *The 1922 Committee: Power Behind the Scenes* (Manchester University Press).

42  S. Levitsky and D. Ziblatt and (2018) *How Democracies Die: What History Reveals About Our Future* (Crown).

43  T. Paine (1791) *The Rights of Man*, https://www.gutenberg.org/files/3742/3742-h/3742-h.htm, accessed 25 October 2022.

44  This statement is, I believe, attributed to Sir Robin Butler by Professor Peter Hennessy.

45  R. Stewart (2023) *Politics on the Edge* (Jonathan Cape), p. ix.

46  M. Thomas (2021) 'Malice in Plunderland: a new kind of government?', 99% Organisation (15 September), https://99-percent.org/malice-in-plunderland-a-new-kind-of-government, accessed 5 September 2022.

47  S. Bush (2021) 'The testimony from Foreign Office whistleblower directly blames Dominic Raab's lack of grip', *New Statesman*, 7 December, https://www.newstatesman.com/afghanistan/2021/12/the-40-page-written-testimony-from-the-foreign-office-whistleblower-directly-blames-dominic-raabs-lack-of-grip, accessed 20 November 2022.

48  G. Orwell (1941) *The Lion and the Unicorn: Socialism and the English Genius* (Orwell Foundation), https://www.orwellfoundation.com/the-orwell-foundation/orwell/essays-and-other-works/the-lion-and-the-unicorn-socialism-and-the-english-genius, accessed 19 November 2022.

49  House of Commons Committee of Privileges (2023) 'Matter Referred on 21April 2022 (Conduct of Rt Hon Boris Johnson): Final Report' (Report of Fifth Session 2022–23), 15 June, HC 564.

50  *Daily Mail* (2023) 'Mail unveils Boris Johnson as our new columnist', 16 June.

51  P. Walker and S. Gecsoyler (2023) 'Boris Johnson allies threaten to target Tories who back Partygate report for deselection', *The Guardian*, 15 June.

52  Levitsky and Ziblatt, *How Democracies Die*.

53  These arguments are discussed at greater length in W. E. Bulmer (2020) *Westminster and*

*the World: Commonwealth and Comparative Insights for Constitutional Reform* (Bristol University Press), ch. 4.

54 S. Kuper (2023) *Chums: How a Tiny Caste of Oxford Tories Took Over the UK* (Profile Books), p. 179.

55 E. Plischke (1962) *Contemporary Government of Germany* (Houghton, Mifflin and Co.).

56 D. Easton (1975) 'A reassessment of the concept of political support', *British Journal of Political Science*, Vol. 5, pp. 435–457.

# 2

# Unravelling of the United Kingdom

## (a) Who are 'the people'?

Sir Ivor Jennings, perhaps the greatest practitioner-scholar of Commonwealth constitutionalism, recognised that questions of identity, boundaries, and demographics precede questions of institutional design. In other words, before we can ask 'How should the people govern themselves?' we must first ask 'Who are the people?'[1] The development of a written constitution must therefore start, as the Canadian constitutional lawyer Sujit Choudhry put it, with 'the existential question of whether a multinational polity' – in this case, the United Kingdom – 'should exist at all'.[2]

This matters because the demographic, physical, and cultural boundaries of the state – who is included, who is excluded, its territorial extent, and whether the resulting population is homogeneous or heterogeneous – determine the range of viable and acceptable constitutional options. The constitutions of Canada and Jamaica, for example, both descend from a common Westminster Model heritage. Their institutions and principles of government are very similar. The fundamental difference between them is that Canada has a complex federal system, while Jamaica is a simple unitary state. This reflects the different constitutional needs of the two countries, based on their different physical, demographic, and cultural contexts. The intricate federalism necessary for Canada, with its provincial autonomy and special guarantees for Quebec and the French-speaking minority, would be unnecessary in Jamaica, a small and relatively homogenous island country, with no major cultural or linguistic divisions. In the same way, a constitution for the whole United Kingdom – consisting of four countries, with distinct histories, cultural identities, legal systems, religious settlements, and languages – would necessarily be a longer, more complex, and more intricate document than a constitution for England alone.

The argument advanced in this chapter is that the costs, complications, and inconveniences of trying to keep the United Kingdom together in its current form outweigh any advantages. The game is no longer worth the candle. If the Union is to continue at all, it must be in a radically different form – as an equal, voluntary, 'unincorporating' Union, not as a single United Kingdom under one Government and one sovereign Parliament. This would be a positive step for England. The recovery of English statehood, lost for three centuries in the British imperial state, offers new life to England, a chance to come to terms with its own past, and an opportunity to make a fresh start as a flourishing democracy.

## (b) Englishness and Anglo-centric British nationalism

The United Kingdom, as currently constituted on the back of the devolution arrangements of the late 1990s, has become untenable. Besides those with pro-independence sentiments in Scotland and Wales, and those seeking a united Ireland, many more are dissatisfied with the devolved Union from an English perspective. Devolution offered quick-and-dirty fixes to accommodate Scotland, Wales, and Northern Ireland, but without any coherent plan of how the new United Kingdom would fit together. It ignores England, and treats England as a geographical expression, devoid of political significance.[3]

Covid lockdown messaging in 2020–2021 illustrated the anomalies arising from this lopsided structure. While the UK Government acknowledged the right of Scotland and Wales to make their own rules, the London-based media, and much of the English political class, were confused. The Scottish and Welsh Governments repeatedly had to justify the audacity of diverging from the UK Government's policy, which applied only in England.[4]

Accounts such as 'That's Devolved' and 'Just Say England' on Twitter/X often have to correct official statements, across the whole range of devolved policy areas – health, education, housing, policing, and more – where the UK Government forgets that its power ends at the Scottish and Welsh borders.

As well as being confusing, devolution strikes many English people as unfair on principle. Among those who identify most strongly as English, there is a sense of 'devo-anxiety', or 'a perception that England is unfairly treated within the territorial settlement that now exists in the United Kingdom'.[5] 'Political Englishness' presents itself as the voice of those who consider themselves to be alienated, left behind, disenfranchised, and ignored – economically, culturally, and politically – by the British state.[6] Henderson and Wyn Jones recognise that those most likely to identify as English (rather than British) are characterised by 'low trust' and a sense of 'low efficacy'. In other words, the English-identifiers are those who feel that the British Government neither knows nor cares about them ('low trust') and who feel that they cannot make an effective difference, through democratic action, to the public life of the British state ('low efficacy').[7]

The members of this low-trust, low-efficacy section of society are most likely to vote for the far right, and also to express their rage at the erasure of English identity and at perceived institutional anti-Englishness in the most violent, lawless, and misdirected ways.[8] To them, Englishness is a tribal identity – defined in exclusive and ethnic terms – which used to be culturally dominant, but has now lost its primacy in modern multicultural Britain. The English are an 'unspoken people', whose 'separate sense of English grievance' has become a 'powerful and rather unbiddable force'.[9]

It is also remarkable that English identity is weakest in London.[10] Daily life in London is closer, in geographic if not in class terms, to the centre of British power. Moreover, for the past twenty years there has been a highly visible form of devolution, the Greater London Authority, that has allowed Londoners to have some sense of collective agency. Identifying as a 'Londoner' is now a way of being (civically) British without being (ethno-culturally) English.

Resurgent English nationalism could pose an existential threat to the United Kingdom. As argued by Gavin Esler, while the United Kingdom 'can survive Irish, Scottish and Welsh nationalisms, it cannot survive English nationalism'.[11] Those who primarily identify as English are indeed more likely (compared with those resident in England who primarily identify as British) to believe that 'the current structure of the UK is unfair' and to support 'a particularly English dimension to the governance of England'.[12]

However, in marked contrast to the situation in Scotland and Wales, this sense of English grievance does not entail the abandonment of Britishness, nor does it necessarily translate into a rejection of the United Kingdom as a political entity. British and English identities are rarely mutually exclusive. Rather, they are nested within one another, in a way that places England at the core of the Union and the Union as an extension of English power. Henderson and Wyn Jones use the analogy of a castle, with English identity as the inner keep and British identity as the inner curtain wall, and a wider imperial identity, shared with the 'kith and kin' of the old Dominions, as the outer wall.[13]

Mainstream English public opinion is still ashamed of English national identity, and repulsed by the implications of political Englishness. The parading of English identity by rioters, and by certain far-right politicians, only strengthens middle-class fear of Englishness. It is a low-status identity, fit only for the brick-chucking classes. St George's flags easily blur, in the public imagination, with flaming wheelie bins and glass bottles bouncing off riot shields. Alternative, more progressive and inclusive, accounts of Englishness are few – *The Progressive Patriot* by Billy Bragg and *Another England* by Caroline Lucas are partial, notable, exceptions.[14]

Support for English independence remains a niche cause.[15] Those who wish to establish an independent English state, on similar lines to those proposed for Scotland by the Scottish National Party, have negligible political influence. No political party speaks for them. According to the 2022 British Social Attitudes Survey, 25% of people in England support the dissolution of the Union between England and Scotland, but this figure demonstrates only their indifference to the Union, rather than active support for English independence.[16]

In other words, much of English nationalism today is still focused on maintaining a centralised United Kingdom in which the non-English fringe is dominated by the English core. It nurses grievances against the Scots and the Welsh, both for their rejection of English dominance and for their alleged overuse of English resources.

The awakening of the other countries in the United Kingdom has, as Arthur Aughey puts it, 'disordered the senses' of the English, because it forced them to discover the rest of the Union 'not as appendages to England but as assertive political communities' whose existence challenges the Englishness of Britain and Britishness of England.[17] This resentment is combines, in poisonous ways, with a fear of perceived threats to Englishness from the European Union and from minority groups it regards as 'non-English': Muslims, immigrants, and asylum seekers. This right-wing form of English nationalism clings to an exclusionary, reactionary, and authoritarian form of 'English Britishness' and 'British

Englishness', which puts the Scots, Welsh, Irish, immigrants, and foreigners in their place.[18] It lies behind the hopeless logic that has driven Government policy in recent years: Brexit, hard borders, forced deportations, the 'hostile environment' regime, 'muscular Unionism', and the stony-faced denial of another Scottish independence referendum.

This form of English nationalism – a form that tries to suppress Scotland and Wales, rather than partner with them on equal terms as good neighbours – has changed the face of the Union. According to Wyn Jones and Henderson, the view that Scotland, Wales, and England are distinct nations, and that the United Kingdom is therefore a 'partnership of nations', is 'centuries old' and 'remains very widely shared'.[19] It was not controversial, and 'was not confined to a particular part of the state or political spectrum'; rather, it was 'an utterly mainstream opinion'.[20] Indeed, a decade ago Conservatives were most likely to regard England as a nation (84% of English Conservatives, compared with 78% of English Labour and 68% of English Liberal Democrats). The same view of the Union, as a broadly equal partnership of distinct nations, was also held by Conservatives north of the border, with 83% of Scottish Conservatives in 2011 regarding Scotland as a nation rather than as a mere region of Britain.[21]

With the 2016 Brexit vote and the subsequent rightward shift of the Conservative Party, that position has reversed, and the partisan split on attitudes to the Union has widened. Whereas in 2011 broadly equal numbers of Labour (25%) and Conservative (24%) supporters were in favour of Scottish independence, this figure has diverged, with support for the dissolution of the Union now nearly twice as high among English Labour supporters (30%) as among English Conservatives (16%). Labour, despite its ingrained British-mindedness, has a likely electorate that is now much more open than Conservative voters to accept the possibility of the dissolution of the United Kingdom. The Conservatives in Scotland, in a staggering aberration from their tradition, are most likely to deny Scotland's existence as nation and to regard Scotland merely as a region in a British nation – a view held by 48% of them.[22] The old Conservative idea of Scottish Unionism, as distinct from British nationalism, is effectively dead. However, only 28% of Conservative supporters in England share this belief that there is only one British nation – they are much happier to own an English *national* identity, even while loyal to the United Kingdom.[23]

This apparent contradiction in Conservative English identity – recognising England as a nation, but not wanting that nation to be independent from the United Kingdom – can only be resolved through what John Denham calls 'Anglo-centric British Unionism'. This approach, according to Denham, is the 'largest and most hegemonic' form of English political identity, and which 'dominates the outlook of the Labour Party in England, the Whitehall civil service machine, the London-based UK media, and England's cultural and arts establishment'. It understands the United Kingdom simply as an 'extension of English institutions and the expression of English interests'.[24]

If the Union is understood merely as an expansion of the English state across a wider territory – an expansion that does not fundamentally change its English character – then the 'institutions, symbols and values that in the rest of the state are regarded as quintessentially British' can be seen in England as properly belonging to the English.[25] For those of this mind, to be English is the normal, default mode of Britishness, the real and original members of the club. The Scots, Welsh, and Northern Irish have reciprocal rights – they may use the facilities, even drink in the Members' Bar – but they do not have a right to feel like they *own the place*.

Yet this English dominance over the United Kingdom has the paradoxical effect of denying England – as *England* – a voice in its own affairs. England, becoming everything, also becomes nothing. Despite its historical position at the core of the Union and the Empire, England remains a curiously underdeveloped nation in constitutional terms. It is the only country of the United Kingdom that has no national Government, Parliament, or political life of its own. It is also – not coincidentally – the only country in the United Kingdom where National Health Service prescription charges apply and where university tuition fees for home students have increased so dramatically.[26] Once again, constitutional structures cannot be disentangled from socio-economic outcomes. *How* we are governed, and not only *by whom* we are governed, makes all the difference. It is no surprise, then, that the Brexit slogan of 'Take Back Control' resonated most strongly in England.

## (c) The Brexit effect

In the aftermath of the Brexit referendum, during that strange time when Theresa May was Prime Minister and political life was consuming itself with the task of trying to make the unworkable work, my wife and I decided to undertake a tour of English cathedral cities. We went into the heart of England, exploring some of its most picturesque medieval cities. Even there, however, not far from the tearooms and the fudge shops, it seemed hard to escape the squalor. Everything looked tired, worn out, shabby. There were a lot of homeless people, beggars, daytime drunks, and people who looked as if they had fallen through the cracks of life without anyone to catch them.

Nearly a decade after the 2008 financial crisis, growth and confidence had not returned. David Cameron's austerity programme had bitten hard. Yet the roots of this distress were deeper. For forty years, much of provincial England had been hit hard by the ideological double whammy of Thatcherism and Blairism: the victory of the neoliberal right in economics and of the neoliberal left in society. The first blow brought with it privatisation, union-busting, precarious employment, factory closures, underinvestment, deep cuts to public services, and, for many, a relative decline in living standards. The second blow brought an erosion of solidarity and of the traditional family, and the undermining of the communal Christian values that had once given resilience and structure to people's lives.[27] Between them, these two forces had unravelled society, and now the effects were showing.

No wonder, then, that so much of provincial England had a desire to 'take back control' over jobs that had been lost, lives that had been stunted, and once-solid communities that had been hollowed out. None of this was the fault of the European Union – Delft and Troyes did not look like that. Still, it was easy for the populist far right to harness that displaced anger and ride it into power. The United Kingdom Independence Party (UKIP) (never, it should be noted, the 'English Independence Party'), its successor parties, and its hard-right Conservative collaborators, very skilfully redirected English anger and resentment outwards, against immigration and the European Union, while ignoring the deficit of English democracy and development within the United Kingdom.[28]

An infamous incident in Oldham in the 2010 general election campaign, when the then Prime Minister Gordon Brown called local Labour supporter Gillian Duffy a 'bigoted old woman' for raising the issue of immigration, appears in retrospect to have indicated a shift in the public mood.[29] It fore-shadowed the Leave victory in the referendum in 2016, and ultimately led to Labour losing the 'Red Wall' of formerly safe seats across the north of England in 2019. Neither should we forget the coastal towns – ageing, dishevelled, with poor infrastructure and low-paying, seasonal jobs – that have been seduced, in their grey despair, by far-right politicians peddling a strand of English national-ism so 'fixated on its borders' that it was willing to accept 'dysfunctional and shocking' misgovernment as the price of sealing them.[30]

For Anglo-centric British Unionists, Brexit might yet turn out to be a pyrrhic victory. In truth, there is not one Brexit, but two. The first is the 'culture war Brexit', or, as Andrew Marr put it, the 'Nostalgia Brexit': the 'flag-waving, sovereignty-fetishising, fever-dream', which rejected Europe in a desperate and futile attempt to bring back the traditional England, undone by the last four or five decades of social, economic, and cultural change.[31] The second Brexit is the 'actual Brexit': the painful legal, political, and economic consequences of that decision, as implemented by Theresa May, Boris Johnson, and his successors. Actual Brexit is a 'corrupt relentless horrorshow of loss, waste, cost, red tape and damage',[32] which has made the whole United Kingdom visibly poorer.[33] In the last quarter of 2021, according to estimates by the Centre for European Reform, the United Kingdom's gross domestic product (GDP) was 5.2% smaller, investment was 13.7% lower, and trade in goods trade 13.6% lower than would have been the case had Brexit been avoided.[34]

It is possible to understand and empathise with the reasons for the 'culture war' or 'nostalgia' Brexit – the heart-cry of provincial England, bewildered, forgotten, ignored, sneered at by a metropolitan cultural elite and a floating, far-away, ruling class – while also recognising that actual Brexit is, and was always going to be, an economic disaster. Brexit, in other words, was the wrong answer to a real problem.

The better answer would have been three-pronged: first, to address the democratic deficit in England through constitutional change; second, to im-plement active industrial and infrastructural development policies that would have brought growth, investment, opportunities, higher-paying jobs, and better public services to English northern cities and provincial and coastal towns (not by Whitehall command, but in a locally accountable, bottom-up way); and third, to encourage a more secure and inclusive sense of civic English identity that, being less frustrated, alienated, and threatened, could again feel at home in its own historical Europeanness.[35]

None of that was done. When the rich and well connected backers of Brexit said that they wanted to 'take back control' they meant it: they meant to take control back into their own hands, into the hands of the Eton and Oxford ruling caste for whom the sovereign Parliament acted as just another private club, where they took orders from no-one.[36] They had no intention of giving power to people in Salford or Sunderland – the sort of people whose schools do not have boat houses or shooting ranges. The ranks of London-based land-lords, financiers, and politicos cared so little about the prosperity of northern England that they could not even bring themselves to build a high-speed rail link from Birmingham to Leeds. The redevelopment of coastal towns and the re-industrialisation of provincial cities lay far beyond their imagination. It was just so much easier to milk the City of London, short the pound, and blame Europe.

This has consequences for the survival of the United Kingdom. For better or worse, Brexit has driven a sharp, perhaps irreconcilable, wedge between its four countries. A majority in England, and a thin majority in Wales, voted for Brexit. Bigger majorities in Scotland and Northern Ireland voted against it. The reasons why Scotland voted against Brexit are complex, with explanations ranging from the long-term impact of the Scottish Reformation (which meant that Scotland maintained closer intellectual links than did England with Protestant continental Europe) to different responses to the end of Empire. Certainly, Scotland does not fetishise the idea of parliamentary sovereignty in the way that England does, and the experience of devolved institutions made it clear to many Scots that Westminster, not Brussels, was the bigger obstacle to a better life. Despite these different dynamics, to which Nicola Sturgeon, then First Minister of Scotland, tried to give voice, the United Kingdom Government made no attempt to reach a compromise with Scotland over Brexit, as it did with Northern Ireland. Scotland was taken out of the European Union against its manifest national will.

To deny, as some do, that Scotland has a 'national will', and to say that it should be treated in that regard no differently from any English region, is to break with the historical position, on which the 'No' vote in the 2014 Scottish independence referendum depended, of seeing the Union as a voluntary and equal Union of nations. Treating the United Kingdom as one whole undif-ferentiated unit, regardless of these national distinctions and contrary to the principles of Scotland's 1989 Claim of Right, is a dangerous innovation – replacing Scottish Unionism with a British Nationalism that denies English as well as Scottish nationhood.

It is worth noting that many supporters of Scottish and Welsh independence see no contradiction between seeking the dissolution of the United Kingdom, on the one hand, and membership of the European Union, on the other. Like many people in other European countries, most Scottish and Welsh nationalists do not see membership of the European Union as an existential threat to their identity or democracy; rather, they see it as a guarantee of their freedom, and of their continued existence and relevance in a big, sometimes bad, world. They are mostly mature enough, and realistic enough, to recognise that independence, in a complex and interdependent world, is always a relative term. Of the two unions on offer, the European Union simply offers a better deal, politically and economically, than the United Kingdom.

In a costly failure of both leadership and imagination, no effort was made to accommodate Scotland's decision to remain in the European Union. This could have been done by pursing a 'soft Brexit' inside the Single Market, or at the very least inside the Customs Union. That compromise would have separated the symbolism of 'culture war Brexit' from the harmful material and economic consequences of 'actual Brexit'. Instead, driven by anti-immigrant sentiment and by the hard right of the Conservative Party, Theresa May's economically self-sabotaging 'red lines' resulted in a 'hard Brexit': leaving the Single Market and the Customs Union, and even ceasing other forms of cooperation that were not directly dependent on membership of the European Union, such as the Erasmus exchange scheme for students. Labour, afraid of its own voters, acquiesced. Locked in adversarial all-or-nothing politics, the British political class showed no ability to work across party lines to find a sensible and acceptable outcome.

The Government's decision to impose a hard Brexit was not a small, incidental policy matter, which might have been overcome by the ordinary ebbs and flows of political dealing. It was a question of fundamental importance to the state, society, economy, constitutional order, and strategic orientation of each constituent country. An Anglo-centric Union, in which England's numerical majority could impose a hard Brexit on the rest of the United Kingdom, against their national wills, was and is no Union of equals. It is hardly surprising that by 2022, 52% of people in Scotland supported Scottish independence, up from 23% in 2012.[37] That figure will undoubtedly wobble. The Scottish National Party's loss of seats in the 2024 general election – dropping from forty-eight in 2019 to just nine – shows that independence is not in the bag. Nevertheless, it is telling that, by 2021, 65% of Scots who had voted Remain in the Brexit referendum supported Scottish independence, up from 44% in 2016.[38] Even if that support is not currently translated into votes for the Scottish National Party, Brexit is an irrevocable act of disrespect towards Scotland, that has made the United Kingdom in its current form more precarious.

At the time of writing, there seems to be a noticeable shift in English opinion against Brexit.[39] At least, there is a growing realisation that Brexit was based on false premises and on a tragic overestimation of British power. There is also an emerging recognition that Brexit has had severely damaging economic effects, the full impact of which is gradually becoming apparent. Sooner or later, relations with the European Union will have to be repaired, and then, in time, the borders reopened to frictionless trade. Despite the urgent economic imperatives, such action cannot be taken overnight. Reaching the cross-party consensus needed to rejoin the Customs Union will not be easy or quick. Brexit is likely to remain a divisive and emotive issue for some time.

Even if there is a consensus for some degree of reintegration with Europe both in Parliament and in the country, there is no guarantee that the United Kingdom will be allowed back in. Influential people in other European capitals, as well as in the institutions of the European Union, would have to be convinced of a sincere change of heart, a willingness to reform in order to meet all the criteria of membership, and a genuine commitment to play by the rules. A new constitution like that proposed here might help. It would signal to Europe the end of British exceptionalism, the renunciation of the tragic imperial hubris that thought the United Kingdom was too big and too powerful to have to fit in with everyone else, and a clearer constitutional commitment to European values.

### (d) The end of Empire: end of the Union?

Pressure upon the Union arises not only from recent factors like Brexit. It arises, more profoundly, from the nature of the United Kingdom as an imperial rather than national state. To say that the United Kingdom is an 'imperial state' is not to say that English rule over the other countries of the Union has the same colonial dynamic as British rule over, say, Kenya or Ceylon had (although there are many parallels, not least in the co-optation of local elites, who were Anglicised through access to exclusive educational institutions). It is, rather, to say that the logic, the *raison d'être*, of the United Kingdom was to provide a safe domestic island base from which to launch a maritime Empire, and that 'Britishness' acquired meaning and value only in that imperial context.[40]

George Chetwynd Griffith's book *Men Who Have Made the Empire* (1897), a stirring collective biography of moustachioed imperialists written for the inspiration of late-Victorian schoolboys, included figures such as Edward Long-shanks, Oliver Cromwell, and William of Orange, whose part in the imperial drama was to solidify English control over the 'inner Empire' of the British Isles, as well as people such as Gordon of Khartoum, Cecil Rhodes, and Clive of India, whose part was to expand that power into Africa and Asia.[41] Griffith saw the shared hardship and rewards of the imperial adventure as knitting the four home nations together:

> There are two kinds of patriotism, a smaller and a greater, a National and an Imperial. Both are equally good and noble, and it is necessary that the first should precede the second. But it is equally necessary that it should not supersede or obscure it, and it is to this later and greater, this Imperial patriotism that I shall appeal, and I would ask my readers, whatever their nationality, to remember that on the burning plains of India and the rolling prairies of Canada, in the vast expanses of the Australian Bush and the African Veld, there are neither Englishmen nor Scotsmen, Welshmen nor Irishmen; but only Citizens of the Empire, brothers in blood and speech, and fellow-workers in the building up of the noblest and stateliest fabric that human hands have ever reared or God's sun has ever shone upon.[42]

During the British imperial age (say, from the Treaty of Union in 1707 to the loss of Hong Kong in 1997), most Scottish people could hold these two patriotic identities side by side, without ever losing sight of the crucial distinction between them. A Scotsman serving in a Scottish regiment in the British Army was no less Scottish for being British, and only a little less British for being Scottish.[43] These 'Scottish' and 'British' labels denoted distinct and parallel identities, one cultural and national, the other official, institutional, and imperial. There was little or no tension between them, but they were different, and emphasised in different situations. The same could be said for the Welsh, who, like the Scots, 'never fully extinguished their identity within the idea of being British'.[44] Ireland's different experience of the Union, in contrast, meant that many in that country ultimately had to choose between identities which had become irreconcilable: by the time of Home Rule, they could be either Irish or British, but not easily both.[45]

The English, on the other hand, wore their Britishness with such effortless ease that the conscious distinction between these two identities was often lost. As England was the politically and economically dominant core of the United Kingdom and of the British Empire, Englishness could be wholly subsumed within these wider British and imperial identities, without any sense of pain or loss. As Jeremy Paxman noted, 'it was because the English so dominated the organization which dominated so much of the world that the words "England" and "Britain" were soon being used interchangeably'.[46] Indeed, the prevailing English notion of Britain and the Empire as 'greater England' increased, not diminished, English national pride.[47]

The cascade of decolonisation began in earnest soon after the Second World War, with the independence of India, Pakistan, Burma, and Ceylon. In response to the loss of the Empire, the British Government under Clement Attlee tried to create a unified British national identity. Instead of a Union of distinct home nations at the core of a global British Empire, there would henceforth be one insular 'British nation'.[48]

However, this was not entirely successful. Creating a national, rather than imperial, Britishness meant the erasure of Scottish and Welsh national identities. Scottish and Welsh nations could continue to exist, as cultural if not as political units, within a *British Union* and a *British Empire*, but they could not exist within a *British nation*. It would reduce Scotland and Wales, proud nations in their own rights, to being but 'regions' of Britain. In this way, the rise of Scottish and Welsh nationalism is intimately linked to the decline of the Empire and to the pressure the 'end of Empire' put upon the British state to redefine itself in national terms.[49]

By 2022, when Liz Truss stepped briefly into power, it was clear that the United Kingdom faced not only a crisis of trade, economics, and diplomacy, but a complex, multidimensional, 'omni-crisis': a crisis of governance, democracy, politics, identity, integrity, values, principles, and public ethics. This crisis is still unresolved, despite a change of Government. The legacy of Brexit continues to harm the economy, to damage the United Kingdom's international reputation, and to poison our politics. Brexit revealed the United Kingdom's structural economic precarity, exposed its institutional and infrastructural fragility, and highlighted the shambolic perfidy of its ruling class. This damage was done not only by the initial act of voting to leave the European Union (an excusable moment of unthinkingness), but also by the panicked and inept way in which the political leadership tried to handle the contradictory implications of the vote.

All these elements of crisis are indicative of an underlying constitutional failure: a justified loss of faith in the credibility and suitability of the institutions, ground rules, and principles of government that have shaped the British imperial state since its formation.

Much of what we see today is a result of the failure of an imperial state to satisfactorily reconstitute and reinvent itself for a post-imperial world. Arguably, there is no longer even such a thing as 'British politics', if by that we mean a shared British space of political participation where the same British parties compete on the same British issues, with an intent to win a majority of seats across Britain and to form a British Government. Of course, Northern Ireland had always been an outlier, but during most of the twentieth century that was how British politics worked. According to the old textbooks that formed my introduction to the study of British politics, the borders between England, Wales, and Scotland had some small cultural significance (and, in Scotland's case, also legal significance), but the British electorate was seen as being politically divided mainly by class, party, and ideology.[50] The parties held 'safe seats' in different geographical areas, but these were determined by industrial and economic factors, not by divisions of nationality or identity.[51]

Such homogeneity seems long ago and far away. For three general elections in a row (2015, 2017, 2019), different parties won in each constituent country of the United Kingdom: the Conservatives in England, the Scottish National Party in Scotland, Labour in Wales, and the Democratic Unionists in Northern Ireland. The Democratic Unionists were overtaken by Sinn Féin in the 2022 Northern Ireland Assembly elections: an even more significant development in the centrifugal tendencies of the Union. In 2024, Labour regained ascendency in England, Scotland, and Wales. It is not possible to tell whether that is a fluke or the start of a trend. Even so, there is a distinct pattern of party competition in each country, responding to different interests and priorities. The Liberal Democrats picked up swathes of seats in southern England, but only one seat in Wales. Likewise, if we look at who came second in each seat, as the main challenger to Labour's brand of Unionism, differences between the four nations are stark. The Scottish Nationals, rather than the Conservatives, are still the main challenger to Labour in urban Scotland.

To claim that the United Kingdom is in constitutional crisis, is not just to refer to specific incidents – the prorogation dispute in 2019, the chipping away of devolution, the backlash against the Supreme Court, the erosion of rights that in other countries would be more securely protected, or the fact that in 2024 Labour won a two-thirds majority of the seats – and absolute power – with only about a third of the votes. Those are details. Rather, it refers to the fact that the British unwritten constitution, and the Union itself, has outlived its original purpose and has failed to adapt to new realities. Without an Empire to hold it together, the United Kingdom is a state out of place, out of time, out of puff, out of ideas, out of kilter.

Of course, this is not to say the United Kingdom will collapse tomorrow. Even an old state, if blessed with bold statecraft, can sometimes reform itself. The Austro-Hungarian Empire is instructive on this point. Parallels between the post-imperial British state and the Austro-Hungarian Empire have been drawn ever since Tom Nairn's *Break-Up of Britain* (1977).[52] The sprawling Austro-Hungarian Empire, held together by historic and dynastic ties, was in some ways a success story of multinational constitutional state-building. After various failed attempts at repression in the 1850s, a liberal and confederal constitutional settlement was hammered out in 1867 that offered a fair degree of political and cultural autonomy for the Empire's component nations.[53] From that date until its final collapse after the First World War, the Austro-Hungarian Empire existed as dual entity: presenting itself to the outside world as one state, for the purposes of foreign relations and defence, while allowing maximal internal self-government. Despite its weaknesses, and although it could not ultimately withstand the shock of total war, that Empire survived – and in some ways thrived – for another fifty years, thanks to its life-saving constitutional surgery.[54]

Avoiding such surgery on the constitution – or merely treating it with sticking plasters – prolongs the pain and increases the chance of fatal outcomes. It increases the risk that the United Kingdom will try to hold its inner Empire intact by force or coercion. Even if things do not deteriorate into violence, the Union as currently constituted continues to be a source of distraction and division, a stumbling block to constitutional reform, and a hindrance to socio-economic regeneration, in all four parts of the United Kingdom. We must do better.

Any Union must have a credible reason to exist. It must have a purpose beyond mere inertia, and a common identity that makes emotional as well as practical sense to its people. Again, the Austro-Hungarian (Hapsburg) Empire is a useful guide. Despite the constitutional compromise of 1867, it could not come up with a story and a vision that would salvage its moral sense and purpose. Living in the United Kingdom today is much like living in 'Kakania' – Robert Musil's fictionalised name for the pre-First World War Austro-Hungarian Empire in his novel *The Man Without Qualities*.[55]

There might be good reasons – pragmatic as well as sentimental – for the British nations to continue to have a common defence and foreign policy, through some sort of looser Union. That does not mean, however, that there is a convincing answer to the question of why we should all be bundled up together in this dynastic and imperial relic called the United Kingdom, under one sovereign Parliament.

We suffer from the same late-Hapsburg listlessness and disorientation: a queasy feeling that nothing makes sense anymore; the old ways that once defined us have become meaningless; the pomp and parades are still there, but are increasingly hollow; politics under Cameron, May, Johnson, Truss, and Sunak veered from tragedy to farce; even religion has dissipated, with the Church of England beset by scandal and division, while society drifts into a moral morass. By the end of Sunak's premiership, public life in the United Kingdom had become so staid, changeless, and hopeless, yet in such ceaseless turmoil, as to be almost unbearable by any person of moral or intellectual integrity.

It remains to be seen whether Sir Keir Starmer can bring about change that will percolate down to ordinary people, but it will take more than housing and growth to give people a sense of belonging, meaning, and purpose, as citizens and as members of a political community. That – if it is not to take the wholly reactionary and farcical form now being offered by Reform UK – demands constitutional change. As in the Austro-Hungarian Empire, official Union identity, built upon the political abstraction of the Union state, goes only so far. Unless the state can respect the historical and organic national identities of its constituent countries, and can harness those national identities to a civic, democratic, and constitutional project, there is a risk that a darker, more visceral and destructive, form of nationalism will emerge from the void.

### (e) Is there a federal solution?

Federalism has long attracted the interest of constitutional reformers across the United Kingdom. It is offered as a more stable and comprehensive solution to the problems of British territorial politics, addressing many of the shortcomings of the present devolved arrangements.

A federal system is one in which there are at least two layers of government, each constitutionally established and protected, and each having its own sphere of legislative and executive activity.[56] People are directly subject to two governments at once: to the federal or Union level for those matters within its charge, and to their state, provincial, or regional government (terminology varies between countries, but the essence is similar) for those matters within its charge. The institutions of government are duplicated, with a federal or Union Parliament and Government, elected by the whole federation, and state, provincial, or regional Parliaments and Governments elected by the people in each of those entities.

In contrast to the post-1997 devolution arrangements, federalism offers two main advantages. Firstly, a federal system would apply across the United Kingdom. The current anomaly, in which Scotland, Wales and Northern Ireland have institutions of self-government, but England does not, would end. As will be explained below, this could take the form of an English national Parliament, but more often the proposal is for England to be divided up into large regions.

Secondly, federalism solves the problem that *power devolved is power retained.* Under devolution, the powers of Scottish, Welsh and Northern Irish institutions depend upon the goodwill of the United Kingdom Parliament, which can – and sometimes does – override or curtail them at will, as best suits the United Kingdom Government. The so-called 'Sewel' convention, which states that the UK Parliament should not normally legislate in devolved areas without the consent of the devolved legislature concerned, has often been breached. There is reasonable fear, in Scotland especially, that the gains of devolution are being stealthily and incrementally undone. Since the Brexit referendum, we have witnessed a gradual rolling back of devolution and the increasingly high-handed and dismissive treatment of the devolved administrations. A federal system, in which the powers and responsibilities of the different levels of government are defined and protected by an entrenched constitution, would offer reassurance.

Although federalism seems to have no place in the current Government's policy agenda, certain senior Labour figures, most notably former Prime Minister Gordon Brown, offered detailed proposals for British federalism, or at least something very close to federalism, in the run-up to the 2024 election.[57] For Brown, the intention of federalism is to make the Union stronger; there is no place in this scheme for a self-governing English nation, only for federalised British regions.

Federalism has occasionally featured in the Scottish debate. In September 2014, on the eve of the independence referendum, the leaders of the three main Unionist parties – Conservatives, Labour, and Liberal Democrats – made a public 'vow', promising in vague and sweeping terms that if independence was rejected, 'faster, safer and better change' would follow.[58] The vow enticed Scotland with the prospect of a federal Union based on mutual cooperation and mutual respect, although the reality – what became the Scotland Act 2016 – fell very far short of that expectation. For a long time, federalism was the preferred position of the Scottish Liberal Democrats, but they have gone very quiet on the subject.

Some of the best thinking on federalism comes from Welsh Labour. In its 2019 report *Reforming Our Union: Shared Governance in the United Kingdom*, the Welsh Government said that 'Future constitutional developments in the United Kingdom should be considered on a holistic basis and on the basis of constitutional principle, rather than by way of *ad hoc* reforms to particular constitutional settlements'. It argued that 'This should be undertaken by a constitutional convention' and that 'The case for a written constitution, and a debate about the nature of such a written constitution should, we believe, form part of the deliberations of a constitutional convention'.[59] In 2021, the Welsh Government set up the Independent Commission on the Constitutional Future of Wales, co-chaired by Professor Laura McAllister and a former archbishop, Rowan Williams. This had a remit to 'consider and develop options for fundamental reform of the constitutional structures of the United Kingdom' and 'to consider and develop all progressive principal options to strengthen Welsh democracy and deliver improvements for the people of Wales'.[60] One of the options it considered was a federal United Kingdom, with Wales as a constituent state, and parallel institutions 'either for England as a whole, or for regions of England'.[61]

There is nothing intrinsically alien about federalism. Stanley Alexander de Smith, a leading comparative scholar of Commonwealth constitutionalism in the decolonisation era, recognised 'a characteristic British bias in favour of federalism'.[62] Federalism – in Australia, Canada, India, Pakistan, Burma, Malaysia, and elsewhere – was a standard part of the British post-imperial constitutional toolkit. Although de Smith noted that this bias towards federalism 'corrects itself north of the channel',[63] these Commonwealth examples show that it would not be hard, on a purely technical level, to design a federal constitution for the United Kingdom.

There are, broadly speaking, two principal approaches to a federal United Kingdom: (1) the 'nations and regions' approach; and (2) the 'four nations' approach.[64] The former typically envisages a federal system based on the NUTS1 statistical regions – the same as those used, from 1999 to 2019, for elections to the European Parliament. Under this scheme, the Union would consist of twelve units: Scotland, Wales, and Northern Ireland (the 'nations'), and the nine English regions (the 'regions'). Each of these might have structurally similar institutions, albeit with different powers and different names (a 'Parliament' for Scotland and Wales, and 'Assemblies' for English regions, and perhaps for Northern Ireland).

The different powers – greater for the 'nations' than for the 'regions' – reflects the fact that powers adequate to meet the demands of Scotland, Wales, and Northern Ireland would be far beyond what any English region would want or need. Criminal law, for example, could not be handled on a federal level, because of different histories, legal systems, and policy considerations in each of the four countries. Neither could it be handled, within England, on a regional level. So it would need to be handled on a national level, in England as a whole, and in Scotland, Wales, and Northern Ireland.[65] In the same way, provision for language rights – for Welsh, Irish, Gaelic, and Scots – would be relevant to Scotland, Wales, and Northern Ireland, but not to English regions (with the possible exception of some recognition of Cornish in the South West).

Powers and responsibilities in a 'nations and regions' federation would therefore have to be divided according to a tripartite scheme. There would have be: (1) 'Union' matters (e.g. defence, foreign affairs, citizenship, passports, shipping, external trade, overseas aid, currency and coinage, perhaps certain aspects of economic policy); (2) 'National' matters (e.g. ecclesiastical law, much of civil and criminal law, language rights, most aspects of education); and (3) 'Regional' matters (e.g. economic development, planning, much of transport policy, police, and so on). In this scheme, the Parliaments of Scotland, Wales, and Northern Ireland would have power over both 'national' and 'regional' matters, while the English Regional Assemblies would have only 'regional' powers.

Since the 'nations and regions' approach rules out the creation of an English Parliament, the 'national' powers in England would have to be given to the Union Parliament. It is not impossible to draft such a constitution – I sketched out several examples to test the concept – but it does make for a lopsided and unbalanced system of government, which reintroduces all the asymmetries and inconsistencies of the current devolved arrangement. It does not solve, for example, the West Lothian Question. There might still be some need for an 'English votes for English laws' procedure. Making it work in practice could be tricky.

Another reason for rejecting a 'nations and regions' federation is that these regions – which, to balance Scotland, Wales, and Northern Ireland, have to be fairly few and fairly large – are not very well loved. They are rejected as artificial, bureaucratic creations, too big and distant to serve as sites of genuine local empowerment. The most compelling objection to a 'nations and regions' federalism, however, is simply that England is a nation and ought to be treated as such.[66] If England is to develop in healthy, civic and democratic ways, it needs an institutional means of collective political self-expression. To dismember England into 'mere regions', and to prevent the establishment of an English Parliament, is to deny English national agency, and so to deprive England of the chance to become a normal, mature, democratic nation. If that is done simply for the sake of saving the Union, then it makes one wonder if the Union is worth saving. Are we really willing to kill England, just so that the United Kingdom can live?

That brings us to the second potential form of British federalism: a symmetrical Union of 'four nations'. Under this arrangement, the United Kingdom would be a federation of four equal states – England, Scotland, Wales, and Northern Ireland. Each would have its own Parliament and Government, with equal powers and equal status. Above these would sit a Union Parliament and Government – in a way that would be instantly recognisable to Australians, Canadians, or Indians – exercising authority over the whole, in respect of certain constitutionally enumerated matters.

It has often been asserted that such a four-nation federation cannot work, because England is so much bigger than the other three parts put together. However, that need not in principle hinder such a scheme – indeed, the tension and competition between the Prime Minister of the United Kingdom and the First Minister of England, pushing against each other, might create the 'space' in which Scotland, Wales, and Northern Ireland would have room to breathe.

On federal matters, England's votes would of course, by sheer numerical superiority, outweigh those of the other three nations, but the four countries would be equally autonomous in the exercise of their own national powers. There might also be deeper forms of representation and cooperation at the centre. These might include, for example, a reformed second chamber, most of whose members would be indirectly elected by the four State Parliaments. There could also be a Federal Council, bringing together the Prime Minister of the United Kingdom and the First Ministers of the four nations to coordinate their activities in a cooperative way.

England is too big and too diverse to be governed – or, at least, governed well – as one centralised state. Even in a four-nations federation, many policy issues, such as public transport, infrastructure, planning, redevelopment, policing and education, would need to be transferred from an all-England level to lower levels of government. An advantage of the 'four nations' model, over the 'nations and regions' model, is that these units – being devolved from an English nation-state rather than being constituent units in their own right of a federation – could be greater in number, and smaller in size. For example, within an English state, the primary level of devolved government could be Counties and Cities (about fifty in number), which many people feel to be more natural and historical units, and more in keeping with existing identities.

There are two further features to be included in any federal United Kingdom constitution. The first is a mechanism that protects the voluntary nature of the

Union and recognises the distinct claims of national sovereignty within it, such as the Scottish Claim of Right. That means establishing a process for any state to leave the Union in a peaceful, democratic, and orderly manner, if the majority of its people so wish, in the future. Again, there are no major difficulties from a technical point of view; there are examples of constitutional provision for independence referendums in other constitutions based on the Westminster Model, such as constitution of Saint Kitts and Nevis and the former (1947) constitution of Burma. Similarly, so long as Northern Ireland is part of the Union, there would be a need to reaffirm and protect the Good Friday Agreement, including provision for a poll on Irish unification.

Secondly, it would need a constitutional amendment rule that recognises and protects the authority of the states. Professor Jeffery King, working on the basis of a belief in popular sovereignty, has suggested that any new written constitution should be amendable – as, for example, the Irish constitution is – by a majority vote in a referendum.[67] Even setting aside, for a moment, concerns about the tyranny of the majority and the need for the protection of minorities, that works only if there is one people with one undivided national sovereignty. It does not work when the constitution is designed to bring together four countries on a federal basis. A constitutional amendment rule similar to that of Canada (where certain fundamental changes can be made only with the agreement of every province) or Australia (where voters in four of the six states, as well as a majority of the voters across Australia as a whole, must agree to constitutional amendments) would probably be more appropriate.

Given Drafting Instructions to that effect, a competent constitutional drafter would be able to produce a technically sound constitution for a federal United Kingdom without much trouble. In *Westminster and the World*, I entered into the federal debate in good faith, and even sketched out in some detail how a four-nations federation might be designed.[68]

However, one does wonder what, exactly, a federal United Kingdom Parliament and Government would do. In the 'nations and regions' model, it would spend much of its time acting as a *de facto* English Parliament, dealing with the all-England matters that could not be transferred to Regional Assemblies. Under the 'four nations' model, it either has to interfere in a range of matters that would be better handled by each nation, or else be left with little to do. An Indian, Australian, or even Canadian approach to federalism would necessarily give the Union Parliament and Government a lot of power over the four nations, over a range of domestic and fiscal policy areas. This would cause confusion in England, with the competing mandates of the English and Union Parliaments, while failing to satisfy the demands of Scotland, Wales, and Northern Ireland. If, on the other hand, the range of federal matters were to be reduced to just essentials – defence, foreign affairs, citizenship – then why bother with the panoply of federal institutions, with their cost and duplication? Would it not be better, in that case, to find other forms of simpler, and looser, Union?

Another problem facing federalists is that of political divergence. Again, comparative examples are instructive. Nigeria's federal constitution of 1960 was by no means a bad one. It was a good example of the Westminster Model being exported and adapted to a federal context. There was much about it that might serve as a model for a federal United Kingdom. Under it, however, Nigerian democracy lasted just six difficult years before the country fell prey to a military coup. The slaughter of democracy by military usurpers was not an unusual occurrence in post-colonial Africa, but in Nigeria's case the weakness of the democratic state was exacerbated by the absence of federation-wide parties. Each Region became a virtual 'ethno-state', dominated by one party representing its own regional interests. Elections were little more than censuses of identity, and politics was reduced to a game of patronage distribution.

If each nation-state in a federal United Kingdom were to be dominated by a party which is virtually excluded from power in the other states, then no clever federal constitutional engineering could make up for it. Federalism will not work if a British Government is always to be dominated by English-centred parties that the Scottish people reject time and time again. As previously noted, the success of Labour in Scotland and Wales, as well as in England, in the 2024 general election does not overcome the fact that the structure of party competition in the 'home nations' has diverged: the Conservatives were wiped out in Wales, while the Scottish National Party came in second place in much of Scotland.

A further disadvantage of federalism is that it tends to encourage the judicialisation of politics. Those who oppose written, supreme and fundamental, constitutions often do so on the grounds that they bring the judiciary into political decision-making and turn every political question into a legal one. While rejecting that criticism, it is certainly more true of federal constitutions than of unitary (or devolved) ones. If one has a concern about this aspect of constitutional government, then options other than federalism should be considered.

Moreover, federal systems are inherently clunky and inefficient. Lines of accountability are blurred. Governments at different levels can work against each other. Although England needs stronger local government and more effective decentralisation, a rigid federal structure may hinder economic redevelopment and make the provision of public services more expensive; a flexible devolved arrangement would be better.[69] The experience of Belgium, a country burdened by the overheads of seven different Governments in a complex, overlapping, system of federalism, should serve as a salutary warning.[70]

The greatest difficulty facing federalism is that almost no one in England, of any political significance, is willing to back it. Despite the aggressive and domineering aspects of post-Brexit British nationalism, most English people remain decent and fair-minded, and recognise that the constitutional futures of Scotland, Wales, and Northern Ireland must be settled by their respective peoples. They might be saddened by the end of the Union, but would not seek to hold any part of it by force, against the will of its people. However, to accept a federal United Kingdom is quite another matter. The underlying problem is the Anglo-centricity of England's British Unionism. In other words, the English will accept the Union if they are supreme within it, and on no other terms.

Federalism is a balance of self-rule and shared-rule.[71] A federal United Kingdom means that England would have to share power with Scotland, Wales, and Northern Ireland. On some issues, English views might not prevail. The wider the range of federal powers, the more this possibility arises. As long as the majority of English people continue to see the United Kingdom as 'greater England', neither understanding the distinctiveness of the other home nations, nor giving them with equal status and respect, all attempts to reform the United Kingdom on classically federal terms will fail.

We come back to the inherent problem of the Union: a majority in Scotland – and many people in Wales too – will accept no master, while England will accept no equal. This means the United Kingdom cannot reconstitute itself in a way that recognises each country's identity and interests in a federal Union. From an English perspective, a federal Union – one that is democratically acceptable to Scotland and Wales, and that can accommodate the needs of both communities in Northern Ireland – is just not worth the effort or the political cost. Most English people simply do not care about 'saving the Union' to the point of being willing to make that sacrifice.

Here is the fatal dilemma of federalism: any federal constitutional renewal big enough to fix the United Kingdom is also big enough to bust it wide open. If a federal United Kingdom cannot constrain English power, and protect the autonomy of its distinct countries, it is finished: Scotland and Wales – and perhaps Northern Ireland, too – will not stand for it. But as soon as genuine federalism threatens to constrain rather than to project English power, and to end the primacy of England, it is finished: England will not stand for it. So the Union can neither continue as it is, nor can it reform itself as a normal federation. Either way, it is finished, unless a way can be found to protect English primacy, while limiting its power.

### (f) Federacy, associated statehood, and the United Kingdom

In many ways, the easiest and most straightforward solution would be to dissolve the Union: embrace 'independence all round', and establish England, Scotland, Wales, and a united Ireland as four separate nation-states. That possibility will be discussed in the next section. For now, however, we must acknowledge that, although many people across the United Kingdom want more recognition and autonomy for their respective nations, there is no settled and sustained majority, in any part of the United Kingdom, for its total dissolution. Even in Scotland, the level of support for independence has long hovered at or around 50%. Those polling figures are no basis for an all-or-nothing, in-or-out, decision. Even if one is convinced that a bare majority would have enough democratic legitimacy, it would be difficult, in practice, to consolidate stable constitutional democracies in newly independent states without broad public and political backing. It would be wise, in such circumstances, to seek constructive compromises, not to insist on divisive absolutes.

The draft Constitution presented in the annex to this book does not therefore directly envisage the dissolution of the Union. That, however, just takes us back to the problem. We cannot continue with the status quo, nor roll back time to a pre-1997 Union, nor adopt classic federalism, in either its 'nations and regions' or its 'four nations' form. So what is the way ahead?

What is needed is a constitutional solution that meets these criteria: it should maximise the autonomy of England, Scotland, Wales, and Northern Ireland as distinct national political entities, but maintain a real Union between them for matters like foreign affairs, defence, and citizenship, while also upholding the primacy of England within that Union.

That solution is not federalism, but a different type of Union, one known to political scientists as *federacy*. This is way of maximising autonomy without requiring the relationship to be symmetrical or reciprocal. Whereas federalism would always bump up against the problem of 'Anglo-centricity', and the consequent unwillingness of England to share power with Scotland, Wales, or Northern Ireland, federacy makes a virtue of necessity. It would uphold England's pre-eminence over shared policy areas, while limiting the range of shared areas to a minimum – little more than foreign affairs, defence, and common citizenship, although with scope for voluntary cooperation in other policy areas by mutual agreement.

Such a federacy might be quite hard to imagine. Yet it already exists, although we rarely notice it. The solution for Scotland, Wales, and Northern Ireland – and therefore the solution for England, and for the Union as a whole – can be found in the Crown Dependencies (Jersey, Guernsey, and the Isle of Man) and in those British Overseas Territories having advanced levels of self-government (such as Bermuda, the Cayman Islands, the Falkland Islands, and Gibraltar).

In most regards – the exceptions being defence and foreign affairs, the shared Crown, and British citizenship – the Crown Dependencies are virtually independent states: they have their own Governments, their own Parliaments, courts, laws, administrative agencies, and fiscal systems. Although part of the Common Travel Area, they even manage their own immigration and customs policy. Self-governing British Overseas Territories, likewise, have a degree of autonomy far beyond that usually allowed to the member states of a federation. Insofar as their Governors have certain reserve powers to act in matters of domestic politics and administration, those powers are set by the constitutions of the Territories concerned; they are mostly about ensuring good governance, and do not greatly limit the autonomy of the Territories in policy or legislation.

The crux of the federacy proposal is therefore that Scotland, Wales, and Northern Ireland should have a similar degree of autonomy, including fiscal autonomy, to that enjoyed by the Crown Dependencies and self-governing British Overseas Territories. In place of the current *incorporating Union*, which sees England, Scotland, Wales, and Northern Ireland folded up into one sovereign United Kingdom, represented in one Union Parliament, there would be an *unincorporating Union*: that is, a Union in which there is no one central Parliament.[72] Just as the Crown Dependencies and British Overseas Territories are not represented in the British Parliament, so Scotland, Wales, and Northern Ireland would, under these proposals, cease to be represented at Westminster. In those matters for which the United Kingdom is responsible, the established processes of intergovernmental consultation to ensure that the interests of the Dependencies and Territories are considered would, in the same way, extend to Scotland, Wales, and Northern Ireland. The Westminster Parliament would become in law what it often is in fact: an *English* Parliament. Scottish, Welsh, and Northern Irish votes would not have any direct bearing on English affairs. Instead, English relations with Scotland, Wales, and Northern Ireland would take place on an intergovernmental basis. In this way, the West Lothian Question would no longer arise.

This approach also recognises that British identity is not confined to Great Britain and Northern Ireland alone. Places like Gibraltar and the Falkland Islands show that it is possible to be unmistakably British while not being English, Scottish, Welsh, or Northern Irish. Likewise, these places show that it is possible to be British, and proudly and loyally so, while enjoying the broadest possible autonomy from London rule.

A reconstituted United Kingdom, as envisaged by the constitution proposed in this book, would therefore consist of: (1) England; (2) Scotland, Wales, and Northern Ireland, to be known as 'Associated States'; (3) the Crown Dependencies; and (4) the self-governing British Overseas Territories.

These jurisdictions would be united under the Crown (although the powers and rights of the Crown, and perhaps even the titles of the monarch, would be different in each jurisdiction, according to their respective constitutions and laws). There would be a common British citizenship. The provisions in the draft Constitution relating to citizenship are complex, but the essence of it is that there would be one British *citizenship* for the whole United Kingdom, and an English *nationality* for those born or resident in England. All British citizens would have the right of abode in England, but English nationals would not necessarily have the right to reside in other parts of the United Kingdom, since each Associated State, Crown Dependency and self-governing British Overseas Territory would be able to determine its own laws of nationality, residency, or 'belonger' status.[73]

The English Parliament would have authority to make laws for the whole or any part of the United Kingdom in relation to foreign affairs, defence, and citizenship. Before introducing such legislation, the English Government would have to consult, as far as possible, with the Governments of each jurisdiction to which the legislation would apply.

The English Parliament would also be able to make laws for the whole or any part of the United Kingdom on a range of other matters, including international development, disaster relief, currency, cross-border services, the internal market, and customs. Crucially, however, it would be able to do so only with the consent of the Governments of each of the jurisdictions concerned. The extent of cooperation would therefore depend upon the degree of mutual agreement. The pattern for this is well precedented, because it substantially replicates the relationship between the Imperial Parliament and the Dominions under the Statute of Westminster.[74]

Under section 172 of the draft Constitution, this power to legislate with consent may extend to any matter mutually agreed between the English

Government and the Government of the Associated State, Crown Dependency, or self-governing British Overseas Territory, to which it applies. In other words, the United Kingdom would be infinitely elastic. The scope of powers exercised at the British level could be more or less, according to the wants and needs of each jurisdiction. For example, it makes little sense for the Cayman Islands to have a common currency with England, but Scotland might take a different view, and decide to keep the pound in a currency union.

There would be no British Government as such, but the English Government would represent the whole United Kingdom externally (just as the British Government, under current arrangements, represents the Channel Islands and the British Overseas Territories). Treaties would bind the United Kingdom in international law, but would not necessarily be adopted into the domestic legislation of any part of the Union except in accordance with an Act of its own legislature.[75]

Defence, likewise, would be managed on behalf of the whole Union by the English Government. The United Kingdom would have common Armed Forces – the Royal Regiment of Scotland, for example, being integrated into the British Army in the same way as the Royal Bermuda Regiment or the Royal Gibraltar Regiment. The Royal Navy and the Royal Air Force would be Union-wide institutions. Scots, Welsh, and Northern Irish would be eligible to serve alongside the English in the Armed Forces, in the same way as people from the Crown Dependencies or British Overseas Territories, by virtue of their common British citizenship.

There would be a Council of the United Kingdom, to consist of the Prime Minister of England (who would chair the Council, as first among equals) and the First Ministers, Chief Ministers, or Premiers of each Associated State, Crown Dependency, and self-governing British Overseas Territory. The Council of the United Kingdom would be a consultative and advisory, rather than an executive body, but it would be assisted by a secretariat to manage certain common policies.

In the absence of a Prime Minister, First Minister, or Chief Minister, a jurisdiction might be represented by another minister of Cabinet rank. It is expected that the norm would be for the heads of government to meet in person, perhaps annually, and for other working sessions to take place either through a Minister for United Kingdom Affairs in each Government, or through the ministers in each Government responsible for the policy area under discussion.

This proposal would recast the Union in a way that recognises the statehood and national identity of England, Scotland, Wales, and Northern Ireland, while maintaining a flexible, equitable, and voluntary Union, not only among the home nations, but also among the wider British family.[76]

Such a United Kingdom is a pragmatic compromise between Unionists and independence supporters. Unionists get to keep the things that matter to them: British citizenship, the British Armed Forces, and a unified British presence on the world stage, including a seat in the United Nations Security Council. They also get to keep the pound sterling, and to stay in the Common Travel Area. There is potential for further bilateral or multilateral cooperation between the

British nations in other areas, if there is mutual agreement, and if it works to the benefit of all involved. For those seeking independence, on the other hand, this federacy would give 90% or more of the substance of independence, including full fiscal autonomy and powers over swathes of domestic and economic policy that are currently reserved to Westminster.

### (g) Becoming a normal country

To reconstitute the United Kingdom on the above lines is not driven by any animosity towards the other home nations. It looks not necessarily for complete *separation* for England, but for a different way for British countries to live together, on an equitable and consensual basis, beyond the unitary sovereignty of the United Kingdom as currently constituted.

For some, this might be the last chance to hold the Union together. Those favouring Home Rule or 'Devo-Max' might regard federacy as an acceptable end-point. Indeed, a reconstituted United Kingdom, on the lines outlined above, might best be thought of as a form of 'Home Rule all round'. The United Kingdom would present itself to the outside world as one; within, it would consist of many jurisdictions, each substantially self-governing.

For those who wish to go further, on the other hand, this solution might be a convenient staging-point on the road to full independence. A vital part of this compromise is that it recognises the *right* of each part of the United Kingdom to decide its own future, and become an independent country, if it so wishes, on largely its own terms, in its own time.[77]

The draft Constitution (section 181) therefore provides an orderly, democratic path to independence, with clearly defined steps. It would begin with the Government of the Associated State, Crown Dependency or Overseas Territory proposing independence. This would have to be backed by a resolution in its legislature, by a three-fifths majority vote. This is not a high hurdle, but it is high enough to ensure that there is solid support for independence. If this resolution is passed, a period of negotiation would be initiated, in which the terms of the independence package are agreed, including the division of assets and debts, the disentanglement of the Armed Forces, and arrangements for post-independence cooperation. The final stage would be to hold a referendum in the jurisdiction concerned on the terms of the independence deal. This three-stage process means that voters would not be voting on the vague rhetorical idea of independence, but on a settlement with known and public terms, giving greater clarity and legitimacy to the result.

English reformers seeking a democratic constitutional refoundation should be open to the idea that the Union will have to change very radically, and perhaps even one day disappear. Loosening England's grip on Scotland, Wales, and Northern Ireland – maximising their internal autonomy, and providing a democratic mechanism for them to go their own ways if and when they so wish – is integral to the task of reconstituting England as a normal, healthy, democratic country. As a former First Minister of Scotland, Alex Salmond, said, in his final public speech before he died in 2024, 'Respect for legitimate democratic aspirations leads to good outcomes; disrespecting it, in one way or another, and often surprisingly, can lead to bad outcomes for everyone'.[78]

Yet, if nothing else, this proposal solves the problem of *sequencing*. Raising Scotland, Wales, and Northern Ireland to the status of Associated States, and transforming the United Kingdom in the manner set forth in this chapter, means that the two processes – reconstituting a democratic English state, and dismantling England's 'inner Empire' – do not have to be undertaken at the same time.

This willingness to *let go* – to let Scotland and Wales, as well as Northern Ireland, choose their own futures, and to relate to England on their own terms – is vital to the cultural, as well as to the political and economic, health of England. If the draft Constitution were to be adopted, then it is possible that we could all get along peacefully and harmoniously, in a spirit of mutual respect, within a new United Kingdom. On the other hand, if in the fullness of time Scotland, Wales, and Northern Ireland were all to leave the United Kingdom, that is not something to be resisted or regretted. On the contrary, it would allow England to focus on what matters now, free from the historical burden of British greatness. The peaceful, orderly, and democratic dismantling of the Union – if that is what people in Scotland, Wales, and Northern Ireland want – would offer England a chance to move on: to be at home in itself, make peace with its past, and become a normal, stable, prosperous, decently governed, free, democratic country.

Another advantage of the federacy model is that the United Kingdom would survive, as an entity, even if some of its members were to leave it. Scottish independence from the United Kingdom as currently constituted creates all sorts of knotty constitutional problems – such as whether the United Kingdom would cease to exist, or would continue as a state within different borders. In other words, would Scotland in that case be seceding from a unitary state (the Anglo-centric British Unionist position), or withdrawing from a Union-state (the Scottish nationalist, and historic Scottish Unionist, position)? Under the proposed arrangements, no such issue arises. The United Kingdom could continue, as a Union of its remaining parts, even if Scotland, Wales, or Northern Ireland – or Jersey or Gibraltar, for that matter – were to leave it.[79]

The Union has had a good innings: three centuries. If it is finally caught out, the only honourable thing to do is humbly to accept the judgment of the Great Umpire of the Universe and walk gracefully back to the pavilion of history.

If that were to happen – if Scotland and Wales were to become independent, and Ireland were to reunify – that that need not be the end of cooperation between us. The end of the Union need not break the social, historical, or cultural connections between our closely related nations, nor would it alter the geographical realities and economic imperatives of their proximity. It need not even be the end of some kind of shared British identity. After all, groups of similar nations in Europe – the Nordic countries, the Low Countries, those of the Danubian basin and former Austro-Hungarian Empire – continue to have some lingering shared identity, although the countries are independent from one another. The end of the Union need not be the end, either, of shared institutions, established by international agreement in matters of mutual interest. Cooperation would be possible, for example, through a revamped British-Irish Council, a body established by the Good Friday Agreement in 1999 to provide 'a forum for consultation and co-operation' and to 'promote positive, practical relationships among the people of the islands'.[80]

It might further be assumed that Scotland, if it were to become an independent state, would seek to maintain close defence cooperation with European allies.[81] Also, independent post-British countries would most likely remain in the Commonwealth, which would provide a basis for continued sporting and cultural relations, as well as cooperation in areas such as international development. These are assumed likelihoods, not predictive certainties. Nevertheless, they illustrate some ways in which, with a bit of mutual goodwill and some creative negotiation, constructive post-Union cooperation could be secured.

The prospects for such cooperation depend, in large measure, on whether England, by its conduct towards Scotland, Wales, and both communities in Northern Ireland, makes friendly and contented neighbours, or provokes fear and resentment. To be a good friend and neighbour, England first needs to make peace with its own past: not to forget it, not to obliterate it, neither to be too proud of it nor too ashamed of it, but to put it down, take honest stock of its diminished present, and to look to the future.

Post-imperial nationalisms, when they try to cling on to a past glory that has slipped away, often descend into chauvinism, bitterness, isolation, aggression, xenophobia, and authoritarianism. Those formerly imperial countries that have gone through the process of coming to terms with the end of Empire, and have learned to accept themselves as nation-states with relatively modest ambitions, have then been able to concentrate on domestic development and on improving the quality of life of their citizens. The Dutch have done it. The Swedes have done it.[82] The English can do it too. On the other hand, those countries – like Russia and Turkey – that have not made this mental and cultural shift to normal nationhood, but have instead clung to old grandiose imperial attitudes, are paying the price. Their governments swagger while their people suffer. They bluster around on the world stage desperate to recapture former glories, but in so doing they make themselves despised and ridiculous.

England can choose to have a 'Dutch future', where a European former imperial power with a strong maritime and mercantile tradition remains true to its principles of liberty and democracy, and adjusts to its new post-imperial realities in ways that promote good neighbourliness in Europe and a decent quality of life at home. Or it can – heaven forbid – have a 'Russian future', where the unprocessed pain of lost imperial power is sublimated into an aggressive national chauvinism that menaces its neighbours and keeps its own people trapped in a mire of poverty and authoritarian rule.

How quickly and willingly British exceptionalism can be ditched in favour of a more modest civic-democratic sense of English nationhood will therefore have profound effects on the peace, stability, and prosperity of these islands for generations to come. Holding the United Kingdom together through coercive techniques of 'muscular unionism' is likely to be self-defeating.[83] Instead of the friends and allies that will emerge from mutual respect of national sovereignty, denying Scottish and Welsh self-determination is likely to create a long-lasting enmity on both banks of the Tweed and of the Severn.

The question that Scottish and Welsh independence supporters should put to the English is that once put by D. S. Senanayake, the first Prime Minister of Ceylon, to the British when negotiating for his country's independence: 'We ask [for independence] because it is in your interest as well as ours. We want to keep your friendship. Do you not want to keep ours?'[84]

Becoming a normal country and a good neighbour means setting England free from its obsession with Britain's past greatness. England should be unashamed of the British centuries in its history, and celebrate belonging to a family of interlaced cultures and nations that, through the historical experience of the British Empire, has become global. At the same time, England must make peace with the fact that the sun has finally set on that Empire. It needs to accept that Britain's relative power and significance have declined to the point where bluster, pretence, and 'punching above our weight' look absurd. England has no choice but to face reality: British global dominance is over and – for good or ill, better or worse – it is not coming back. The future well-being of England depends upon coming to terms with that fact.

In terms of its geostrategic posture and sense of self, the United Kingdom is still trying (though not very well) to be a 'small United States': a great power with global reach. It would do better to aim to be a 'big Netherlands': a state with more modest, although still considerable, geostrategic ambitions, but which has accepted its place in the global and European order, and has turned its attention inwards, towards domestic and economic developmental priorities.

England must move beyond its lazy attachment to post-imperial rentier capitalism, with all that means in terms of low productivity, low median wages, and deep inequality. Instead, it needs a new state, constitutionally oriented to the economic and industrial redevelopment of the country. Then Newcastle could be as rich and flourishing as Nijmegen, and Sheffield could hold its head up as an equal to Strasbourg.

That is more than a matter of just different policies or spending priorities. It requires a fundamental change in the orientation, nature, and purpose of the state itself, reflected at the constitutional level in the structure of its institutions and in the principles that motivate them. Bluntly put, the British state was built by and for a thalassocratic mercantile empire. A new constitution can be oriented to England's flourishing and the common good: 'Be ye transformed by the renewing of your constitutional foundations', as it were.

This does not mean that England cannot be great anymore. Far from it. It simply means shifting the concept of greatness, away from being a 'great power' and towards being a 'great country'. A great country does not necessarily have the most wealth, but the least poverty. It does not necessarily have the most aircraft carriers, but the best hospitals. It is not a country on whose Empire the sun never sets, but one whose children never go to bed cold or hungry. The greatness of the Netherlands, to which England should aspire, is demonstrated in the fact that it is about 25% richer per head than the United Kingdom, with shorter working hours, a more even distribution of income, less poverty, and much better public infrastructure.[85]

Even Peter Hitchens, hardly a figure of the liberal left, recognises that there is a virtue in seeking a more modest and domesticated form of national happiness – the flourishing and well-being of the people – rather than living in the past and hankering after bygone glories:

> Look around Europe and see those nations that are happiest. They are the small compact ones which concentrate on their own business and contentment rather than stomping about the world pretending to be great powers when they long ago ceased to be so.[86]

Just as the concept of national greatness must change to meet post-imperial realities, so must the notion of personal greatness. For those with a sense of adventure, whose hearts are filled with a desire to build, serve, and improve, and who wish to emulate the heroes of the past, there is plenty of work to be done in rebuilding England. The days of serving the Raj are long gone, but there is an urgent call for good and capable people to serve Runcorn, Rochdale, or Reigate – where the need for good government, railways, education, economic development, and, yes, even Christian missions is surely just as pressing as ever it was in any corner of the former Empire.

Under a democratic and decentralised constitution this call would come not from without, but from within; cities and counties would, to a large degree, be able to take charge of their own resources, take responsibility for their own environments, nurture their own talents, develop their own local economies, and enjoy their own civic and local identities. There might not be a chance, in a normal England, for the aspiring chap of courage and tenacity to be a District Commissioner in Sudan or Nyasaland, but there is plenty of good, honest, and worthy work for a future mayor of Liverpool or Bristol to do.

## Notes

1 W. I. Jennings (1956) *The Approach to Self-government* (Cambridge University Press).
2 S. Choudhry (2007) 'Does the world need more Canada?', *ICON*, Vol. 5, No. 4, p. 634.
3 The official legal definition of England, as laid down in the Interpretation Act 1978, is as follows: '"England" means, subject to any alteration of boundaries under Part IV of the Local Government Act 1972, the area consisting of the counties established by section 1 of that Act, Greater London and the Isles of Scilly'.
4 P. Gourtsoyannis (2020) 'Nicola Sturgeon: Scotland "will not hesitate" to diverge from UK on lockdown', *Scotsman*, 13 April.
5 A. Henderson and R. Wyn Jones (2021) *Englishness: The Political Force Transforming Britain* (Oxford University Press), p. 65.
6 G. Esler (2021) *How Britain Ends: English Nationalism and the Rebirth of Four Nations* (Apollo), p. 79.
7 A. Henderson and R. Wyn Jones (2021) *Englishness: The Political Force Transforming Britain* (Oxford University Press), p. 49.
8 It is notable that in the summer of 2024, when much of England experienced riots in

response to a stabbing in Southport – erroneously believed to have been committed by a Muslim immigrant – rioting did not break out at scale in Scotland or Wales, where national political institutions had created a more inclusive civic national identity transcending ethnicity.

9 J. Denham and G. Young (2018) 'England: the nation that is not to be named?', Open Democracy website (29 October 2018), https://www.opendemocracy.net/en/opendemocracyuk/england-nation-that-is-not-to-be-named, accessed 25 October 2022.

10 In 2016, 26% of London's population, the highest figure of any English region, either ranked their British identity above their English identity (17%), or denied an English identity altogether (9%) (Henderson and Wyn-Jones, *Englishness*, p. 47). Without detracting from the argument above, it must be recognised that some of this rejection of Englishness can be explained by high levels of immigration and immigrant-descended populations, who have until recently tended to identify as 'Black British' or 'Asian British', rather than as 'Black English' or 'Asian English'.

11 Esler, *How Britain Ends*.

12 Henderson and Wyn Jones, *Englishness*, p. 49.

13 Ibid., p. 206.

14 B. Bragg (2007) *The Progressive Patriot: A Search for Belonging* (Black Swan); C. Lucas (2024) *Another England: How to Reclaim Our National Story* (Penguin).

15 J. Denham (2021) 'Who speaks for England: how the people of England view England, Britain and the Union', https://j-denham.medium.com/who-speaks-for-england-do87abde142e, accessed 21 November 2022.

16 National Centre for Social Research (2022) *39th British Social Attitudes Report*: Britain more politically polarised than ever over Scottish independence, https://natcen.ac.uk/news/british-social-attitudes-britain-more-politically-polarised-ever-over-scottish-independence, accessed 7 May 2025.

17 A. Aughey (2008) 'Imagined nation: England after Britain', Open Democracy website (16 June), https://www.opendemocracy.net/en/imagined-nation-england-after-britain, accessed 22 November 2022.

18 The word order here is deliberate: 'British Englishness' and 'English Britishness' are closely linked, but distinct. It is for the sake of preserving 'British Englishness' (a way of being English in the British state) that this section of society wishes to double down on 'English Britishness' (a British state that is Anglo-centric to its very core). A 'British Britishness', which a federal United Kingdom would require, would force the English to share power and esteem on equal terms with the Scots, Welsh, and Northern Irish, which for the most part they do not wish to do. An 'English Englishness', in an independent state, would deprive them of their sense of British imperial superiority.

19 R. Wyn Jones and A. Henderson (2022) 'The Conservative Party's national question', UK in a Changing Europe website (15 September), https://ukandeu.ac.uk/the-conservative-partys-national-question, accessed 21 November 2022.

20 Ibid.

21 S .Butt, E. Clery, and J. Curtice (eds) (2022) *British Social Attitudes: The 39th Report* (National Centre for Social Research), https://bsa.natcen.ac.uk/media/39477/bsa39_constitutional-reform.pdf, accessed 11 November 2022.

22 Wyn Jones and Hunderson, *The Conservative Party's national question*.

23 Ibid.

24 Denham, 'Who speaks for England'.

25 Henderson and Wyn Jones, *Englishness*, p. 56. For an excellent and detailed account of the formation of the United Kingdom as an extension of English institutions writ large, absorbing rather than uniting with the other nations, see V. Bulmer-Thomas (2023), *Internal Empire: The Rise and Fall of English Imperialism* (Hurst).

26 T. Winter, and S. Keegan-Phipps (2015) *Performing Englishness: Identity and Politics in a Contemporary Folk Resurgence* (Manchester University Press), p. 106.

27 P. Blond (2010) *Red Tory: How Left and Right Have Broken Britain and How We Can Fix It* (Faber and Faber).

28  Esler, *How Britain Ends*, p. 14.

29  J. Cowley (2022) *Who Are We Now? Stories of Modern England* (Picador).

30  M. Bunting (2023) *The Seaside: England's Love Affair* (Granta), p. 14.

31  A. Marr, 'Brexit is behind Liz Truss failure', *New Statesman* YouTube channel (2023), https://www.youtube.com/watch?v=v3M00yKCVww, last accessed 16 April 2025.

32  S. Murphy, post on Twitter (@13sarahmurphy), 3 June 2022, https://x.com/13sarahmurphy/status/1532625669586399234 , last accessed 16 April 2025.

33  H. Lambert (2022) 'Brexit is making us poorer – and Rishi Sunak agrees', *New Statesman*, 29 March, https://www.newstatesman.com/politics/brexit/2022/03/brexit-is-making-us-poorer-and-rishi-sunak-agrees, accessed 26 October 2022.

34  J. Springford (2022) *What Can We Know About the Cost of Brexit So Far?* (Centre for European Reform), https://www.cer.org.uk/publications/archive/policy-brief/2022/cost-brexit-so-far, accessed 26 October 2022.

35  After all – although this is a hard saying for some – England was, and remains, a European nation. Despite popular mental geographies that at times seem to imagine England as an island halfway across the Atlantic, England is only twenty-two miles from France, and the whole East Coast is just an easy overnight crossing from the Low Countries and Scandinavia.

36  S. Kuper (2023) *Chums: How a Tiny Caste of Oxford Tories Took Over the UK* (Profile Books), p. 160.

37  S .Butt, E. Clery, and J. Curtice (eds), *British Social Attitudes: The 39th Report*.

38  Ibid.

39  Support for rejoining the European Union has increased as the economic consequences of Brexit have become apparent. A poll in late October 2022 put UK-wide support for rejoining at 57%, as against 43% for remaining outside. See J. Stone (2022) 'Brexit: rejoining EU takes record 14-point lead in latest poll', *Independent*, 28 October.

40  L. Colley (2009) *Britons: Forging the Nation 1707–1837* (3rd edn) (Yale University Press).

41  For an account of the creation of the Union as England's 'inner empire', and of the continuity of the imperial impulse between the 'inner' and 'outer' empires, see Bulmer-Thomas, *Internal Empire*.

42  G. C. Griffith (1899) *Men Who Have Made the Empire* (3rd edn) (C. Arthur Pearson), p. xvi.

43  There is a very revealing line in Jim Mackie's account of his work as a colonial agricultural inspector in Sudan during the Second World War, where he was in charge of a government irrigation and plantation scheme which produced wheat to feed Montgomery's armies in Egypt. He noted that 'Most Sudanese recognised that "Scottish" and "English" were separate tribes'. See J. Mackie (1994) *Trek into Nuba* (Pentland Press), p. 72.

44  J. Paxman (2007) *The English: A Portrait of a People* (Penguin), p. 13.

45  This, too, is arguably changing. The 1998 Good Friday Agreement has opened the possibility, for some people, of finding an Irish way of being British, and, for others, a British way of being Irish. Whether this mollification of previously harsh attitudes will survive the post-Brexit arrangement for Northern Ireland and the strain that puts on the Good Friday Agreement remains to be seen.

46  Paxman, *The English*, p. 53.

47  Bulmer-Thomas, *Internal Empire*, p. 138.

48  D. Edgerton (2018) *The Rise and Fall of the British Nation: A Twentieth-Century History* (Allen Lane).

49  Ibid.

50  A. Birch (1969) *The British System of Government* (2nd edn) (George Allen and Unwin).

51  W. I. Jennings (1965) *The Queen's Government* (revised edn) (Penguin).

52  T. Nairn (1977) *The Break-Up of Britain: Crisis and Neonationalism* (NLB).

53  A. J. P. Taylor (1990) *The Habsburg Monarchy 1809–1918* (Penguin); J. Deak (2015) *Forging a Multi-National State: State Making in Imperial Austria from the Enlightenment to the First World War* (Stanford University Press).

54  J. Deak (2015) *Forging a Multinational State: State Making in Imperial Austria from the Enlightenment to the First World War* (Stanford University Press).

55  A. Aughey (2002) 'Britain's Hapsburg question? Tom Nairn, Sir Ernest Barker, and the multi-national state', *Scottish Affairs*, Vol. 38, No. 1, pp. 81–93.
56  W. E. Bulmer (2017) *Federalism* (Constitution Building Primer No. 12) (International IDEA).
57  G. Brown (2020) 'We need a new way to run a truly United Kingdom', *The Guardian*, 18 October, https://www.theguardian.com/commentisfree/2020/oct/18/we-need-a-new-way-to-run-a-truly-united-kingdom-gordon-brown, accessed 22 October 2022.
58  'UK party leaders issue joint pledge to give Scottish parliament new powers', *The Guardian*, 16 September 2014. https://www.theguardian.com/politics/2014/sep/16/cameron-miliband-clegg-pledge-daily-record, accessed 1 November 2022.
59  Welsh Government (2019) *Reforming Our Union: Shared Governance in the United Kingdom*, https://gov.wales/sites/default/files/publications/2019-10/reforming-our-union-shared-governance-in-the-uk.pdf, accessed 21 November 2022.
60  Independent Commission on the Constitutional Future of Wales (2022) *What We Do* (Welsh Government), https://gov.wales/independent-commission-constitutional-future-wales, accessed 21 November 2022.
61  Independent Commission on the Constitutional Future of Wales (2024) *Final Report*, https://www.gov.wales/sites/default/files/publications/2024-07/independent-commission-on-the-constitutional-future-of-wales-final-report.pdf, accessed 21 November 2022.
62  S. A. de Smith (1964) *The New Commonwealth and Its Constitutions* (Stevens), p. 254.
63  Ibid.
64  In 2018, the Constitutional Reform Group, a Unionist think-tank, drafted a new Act of Union Bill, which – although a very flawed document, which is too wedded to the principle of parliamentary sovereignty to be effective – did at least clearly set out these two options: a 'nations and regions' option, and a 'four nations' option.
65  This is on the assumption, of course, that Wales wishes to have its own legal jurisdiction; otherwise, the picture becomes even more complicated and absurd, with 'England and Wales' forming one legal jurisdiction, but having no shared legislature except for the federal Parliament.
66  In 2024, the Labour Government created the Council of the Nations and Regions, which revealed the inadequacy and unacceptability of the 'nations and regions' idea. It brought together the national administrations of Scotland and Wales, as well as Northern Ireland, with English city/regional mayors. This measure was insulting at once to England, which was denied national representation, and to Scotland, Wales, and Northern Ireland, which were treated on a par with mere regions of England.
67  J. King (2019) 'The democratic case for a written constitution', *Current Legal Problems*, Vol. 72, No. 1, pp. 1–36.
68  W. E. Bulmer (2020) *Westminster and the World: Commonwealth and Comparative Insights for Constitutional Reform* (Bristol University Press).
69  The system of constitutionally-embedded devolution within England in the draft Constitution differs from federalism in that, while certain powers are devolved, and not merely in the gift of the English Parliament, these powers are exercisable only within the terms prescribed by Parliament. When Parliament considers there to be a compelling national interest to do so, it can enact English-wide legislation, even in devolved areas. There is a flexibility built into this model that true federalism usually lacks.
70  P. Popelier and K. Lemmens (2015) *The Constitution of Beligum: A Contextual Analysis* (Bloomsbury).
71  D. Elazar (1987) *Exploring Federalism* (University of Alabama Press), p. 5.
72  For a historical perspective on the difference between an 'incorporating union' under one Parliament, and an 'unincorporating union' under separate Parliaments, see A. Fletcher (1706) *State of the Controversy Betwixt United and Separate Parliaments* (Forgotten Books, 2010).
73  Another quirk is that certain rights would be retained by citizens of the Republic of Ireland, who, under agreements going back to Irish independence, have the right of residence and the right to work in England.

74 On the relationship between the UK and the Dominions, see A. B. Keith (1932) *Speeches and Documents on the British Dominons 1918-1931: From Self-Government to National Sovereignty* (Oxford University Press).

75 If, say, the United Kingdom ratified a treaty, but the Welsh Parliament refused to incorporate it into Welsh law, then the treaty would not apply in Wales as part of the domestic law of Wales, but would still be binding on the whole of the UK in international law. It looks messy but it works. Ireland had pretty much this arrangement under the Free State.

76 The Crown Dependencies and the British Overseas Territories are not, at present, part of the United Kingdom; they belong *to* it, not *in* it. That would change under the proposals outlined here.

77 Northern Ireland already has a legal, as well as a moral, right to determine its own future, guaranteed by the Good Friday Agreement. That right would have to be constitutionally recognised, but not created. Scotland's right to self-determination has been asserted and recognised in the Claim of Right, but this does not yet have effect in law. On democratic principles, the same right should be extended to Wales, as well as to the Crown Dependencies and to the self-governing Overseas Territories.

78 A. Salmond (2024), Panel Discussion 1: OHRID Academy for Cultural Diplomacy Forum (10–13 October), available at https://www.youtube.com/watch?v=KfzhzVwoGhg, accessed 12 May 2025.

79 There is also nothing to stop other countries from joining the United Kingdom (by agreement, and with a small amendment to the Sixth Schedule to the Constitution). It is hard to imagine circumstances in which that would happen, but it is not inconceivable that some small states might find the protection granted by membership of the United Kingdom to be worthwhile, given the very small sacrifice of sovereignty. For those who do still dream of a restoration of British imperial greatness, this paradoxical loosening of the Union, and turning it into an organisation with benefits that small-island jurisdictions, in particular, might want to share, is the way to do it.

80 British Irish Council (2022) 'About the Council', https://www.britishirishcouncil.org/about-council, last accessed 16 April 2025.

81 Earlier drafts of this book mentioned NATO by name. At the time of submitting the final manuscript, the Trump administration was blowing the North Atlantic alliance apart, and all the calls were for closer European defence integration. We shall have to see how all that shakes out.

82 The Swedes have been so successful in coming to terms with the end of their inner Empire that we rarely think of them today as a former imperial power. However, it is as well to remember that the Swedes ruled Norway (1814–1905) in much the same way as England rules the United Kingdom, and that the friendship and cooperation between them today, through institutions such as the Nordic Council, is a model for the British islands.

83 A. Henderson and R. Wyn Jones (2023) *The Ambivalent Union: Findings of the State of the Union Survey* (Institute for Public Policy Research), p. 41.

84 Kumarasingham, H. (ed) (2015) *The Road to Temple Trees: Sir Ivor Jennings and the Constitutional Development of Ceylon* (Colombo: Centre for Policy Alternatives), p. 17.

85 J. Cliffe (2022) 'The failure of Trussonomics shows Britain is European, not American, at heart. The UK should look to the Netherlands for inspiration: it is both richer and more equal', *New Statesman*,19 October, https://www.newstatesman.com/comment/2022/10/failure-trussonomics-shows-britain-european-not-american, accessed 31 October 2022.

86 P. Hitchens (2022) 'Why England should leave the UK instead of persuading the others to stay and embrace a golden future', *Daily Mail*, 18 May, https://www.dailymail.co.uk/debate/article-10831007/PETER-HITCHENS-England-leave-UK-embrace-golden-future.html, accessed 19 November 2022.

# 3

# Rediscovering England, reclaiming Englishness

## (a) Visions of England

Accepting normal nationhood calls for a reinterpretation of English culture, identity, and belonging. Some people would welcome such a change, or would adapt to it quickly and easily. For others, it would be a difficult adjustment. England has yet to find a post-British and post-imperial way of being English. What is England, anyway? What might the England that emerges from the unravelling of its 'inner Empire' look like? Does England still have a national identity? How might that identity change with the restoration of statehood, even within a reconstituted United Kingdom as is here proposed?

This chapter does not have any easy answers to these questions. It does, however, seek to survey England and Englishness, to connect the cultural fragments of Englishness into a recognisable whole, then to imagine the development of an inclusive – constitutional and civic – English identity.

\* \* \* \* \*

England – the England I know and love – is country pubs, real ale, ploughman's lunches, pork pies, pickled onions, and smelly dogs sleeping by open fires. It is old market towns, antiquarian bookshops, castles, museums, and heritage sites. The National Trust. Follies. Preserved steam railways, steam engine rallies, steamed pudding.

Afternoon tea. Tea rooms. Tea and scones. Proper porcelain pots of tea. Thermos flasks full of tea, sipped in the car overlooking a grey windswept sea while the rain batters against the windows. The common, tacit wisdom that tea solves all problems.

Outdoor summer Shakespeare plays performed in the grounds of ruined abbeys. Pimm's, picnic hampers, and picnic blankets. Rowing on the river, the dabbled morning light sparking on the pencil-fine wake of a coxed four at speed. Cricket, both county and test, but best of all on a village green. Lazy summer late afternoons in the garden, listening to *Test Match Special*. On the subject of radio: *In Our Time, Gardeners' Question Time,* and *I'm Sorry I Haven't a Clue.*

Cooked English breakfasts. Cumberland sausages, Lincolnshire sausages, fish and chips (best on the north-east coast, with Whitby as the epicentre of greatness). Herring. Kippers. Kedgeree. Giant Yorkshire puddings filled with slices of roast beef and gravy. Beef Wellington. Colman's mustard. Rosemary-basted lamb with roast potatoes, braised red cabbage, and lashings of mint sauce. Stilton, marmalade, and Weetabix – although not all at once. Curry nights, with little pots of chutney to go with your papadums.

Pick-your-own strawberries. Russet apples. Cloudy scrumpy so raw and authentic it almost has bits of dead wasp in it. Adge Cutler and the Wurzels. Summer pudding, raspberry jam, clotted cream, sherry trifle. Apple crumble, sticky toffee pudding, plum pudding. Victoria plums, Victoria sponge, 'Victoria' by The Kinks, statues of Queen Victoria.

Magna Carta. The Petition of Right. The Bill of Rights and the Glorious Revolution. Parliamentary government (although not necessarily the current lot). The Speaker shouting 'Division! Clear the lobbies!' The common law. Trial by jury. Habeas corpus. Sir Edward Coke, Sir William Blackstone, Sir Matthew Hale, Baroness Hale of Richmond.

The Palace of Westminster. Gothic architecture. The great English cathedrals: Salisbury, Norwich, Wells, Lincoln, Gloucester, Hereford, Durham. York Minster. Singing 'Jerusalem' in my old school chapel, beneath a stained-glass window that said 'Let us now praise famous men and our fathers that begat us'.

The abundance of ancient village churches with hand-tapestried hassocks, musty smells, memorial plaques, and an almost tangible presence of congregants gone by. The moss and lichen on old gravestones. Ghosts, both in and out of their proper haunting grounds. Choral evensong. The Book of Common Prayer. The King James Bible. Parish councils. The Women's Institute and the Mothers' Union. Memorial benches. Scout huts.

The intellectual and moral rigour of Old Dissent. *The Pilgrim's Progress*. Thunderous lay preachers in Methodist chapels. The Wesley brothers' soul-stirring hymns. The Nonconformist social conscience. Temperance halls and friendly societies. The Tolpuddle martyrs, abolitionists, Chartists, and suffragettes. Salvation Army bands.

Bandstands. Well tended municipal flowerbeds. Maypoles. Morris dancers. Morris Minors. Summer fetes. Whack-a-rat. White-elephant stalls. The piercing scream of a little glo-plug engine as it pulls a balsawood model aircraft up in a gentle spiral through the still August afternoon sky.

Foggy autumn evenings when the clocks go back. That strange spooky week between Halloween and Bonfire Night. Apple bobbing. Frosty Sunday morning walks on ancient public footpaths through wintering Wessex woods. Mulled wine. Pantomime. Traditional English Christmas dinners with all the trimmings – except sprouts. Mince pies, brandy butter. Chocolate oranges. Boxing Day. Cordite and gun-oil. Badgers, otters, robins, hedgehogs, spaniels.

The breadth and variety of knowledge in unlikely places. Amateur inventors, part-time palaeontologists, weekend archaeologists, autodidactic experts in obscure subjects, local historians in M&S cardigans, bearded folk musicians, bee-keepers, brass-rubbers, bell-ringers, artisan mead-makers, home brewers, organic smallholders, potting-shed horticulturalists, flower arrangers, hobbyists, tinkerers, classic-car restorers, model-railway enthusiasts, Sealed Knot re-enactors, narrow-boaters.

Big old draughty houses full of books and paintings, wardrobes, and dust. The way the colours and textures of villages and cities vary with local stone types. Lychgates. Country cottages with chintz curtains and a trellis of roses growing around the door. Foxgloves and delphiniums. Thatched roofs. High hedgerows enclosing winding country lanes. Raindrops hanging heavily on the cobwebs of bramble bushes along railway cuttings and canal banks.

Medieval city streets with rude names. Inter-war Tudor-revival suburban redbrick semi-detached houses with bay windows, rooting middle-class aspiration in a sense of time and place – a proudly earned patch of ground to call home. Garden sheds. Garden gnomes. Garden centres. Allotments. Buttercups and daisies. Prize-winning turnips judged by local worthies at county shows.

The English language with its convoluted history, diglossic vocabulary, and many accents. Its mongrel mix of Celt, Anglo-Saxon, Norse, and Norman French. Its indiscriminate plundering of Latin, Greek, Hindi, Arabic, and Malay – and any other language it meets.

William Shakespeare, John Milton, William Blake, Samuel Taylor Coleridge, Mary Shelley, Rudyard Kipling, Anthony Trollope, Thomas Hardy, C. S. Lewis, J. R. R. Tolkien, Agatha Christie, Arthur Ransome, George Orwell, Eleanor Scott, and Terry Pratchett. M. R. James and all his gang of spook-hunting scholars. Sir John Betjeman, with his war on Slough and his tirades against the seaside bungalows so many of us secretly covet. Winnie-the-Pooh, Thomas the Tank Engine, Postman Pat, *The Secret Garden*, Brambly Hedge, *The Wind in the Willows*.

The distinctly English humour of Monty Python, Blackadder, Fawlty Towers, Victoria Wood, Reginald Perrin, and Alan Partridge. *Private Eye*.

Self-deprecation. Struggling through noble failure. Eddie 'the Eagle' Edwards and his have-a-go spirit. Good sportsmanship. Playing the game. A 'swift half' on the way home. Banter. Amateur dramatics. Nursery rhymes.

The music of Elgar and Vaughan Williams. 'Barwick Green'. Gilbert and Sullivan's giddy operettas, especially *The Pirates of Penzance* and *H.M.S. Pinafore*. Sea shanties. Tall tales of the sea. Pictures of ships, not just Turner's *The Fighting Temeraire*, but that above all the rest. *The Shipping Forecast*. Navy Days and the Field Gun run (sadly defunct, *sic transit* etc.). Gin and tonic at six o'clock sharp in the Wardroom scruffs' bar. Passing the port.[1]

Little seaside towns. Piers, lighthouses, lifeboat stations. Pubs again, with names like The Ship Inn, The Crown and Anchor, or The Pig and Whistle, smelling of salt, vinegar, fishing nets, and seaweed. Eerie stretches of empty coastline. Windswept out-of-season beaches. Groynes. Martello towers, Palmerston forts, and the relics of pill boxes and coastal batteries. Beach huts.

The great English seafarers and explorers: Sir Walter Raleigh, Sir Francis Drake, Sir Martin Frobisher. The scientists, engineers, and architects: Sir Isaac Newton, Charles Darwin, Isambard Kingdom Brunel, Richard Trevithick, Robert Stephenson, Sir Christopher Wren, Sir Charles Barry, John Harrison and his chronometer. The humanitarians: Florence Nightingale, Elizabeth Fry, and Catherine Booth. (Let there be little blue plaques halfway up walls for all of them, and pictures on banknotes for the lucky ones.)

High-quality costume dramas. Low-budget Hammer horror and *Carry On* films. David Attenborough's wildlife documentaries. *Old Country* with Jack Hargreaves. Sunday afternoon BBC television as I remember it from childhood: *Songs of Praise*, *Antiques Roadshow*, and *Time Team* – all serving to remind the English that they live in an old country, with bats in the belfry, secrets in the attic, and bones under the soil. John Simpson and Kate Adie reporting from somewhere very dangerous, but reassuringly far away.

Landscape artists from John Constable to Eric Ravilious, Gordon Beningfield, and Ronald Lampitt. The gentleness of the Devon hills, the majesty of the Lake District, the ruggedness of the Cornish coast. The view from the East Coast mainline. The Abbey and East Cliff at Whitby. 1930s Great Western Railway posters inviting travellers to 'Visit Sidmouth'. The red rocks of the South Devon coast. Teignmouth. Shaldon, with The Ness and its Smugglers' Tunnel. Dartmoor ponies. Dawlish Warren. The bluebells on Exmoor that my father told me to remember. Dartmouth to Totnes in a picket boat. The Parson and the Clerk. Wookey Hole. Cheddar Gorge. Stonehenge. Avebury Stone Circle. Glastonbury Tor. The Cerne Abbas Giant. The Beast of Bodmin Moor. The Lincoln Imp. The Lambton Worm.

* * * * *

In the absence of a democratic constitutional state and national public in-stitutions upon which to ground 'civic Englishness', English identity can be described and defined only through such a kaleidoscope of cultural fragments. Everyone's list will be different, with variations of detail and emphasis, accord-ing to region, religion, sex, class, and age. Others will include things that are not on my personal list – football terraces, London buses, the Tube – things from the counties I know nothing about, like Surrey, Shropshire, or Bedfordshire.[2]

Nevertheless, recurring images of Englishness do seem to resonate across the political spectrum. For George Orwell, England was 'the to-and-fro of the lorries on the Great North Road, the queues outside the Labour Exchanges, the rattle of pin-tables in the Soho pubs, the old maids biking to Holy Communion through the mists of the autumn morning' and 'solid breakfasts and gloomy Sundays, smoky towns and winding roads, green fields and red pillar-boxes'.[3] Clement Attlee, Labour Prime Minister in 1945, proclaimed his love of England in terms of 'trees, hedges, grass and lie of the land … railways, towns and lighted streets. And above all, the lit pavements shimmering with rain.'[4] The former Conservative Prime Minister John Major, perhaps deliberately echoing the sentiments of his inter-war predecessor Stanley Baldwin, described England as 'the country of long shadows on county grounds, warm beer, invincible green suburbs, dog lovers and pools fillers' – scenes of a domesticated, settled, quiet English life.[5]

These familiar fragments of Englishness – Orwell called them 'character-istic fragments' – keep on cropping up in the imagination. They somehow fit together in ways that construct a recognisably familiar 'collage of Englishness'.

In these sad late days, when a legacy of corruption and misrule have made people more ashamed than proud of what England has become, that collage of Englishness no doubt offers some comfort. One may bemoan the stench of public life or lament the relative decline of living standards, while still finding some anchor of meaning in those few fragments of cultural Englishness that are not yet ruined.

Cultural nationalism is not necessarily a bad thing. A civic approach to cultural nationalism sees national cultural traditions as absorbing, not excluding. It does not matter if your middle name is Amy, Aisha, or Agnieszka, or whether your grandparents came from Bognor Regis, Bombay, or Bydgoszcz, you can be equally included in an English nation that is defined by its shared culture and customs, not by a shared ethnicity.

Even so, cultural nationalism based on cream teas, country inns, and all the curious charm, clichés, and contradictions of 'Quaintshire' – reassuring and comforting though that mythological England might be – will not help the real England overcome its profound crisis of policy, governance, institutions, socio-economic performance, and public ethics. The imaginary England, with its rose-tinted nostalgia, is no substitute for a thriving democratic political community – a Government, Parliament, and above all a decent written constitution, of England's own. Without its own legitimate and democratic constitutional voice, English identity is trapped in these clichés, and cultural nationalism, so stifled, can become 'nativist and somewhat reactionary'.[6]

Besides, many of these things are either already lost or endangered. Idiosyncratic country inns have closed down, or been replaced by bland noisy chain pubs, and once thriving towns have been eviscerated by big-box shopping centres.[7] Everywhere, the pleasant façade is cracked. Behind it, there is another England, a real England, more grim and dismal than this kaleidoscope of comforting cultural fragments. Behind what is left of the pretty scenery, the real England is in a wretched state. It is a land of sporadic buses, expensive, overcrowded trains, low wages, unfair taxes, long hours, damp houses, expensive energy bills, sink estates, drug crime, knife crime, racial prejudice, two-tier policing, obesity, food banks, permanently closed libraries, bleak playgrounds covered in broken glass and used condoms, pawn shops, potholes, payday loans, churches turned into discount carpet warehouses, grey concrete towers burning like infernos of neglect and mismanagement, and all kinds of unremitting misery never to be depicted on the cover of a Ladybird book.

By the time of the Brexit vote, England had lost its way, forgotten its values, corrupted its public institutions, betrayed its history, and abandoned many of its own people. Austerity meant the decline of quality of life, life expectancy, and real wages. Opportunities are narrow, poverty on the rise, and the gap between the 'haves' and the 'have-nots' is widening to a dangerous and morally shameful degree. Despite England's record of outstanding contributions to human civilisation, it has become a nation in grave distress. If Labour can reverse these trends, hallelujah. If not, England is in danger of becoming a Ruritanian parody of itself: a poor, dismal, isolated, and backward country, ruled by a stupid, corrupt, and authoritarian state.

To recover, and to avoid this plight, England first needs to accept itself. Englishness is nothing to be embarrassed by or ashamed of, and English nationhood does not need to be hidden or denied. A healthy, civic, democratic sense of Englishness is to be welcomed. But to get there, England must come to terms with the fact that, economically and socially, and in terms of its ability to provide most of its citizens with a good quality of life, it is falling behind the rest of the Western world. It needs to accept that it is no longer a great world power and can no longer dictate terms to other countries – not to Scotland, Ireland, or Wales, not to its former colonies, and not to the rest of Europe. It needs to accept, above all, that its political institutions are broken, its public life is degraded, and its unwritten constitution is no longer fit for purpose – no matter which party is in power. Its economic model – which since the 1980s has been based on speculation in the City of London rather than productive industrial investment – has benefited a few, but failed many. England's great and honourable tradition of civil liberties and parliamentary democracy has been sorely strained.

The gap between the bucolic English imagination and the bleak English reality is now too wide to be ignored. That stark realisation of how far England has fallen – that moment of piercing clarity that hits when one realises it has all gone so horribly wrong – should shake off complacency and focus English hearts and minds on the building of a movement for democratic national reform, renewal, and restoration.

## (b) The hauntology of Englishness

There is a growing literature on England and Englishness, and on the academic study of Englishness as a political force. Arthur Aughey's *The Politics of Englishness* is now somewhat dated – having been written before the Brexit vote – but still an excellent introduction to the subject.[8] Aughey identified 1996 ('sometime between New Year and football's Euro96') as the moment when an English national identity burst into public consciousness.[9] The English flag, which had been 'for centuries confined largely to the spires of rural parish churches', suddenly 'flew from cars, pubs and shops'.[10] Two years earlier, Julia Stapleton's *Englishness and the Study of Politics* had already noted 'the erosion of a particular sense of Englishness' associated with middle-brow, mid-twentieth-century thought and culture.[11] By the late 1990s, Englishness was back – in a different guise. It had taken off its tweed jacket with leather elbow patches, stepped out of its dreaming spires, and morphed into a brash, popular, laddish, working-class form. The porky Englishry – drinking beer, singing football chants, throwing punches, and waving the cross of St George – had 'come out of the national closet and declared a patriotic love that could now speak its name'.[12]

The timing was significant. This resurgence of popular Englishness occurred shortly before devolution to Scotland and Wales had happened, but at the time when it was being hotly debated. The return of the Stone of Destiny to Scotland in 1996 was a merely symbolic gesture by Sir John Major, but it brought Scottish discontent with the constitutional status quo to the attention of English voters. In 1997, Hong Kong was handed to China, and so the final curtain of the Empire fell in a ceremony of poignant powerlessness. Englishness thus emerged as a publicly visible political identity just at the time the Union and Empire were collapsing. After winning the 1997 general election, Tony Blair introduced devolution, which forced the English, on the one hand, to 'recognise themselves as different from the Welsh and Scots' and, on the other hand, to 'acknowledge their role as a dominant power whose annexing of these nations over many centuries is slowly being undone'.[13]

More recently, the study of English identity has been dominated by the duo of Alisa Henderson and Richard Wyn Jones, whose *Englishness: The Political Force Transforming Britain* provides a rich source of crunchy data on how the English see themselves and others.[14] The relationship of England to Britain, and the role of Englishness in splitting apart the Union, is also examined by Gavin Esler in *How Britain Ends: English Nationalism and the Rebirth of Four Nations*.[15] John Denham, a former Labour MP, has contributed many interesting articles and opinion pieces on the English question, and is one of the few voices to support England and Englishness in the spaces that bridge policy and academia.

Perhaps the most interesting contribution, insofar as it explicitly addresses English constitutional thought, is Ian Ward's *The English Constitution: Myths and Realities*.[16] Ward's constitutional proposals are radical, going beyond the tame, moderate, reformist proposals of this book. Nevertheless, by connecting the socio-economic problem to the constitutional problem, and by advocating institutions that seek to promote the common good and to maintain the public-ness of the state against corrupt private interests, Ward is very much on the right lines. He points to the creation of a civic, democratic, idea of Englishness, which is vital if England is ever again to flourish. Where he errs is only in not reconciling that vision, on an aesthetic and symbolic level, with older, deeper English identities, so that people across the political spectrum, including moderate conservatives, can share in it.

Besides these academic and political analyses, there has also been a flower-ing of historical, cultural, personal, and literary explorations of England and Englishness. Peter Ackroyd's *Albion: The Origins of the English Imagination*[17] and Roger Scruton's *England: An Elegy*[18] have become standard sources. More critical, left-leaning, accounts of Englishness include James Hawes' excellent *The Shortest History of England*.[19] Jeremy Paxman's *The English: A Portrait of a People*[20] probably sits ideologically somewhere in the middle, and is perhaps the best starting point for those seeking an introduction to the subject. To these must also be added the anthropological observations of Kate Fox's *Watching the English*,[21] the heartfelt lamentations of Paul Kingsnorth's *Real England*,[22] and the historical analysis of Victor Bulmer-Thomas' *Internal Empire*.[23]

Jason Cowley's *Who Are We Now? Stories of Modern England* stands out for its portrait of what might yet come to be called 'New Elizabethan' England, span-ning the period of rapid social change from 1952 to 2022. He describes, through snapshots of his home town of Harlow in Essex, how 'thrilling possibilities' of

Attlee's post-war New Jerusalem have been dashed. Cowley describes the world the world he grew up in:

> The National Health Service was established; the National Insurance Act abolished the hated means test for welfare provision; essential industries such as the railways and mining were nationalized; the Town and Country Planning Act was passed, opening the way for mass housebuilding and the redevelopment of huge tracts of land, as well as the creation of the Green Belt; [...] the gap between rich and poor narrowed. [...] It seemed everything we needed was provided by the state: housing, education, health care, libraries, recreational and sports facilities. There were play schemes (summer camps) where we gathered to take part in organized games during the long school holidays.[24]

Returning to Harlow in recent years, after Thatcherism, and then Cameron's austerity, Cowley was 'shocked at how shabby and neglected it was':

> In the pedestrian precinct, pound and charity shops – the RSPCA and Salvation Army occupied what were once prime sites – and scrappy fast-food joints proliferated. There was a tattoo and body-piercing shop. A Thai massage parlour was adjacent to an undertaker.[25]

One cannot make sense of England without recognising this picture. The New Jerusalem *was* built. While surely not perfect, it was in many ways very good. But it was abandoned where it was not destroyed. The broken hope of England's lost future haunts the ruins of its New Towns, no less than it haunts the pretty houses (which locals cannot afford to live in) of its ancient cathedral cities.

Much of the literature about England focuses on what one might call the 'deep England', rooted in English landscape and folk culture. Works such as *Landscape and Englishness* by David Matless,[26] and *How England Made the English* by Harry Mount,[27] explore this relationship between land, people, and culture, going back into geological time.

England is now in the middle of a quiet folk revival – a sign of an English search, in a changing and increasingly uncertain world, for a deeper identity and more rooted sense of belonging.[28] In *Performing Englishness*, Trish Winter and Simon Keegan-Phipps examine how the revival of folk music and folk dance has given voice to a repressed but resurgent English identity. Henry Buckton's *Yesterday's Country Customs* likewise notes that hobbyhorses, cheese-rolling, Strove Tuesday mob football, wassailing, and other old folk traditions, which in many places almost disappeared in the twentieth century, are coming back into fashion.[29]

It is not all beer and skittles, though. Englishness has long had an uncanny side, evident in folk-horror, gothic literature, ghost stories, and an obsession with the mysteries of the ancient landscape. All these genres and their associated themes have had enduring resonance in English popular culture. They were particularly popular in Victorian times, as the country came to terms with urbanisation, industrialisation, modernity, and the challenge posed to traditional theology by scientific materialism.[30] That era was also the heyday of Gothic Revival architecture, which was presented as an authentically English (and

Anglican) style, in contrast to continental Catholic baroque and New World puritan classicism.

Since the late 1960s, when initial post-war optimism and certainty began to dissipate, there have been recurring waves of revival of folk, gothic, and gothic-adjacent genres in England. When England was forced to confront the end of Empire, persistent economic woes, the looming European question, The Troubles in Northern Ireland, and the rise of Scottish and Welsh nationalisms challenging the Anglo-centricity of the Union, much of the cultural output was 'born of an obsession with the past as a repository of national mythologies', which revealed a national character that was 'weirder, more eldritch and more conflicted than anyone might have expected'.[31] This trend was exemplified by Hammer horror films, the BBC's 'A Ghost Story for Christmas' series, Usborne's 'World of the Unknown' series, which inspired the dark imaginations of a whole generation of children,[32] and much else besides.

In the 1980s, as inequality widened and as industrial communities endured the living death of long-term unemployment, this resurgent interest in all things gothic was made visible by the emergence of New Romantic and Goth subcultures. It is quite understandable, when the financial sector sucks the life blood out of the real economy and your life is spent wandering through the desolate graveyard of abandoned factories, to want to dress in black and listen to The Cure's moody chords. It is no surprise, then, to find that in similar conditions today many people return to this 'Englishness of the uncanny' to make sense of their nation. The dark side of English nationalism comes from these ghost towns.[33]

The gothicism of England, as a numinous land of mystery and the weird, is explored in recent books such as Edward Parnell's *Ghostland: In Search of a Haunted Country*,[34] Jack Strange's *It's a Strange Place, England*,[35] and H. E. Bulstrode's 'Curious England' series.[36] It can also be seen in folk horror films such as the cult classic *Penda's Fen* (1975), or Ben Wheatley's peculiar account of the English Civil War, *A Field in England* (2013). According to the Hookland project, a creative endeavour dedicated to 'High Weirdness from the Lost County of England', 'England is strange. Inescapably strange. [...] Anywhere you go, this country is an enfolding of eerie.'[37]

Jason Cowley identifies the root of English eeriness in a pervading sense of absence and loss: 'From ruined castles and dissolved monasteries to the enclosures of common land, the English landscape is haunted by the presence of what is absent'.[38] The most chilling absence of all, of course, is that of a constitution. The Palace of Westminster is truly gothic not because of its pointed arches, or Gormenghastian rituals, but because it sits, as an institutional relic, amidst the empty ruins of an unconstituted and de-constituted state.

So long as there is no living constitution to embody England's wandering spirit, one must look for it in these apparitions. The stateless and constitutionless politics of England is weirdly rooted in a dark 'constitutional hauntology' – that is, in twisted reflections of its own past.[39] Seen or unseen, English constitutional debates are deeply embedded in folk stories, theatrically and rhetorically replaying, like a stone tape, the unresolved trauma of old fights: Saxons and Normans,

King John and the barons, Robin Hood and the Sheriff of Nottingham, Roundheads and Cavaliers, Chartists and yeomanry, suffragettes and King's Horses, striking miners and Thatcher's police.

The works of M. R. James, R. H. Malden, E. G. Swain, L. T. C. Rolt, Sir Andrew Caldecott, H. R. Wakefield, the Benson brothers, Arthur Gray, and others of that ilk, all show England 'through a glass darkly'. These Victorian or Edwardian learned gentlemen, most of them Anglican clergy or academics, living comfortable lives as the cultural elite of an imperial society, set the canon and the defined the genre of the classic English ghost story. These stories are relevant today not primarily for their supernatural element, nor for the simple 'pleasing terror' of a chilling spook-tale on a winter's night, nor even because they demonstrate England's weirdness, its uncanniness, its sense of being a strange country haunted by its past. They are relevant because they deal with questions of identity, place, belonging, history, and morality – in other words, unsettled constitutional questions.

The theme of ancient Englishness can be found in the works of Francis Young, whose research on Saint Edmund points to a reconstruction of an English identity based not on '1066 and all that' but upon the Christian Anglo-Saxon state that preceded the Norman Conquest.[40] Young's work on Merlin – the wizard advisor to the legendary King Arthur – goes back even further, to a not-yet-England suffused with myth, magic, and mystery. This ancient, buried England, beautiful and strange, keeps reminding us of its presence, like unruly wild flowers poking through the cold, charmless paving slabs of official Britishness.

Englishness asserts itself in reaction against modern architecture, resisting the destruction of so much of England under ugly concrete piles. The old land must have its revenge on the 'monstrous carbuncles' of brutalism – as King Charles once famously described them – and restore the traditional, local, and vernacular. There are also echoes of a long-lost, latent but resurgent England in J. R. R. Tolkien's great English mythology, *The Lord of the Rings*. 'The Shire' can be interpreted as an idealised pre-Conquest England that, in the end, becomes tragically ruined and in need of restoration.[41] Perhaps the best recent evocation of this buried England is the TV series *Detectorists*, a heart-warming comedy about people digging for gold and old buttons in a gentle Engle-land that might still exist, somewhere, beneath all the layers of British and imperial history.[42]

All this, too, has constitutional implications. England is not a virgin land, where things can just be created and destroyed. The tangled wood where developers want to build 'an exclusive development of luxury homes' is an old place; there are stories about it, which for all we know could be true, and it would be folly to uproot it without expecting consequences.[43] The parish and the county matter. Freedom and democracy are not abstract concepts, but a historical inheritance, embedded in institutions – not only legal and political institutions, but also social and cultural ones. It may come down to the right to walk along a particular public footpath that a farmer wants to close off. It might be saving a local pond or park from destruction. It might be defending 'an Englishman's right to play cricket on his village green'.[44]

When radicals or reactionaries purpose to uproot old-growth constitutional conventions, chop down inherited rights and freedoms, or pave over cherished institutional norms, we would do well to hear and heed the warning given by Dr Ayloff in M. R. James's 'An Episode of Cathedral History': 'You ought not to touch it, you don't know what mischief you may do'.[45]

### (c) Looking for three Englands

Another good place to go 'looking for England' is in travel writing. It is as well to start with the modern classics: Paul Theroux's grimly serious *A Kingdom by the Sea* (1983) and Bill Bryson's more cheerful, but no less acute, *Notes from a Small Island* (1995). Although these two books are now somewhat dated, much of what they describe has not changed, at least not for the better. Both are written by Americans living in England, who have close familiarity with their subject matter combined with an incomer's knack for spotting what natives might not notice. They both cover Great Britain as a whole, but naturally devote most of their pages to England.

Reading now like social history with a prescient edge, Theroux and Bryson describe the long-term decline afflicting parts of England: the sad state of its post-industrial northern cities, the lack of investment outside of London and the South East, the stagnation of its tawdry coastal towns. They depict the poor infrastructure, the long-brewing sense of loss, the resentment against unwanted social change and economic dislocation, the desire of those outside the metropolitan centre to be heard and recognised, and to 'get their country back'. All these trends are, of course, signs of constitutional failure – the failure of the state to make and implement policy in ways that meet the needs of ordinary people – that are now so skilfully, but so duplicitously, mobilised by far-right movements. Re-reading Theroux and Bryson in the aftermath of Brexit, one would think that they could see what was coming.

Sociological travel writing as a means of discovering England has a good pedigree. During the inter-war years – when the British Empire was at its territorial apogee, but England was reeling from the General Strike and the Great Depression – a new genre of travel writing sprang up, exemplified by titles such as J. B. Priestley's *English Journey*[46] and H. V. Morton's *In Search of England*.[47] The great age of exploration was over, so instead of exploring Africa or the Indus valley, these writers turned to the well ploughed gentle shires of the south of England and to the windswept hills and mill towns of the north, to study their pasty-faced pudding-fed tribes. Even George Orwell's classic wartime essay on Englishness, *The Lion and the Unicorn: Socialism and the English Genius*, might not have been written without the impressions described in his *Road to Wigan Pier*, a travelogue of despair through the industrial north in the midst of the Depression.

J. B. Priestley, himself a northerner, discovered not one England, but three Englands.[48] The First England was that picturesque and mostly southern country, idealised by tourist boards and postcard printers. He called this 'Old

England, the country of the cathedrals and minsters and manor houses and inns, of parson and Squire; guide-book and quaint highways and byways'.[49]

Priestley's Second England, which made up 'the larger part of the Midlands and the North', was 'nineteenth-century England, the industrial England of coal, iron, steel, cotton, wool, railways; [...] sooty dismal little towns, and still sootier grim fortress-like cities'.[50]

The Third England Priestly discovered was that of the twentieth century, 'belonging far more to the age itself than to this particular island'. This new middle England, which was, in Priestley's view, 'as near to a classless society as we have yet got', was shaped neither by traditional village agricultural life nor by the Dark Satanic Mills of the first industrial revolution, but by newer and cleaner forms of high-tech light industry, giving rise to better-paid jobs and more disposable income. This was the England of 'by-pass roads', 'cinemas and dance halls and cafes', 'semi-detached bungalows, all with their little garages', 'wireless sets', 'periodicals about film stars', 'swimming costumes and tennis rackets and dancing shoes'.[51]

Priestley's 'three Englands' typology is rarely used today as a descriptive framework of analysis, but perhaps it should be. Politically, these social, cultural, and geographical divisions are still highly relevant. James Hawes identifies embedded 'tribal' patterns in English voting behaviour, which map quite neatly onto Priestley's three Englands. The First England has normally been solidly Conservative – while it has always had some Liberal presence, which emerges occasionally in local elections or by-elections, there has been little depth of Labour support. The second England was largely Liberal in the nineteenth century and Labour in the twentieth. The Third England has normally voted Tory with the First England, rather than anti-Tory with the Second, and this has been a main reason for long-term structural Tory dominance.[52]

The Third England's support for the Conservatives has wavered on a few occasions, when the Tories have been discredited and divided, or when they are dangerously out of step with the public mood – as in 1945, 1966, 1997, and 2024. This has made the Third England – the middle-English, mixed-class, swing constituencies, filled with such pollsters' stereotypes as 'Mondeo man' and 'Worcester woman' – the key battleground on which general elections have been decided.[53]

Even if these voting patterns are changing, the North–South divide – in economics, culture, and politics – persists. There is a lingering sense, at least among many southerners, that the South (not the real South, but an idealised 'Quaintshire', with its pretty villages and thatched cottages) is the 'real England'. The North is another country: a second-class England; a not fully, properly 'English' England. Of course, what they mean is that the North is a less Normanised England: a colder, harsher, thinner-soiled, upland England, in which Norman patterns of feudal village agriculture and settlement were less feasible. Long before the industrial revolution, hill farming and extractive work like mining bred a different sort of folk – more independent-minded and less deferential to imposed authority, yet more communal in their mutual reliance; less polished, but bolder and more outspoken.[54]

All this means that, although England is a nation, it is not an *undifferentiated* nation. Rather, it contains important regional variations, which go back at least a thousand years. England consists of real people in real places, some of which are beautiful Cotswold villages where no one can afford to live, and some of which are grim ex-mining towns where few would choose to live if they had a way out. Both are, in their different ways, victims of a class-bound neoliberal and post-imperial state that fails to serve the common good. Yet each demands different policy solutions. They must each be able to 'take back control' if their problems are to be overcome. Any governmental structure for England that fails to take account of that, and that tries to impose a centralised uniformity on the country and to keep power and resources in London, will fail to meet the country's deepest needs.[55]

### (d) The Anglo-scepticism of the Anglo-British elite

It has already been noted that Englishness has become a low-status identity, which sits awkwardly with England's ruling Anglo-British elites. The billionaire, banker, and rentier class, of course, have little sense of place, national identity, or belonging, and not much sympathy for the English. Those who understand Brexit-era politics in terms of the division between *Somewheres* (who have a strong sense of belonging to a place) and *Anywheres* (who live in a post-geographic, distanceless world) are correct at least to that extent.[56]

However, the English desire to be recognised as being from somewhere has, so far, mostly been weaponised by the populist anti-European far-right, rather than by democratic reformers calling into question the continued justifiability of the British state in its present form. This is a regrettable quirk of Anglo-British nationalism; elsewhere, European identities can happily coexist with strong national, regional, and local identities. Those pushing the narrative of a popular revolt against 'cosmopolitan elites' might wallow in a nostalgic cultural sense of Englishness, but they have little time for civic, democratic, constitutional, ideas of English nationhood.

The response of the British Governments, both Labour and Conservative, to English political nationhood has been to ignore or denigrate it, and to keep the idea as far as possible out of the orbit of respectable discourse. English national identity remains 'unsupported by those in positions of power'.[57] Instead, the Government has sought with an increasing desperation to reinforce a brittle, official version of Britishness, chiefly through 'Union Jackery' and pageants like the Diamond and Platinum Jubilees and Armed Forces Day.

The erasure of England from political debate goes so far as the use of euphemisms like 'this country' rather than risk drawing attention to England's existence. In the past, 'England' was often used as shorthand for 'Britain', 'the United Kingdom', or even 'the British Empire'. Now it has flipped: 'Britain', or increasingly 'the United Kingdom', is often used when really the speaker is thinking of England.[58] This elite suspicion of Englishness has deep roots. Ever since the Norman Conquest, England's owners and rulers have been distinguished from the great mass of native English people by language and culture. For centuries, the descendants of Norman knights have, in the words of James Hawes, been 'firmly in the saddle, on their high horses, talking their fancy foreign, looking down their noses at the English'.[59]

The Normans and Anglo-Saxons slowly merged, through centuries of inter-marriage and glacial but unstoppable social mobility, into an English nation. Nevertheless, this distinction between the ruling Norman-infused few and the ruled Anglo-Saxon many remained – albeit on class, rather than ethnic, lines. Ultimately, the English elite came to be 'distinguishable from the general popu-lation not by genealogy, but by learnable language and culture'.[60] This meant that the door was always at least potentially open to those with the means to assimilate themselves, through the schools and the universities, to the culture of the rulers.[61] In so doing, however, the aspiring new members of the elite set themselves apart – by accent and manners – from the ordinary English folk, whose 'ancient national culture had been abandoned'.[62]

This helps explain the Anglo-scepticism not only of the British Government, but also of the wider British political, media, cultural, and academic establish-ments. When Robert Jenrick tried to speak, ever so hesitantly, for England in the 2024 Conservative leadership election, he was roundly shouted down and mocked for it. For members of the 'Norman' ruling caste to speak for England, and even to hint at England's claim to exist as a cultural nation, is to align themselves with the lowly Saxons, and thereby to commit what any imperial elite regards as the most grievous sin: to 'go native'.

Much of the British ruling class during the heyday of imperial power barely knew the real 'England of the English'. Sweating through the fevers of India or the dust storms of Africa, they knew England only as a bucolic, idealised, half-remembered, half-imagined place, which had been glimpsed briefly from the nursery of a country house, from behind the walls of a boarding school, or from the safe confines of a university college or a London club. That was the England of which they dreamed, and which has percolated through to the English cultural imagination.

Even those members of the ruling class who stayed behind to run the core institutions of the Empire rarely got to know more than a thin, privileged wedge England. By 'England' they meant 'Imperial HQ', which was described by James Hawes as 'a network of exclusive southern spaces [...] a South of the mind, a vision, as unconnected to any real place as the RP accent in which they all spoke'.[63]

In *England: An Elegy*, Roger Scruton described getting his 'first real glimpses of England' from his schoolmaster, Mr Chapman. Mr Chapman had previously been a colonial administrator in Nigeria. He spoke Ibo and had tribal masks and elephant tusks on the walls of his home. The England Chapman repre-sented was not really English at all. It barely touched the reality of life between the Tweed and the Channel. Chapman's was an imperial British Englishness, a culture portable in a steamer trunk, whose traditional national dress was the solar topee and khaki drill shorts, and whose national habits were forged over sun-downers at the club, brought on silver trays by turbaned servants.

Scruton recognised the tragedy of belonging to a place that has ceased to exist. After the end of Empire, Mr Chapman lived mentally in an England that was 'no longer a real place, but a consecrated isle in the lake of forgetting, where the God of the English still strode through an imaginary Eden, admiring his works'.[64] Yet, physically, he was 'destined to wander without roots in a country which neither acknowledged nor remembered the mission which it had sent him abroad to perform'.[65]

Mr Chapman's experience was not unique. The very tail end of it has not quite passed from living memory, or at least from recent family histories. I grew up in a house with Indian pig-sticking spears on the wall. I also remember an umbrella stand made of an elephant's foot (a horrible ugly thing, it was, and it gave me the shivers). My mother-in-law grew up in India and remembers being terrified by monkeys bursting into the nursery and being chased out by her *ayah*. I once found an entry in one of my father's old diaries noting his attendance at the Suva Yacht Club dance for Fiji's independence celebrations.

Although Indian independence in 1947 meant the Empire had lost its core and its coherence, the show was still kept on the road, to a point, even after the Suez Crisis in 1956. One might argue that the British imperial age finally ended as late as 1997. In that year, Hong Kong was handed over to the Chinese, marking a shift in global power. Perhaps even more symbolically, 1997 saw the closure of Greenwich Naval College, which was once the intellectual nerve centre of British sea power. In the same year, the Royal Yacht *Britannia* was retired from service and not replaced. The sun had finally set. The pretence of greatness could no longer be maintained. It was Game Over. The English are all Mr Chapmans now: trapped in a strange, faded little England, looking at museum pieces, wondering what imperial Britain was all about, what has become of it, and where its demise has left them.

Disdain towards a civic, democratic Englishness is not confined to imperial nostalgists on the right. It is perhaps even stronger among progressive intellectual and cultural elites on the left, many of whom look down on common-or-garden Englishness as provincial, insular, parochial, vulgar, or reactionary. Julia Stapleton traces this attitude to the inter-war years, when those associated with the *New Statesman* and the Left Book Club effected an 'almost complete rejection of the inherited nation', motivated by 'their scorn for the parochialism and class hierarchies of England'.[66]

Part of the left's dull adherence to Britishness comes from the belief that British patriotism is associated with the ideals of modernity – 'positivism, science and utility' – while Englishness continues to be poetic, mythical, and historical, in a sense pre-modern, or even anti-modern.[67] Much of the metropolitan cultural left is (or was) more at home with the buzzword-laden and faux-inclusive – but ultimately vacuous – official Britishness, of the sort presented by the opening ceremony of the 2012 London Olympics.

However, far from being a reactionary movement, English nationalism – if it takes a civic and constitutional form – could be a liberating, integrating, democratising, reforming force. Nationalism scholars have distinguished between two varieties nationalism: 'ethnic nationalism', which is motivated by 'blood and soil' tribalism, and often encourages authoritarian and xenophobic attitudes; and 'civic nationalism', which is rooted in citizenship, in shared membership of a democratic state, and in the shared enjoyment of civil rights.[68] Ethnic nationalism taken to extremes leads to genocide. Civic nationalism, on the other hand, leads to a strong sense of public duty in which citizens see themselves as morally obliged, as members of one constituted body-politic, to love and serve one another by promoting the common good, resisting corruption, and protecting their liberties.[69]

To adopt a civic nationalism is to think of the English nation as consisting of its citizens, which includes everyone who calls England home: people of all classes, regions, religions, and ethnicities – not only those who happen to be pale-skinned and rosy-cheeked, and not only those who come from the best families and who went to the right schools.

There is an authentic tradition of English radicalism. Even cultural manifestations of Englishness that seem deeply traditional, such as folklore, folk music, and folk song, might be more radical than they appear. It is not far from the quaint trivialities of 'All around my hat, I'll wear a green willow' to 'Stand up now, ye Diggers all, stand up now!' Nor does it take much digging to discover that a seemingly quaint, trivial song about green willow on a hat is itself a protest song. Its lyrics decry 'the cruel judge and jury' and rail against the needless poverty that drove honest people into petty criminality, resulting in transportation to Australian penal colonies.

The tragedy for the Labour Party – hidebound by its industrial-era thinking, its roots in Scotland and Wales, and its British nationalism – is that it is incapable of tapping into this cultural stream of English radicalism. It too easily cedes all that territory to the populist right. Nigel Farage, although he speaks more of Britain than of England, seems instinctively to understand the mobilising appeal of Anglo-folksiness. The policies of Reform UK may be tailored to the interests of the barons, but the tone is Anglo-Saxon, anti-Norman, rebellion.

Allied to this left-leaning suspicion of Englishness is the false but pervasive idea that only British nationalism can be civic in nature, whereas English nationalism must be ethnically exclusive. Support for Britishness among people in England of Asian or Afro-Caribbean descent or from other recent immigrant backgrounds seems to stem from the assumption that Britishness can be assimilated into: one can pass the 'Life in the UK' test, take an oath, and eventually get British citizenship – whereas Englishness, they feel, is something one must be born with. Whatever the cause, Black, Asian, and minority ethic (BAME) citizens of the United Kingdom are more than twice as likely to consider themselves as more or exclusively British, and not English – about 44% having that identity – in comparison with around 21% of the total population.[70]

Britishness, too, is tainted in many people's eyes by its associations with the Empire, but at least it has taken the form of a civic nationalism, which is open to a multi-ethnic, cosmopolitan society. The British imperial state absorbed and accommodated many nations, cultures, languages, and ethnicities within it, and united them not through ethnic nationhood but by a common political allegiance represented by the Crown and embodied in certain institutions and principles of government. We see this in official symbols of Britishness. For example, the United Kingdom's so-called 'national' anthem is a royal hymn, and it says nothing at all about the nation, land, or people; it is solely focused on common allegiance to the Crown, and – as Sir Ivor Jennings could put it as late as 1965 – 'is sung wherever men serve in the Queen's name'.[71]

The status of 'British subject' extended not only to the insular British, but – until 1948 at least – to all in the Empire. This is not to deny that there was a pervasive racial hierarchy in the Empire. In principle, however, and in law, a street vendor from Calcutta and a villager from Kenya's Rift Valley were just as British as any Scotsman, or, indeed, as any Englishman. When Elizabeth II came to the throne, she had more brown Muslim than white Christian subjects.

Civic nationalism can be seen, too, in popular expressions of British identity. James Thomson's 1740 patriotic song 'Rule, Britannia!', the perennial favourite of the last night of the Proms, is often misunderstood by its critics on the left as mere jingoism. The words, however, reveal a different story: the song is not an expression of ethnic nationalism, but of civic patriotism grounded in constitutional liberty. It is a presentation, in six short verses, of the ideological basis of the British Empire. This might best be described as 'thalassocratic Whiggery': the inseparable union between freedom (understood in the Whig tradition), sea power (thalassocracy), and commercial prosperity.

'Rule, Britannia!' presents, as the true foundation of Britain's glory, a constitutional settlement that was far in advance of other European powers at the time: rights rooted in Magna Carta and secured by the Glorious Revolution, government by a responsible Cabinet and Parliament rather than by a monarch's capricious will, and a liberty under the law rather than submission to arbitrary power. This constitutional freedom – the energy and dynamism it unleashed, the confidence it gave to people, the sound basis it provided for trade and investment – was the springboard for scientific advancement, trade, naval dominance, industrial prowess, public spirit, and healthy national pride.[72] Britain could 'flourish great and free, / The dread and envy of them all' only because it was secured by 'the charter of the land'. The Great Charter, and all it stood for, assured that Britons 'never will be slaves' ('slavery' in this sense, of course, meant subjection to the arbitrary power of a despotic regime). Meanwhile, the 'nations, not so blessed as thee, / Must, in their turns, to tyrants fall'. In the same way, 'Heart of Oak', the great naval song, proclaimed 'To honour we call you, as freemen not slaves, / For who are so free as we sons of the waves?' No matter how far removed from the reality of a pressed sailor's life, this is as much a hymn to constitutional liberty as to sea power.

It is astounding that those liberal Conservatives who regard themselves as heirs to that tradition of thalassocratic Whiggery should so willingly have thrown in their lot with a Government that isolated Britain from its main trading partner, restricted freedom of protest, sought to repeal the Human Rights Act and to limit access to judicial review, and wanted to deport refugees to Rwanda. The principle that constitutional freedom is the foundation of the public good has been forgotten. The value of an open, inclusive society, where dissent is permitted and where people of all types are free to be themselves, was cast aside in favour of populism.

Reclaiming, preserving, and defending this tradition of constitutional liberty will take more than nostalgic flag-waving. It requires a return *ad fontes*, to the foundation of it all, in the search for a restored constitutional settlement embodied in a written constitution that clarifies, declares, and protects our constitutional heritage, while incorporating within it those reforms that have been found by experience, across the Commonwealth, to be helpful and beneficial.

Instead of reinterpreting and reinvigorating this constitutional tradition, the Conservatives from 2016 to 2024 doubled down on exploiting the flaws and weaknesses of British institutions. One of the symptoms of 'dying empire syndrome' is that countries assume that clinging to the signs of past greatness will make them great again, despite different needs for very different times. This is the same tragic miscalculation made by those Brexiteers who thought that being outside of the European Union would allow the United Kingdom to become 'global' again by returning to its former swashbuckling ways. That was an unrealistic expectation in the 1970s, when the United Kingdom joined Europe out of sheer economic necessity, although it still had the third biggest navy in the world and an economy bigger than that of China. By 2016, it had become a proposition of preposterous delusion, but no less tempting to those whose sense of what can be done was clouded by misplaced faith in past glories.

It is hard to flourish in the twenty-first century with twentieth-century parties and nineteenth-century ideologies, operating eighteenth-century institutions. This is not to think we are wiser than our ancestors; it is merely to recognise that we must adapt to meet the challenges of our own times. If the people of England are ever to enjoy the sort of practical, everyday flourishing that the people of, say, Sweden or the Netherlands enjoy (dependable institutions, good schools, warm houses, safe and well paying jobs, clean streets, decent pensions) it is necessary to think differently. England must move on from British exceptionalism and from delusions of 'Global British' neo-imperial power, and learn to embrace a healthy, democratic, civic, form of English nationalism. That means creating an English state that serves the public good.

This is not an appeal for 'Year Zero' modernity. As Emma Trimble put it in a powerful speech to the National Conservatism Conference in 2023, 'abstraction is violence'.[73] Adopting a written constitution for England is not about building a new society from scratch, to an abstract blueprint, without loyalty to particular places, reference to the common past, or reverence for tradition. A reconstituted English state would draw, structurally and symbolically, on the pre-Union English state. A civic English nation would be linked in the imagination to the depths of England's past. It would honour England's historic institutions by reforming them, and celebrate its illustrious history of constitutional freedom by trying to bridge the gap between myth and reality. It would cherish England's heritage and seek to build upon it, in a way that is not unthinking or merely imitative, but creatively faithful to its best elements and highest principles. The process of democratic constitutional refoundation must be lovingly restorative as well as devotedly reforming.

### (e) Civic, democratic, constitutional nationalism

One of the purposes of a written constitution is to provide a framework for the development of civic nationalism by declaring the basic principles and values which bind society together and upon which the state is founded. These principles and values can usually be found in the preamble to the constitution, or else in its opening declaratory clauses. For example, a citizen of the French Republic can point to didactic statements, in the constitution, plainly written down for all to see, in which a common political identity is defined: 'France shall be an indivisible, secular, democratic and social Republic. The maxim of the Republic shall be Liberty, Equality, Fraternity. The principle of the Republic shall be: government of the people, by the people and for the people.'[74]

However, it is not necessary for these statements to have such a Jacobin tone. In the Commonwealth, written constitutions often appeal to more moderate and less abstract values: free and democratic, but not revolutionary. The constitution of Barbados, to cite a very typical example from the Westminster constitutional tradition, declares that the state is founded upon 'the supremacy of God, the dignity of the human person, [...] unshakeable faith in fundamental human rights and freedoms, the position of the family in a society of free men and free institutions, [and] respect for moral and spiritual values and the rule of law'.[75] The preamble to the draft Constitution presented at the annex draws upon this tradition.[76]

Foundational principles may also be implicit in the substantive and structural content of the constitution. In Canada, for example, the principle of democracy is evident in regular, free, and fair elections based on universal suffrage; the principle of federalism is evident in the constitutional division of powers between the federal and provincial institutions; the principle of biculturalism is evident in the language and cultural rights extended to Quebec and the Francophone minority; the principles of human rights and the rule of law are evident in the Charter of Rights and Freedoms and in the guarantees of the independence of the judiciary.[77]

England has none of that. Without a Parliament and a Government of its own, and crucially without an English constitution to hold it all together, there are no officially endorsed and constitutionally recognised principles, rights, institutions, or values, to define 'civic Englishness'. These things might be built into a new written constitution, in its preamble or opening clauses, embodied in its structural and substantive provisions, and even reflected in the official symbolism of a future English state.[78] For the time being, however, England has almost no formal recognition as a national community. The institutions, symbols, and icons of political identity are British. Even the banal markers of national identity that people might have in their pockets – coins, stamps, their passport – are British, not English.

The absence of that constitutional common ground in England means that English national identity has high 'barriers to entry'. It makes it harder for new English people to fit in. A written constitution provides a clear and shared basis for civic and political integration, without requiring total cultural assimilation.

In some constitutionally relevant ways, the United Kingdom today is less similar to the United Kingdom of, say, 1950 than it is to India and other decolonising countries at that time. Obviously, the levels of economic development, literacy, and democratic experience are very different, but the socio-cultural homogeneity of Britain in the 1950s, and the resulting assumed unity of underlying values, have gone. We are now a multi-ethnic, multi-religious, socially fragmented society, with all that entails. The United Kingdom in the 1950s could do well enough without a written constitution. The basic rules did not have to be agreed and written down, because they were understood and respected. The devices that made democracy possible in more divided societies in the Commonwealth – guaranteed minority rights, on the one hand, and, on the other, attempts to build inclusive civic and constitutional identities that would bridge 'communalism' – were not needed in the United Kingdom then. They are now.

If a driver of authoritarian right-wing populism is a feeling that certain people no longer want to live together – that minorities ought to be excluded from the nation defined in terms of 'real people',[79] then constitutionalism can be an antidote. One response to the effects of mass immigration and Islamification is to retreat into racism and exclusionary forms of ethnic Englishness. The other response starts with allowing 'English' to be a civic and constitutional identity, expressed through English democratic institutions. Only the second way offers hope of integration, peace, and democratic stability. It would not matter whether your family eat samosas or gefilte fish, or whether you speak to your grandmother in English, Urdu, Bengali, or Polish, because the basis of belonging is constitutionally defined, in ways that encourage civic rather than ethnic nationalism. The kaleidoscope of characteristic cultural fragments can be broadened, to accommodate diversity, without losing the essential core of values that hold everyone together as a distinctively English civil polity.

There is a reciprocal relationship between civic nationalism and the democratic constitutional state. Civic nationalism can exist only in a free society. It nurtures this freedom and is in turn nurtured by it. Civic nationalism is associated not so much with the *natio* (the physical place where one is born, and the accidents of landscape, language, and culture), but with the *patria* (the polity in which one enjoys the rights of citizenship and can participate in public life). True patriotism – the patriotism that expresses itself in public service and not in manic flag-waving or hatred of others – is possible only for citizens whose constitutional rights in a democratic polity are secure, and who therefore feel that they *have a country of their own*, a country that in some important sense belongs to the public (in the best and original of the term, a *res publica*), not a country treated as the fiefdom of dictators, oligarchs, supermarket chains, property developers, or a corrupt class of self-interested politicians.[80] Public duty has no meaning to the subjects of a kleptocratic regime. The free citizens of a well constituted country, in contrast, can value and respect their country because it values and respects them. They will be willing to serve their country, because they see that their country is, on the whole, good, decent, honourable, just, and free, and therefore worthy of their service. This, by the way, is one of the reasons why liberal democracies are so good at winning wars against authoritarian powers: people are willing to make sacrifices when they have a country worth living for and dying for.[81]

Such a civic national identity cannot be created by decree. These things emerge and evolve over time, when the circumstances are favourable. Progress is slow. Results are limited and patchy. Culture is sticky. Human nature is flawed. Nevertheless, experiences in some Commonwealth countries show that constitution-building can help to create those favourable circumstances, with practical and tangible results. In India (1947–1950), South Africa (1990–1996), and Kenya (2007–2010), coming together to adopt a new constitution was an integrative process, through which diverse societies were not entirely, but at least partly, fused into a more civic, inclusive, national identity. The result was not only new constitutions, but also the emergence of a civic, political, constitutional identity that partially transcended, and eclipsed, even if it did not remove, other identities of ethnicity, religion, tribe, or caste.

### (f) Can the tide be turned?

One surprising conclusion of this chapter is that England is a colonised country. Of course, it was also a coloniser and an imperial power, but it was never really the common people of England, the ordinary beef-eating, beer-swilling, pink-gutted English, who led or benefited from the Empire. As the historian Colin Cross wrote, 'It was largely members of the upper and upper-middle classes who administered the Empire'; although traders and missionaries came from the lower middle class, and soldiers and settlers mostly from the lower orders, when it came to actually running the Empire, 'the majority of the British population had very little to do with [it]'.[82]

That is not an attempt to evade responsibility, merely a recognition that the primary colonising force was a specific ruling class: the 'old public-school men'.[83] Their ancestors colonised England first, and they and their successors have been running it, more or less unimpeded, ever since. England's swaggering domination, first of the British Isles and then of the British Empire, was rooted in, and sustained by, this ruling class that was quite distinct from the ordinary people. They are the cultural and political, if not always the biological, successors to the Normans.

The real England, where 'The People of England' live, has never really been able to be itself. English nationhood was obscured by, and absorbed into, this imperial identity, which was curated by and for its imperial ruling class. England did not come into political maturity, nor develop a modern, civic, and constitutional, sense of national identity. The result is that England, now that it has lost its Empire, is left bereft, and does not know who it is or what to do with itself. The psycho-geography of England has become haunted and liminal; it is a land of dispossession, of lost pasts, and abandoned futures.

Perhaps Brexit can best be understood through this lens. It was not really an English rejection of Europe, but a symptom of English national dispossession.

It is a faint echo of Hereward the Wake's rebellion: the sullen, angry protest of landless ale-soaked Saxons, who 'just want their country back' from their landowning, wine-quaffing, Norman rulers.

The tragedy, of course, is that this was a sham revolution. The rulers just shifted the folkwrath elsewhere, away from the failings of the British state and of the ruling class, and towards Brussels and Strasbourg. Brexit was all a game, played by one set of Eton–Oxford Normans against the other, in which ordinary people were both peripheral and expendable.[84] Posing as populist – even as 'anti-elitist' – Brexit was the ultimate counter-revolution against English democracy. It reseated the old school elite on their thrones: no longer would humourless trilingual Eurocrats, with doctorates in European law but not a clue about cricket, tell the chaps and the chums how to treat their unruly natives.

Reconstituting an English state is about democracy, good government, public ethics, power-sharing, devolution, and protecting rights. Above all, it is about increasing the legitimacy and capacity of the state to get good things done, to serve the public interest, and to deliver development. Those things are of vital importance if England is to become a flourishing and prosperous country, in which ordinary people can have good, happy, and healthy lives. It also about cultural regeneration, becoming a mature country that has come to terms with its own past. More deeply, constitutional refoundation is an opportunity for the English to become a civic nation, a *res publica*, a people united neither by conquest nor by ethnic exclusivism, but by a constitutional covenant.

Much has been made in this chapter of the gothicness of England. England inhabits the ruins of the British Empire. That imperial state is lost, doomed, beyond repair. It cannot be revived, and yet it refuses to pass quietly. It has no future, only a fading, haunted, and at times bloody, past. The English are stuck in a zombie state, a vampire economy, a ghost town.

Somehow, a living, revitalised England must be disentangled from this monstrous corpse. That is not easily done. Yet we must live by faith and not by sight. Nations that turn from foolish ways may be restored. New civic and democratic life can walk out of the grave of dead empires. When the foundations on which things have long rested are disturbed, it is possible to reset them through a new constitutional settlement – as the English did in 1215 and 1689. We should not shy away from that. As Edmund Burke put it, 'A state without the means of some change is without the means of its own conservation'.[85] The challenge is to make reforms that are bold enough to restore the best of the nation's heritage. Mere tinkering is not true repentance.

So England's story does not have to end with '... and then we lost the Empire, flounced out of Europe, and slowly degenerated into an exhausted, impoverished, chronically dysfunctional, Argentina of the North'. Through the process of reconstituting the state, we can find new ways of being English, and imagine a post-imperial Englishness.

A new constitutional settlement is not only a matter of overdue democratic institutional reform, but an opportunity to reconnect 'Quaintshire' and 'Grimsdale' – to tie together, through constitutional renewal, the two strands of England's national story: the Norman-Cavalier-Anglican-Tory-Rural-Southern story, and the Saxon-Roundhead-Dissenter-Whig-Urban-Northern story. There is room enough in all the broad acres of England for cakes and ale, maypoles, and the 'Merrie England' of the Tory imagination. There is room, too, in our city squares, for the Whig tradition of Magna Carta, Glorious Revolution, Reform Acts, Chartists, trade unionists, and suffragettes. At the same time, a compelling English national story should not be so tightly constrained by either of these two tropes that it cannot weave into itself other threads – such as those of the 'new English', who have been made co-heirs by immigration and naturalisation.

There must be space, too, to write new and better chapters of the story, to imagine a future that is better than the perilous present or the romanticised past. The challenge now facing England is to grow up, and to become a decent, prosperous, developed country, with an inclusive sense of civic nationhood, a sound democratic constitution, and well functioning public institutions that are willing and able to deliver a First World quality of life to all its people.

Left and right should be able to find aesthetic and imaginative common ground in this synthesis: nationalised railways *and* real ale in country pubs; active industrial development policies *and* gothic architecture; a well funded National Health Service (with matrons in starched aprons) *and* bluebells in the bridleways; a reassuringly familiar idea of English national and political identity, *and* the closest possible relationship with Europe; the preservation of the best traditions of the Westminster Model *and* a written, reformed constitution that can actually deliver good government.[86]

That, at least, is the hope and the aspiration. That aim set, the rest of this book considers how, in practical terms of substance and process, it might be achieved.

## Notes

1 It might be said, and perhaps very rightly, that the Royal Navy is more British and imperial than English. Indeed, it is perhaps the most British of all institutions – far more so than the Army, whose regimental system retains traces of national difference. However, the British Empire was itself an expansion of English maritime power, which was established before the Union.

2 The parts of England I know best are the West Country and the North East: the extremes, as far away from London as possible. The England that lies within 100 miles of the M25 is another world. If that prosperous core were the only England one knew or cared about, the claim that everything is broken and in desperate need of repair might appear unnecessarily alarmist. Yet even there the rot is increasingly visible. South East England has deep and festering pockets of poverty amidst its wealth.

3 G. Esler (2021) *How Britain Ends: English Nationalism and the Rebirth of Four Nations* (Apollo), p. 68.

4 Attlee quoted in a post by English Radical History (2022), 9:06 pm, 3 Jan 2022, https://x.com/EnglishRadical/status/1478110549976174594, last accessed 16 April 2025.

5 J. Major (1993) 'Mr Major's Speech to Conservative Group for Europe – 22 April 1993', https://johnmajorarchive.org.uk/1993/04/22/mr-majors-speech-to-conservative-group-for-europe-22-april-1993/, last accessed 16 April 2025.

6 G. Young (Campaign for an English Parliament), personal communication, 14 June 2022.

7 P. Kingsnorth (2008) *Real England: The Battle Against the Bland* (Portobello Books).

8 A. Aughey (2007) *The Politics of Englishness* (Manchester University Press).

9 Ibid., p. 1.

10 R. Weight (1999) 'Raise St George's standard high', *New Statesman*, 8 January. Cited in Aughey, *The Politics of Englishness*, p. 2.

11 J. Stapleton (1994) *Englishness and the Study of Politics: The Social and Political Thought of Ernest Barker* (Cambridge University Press), quote from the back cover of the hardback edition.

12 Aughey, *The Politics of Englishness*, p. 1.

13 T. Winter and S. Keegan-Phipps (2015) *Performing Englishness: Identity and Politics in a Contemporary Folk Resurgence* (Manchester University Press), p. 107.

14 A. Henderson and R. Wyn Jones (2021) *Englishness: The Political Force Transforming Britain* (Oxford University Press).

15 Elser, *How Britain Ends*.

16 I. Ward (2004) *The English Constitution: Myths and Realities* (Hart).

17 P. Ackroyd (2004) *Albion: The Origins of the English Imagination* (Vintage).

18 R. Scruton (2006) *England: An Elegy* (Bloomsbury Continuum).

19 J. Hawes (2021) *The Shortest History of England* (Old Street Publishing).

20 Paxman, J. (2007) *The English: A Portrait of a People* (Penguin).

21 Fox, K (2005)*Watching the English: The Hidden Rules of English Behaviour* (Hodder and Stoughton).

22 Kingsnorth, P. (2008) *Real England: The Battle Against the Bland* (Portobello Books).

23 V. Bulmer-Thomas (2023), *Internal Empire: The Rise and Fall of English Imperialism* (Hurst).

24 J. Cowley (2022) *Who Are We Now? Stories of Modern England* (Picador), pp. 144–145.

25 Ibid., p. 137.

26 Matless, D. (2016) *Landscape and Englishness* (2nd ed) (Reaction Books).

27 Mount, H. (2013) *How England Made the English* (Viking).

28 R. R. Lall (2023) 'Folk traditions are back, with bells on', New European, 2 April, https://www.theneweuropean.co.uk/folk-traditions-are-back-with-bells-on, accessed 6 April 2023.

29 H. Buckton (2012) *Yesterday's Country Customs: A History of Traditional English Folklore* (History Press).

30 'Oh Whistle and I'll Come to You, My Lad', a short story by M. R. James, published in 1904 (in his collection *Ghost Stories of an Antiquary*), just after the end of the Victorian era, illustrates this point. It features a young protagonist, Parkins, Professor of Ontography (an invented subject, which means something like 'the description of things as they actually are'), who is spooked by a *jinn* released from an incautiously blown whistle that he had found in the ruins of a Templar preceptory. It is a bluff retired colonel, with 'views of a pronouncedly Protestant type', who eventually comes to the rescue. The implication is clear: there are more things lurking in the Christian ruins of England, Prof. Parkins, than are dreamt of in your philosophy.

31 J. Coe (2022) 'Ghost ions', *London Review of Books*, Vol. 44, No. 16 (18 August), https://www.lrb.co.uk/the-paper/v44/n16/jonathan-coe/ghost-ions, accessed 21 November 2022.

32 A. Flood (2019) 'Ghosts shaped my life: out-of-print children's classic to be resurrected', *The Guardian*, 12 June, https://www.theguardian.com/books/booksblog/2019/jun/12/ghosts-shaped-my-life-out-of-print-childrens-classic-to-be-resurrected, accessed 12 January 2023.

33 L. Telford (2022) *English Nationalism and Its Ghost Towns* (Routledge).

34 E. Parnell (2019) *Ghostland: In Search of a Haunted Country* (William Collins).

35 J. Strange (2017) *It's a Strange Place, England* (Next Chapter).

36 H. E. Bulstrode (2021) *Curious England: A Guide* (independently published through Amazon).

37 HooklandGuide post on X quoting Trippy Pete, https://x.com/HooklandGuide/status/1628043832519544832, last accessed 16 April 2025.

38 Cowley, *Who Are We Now?*, p. 172.
39 R. Edgard (2022) 'British folk horror, hauntology and the terrifying nature of the ordinary', *The Conversation*, 28 October.
40 F. Young (2021) *Edmund: In Search of England's Lost King* (Bloomsbury Academic).
41 See the chapter 'The scouring of the Shire' in J. R. R. Tolkien (1955) *The Lord of the Rings* (Allen and Unwin).
42 One has to be careful with all this. It is all very well to take the English dimension to constitutional reform seriously, to rehabilitate Englishness, and to consider the cultural as well as constitutional implications of English nationhood. But there is an ever-present danger, when one immerses oneself in the weirdness that is England, of turning into one of those strange people who walks up to the top of Glastonbury Tor at solstices. Either that, or you end up with a model railway, spending every evening in your attic or shed painstakingly recreating a section of a branch line on the Somerset and Dorset Joint Railway in OO scale. In extreme cases, if untreated, interest in Englishness may result in Morris dancing, bell ringing or an addiction to Choral Evensong. Let the reader beware. The author accepts no liability.
43 Miller, J. (2020) 'Introduction', in J. Miller (ed.) *Weird Woods: Tales from the Haunted Forests of Britain* (British Library Tales of the Weird).
44 T. Fort (2015) *The Channel Shore: From the White Cliffs to Land's End* (Simon and Schuster), p. 108.
45 D. Jones (ed.) (2011) *M. R. James: Collected Ghost Stories* (Oxford University Press), p. 257.
46 J. B. Priestley (1934) *English Journey* (William Heinemann).
47 H. V. Morton (1927) *In Search of England* (Methuen).
48 Priestley, *English Journey*, p. 397.
49 Ibid., pp. 397–398.
50 Ibid., pp. 398–399.
51 Ibid., p. 401.
52 Hawes, *The Shortest History of England*.
53 W. I. Jennings (1965) *The Queen's Government* (revised edn) (Penguin Books), p. 56.
54 Hawes, *The Shortest History of England*.
55 Chapter 5 proposes a system of devolved governance for England, operating primarily at the county and city level. This would provide the institutional structure to make so-called 'northern powerhouses' a reality and 'levelling up' more than just a campaign slogan. The draft Constitution also proposes proportional representation for the House of Commons. That would make the whole country more electorally competitive and force parties to address public needs beyond a just handful of marginal swing constituencies in middle England.
56 D. Goodhart (2017) *The Road to Somewhere: The Populist Revolt and the Future of Politics* (Hurst).
57 Winter and Keegan-Phipps, *Performing Englishness*, pp. 105–106.
58 J. Denham and G. Young (2018) 'England – the nation that is not to be named?, Open Democracy website (29 October), https://www.opendemocracy.net/en/opendemocracyuk/england-nation-that-is-not-to-be-named, accessed 25 October 2022.
59 Hawes, *The Shortest History of England*, p. 41.
60 Ibid., p. 55.
61 Ibid., p. 55.
62 Ibid., p. 55.
63 Ibid., p. 183.
64 Scruton, *England*, p. 32.
65 Ibid., p. 29.
66 J. Stapleton (1994) *Englishness and the Study of Politics: The Social and Political Thought of Ernest Barker* (Cambridge University Press), p. 5.
67 I. Ward (2004) *The English Constitution: Myth or Reality?* (Hart), pp. 200–201.
68 J. Coakley (2018) 'National identity and the "Kohn dichotomy"', *Journal of Nationalism and Ethnicity*, Vol. 46, No. 2, pp. 252–271; U. Ozkirimli (2000) *Theories of Nationalism: A*

*Critical Introduction* (Macmillan); G. Zubrzycki (2002) 'The classical opposition between civic and ethnic models of nationhood: ideology, empirical reality and social scientific analysis', *Polish Sociological Review*, No. 139, pp. 275–295.

69 M. Viroli (1995) *For Love of Country: An Essay on Patriotism and Nationalism* (Clarendon Press).

70 Opinium (2020) 'UK: National identity in Britain' (9 March), https://www.opinium.com/resource-center/national-identity-in-britain/, accessed 21 November 2022.

71 Jennings, *The Queen's Government*, pp. 33–34.

72 Padfield, P. (2000) *Maritime Supremacy and the Opening of the Western Mind: Naval Campaigns That Shaped the Modern World, 1588–1782* (New York: Overlook Press).

73 E. Webb, E. (2023) 'Against Year Zero', address to the London National Conservatism Conference, 17 May, https://www.youtube.com/watch?v=4HMCpNecC7c, accessed 19 May 2023.

74 Constitution of France (1958), English translation at https://constituteproject.org/constitution/France_2008, accessed 10 May 2025.

75 Constitution of Barbados (1962): preamble.

76 The preamble to the draft Constitution borrows from other constitutions that follow the Westminster Model and from iconic documents in English history, from the Statute of Westminster of 1275 to the Mayflower Compact of 1620. It weaves these together in a Whiggish compromise. It refers not only to the European Convention on Human Rights and the United Nations' Universal Declaration of Human Rights, but also to the Charter of the Commonwealth, a document signed by Queen Elizabeth II, as sources of its meta-constitutional values.

77 Reference re Secession of Quebec [1998] 2 S.C.R. 217, https://scc-csc.lexum.com/scc-csc/scc-csc/en/item/1643/index.do, accessed 21 November 2022.

78 See section 1, subsection (2), of the draft Constitution in the annex.

79 J.-W. Müller (2021) *Democracy Rules* (Penguin Books), p. 23.

80 M. Viroli (1995) *For Love of Country: An Essay on Patriotism and Nationalism* (Clarendon Press).

81 V. D. Hanson (2002) *Why the West Has Won: Nine Landmark Battles in the Brutal History of Western Victory* (Faber).

82 C. Cross (1970) *The Fall of the British Empire* (Paladin), pp. 34–39.

83 Ibid., p. 38.

84 S. Kuper (2023) *Chums: How a Tiny Caste of Oxford Tories Took Over the UK* (Profile Books), p. 162.

85 E. Burke (1791) *Reflections on the Revolution in France.*

86 This might be described, only half-jokingly, as 'social democracy with Village Green Preservation Society characteristics'. In some ways, it is close to the point where Blue Labour, Red Tory, and Anglo-futurism meet, while categorically rejecting the Europhobia, the British nationalism, and the authoritarian populist reaction.

# 4

# Liberty according to English ideas and on English principles

## (a) The constitutional tradition of the Westminster Model

Constitutions are made for real people, living in a particular place, with their own culture, society, beliefs, habits, and traditions. Moreover, culture changes slowly, in organic ways, and wonderfully resists attempts to force its course. A discussion of the constitutional refoundation of England must begin, therefore, with an appreciation of the cultural and constitutional treacle in which England swims.

England's constitutional tradition is interwoven with its national identity. Ian Ward suggests that there is 'a distinctive, if dormant, English identity' which is 'rooted in the idea of an English common law and a distinctive English constitutionalism'.[1] That tradition, based on a mythologised Whig view of Anglo-British constitutional history, includes such milestones as Magna Carta, the Petition of Right, the Habeas Corpus Act, the Glorious Revolution, the Bill of Rights, the Act of Settlement, the Great Reform Act and other Representation of the People Acts, and the Parliament Acts. This tradition is also embodied in conventional practices of Cabinet government, parliamentary democracy, and responsible parties, in the customs and traditions of Parliament, and in the principle of a neutral, permanent, and professional Civil Service.

In the early twentieth century, these things all came together, in the United Kingdom and its Dominions, to form a coherent, historically derived, culturally embedded, set of institutions, rules, practices, and norms, which in turn became a model for the world.[2]

George Orwell saw England as a country where 'the totalitarian idea that there is no such thing as law, there is only power, has never taken root'; he recognised 'respect for constitutionalism and legality' and 'the belief in the law as something above the State and above the individual', as 'an all-important English trait'.[3] This clashes hard against the idea of parliamentary sovereignty, which claims that there is no law binding on Parliament. It clashes even harder against the authoritarian populist tendency to assert the Prime Minister's personal, plebiscitary mandate, regardless of the rule of law, the independence of the judiciary, the rights of individuals, and the norms of parliamentary scrutiny and accountability.

It is upon this tradition that an English constitution should be built. It should, in the words of Edmund Burke, be 'not only devoted to liberty, but to liberty according to English ideas, and on English principles'.[4] That means a constitution on the Westminster Model, based upon institutions and ideas that descend from Runnymede, not from Rousseau.[5]

The Westminster Model is not, though, narrowly insular. Although its roots are formed of old English oak, its branches spread across the world thanks to iron hulls, steam engines, and undersea telegraph cables. Indeed, the Westminster Model, as a *model* that could be adopted, adapted, and emulated, reached maturity only through the transformation of the British Empire into the Commonwealth.

Decolonisation came not to destroy the Westminster Model constitutional tradition, but to fulfil it. By 1926, it was recognised as a matter of settled policy that the Dominions were 'autonomous Communities within the British Empire, equal in status, in no way subordinate one to another in any aspect of their domestic or external affairs, though united by a common allegiance to the Crown, and freely associated as members of the British Commonwealth of Nations'.[6] This was reflected in law in 1931, with the enactment of the Statute of Westminster. After the Second World War, colonies began to follow this path to independence: India and Pakistan in 1947, Ceylon (Sri Lanka) in 1948, and then a steady stream of countries in later decades. While British colonies wanted to be free from British rule, they did not necessarily wish to depart from the British *way of ruling*, which was then held in justifiably high regard.[7] Postcolonial leaders were understandably keen to adopt the principles and practices of the Westminster Model as the basis for their new countries.

The English constitutional tradition is far wider and grander than anything that can be contained within England, or the United Kingdom, alone. The Westminster Model has been able to adapt itself to many climates, in different ethnic and religious contexts. It is a bit like cricket: the format can vary, but when you play by the laws and in the spirit of the game, it works in recognisable ways. It depends, however, upon the preservation of a particular political or institutional culture, embedded in a large body of sub-constitutional rules, practices, and norms that give flesh, blood, and life to the skeleton of a constitution. This includes the customs and traditions of Parliament, the norms of Civil Service impartiality, the recognition given to the Leader of the Opposition, and respect for the rule of law and judicial independence. This institutional culture is portable, adaptable, and capable of being learned and taught. It is also, however, capable of being lost, if it is not enshrined in robust constitutional forms that, while adjusting changing times and situations, can be passed on from generation to generation.

Britain's imperial past is, of course, a politically divisive subject. The left want nothing to do with the British Empire and will not hear a good word said for it; the right are nostalgic for the Empire and will not hear a bad word said against it. It is no part of my purpose to enter into this partisan debate, nor to sit in judgment upon the Empire – neither to condemn it nor to defend it. Describing the British state as 'imperial' simply acknowledges an undeniable fact: the Westminster Model of parliamentary democracy, about which Dicey and Bagehot wrote, was not developed in a small north-western European archipelago alone: it emerged in the context of a vast sea-borne Empire, and was carried around the world on the shipping lanes of imperialism. Elected parliaments, independent judiciaries, professional civil services, electoral and boundaries commissions, political parties, local councils, *Hansard*, Leaders of the Opposition, *Erskine May*, ceremonial maces, and votes of no confidence are as much a part of the imperial legacy as the abolition of slavery, the suppression of *suttee*, or the Plimsoll line. The Caribbean jurist Professor A. Ralph Carnegie said, 'When we speak of our Westminster Model constitutions, we are not being lawyers or even political scientists. We are at best being poets.'[8] If so, it is as much the poetry of Kipling as of Shakespeare.

The English language would be much poorer without words imported from Hindi, Malay, Egyptian Arabic, and a host of other languages. Anglicanism would be diminished without the vibrancy of Caribbean and African churches. Rugby and cricket would be obscure schoolboy games, if it were not for the contribution made by players from many of the lands over which Queen Victoria once reigned. These English inventions, so central to England's national heritage and identity, were all honed, developed, and matured only in the wider context of the British Empire. Likewise, the Westminster Model of parliamentary democracy would be deficient, unfinished, incomplete if not for the metamorphic change that the Empire wrought upon it.

Looking at the condition of British institutions today, it is easy to see why many constitutional reformers reject the Westminster Model and look to continental Europe or to Scandinavia for inspiration. Since constitutional reform has traditionally been the preoccupation of the centre-left, they have sometimes regarded the Westminster Model as a tainted legacy – all a bit too much 'Land of Hope and Glory' for their liking. But what if the Westminster Model only has to be applied in its fullest, best, most developed, form? What if we can learn a thing or two from those we once taught?

The Westminster Model remains one of the most stable, durable, and successful forms of democracy in the world. Its constitutions can be found in large, complex, and diverse nations like Canada, India, and Malaysia, and in smaller, more homogenous states such as Malta and St Lucia. It is to these independent countries of the Commonwealth, which took the Westminster Model, wrote it down, adapted it, and developed it, that England should look to find examples, models, and precedents for its own written constitution.

Such a constitution would go with, and not against, the grain of England's history, culture, institutions, and traditions. The trick, as the former Liberal Democrat Deputy Prime Minister Nick Clegg noted, 'is to present it as such',[9] disarming those whose hostility to written constitutions is based on the false assumption that they are suspiciously continental innovations. Because English constitutional history has been shaped by the experience of the British Empire and Commonwealth, a written constitution would be as 'pukka English' as sitting in your pyjamas on the veranda of your bungalow, eating chicken tikka masala, and drinking Australian shiraz, while listening to South Africa play the West Indies at cricket.

An English constitution should therefore be a normal Westminster Model constitution, based upon the standard principles of such constitutions:

parliamentary democracy, representative and responsible government, constitu-tionally protected civil liberties, judicial independence, the rule of law, impartial administration, recognition of the opposition as having a legitimate role in holding the Government to account, and the need for ethics and integrity in public life.

Expressed in the institutional forms of Westminster Model parliamentary democracy, these principles ought not be controversial. They are not passing faddish notions, nor strange abstractions suitable only for beret-wearers on Parisian boulevards. They are practical, tried-and-tested, historically rooted, warm-beer and beefsteak foundations for English democratic life. They repre-sent our civilisation's best attempt to establish (in stumbling and imperfect, but real and tangible, ways) an effective system of government that can promote the common good and protect our freedom.

In recent times, regrettably, these principles, and the democratic institutions which were sustained by them, have been neglected. They have been ignored or abandoned by the authorities whose moral responsibility it was to uphold them. In consequence, we have drifted into a fog of moral, political, and constitutional confusion. Even the European Convention on Human Rights, through which the benefits of this tradition of English liberty were shared first with the other nations of Europe and then with many Commonwealth countries,[10] is now under sustained attack in the country that gave it birth.

A new constitution should unapologetically reaffirm the principles of the Westminster Model of parliamentary democracy, and recall us to the values, ideals, and norms on which the peace, order, and good government of the country depend. To that extent, at least, the new constitution should be a work of constructive restoration, generally preferring, in the words Michael Oakeshott, 'the familiar to the unknown' and 'the tried to the untried'.[11] It should not, however, be a work of reaction. The way out of the constitutional morass is ahead, not back. It is neither possible nor desirable to turn back the clock to an imagined halcyon age. Rather, the challenge is to dig deep into these ideals, principles, and values, to plunge into the well of history and tradition, and to build from these old familiar materials a new constitution that meets current needs and future aspirations. This balanced approach neither rejects the tradition that has nurtured us, nor interprets that tradition so narrowly as to limit reform.

Although certain principles and institutional forms are universal across the tradition, the Westminster Model of democracy is not static. Its constitutions can and do embody a wide range of institutional variations. The first genera-tion of Commonwealth constitutions, like those of Canada and Australia, did not include a justiciable Bill of Rights and left much of the actual working of parliamentary democracy to be regulated by unwritten conventions.[12] By the middle of the twentieth century, however, Westminster Model constitu-tions typically included judicially enforced rights.[13] They codified the rules of parliamentary democracy – the rules of government formation and removal, the procedures for votes of no confidence, the rules concerning the summoning, prorogation, and dissolution of Parliaments, methods for resolving deadlocks between two Houses, and so on.[14] They recognised the role of the Opposition in holding Governments to account and providing viable alternatives. They created independent, non-partisan 'fourth branch' institutions (Public Service Commissions, Judicial Service Commissions, Electoral Commissions and Boundary Commissions) to protect the integrity of administrative, judicial, and electoral processes from political manipulation.

Many of these constitutions also established federal systems, or other forms of constitutionally protected regional autonomy. They found ways of accommodating religious differences, recognised minority languages, and protected people from ethnic discrimination. Most kept the monarchy; others replaced it with a figurehead presidency. Some incorporated directive provisions committing the state to economic and social development.

Almost every proposal for constitutional reform that might arise in an English context has already been adopted in one or more Westminster Model constitutions around the world. If we want proportional representation for the House of Commons, we might look to Ireland, Fiji, Malta, and New Zealand. For a reformed second chamber, we might look to Canada and the Caribbean states for examples of nominated Senates, to India and South Africa for indirectly elected second chambers, to Australia for direct election, and to Malaysia for a mixed combination of indirect election and appointment. For federalism we can learn from Australia, Canada, India, Malaysia, Pakistan, and South Africa. If we wish to adopt a justiciable Bill of Rights, modern Westminster Model constitutions provide plenty of examples. We should not try to copy any one of these in its entirety, but we should learn from them: 'test all things, hold fast to that which is good' is a sound principle of constitutional design.

The same principle of borrowing applies to codifying the conventions of parliamentary democracy. The aim is not, necessarily, to codify existing British conventions exactly as they stand, not least because it is rarely clear, after all the bending and battering, which of these conventions are still valid.[15] Rather, it would be wise to codify the best practices, informed by various examples of constitutional codification across the global family of Westminster Model constitutions.

Some of the reforms might address major institutional design choices, such as reforming the electoral system for the House of Commons. Others are relatively minor, such as incorporating the so-called 'Bercow rule' that would allow the Speaker, on the request of one-third of the MPs, to recall Parliament.[16] Yet instead of such reforms being seen as radical innovations, they should be recognised as standard, ordinary, well proven, perhaps even old-fashioned, devices of Westminster Model constitutionalism. They are part of, not alien to, the global-imperial British constitutional tradition, to which England is paradoxically both heir and progenitor. It is bringing the Commonwealth back home. Building on these foundations, with familiar materials, we can have confidence that a Westminster Model constitution, having matured under 'palm and pine', will flourish upon its return to England.

There is, therefore, an important distinction between this wider Westminster Model tradition, which can be open to such reforms, and the narrower 'British

Political Tradition', which is not only a particular subset of Westminster Model institutions, but also a set of ideological assumptions about how those institutions should operate.[17] The British Political Tradition, which 'centralises elite control and perpetuates structured inequalities', is especially 'resistant to reform', 'conservative in its understanding of responsibility, limited in its idea of representation, and offers government by, and frequently for, the elite'.[18] The Westminster Model and the British Political Tradition have often been conflated, so that Westminster Model constitutionalism is presented only in its majoritarian, top-down, centralised, elitist, guise. Seen in that way, real reform, which would transform the state into a more power-sharing, decentralised, inclusive form, becomes almost unimaginable. Yet, what if it were possible to move beyond that specific British Political Tradition without abandoning a Westminster Model constitution? That is exactly what is here proposed. As a package, the reforms outlined in this book would create what Mark Glover and Robert Hazell describe as a 'Westminster Transformed' political system – one rooted in the Westminster Model, but rejecting the majoritarianism, executive dominance, centralisation, parliamentary sovereignty, and elitism, of the British Political Tradition in favour of a broad redistribution of power – between institutions, parties, regions, and classes.[19] Put differently, this is a transformation from a closed, centralised, majoritarian, elitist *governo stretto* version of the Westminster Model to a broad, decentralised, inclusive, cooperative *governo largo* version. The Westminster Model is not abandoned, but it is renewed and transformed.

### (b) Moderation and consensus

George Savile, 1st Marquess of Halifax, the late-seventeenth-century statesman and writer, deserves to be more widely appreciated today. His times were very like our own: the political order was contested, decayed, and distempered; corruption was rife, court politics and jobbery ruled; all problems were to some extent constitutional ones; and the country had been ravaged by plague. His was also a time of scientific, economic, and social change. In the era between the Restoration and the Hanoverian succession, so much of the British imperial world took shape: the Bank of England, the London Stock Exchange, coffee shops, newspapers, Newtonian science, the Royal Society, the victory of Parliament over the Crown, religious toleration, the Treaty of Union, the expansion of naval power, and the whole panoply of Whig thalassocracy.[20]

Halifax's response to navigating these uncertain times was to be a 'Trimmer'. The word, now fallen out of use, acquired for a time a negative connotation, as a person without any principles, who would go where the wind – or the financial rewards and other perks of office – took them. That is not, however, what Halifax meant by the term. To 'trim' a boat is to stow weight around it in such a way that it floats upright and steady, without listing to port or starboard, without being too far down at either the bow or stern, and without being too 'stiff' or 'tender' in its motion. It is, literally, to keep it on an even keel. In the same way, a political Trimmer sailing the ship of state must balance left and right, taking what is good from each, and seeking the 'wise mean' between 'barbarous extremes', to avoid capsize.[21]

When it comes to constitutions, good trim is vital. The constitution is supposed to be the keel and ballast of the state, holding it upright in every storm. The draft Constitution presented in the annex therefore both proposes and assumes a strategic compromise between two broadly defined groups: on one side, moderate reformers, mostly (although perhaps not exclusively) of the centre-left, pursuing a liberal-democratic agenda of constitutional change, based on protecting civil liberties, dispersing power both institutionally and geographically, and promoting a more open, deliberative and accountable style of government; on the other side, moderate conservatives seeking to preserve and restore, symbolically and substantially, as much of our constitutional herit-age as possible, while recognising the need for sensible reforms in order to reinvigorate a system that has become both broken and vulnerable. The aim is to reach a moderate and well trimmed fusion of the reformist approaches of both the left and right, represented by Paddy Ashdown and Lord Hailsham, respectively. If those names seem dated, it is only because this constitutional retrimming is decades overdue.[22]

One difficulty, however, is that constitutional reform has an image problem. Support for constitutional change remains mostly concentrated in the centre-left of the political spectrum, in the Whig-radical-Roundhead ideological space occupied by Liberal Democrats, Greens, and some (but not all) parts of the Labour Party.[23] In the culture war of British politics, it is often seen as the preoccupation of the liberal, metropolitan, university-educated, public-sector middle class, and with the sort of people *The Rest is History* podcast might describe as 'sandal-wearing prune-juice drinkers on bicycles'.

Constitutional reform has no resonance in the white-van England of tabloid newspapers, St George's cross tattoos, ugly dogs, and greasy bacon rolls. The authoritarian populist right have little interest in constitutional change, except in the most reactionary, destructive form. Constitutional reformers are part of the line-up of stock villains whom the far right love to hate, alongside asylum-seekers, environmental protestors, and 'Remoaners'.

Constitutional change has so far failed, too, to appeal to 'natural Tories' in the leafiest parts of England's southern shires. These people are often conventionally conservative and quietly traditional, but not authoritarian or reactionary, and nearly as suspicious of the radical right as of the left. To them, the idea of a constitutional refoundation leading to a new written constitution is anathema. Perhaps this is because they do not yet fully realise the fragility of the things they take for granted, nor recognise the danger posed by the far right.

These pictures are caricatures. Nevertheless, they do reflect an inconvenient truth. The centre-left alone cannot save democracy. Constitutional refounda-tion cannot succeed if it appeals only to those with green hair, and not to those with green wellies. The centre-left must ally, or at least cooperate, with moderate conservatives. A sane, moderate, pragmatic, sensible, and respons-ible centre-right party is the essential ballast of every democratic system. The displacement of the centre right by a strident reactionary populism, combining the worse elements of libertarian economics, corruption, and incompetence, poses a grave threat to our institutions. The politically homeless moderate Conservatives who recognise that threat – those who have been left bewildered and exasperated by signs of how quickly the unwritten norms of the British constitution can collapse – are the crucial centre of gravity for a constitutional renewal.

The association of constitutional reform with the centre-left was a product of the politics of the 1980s, when the top-down, majoritarian, and centralised nature of the unwritten constitution enabled Thatcher to impose her neoliberal policies, without restraint or compromise, on largely unwilling sections of the population.[24] It is hard to understand the rise in support for Scottish devolution between 1979 and 1997, for instance, without reference to privatisation, pit closures, and the poll tax. Socio-economic issues and constitutional issues are often closely intertwined.

Before Thatcher came to power, however, some thoughtful Conservatives had already appreciated the need for stronger constitutional safeguards. Lord Hailsham famously warned about the danger of 'elective dictatorship' in 1976.[25] He proposed an agenda for reform similar to that later adopted by Charter 88 and other reformers, including reform of the House of Lords, a justiciable Bill of Rights, and devolution to regional assemblies.[26] As he put it, nearly half a century ago –

> the real necessity is to limit the unlimited powers of the legislature, partly by establishing a new system of checks and balances, partly by devolution, and partly by restricting the power of Parliament to infringe the rights of minorities and individuals. In other words we need a new constitution, and like all new constitutions its terms must be reduced to writing and defined by law.[27]

Genuine conservatives should recognise that politics is difficult, that states are fragile, that public authority can dissipate, and that corruption is an ever-present temptation. They should support strong, historically embedded, public institutions that stand against the weakness of human nature. They should realise that there are rarely simple solutions to complex problems, and that political institutions should be constructed in such a way as to encourage thoughtful consideration and practical compromise. They should know better than to allow absolute power to accumulate in the hands of one person or clique. They should therefore resist with all their intellectual and moral might the populist-authoritarian distortion of politics which says that traditions, conventions, laws, procedures, norms, institutions, rights, deliberation, evidence, expertise, and compromise do not matter so long as 'the will of the people' – or, rather, that of the leader of the ruling party – is done.

It is also worth remembering that the English Tory aversion to written constitutions is not a universal element of conservative thought. Centre-right parties in other Commonwealth countries, and mainstream Conservative and Christian Democratic parties across Europe, do not object to written constitutions. Indeed, they see written constitutions as indispensable to the stability, integrity, and institutional solidity of the state: a protection against knee-jerk populism and the tyranny of the majority, a guarantee of property, and a foundation for a civic patriotism.

After all, the classical definition of tyranny is not necessarily that it is especially brutal or repressive, nor even unpopular; ancient tyrants were, above all, *populist* leaders. The real essence of tyranny is that it is personal, arbitrary, capricious, unpredictable; it does not allow itself to be bound by institutions, rules, or limits. There was something always potentially tyrannical in the idea of a sovereign Parliament, and it takes very little, once the grip of convention and self-restraint is loosened, for that latent tyranny to be realised.

Moderate conservatives, who want to conserve, not to destroy, and who wish truly to serve the public and not to plunder it – should be, and should *want to be*, included in the process of constitutional refoundation.[28] Many of these people have been left politically stranded, the broad-based party they knew having been eclipsed by hard Brexiteers, authoritarian populists, corrupt oligarchs, and free-market ideologues.[29] All these radical-right factions share a deeply unconservative desire to 'move fast and break things'. They have a lack of respect for inherited rights and liberties, the rule of law, the judiciary, the Civil Service, the norms and conventions of parliamentary government, or even for common decency, competence, and responsibility. In contrast, the restoration and reform of the English constitutional order is a project around which sensible moderates could unite, and to which the more creative and imaginative of them could make a welcome contribution.

This is where the Burkean tradition could be invaluable, if it were properly applied in ways that have regard to the changed circumstances of our times. Edmund Burke, regarded as the father of modern Conservatism, was a Whig, not a Tory. He even sympathised with the American colonies in their grievances against the British Government.[30] His reputation as a conservative, perhaps even as a reactionary, came in response to the French Revolution. Burke recognised that the revolutionary spirit had no natural limits. It quickly turned into 'the Terror' of the guillotine, the convulsion of the whole of social order, the overthrowing of religion, and the destruction of what Burke took to be civilisation.[31]

Burke attacked the French constitution of 1791 as an attempt to transform society, to impose a new-fangled order based on theory and not practice. He looked upon it in the way that we today might look upon Soviet-era constitutions, as a mix of unachievable ideals and plain frauds, but certainly no basis for stable, settled government.

It is wrong to conclude that Burkean conservatives should still object in principle to written constitutions. We do not know whether Burke would have had the same response to, say, the French Constitutional Charter of 1814, but it is not unreasonable to conclude that he would have welcomed it. After all, the Charter of 1814 was modelled upon British institutions, not revolutionary theory. It tried to embody the aspirations of moderate reformist Anglophile French notables, while rejecting the radical impulses of the Jacobins and the

authoritarianism of Napoleon.[32] It is very possible that Burke would have recognised in the Charter something both admirable and familiar: an attempt to
reach a constitutional settlement based on historical compromise.

We know Burke did not object on principle to the existence of a written
constitution. He praised the United States constitution, even though it was
republican and arose out of a revolutionary rejection of the Crown, because he
saw it as an attempt not 'to acquire absolute speculative liberty, but to keep what
they had under the English constitution'.[33]

In the same way, it is hard to argue on Burkean terms against a Westminster
Model constitution. Such constitutions are not based upon abstractions
plucked from the air, but on historically achieved rights, principles, and institutions, the value of which is embedded in our institutional culture and
has been proven by experience. These constitutions provide barriers against
attempts by the Government of the day to undermine these foundations.
They ensure that a common heritage of freedom is not casually forgotten,
nor briskly set aside when the current majority deems it convenient to do so.
In other words, a Westminster Model constitution is, in the best and least
partisan sense of the word, a truly *conservative* constitution – a constitution
that conserves the things that make democracy as we know it work: free, fair,
and regular elections, independence of the judiciary, the neutrality of the Civil
Service, the rights of the Opposition, the ceremonial functions of the head of
state, and so on.

Moreover, Burke was writing before the Westminster Model was fully developed. He could not have anticipated the way in which it would come to
empower the Prime Minister as the head of a disciplined majority party. If
Burke had lived to see the Victorian constitution – with power increasingly
concentrated in the hands of whoever commands a majority in the House of
Commons, so long as they can continue to command that majority – he might
have been horrified by it. Such a constitutional order is always exposed to the
risk that everything could be overthrown in an instant, by a Government
with a majority in the Commons, having no higher law to constrain it. A
Westminster Model constitution would put a framework of Burkean stability
around Bagehot's parliamentary system, to ensure that the inheritance of rights,
liberties, and free institutions can be passed on, intact or better, to future
generations.

Roger Scruton notes that English constitutional crises 'were experienced
as violations of the law' and 'would characteristically end with a reaffirmation
of the law' and the issuing of a charter by which rights would be guaranteed.
Magna Carta, the foremost of these charters, vindicated 'ancient rights and freedoms', denounced and forbade various corruptions and abuses in the exercise of
public power, and 'demanded that the king be subject to the law'.[34] The same
approach was adopted, with a reaffirmation of ancient rights and freedoms,
in the Bill of Rights of 1689. This 'endorsed the ancient writ of *habeas corpus*,
guaranteeing that no subject could be imprisoned without due process of law,
and re-established English law as the common property of the subject, rather
than the private possession of sovereign power'.[35]

A written constitution, being superior to ordinary laws, and harder to change than a mere Act of Parliament, is what keeps the law as the 'common property of the subject', and prevents those who for the time being are in possession of power from placing themselves above the law, or undermining ancient rights and freedoms. The fiduciary relationship that binds the Crown to the people through the law must be reasserted, by means of a written constitution, if that heritage is to be restored and not lost.

A written constitution must be protected from easy or unilateral amendment by the Government of the day with an ordinary majority. Amendment should be possible not on the fleeting whims of those in power, but only when there is a sufficient consensus to do so. To borrow Scruton's words again, the amendment process enables the legal and political system embedded in the constitution 'to grow, like the topsoil of a forest, by slow accumulation over centuries', while ensuring that the law itself, and the underlying constitutional principles of law, maintain an 'authority greater than any temporary sovereign or legislation'.[36] Thanks to a written constitution, those foundational principles of law can remain an 'objective reality', which does not depend upon the capricious will of sovereigns or Parliaments, but stands in judgment upon them.[37]

Scruton did not support a written constitution, but that only shows that he did not follow his argument to its logical conclusion. Without a written constitution to bind it together, all that careful historical accumulation, all those ancient rights and liberties, all that delicate top-soil of good practice and convention and doing the right thing, can be swept away in a mad majoritarian moment. It was to protect against such abuses and usurpations, Scruton argues, that the English 'were constantly reaching for the institutions, the customs, the precedents that would justify them against their oppressors, and would stand up for their rights whenever a powerful person sought to disregard them'.[38] There can be no better safeguard than a written constitution – not that the constitution itself does the work, but it holds together the institutions that do. The constitution defines these institutions, legitimates them, declares the principles according to which they should act, fortifies them when attacked, and recalls them to their proper purpose when they go astray.

All this is to say, firstly, that moderate conservatives are essential to building a broad coalition for constitutional refoundation; secondly, that such a project would be concordant with the best traditions of moderate, reformist English conservatism; and thirdly, that this is a necessary process for the Conservative Party to recover its principles, and to restore their souls, after their disastrous flirtation with far-right populism.[39]

The constitution is the meeting ground, the common ground, of the nation. It does not obliterate our differences. It simply sets down the shared ground rules that bind people together into a civil body-politic, so that we can, despite these differences, live together in peace, justice, freedom, and prosperity. The principle of a written constitution does not, in other words, have to be a culture-war issue. It is far too important (and, if done right, far too boring and mundane) for that. It is perfectly possible for people who wear tweed and admire traditional architecture to recognise the need for a written democratic constitution. It is, likewise, possible for those who would rather tuck into a plate of gammon and chips than to graze on organic edamame salad, and who are more likely to turn to the sports pages of their tabloid newspaper than to read the latest press releases from the Electoral Reform Society, nevertheless to want the basic rules of a free society and democratic state to be fair, clear, agreed, written down, and enforced.

The sociological and political pivot point of 'small-c' conservative England is perhaps best represented by the archetypical National Trust volunteer, sympathetically depicted by Tom Fort in *Channel Shore: From the White Cliffs to Land's End* as the sort of person who listens to Radio 4 and reads Arthur Ransome to their grandchildren: 'unfailingly polite to visitors' but 'firm with people who drop litter'.[40] For the most part, these people have not hitherto supported constitutional reform. They see the constitution in the same way as they see stately homes – as something grand and ancient, to be preserved for the benefit of the nation. Perhaps, now that the wrecking balls have swung, and the towers have fallen, they will come to see that preservation is not enough. Restoration and renovation are also required.

Even so, a political opening for constitutional renewal is likely to arise only after the coming to power of a reformist majority in Parliament which has been convinced, perhaps after sustained public and civil society pressure, to include constitutional change in its manifesto. The expectation is that the reformers, if in a united majority, would be able to achieve much of what they want in terms of structural and institutional change, but that reassuring concessions would have to be made to moderate conservatives, both inside and outside Parliament. It is therefore quite reasonable to presume that the reformers will largely set the *direction*, and conservatives the *limits*, of constitutional renewal.

Above all, a constitution must establish the common ground of public life. It should define and entrench the basic institutional mechanisms of a working democracy, and protect those fundamental rights that are integral to a democratic political order, and to a free, open, and pluralist society. The aim of the constitution is not necessarily to mandate set policies, but to guarantee democratic institutions and procedures that allow policies to be decided by inclusive means, with suitable safeguards and robust mechanisms of accountability. Constitutions that go too far beyond this common ground, and turn themselves into manifestos laden with policy commitments, can become the instruments of a party; they might fail to provide the shared institutional foundation that unites the polity across partisan differences.

The first duty of any constitution, moreover, is not to improve, but to protect; before it can make things better, it must restore what has been damaged and stop things from getting worse. Much of the content of an English constitution should be intended to restore, protect, and entrench existing or former rules, institutions, and practices which have been eroded or are at risk of erosion.[41] These things are precious but fragile, and need to be protected from majorities willing to push the boundaries and overthrow traditional restraints.

With that in mind, a good constitution would chart a middle course, finding the reconciling *via media* between the extremes of reaction and radicalism. It might start from a recognition that, while the unwritten constitution is broken beyond repair, the general principles of the Westminster Model are still sound, and could, if suitably restored and reformed, provide a firm foundation for a renewed English democracy.

## Notes

1 I. Ward (2004) *The English Constitution: Myths and Realities* (Hart), p. 164.

2 The countries of north-western and Scandinavian Europe developed high-quality democratic parliamentary constitutions at or around the same time as the United Kingdom did. These were at least as good as – if not better than –the latter. However, their global-historical influence was minimal.

3 G. Orwell (1941) *The Lion and the Unicorn: Socialism and the English Genius*, available on the Orwell Foundation website, https://www.orwellfoundation.com/the-orwell-foundation/orwell/essays-and-other-works/the-lion-and-the-unicorn-socialism-and-the-english-genius/, accessed 19 November 2022.

4 E. Burke (1775) Speech on conciliation with the colonies (22 March).

5 Runnymede being the place where Magna Carta was signed; Jean-Jacques Rousseau being the much-misunderstood Genevan philosopher whose ideas were appropriated by French revolutionaries.

6 Inter-Imperial Relations Committee (1926) 'Balfour Declaration', Imperial Conference, https://www.foundingdocs.gov.au/resources/transcripts/cth11_doc_1926.pdf, accessed 20 November 2022.

7 S. A. De Smith (1961) 'Westminster's export models: the legal framework of responsible government', *Journal of Commonwealth Political Studies*, Vol. 1, No. 1, pp. 2–16.

8 Regrettably, I have not been able to find a direct source for this quote. It was narrated to me by Professor Tracy Robinson of the University of the West Indies, and I believe it on her authority to be accurate.

9 N. Clegg (2017) *Politics: Between the Extremes* (Bodley Head), pp. 249–250.

10 C. Parkinson (2007) *Bills of Rights and Decolonisation: The Emergence of Domestic Human Rights Instruments in Britain's Overseas Territories* (Oxford University Press).

11 M. Oakeshott (1962) *Rationalism in Politics and Other Essays* (Methuen).

12 Canada's constitution, adopted in 1867, did not include justiciable rights. These were added in the Constitution Act 1982, when the constitution of Canada was patriated and the last tie of dependency upon the Imperial Parliament was cut.

13 Parkinson, *Bills of Rights and Decolonisation*.

14 M. De Merieux (1982) 'The codification of constitutional conventions in the Commonwealth Caribbean constitutions', *International and Comparative Law Quarterly*, Vol. 31, No. 2, pp. 263–277; De Smith, 'Westminster's export models'.

15 As de Smith puts it, writing of the constitutional rules that attempted to capture and specify constitutional conventions across the Commonwealth, 'It cannot be said that any of these rules exactly reproduces the relevant British conventions, if only because nobody can be sure what the British conventions on the matter are; but most of them are consonant with the principles of the British constitution, and some of them would be strong candidates for inclusion in a written constitution for Britain.' See S. A. de Smith (1964) *The New Commonwealth and Its Constitutions* (Stevens), p. 95.

16 House of Commons Library, 'Recall of Parliament', No. 1186, 13 January 2020, https://researchbriefings.files.parliament.uk/documents/SN01186/SN01186.pdf, accessed 19 May 2025.

17 M. Hall, D. Marsh, and E. Vines (2018) 'A changing democracy: the British political tradition has never been more vulnerable', LSE Blog (21 June), https://blogs.lse.ac.uk/politicsandpolicy/bpt-has-never-been-more-vulnerable/, accessed 11 May 2025.

18 Ibid.

19  M. Glover and R. Hazell (2008) 'Introduction: forecasting constitutional futures', in R. Hazell (ed.), *Constitutional Futures Revisited: Britain's Constitution to 2020* (Palgrave Macmillan), pp. 1–25.

20  For a discussion of the relationship between the scientific revolution and the rise of British imperial power, see: S. Irving (2008), *Natural Science and the Origins of the British Empire* (Pickering and Chatto)

21  G. S. Halifax (Marquis of Halifax) (1688) *The Character of a Trimmer*, in J. P. Keynon (ed) (1969) *Halifax: Complete Works* (Penguin Books), pp. 49–104.

22  Everything discussed in this book could have been fixed in the 1990s. I sometimes fear that we have left it a generation too late.

23  Graham Allen, the former MP for Nottingham North, was a dedicated Labour voice in Parliament for a written constitution, especially during the Parliament of 2010–2015. Another former MP who spoke with force, clarity, and good sense on constitutional issues, until her retirement from the House in 2024, was Caroline Lucas: the lone Green Party MP, representing Brighton, one of the most progressive MPs, for one of England's most trendy cities. In the Parliament elected in 2024, strong constitutional reform voices were yet to make themselves heard at the time of writing, although honourable mention might go to Clive Lewis, one of the few Labour MPs to have publicly recognised that there is a democratic deficit problem, demanding a constitutional solution, at the root of many of England's social and economic failings.

24  D. Erdos (2009) 'Charter 88 and the Constitutional Reform Movement: a retrospective', *Parliamentary Affairs*, Vol. 62, No. 4, pp. 537–551.

25  Q. Hogg (Lord Hailsham) (1976) 'Elective dictatorship' (BBC Dimbleby Lecture, 14 October).

26  Q. Hogg (1978) *Dilemma of Democracy: Diagnosis and Prescription* (HarperCollins); see also T. S. Ranvik (2020) 'The many lives of Hailsham's famous phrase, the elective dictatorship' (Master's Thesis, University of Oslo).

27  Hogg, *Dilemma of Democracy*, p. 132.

28  The term 'moderate Conservatives' encompasses pre-Thatcherite 'wets' – in the tradition of Lord Hailsham, Rab Butler, and Sir Edward Heath – mainstream pro-European Conservatives – such as Sir John Major, Lord Heseltine, and Lord Patten – and the anti-Johnson Conservatives who were purged from the party in 2019, such as David Gauke and Rory Stewart. It includes all those Conservatives occupying the broad range between Burkean Whigs, one-nation Tories, and European Christian Democrats. It might also include that thoughtful part of the 'post-liberal' movement which rejects authoritarian populism: Adrian Pabst, John Milbank, Phillip Blond, etc.

29  D. Gauke (ed.) (2023) *The Case for the Centre Right* (Polity); D. Gauke (2022) 'Tax rises. Immigration. The Protocol. The Conservative right stands ready to seek Sunak's destruction', post on the Conservative Home website (24 October), https://conservativehome.com/2022/10/24/david-gauke-the-right-of-the-conservative-party-is-too-powerful-and-is-about-to-destroy-its-own-government/, accessed 25 October 2022.

30  Burke, Speech on conciliation with the colonies.

31  E. Burke (1791) *Reflections on the Revolution in France*.

32  C. Thornhill (2011) *A Sociology of Constitutions* (Cambridge University Press).

33  O. Haivry (2020) 'American restoration: Edmund Burke and the American constitution', online exclusive article, *American Affairs Journal* (17 February), https://americanaffairsjournal.org/2020/02/american-restoration-edmund-burke-and-the-american-constitution, accessed 1 November 2022.

34  R. Scruton (2006) *England: An Elegy* (Continuum), p. 128.

35  Ibid.

36  Ibid., p. 129.

37  Ibid., p. 56.

38  Ibid., p. 54.

39  This applies, of course, only to those Conservatives who see the value in solid institutions, who want to preserve the best of our heritage while accepting necessary reform, and who

approach public life with a sense of moral responsibility founded in a Christian concern for the common good. Those who care nothing for the public interest, and are motivated only by an urge to amass their own wealth and power, while public institutions, public infrastructure, public services, and public ethics, crumble around them, must as far as possible be kept out of power.

40 T. Fort (2013) *Channel Shore: From the White Cliffs to Land's End* (Simon and Schuster UK), pp. 167–168.

41 The list of things to be preserved is a long one. It might include the procedural rights of the Opposition and backbenchers, the protection of fundamental human rights and civil liberties, judicial independence, the impartiality and professionalism of the Civil Service, and the independence of the Electoral cCommission.

# 5

# Restoration and reform

## (a) Institutional reforms

The reformist element of a new constitution would be found in the adoption of the Charter 88 agenda, which has been the recurring demand of constitutional reformers since the tercentenary of the Glorious Revolution. Established at a time when Thatcher was showing just how close the British system could approximate 'elective dictatorship', Charter 88 was a cross-party and grassroots civil society movement for constitutional change. Its ten constitutional demands were as follows: (1) a Bill of Rights protecting fundamental human rights and civil liberties; (2) codifying and regulating Crown prerogatives, the powers of the executive, and constitutional conventions; (3) freedom of information and open government; (4) proportional representation for the House of Commons; (5) a reformed, 'democratic, non-hereditary' second chamber; (6) ensuring the political accountability of the executive to a democratically renewed Parliament, and the legal accountability of all state agencies; (7) ensuring the independence of a reformed judiciary; (8) providing legal remedies for the abuse of state power; (9) guaranteeing 'an equitable distribution of power between the nations of the United Kingdom and between local, regional and central government'; and finally, but vitally, (10) incorporating these reforms into a written, codified, entrenched, constitution.[1]

These reforms are still relevant and necessary today, and should form the basis of any new constitution. They are intended to redistribute power horizontally (mitigating the excessive concentration of power in the hands of a Prime Minister and the House of Commons majority) and vertically (taking power away from Westminster and Whitehall and parcelling it out to counties and cities).

Adopting proportional representation for the House of Commons is perhaps the most politically significant, and certainly the most visible, of these reforms. The immediate effect of proportional representation is to ensure fairness between the parties. This would end the scandal by which a party winning a third of the popular vote can win two-thirds of the seats and all of the power. No longer would a party winning 12% of the vote get more than fourteen times as many seats (seventy-two) as a party winning 14% of the vote (five seats), as happened in the 2024 general election. No matter what one thinks about the relative merits of those parties – the Liberal Democrats and Reform – it is unfair and undemocratic for seats won to be so disconnected from votes cast.

However, proportional representation also has much wider practical consequences. The first of these is to overcome the geographical fragmentation of political tribes, and to make the whole country politically competitive. In place of safe seats and wasted votes, proportional representation ensures votes count everywhere. No part of the country would be politically irrelevant, nor safe for policy-makers to ignore.

Proportional representation would also allow the formation of new parties, able to respond to changing public demands. This prevents the capture of the state by a duopoly that, while competing between themselves, combines to keep new ideas or new interests from being politically expressed. Proportional representation, with lower barriers to the entry of new parties, means more responsiveness and improved policy innovation as we try to navigate rapid social, cultural, economic, technological, and ecological change.

Above all, proportional representation would break the hold of 'winner takes all' majoritarian politics, which, in allowing both exclusivity and recklessness, causes so much chronic misgovernment. First past the post reduces the need to reach out and to form broader agreements: about two-fifths of the votes is usually enough for a party to win all of the power, and to impose its will upon the whole country without having to build consensus. It also, for the same reason, makes it too easy to act first, and think later. The process of negotiation and compromise, which in more proportional systems weeds out bad policies, can be by-passed. That leads to disastrous mistakes. It also results in wild swings of policy. Without the moderating effects of a need to compromise, policy can alternate between extremes. The development of long-term, stable policy is made very difficult. Projects are hurriedly started then arbitrarily cancelled. Things are built then found to be useless. A policy decision is made, on the hoof, found to be unworkable, and then reversed. Every time that happens, money and re-sources are waste, and trust is eroded. Proportional representation helps to limit those irresponsible swings of policy. It encourages a more balanced, moderate, form of politics and policy-making, with more room for dialogue, cooperation, and compromise – and ultimately better governance outcomes.[2]

Proportional representation in a Westminster Model does not change the core operating dynamic of 'Government versus Opposition'. What it can do, though, is soften the edges of inter-party competition by introducing a need to collaborate. Under proportional representation, the Government is often a coalition of two or more parties which work together to advance their common agenda. Normalising coalition politics takes some of the spite and polarisation out of public life. If today's opponent could be tomorrow's coalition partner, it makes sense for parties to treat one another with a little more civility. The Coalition Government in 2010–2015, as well as experience of coalition politics in local authorities, shows that this is possible even in an English context. The Coalition was often criticised at the time, but it is evident, in retrospect, that dialogue and compromise between the coalition partners prevented some of the most destructive policies, while also getting some ideas that would otherwise have been excluded onto the policy agenda.

Proportional representation has a broadening effect on policy: it opens up the field to a wider range of ideas and proposals. At the same time, it has a refin-ing effect. Policy proposals that are extreme, ill-considered, too ideological, or merely self-interested are usually filtered out through coalition negotiations. The recent Dutch experience is instructive: the far-right PVV, led by Geert Wilders, won a plurality of the votes in the 2024 election, which under first past the post would have produced a landslide majority, but the system of proportional representation in the Netherlands, and the need for coalition government, moderated Wilder's power. Inclusive, pragmatic solutions and sensible compromises are favoured. This ability to generate more ideas and to weed out the bad ones is one of many reasons why proportional representation tends to produce better policy outcomes.

There is surprisingly broad support for proportional representation. Much has changed since the referendum on the Alternative Vote in 2011. The 2022 British Social Attitudes survey shows that a majority of people (51%) now want to change the electoral system, while only 44% are in favour of keeping first past the post.[3] Proportional representation has clear majority backing (69%) not only among Liberal Democrat and Labour (61%) supporters, but also among a sizable minority (29%) of Conservative supporters.[4] The 2022 Labour Party conference even endorsed proportional representation for inclusion in the party's manifesto,[5] although the current Labour Government shows no signs of acting upon it.

The precise form of proportional representation is a secondary matter. The most important thing is that the House of Commons, while maintaining some geographic representation, should provide fair representation for each party in accordance with its share of the vote. The main options are the Additional Member System (AMS) and the Single Transferable Vote (STV). AMS has been used for more than twenty years in elections to the London Assembly, Scottish Parliament and Senedd Cymru, and is similar to the system used in New Zealand. It combines single-member constituencies with compensatory lists; list members are allocated to compensate for the disproportional results of the constituency elections. STV is used in Ireland and Malta, and for the Senate and some State/Territorial legislatures in Australia. It is a ranked-choice voting system, where people can number their preferences. Votes that would otherwise be 'wasted', because they go either to a losing candidate or to a candidate who has already received enough votes to win a seat, are transferred to second, third, or subsequent preferences. The main problem with STV is that the counting process is long, complicated, and opaque. It is not always possible for the voter to trace which candidate their vote, after multiple transfers, has ended up supporting.

The biggest difference between AMS and STV is the focus they place on intra-party competition at the local level. STV requires all candidates to stand in large, multi-member constituencies, where they have to compete for preference votes against other candidates from the same party. This can cause MPs to think of themselves – even more so than under first past the post – as 'constituency brokers' rather than as national legislators. In Ireland and Malta this has encouraged hyper-localised, clientelistic politics, while weakening the legislative and scrutiny functions of Parliament. AMS, in contrast, produces two types of MP: those elected by constituencies, and those elected on the list who have no constituency. Breaking the constituency link for about half the MPs means that those MPs would be freed from the endless chore of constituency casework, and so be able to give more attention to important matters of policy and legislation. Parties might even see fit to nominate MPs who are not just local campaigners, but who have some knowledge and experience of key policy areas. That alone would be a great change for the better. We need to strengthen Parliament to focus on its national tasks. Bins and potholes – and a whole lot more besides – should be devolved to local authorities. Do not write to your MP; write to your mayor.

The constitution should also, to the extent necessary and practicable, regulate the internal working procedures of Parliament, in order to strengthen it and make it more effective as a legislative, representative, deliberative, and scrutinising body. As a first step, this means protecting, by constitutional entrenchment, the improvements already made since the Wright report of 2009.[6] These included the election of the chairs of the parliamentary select committees by the whole House, an innovation which has helped make those committees one of the few parts of the current political system to work tolerably well – a place where expertise can be brought to bear, and where policy and administration can be considered in detail, in a less partisan, more constructive, atmosphere.[7]

Another important principle is guaranteed days for backbenchers and Opposition business. The exact number of such days is not specified in the draft Constitution, but at least a quarter of parliamentary time must be reserved for non-Government business, and Opposition days must be shared proportionately between all non-Government parties according to their number of seats. The draft Constitution would make it the duty of the Speaker to ensure that adequate allocation of Opposition Days, Backbench Business Days, and Private Members' Bills is made throughout the session. The Opposition, of course, is formally recognised in the draft Constitution. Specific roles, functions, and privileges are assigned to the Leader of the Opposition, along with the Leader of the Third Party.

All the above provisions are included in the draft as a baseline, and as a constitutional ratchet against backsliding. They are intended to stop things from getting worse. Yet it is clear that Parliament in its current form is not fit for purpose, and much more needs to be done to strengthen it in its legislative and scrutiny functions. Some other proposed constitutional provisions might also help in this regard. Limits on the 'payroll vote' (i.e. limiting the total number of MPs who hold a Government office, and are therefore bound by collective responsibility to support the Government on every division) help to preserve the crucial balancing role of Government backbenchers. Shifting power from the centre to counties and cities will relieve Parliament from some of its legislative and scrutinising burden. However, this does not exclude the need for further change, whether to the Standing Orders of the House, or more generally, to its institutional culture, and to the culture of the political parties, the media, and the Whips' Office.

We must now turn to the other House. Both the IPPR draft Constitution, produced by the Institute for Public Policy Research (IPPR) in 1991, and the draft prepared in 2014 by the House of Commons Political and Constitutional Reform Committee, proposed a directly elected second chamber chosen by proportional representation. However, if we are settled upon proportional representation for the Commons, a second proportionally elected House would be duplicative. Direct election can be good at representing party, opinion, and ideology, but what is needed, in a well tempered and balanced constitution, is a second chamber that provides a complementary form of representation, reflecting the texture of society, in terms of economic, vocational, and professional interests, its regional, cultural, and religious make-up, and its accumulation of expertise and experience. There needs to be a place where partisan politics is more muted, where short-term electoral pressures do not apply, and where people with the requisite knowledge and wisdom can take a longer-term, more objective, view of things.

In developing the draft Constitution, consideration was given to a bolder reform: if not a wholly elected House, for the reasons noted above, then a mixed one, with about half the members being indirectly elected by the members of county and city authorities, and the other half nominated by an Appointments Commission. These proposals were not ultimately adopted. Various arguments can be levelled for, as well as against, such a scheme. In its favour, it would give counties and cities a voice at the centre, and help embed their place in decentralised governance. Against, it would carry the partisanship and parochialism of local government with it. The bottom line is that, of all existing institutions, the House of Lords is the least dysfunctional, and seems to do its job on the whole rather well.[8] There is a risk that more far-reaching reform would undermine the character of the upper House as an assembly distinguished by the independence, expertise, experience, and non-partisanship of its members.[9]

A suitable second chamber might therefore be a reform of, rather than a replacement for, the existing House of Lords. It might even keep the name. 'Senate' is a perfectly respectable term for Commonwealth upper houses, being used in Australia, Canada, and most of the Caribbean, but 'House of Lords' emphasises the continuity of the reformed upper House with its earlier forms. The symbolic trinity of the English Constitution – King, Lords and Commons – is maintained, even as the material constitution is reformed.

The first reform is to fix the number of members, so that the size of the House is not excessive. Complaints against the bloated size of the House of Lords have reinforced public perceptions of it as a sump of political patronage, rather than a working chamber with a vital job to do. The upper House should, in any case, be smaller than the House of Commons; the Lords should be the more exclusive body, where, because of its less partisan nature and scrutinising functions, the style of debate should be more intimate, and less formulaic, than that in the Commons. With a five-hundred-member Commons, a four-hundred-member Lords would be about right.

Secondly, since a fixed maximum size means new peers can be created only when vacancies arise, there must be a retirement age, so that new members can be appointed with sufficient regularity. Although we do not want the House of Lords to be a geriatric ward, the retirement age should not be too low, bearing in mind that those appointed to the Lords will usually have distinguished themselves in former careers, the peak of which they might have reached in their sixties. Therefore, the draft proposes that peers will retire at the end of the session of Parliament following their eightieth birthday. There will, therefore, be a bloc of vacant seats to fill in each session; while the continuity of the House will be maintained, there will be periodic injections of new blood.

The third and most significant reform is to change the appointment process to ensure selection on merit, according to experience, expertise, wisdom, and character. This is needed to ensure the legitimacy of the House, which hangs on the quality of its members. This calls for a reduction in the use and abuse of partisan patronage, as well as a broadening of appointments beyond the 'Westminster bubble'.

A Bill introduced into the House of Lords by Lord Norton of Louth, a Conservative Life Peer, in 2023, proposed an Appointments Commission of nine members. These would be jointly appointed by the Lord Speaker and the Speaker of the House of Commons; of these nine, at least four would be political independents, while the others would be 'politically balanced' between the political parties.[10]

Lord Norton's Bill was a good start and had sound principles, although its details could no doubt be improved. The draft Constitution attempts to do just that. It proposes, in section 76, a Lords Appointments Commission of twelve members. The Lord Speaker would be its *ex-officio* chair. Two members would be appointed by the Prime Minister, one by the Leader of the Opposition, and one by the Leader of the Third Party in the House of Commons. One member would be a serving or former senior judge, appointed on the advice of the Judicial Service Commission. One would be a senior local government leader, appointed on the advice of the National Council of Local Authorities. One would be a serving or retired bishop of the Church of England, appointed on the advice of the Archbishop of Canterbury after consulting the Archbishop of York. Two would be appointed on the advice of the Convenor of Crossbench (i.e. non-partisan) Peers, after consulting the President of the Royal Society and the President of the British Academy. One would be a former senior civil servant, appointed on the advice of the Public Service Commission, and one would be a former senior naval, military or air force officer, appointed on the advice of the Defence Council. All these would serve as members of the Lords Appointments Commission for the duration of one Parliament, but might, if otherwise eligible, be reappointed.

A Lords Appointments Commission so constituted would be broadly representative, including Government and Opposition, MPs and existing peers, clerical and lay, persons from local government, from the legal profession and from the learned societies, the Armed Forces, and the Civil Service. It is intended to produce, on the one hand, a fair balance between the parties, and, on the other, a comprehensive range of suitably qualified and experienced non-partisan voices from various parts of public, civic, and social life. There is also a requirement for appointments to the Lords Appointments Commission to consider gender balance, political balance, and regional representation.

The Commission would make nominations directly to the head of state, without involving the Prime Minister. Also, nomination by the Commission would be the only route into the Lords: the Prime Minister would not be able to by-pass it with political appointments (that power being removed). This does not rule out the Prime Minister from all influence. The Prime Minister appoints two members of the Commission, and there is nothing to stop the Prime Minister from suggesting candidates to the Commission for nomination to the Lords.[11] What the Prime Minister cannot do, under this proposed arrangement, is insist, unilaterally, on getting a seat in the Lords for their favourites or for party hacks. Some of the shameful recent 'Caligula's horse' appointments show the ease with which existing restraints can be by-passed, and the need for the more robust arrangements herein proposed.

Hereditary peers would not sit in the reformed Lords as of right, but there would be nothing to prevent them from being appointed to the House of Lords by the Lords Appointments Commission, if they were suitably qualified and experienced. Bishops would lose *ex-officio* membership of the House of Lords, although provision is made for bishops of the Church of England to be appointed as peers, while also allowing space in the Upper House for leaders of other major Christian denominations, and non-Christian religions,.

To be appointed to the House of Lords it would be necessary to be an English national and at least forty years of age. The Lords Appointments Commission would also be required by the draft to give consideration to representation in terms of socio-economic background, ethnicity, religion, and region, although this should be complementary to, and not placed above, considerations of merit, experience, expertise, wisdom, and character.

Quality is to be assured by having specified qualifying criteria for appointment to the House of Lords. These would be: (1) having held 'Ministerial office or other high political or parliamentary office' (the latter is intended to include people such as former Speakers of the House of Commons, as well as former Opposition leaders); (2) having served 'with merit and distinction' in high administrative, military, diplomatic, or judicial office; (3) representing trade unions, businesses, professional bodies, or other relevant economic or social interests; (4) having made 'outstanding contributions' to academia, the arts, culture, philosophy, jurisprudence, science, industry, technology, philanthropy, or charity work; (5) representing religious communities, including the bishops of the Church of England, but also leaders of other faith communities; or (6) having served as mayor of a county or city, or having held other senior local government office. These categories would structure the choices of the Lords Appointments Commission, and so help to ensure the quality, and therefore the legitimacy, of the House.

The functions of such a reformed chamber would be similar to the present House of Lords. It would be a 'House of review and restraint', bringing expertise and experience to bear on legislation and policy, being a place of 'sober second thought', and acting as a moderating restraint against poorly drafted, hasty, partisan Bills. The draft Constitution specifies the particular duties of the House of Lords as 'improving the technical quality, coherence, and practicality of legislation; giving consideration to future generations and to the long-term public interests; protecting the rights and interests of minorities, and those not otherwise adequately represented; preventing hasty or ill-considered legislation; and protecting the powers, rights, and autonomy of local authorities'.

One area where the House of Lords under this draft would have considerably more power than at present is in relation to constitutional amendments. Constitutions must be capable of amendment, to respond to changing needs and situations, or to correct defects that become apparent through experience. At the same time, they should be harder to change than an ordinary law.[12] The Government, with an ordinary majority in the House of Commons, should not have unilateral power to change the basic rules of the political system for its own advantage. If a constitution embodies a national 'settlement' on the agreed common grounds of the political system, any change should have a similarly broad basis of support.

A two-thirds majority in both Houses of Parliament would be a suitable, and very standard, solution. However, given the unelected nature of the House of Lords, to require a two-thirds majority in that House might be a step too far towards excessive rigidity. The Lords should have a brake, but not a permanent lock. So a two-thirds majority in the Commons and an absolute majority in the Lords could be a suitable rule. In most circumstances, it would mean that any amendment would require, as a minimum, the support of the Government and the Opposition in the Commons, as well as a majority – but not a supermajority – in the Lords.

It can also be prudent to make certain fundamental provisions more difficult to amend than other parts of the constitution. Such two-tier amendment rules, allowing relative flexibility in some aspects of the constitution, and greater resilience to change in other aspects, are common in Westminster Model democracies. In the Solomon Islands, for example, most parts of the constitution can be amended by a two-thirds majority in the unicameral Parliament, but certain fundamental provisions, including those concerning basic rights, can be amended only by a three-fourths majority.[13]

One of the most effective additional hurdles is a requirement to hold a referendum. Some Westminster Model constitutions require a referendum for any amendment, as in Ireland and Australia. Since constitutional referendums are hard to win, that may be an excessive burden, which hinders necessary or beneficial reforms. A better arrangement is to allow a parliamentary supermajority to amend most of the constitution, but to require the people to give their consent, in a referendum, to changes that affect certain fundamental provisions. In Malta, for example, most of the constitution can be amended by a two-thirds majority in both Houses of Parliament, but any change to extend the life of Parliament beyond five years, except as a temporary measure in wartime, requires a referendum.[14] In Jamaica, a referendum is needed to amend the structure of Parliament, the composition of the two Houses, and the role of the monarch as head of state.[15]

Thus, in the draft Constitution proposed in this book, a referendum is required – in addition to a two-thirds majority in the House of Commons and an absolute majority in the House of Lords – for changes to the basic structure of the state. That includes the principle of parliamentary democracy, regular elections, the electoral system, fundamental rights, and the independence of the judiciary. Because they are part of the constitutional identity of the state, a referendum would also be needed to abolish the monarchy or to disestablish the Church of England. The requirement for a referendum means that one big win – a freak two-thirds majority in the Commons – would not give a party the ability to change fundamentals, without going back to the people for a second opinion.

Moreover, certain constitutional rules relating to the rights, status, autonomy, or internal governance of the Associated States, self-governing Overseas Territories, and Crown Dependencies, must be protected. This protection is what distinguishes the security of their status under this draft Constitution from their present precarity, existing (or not) at the grace and favour of Westminster majorities. These rules therefore form a set of 'specially entrenched' provisions, which can be amended only with the approval of the legislatures of the jurisdictions concerned.

Besides the obligatory constitutional referendums noted above, the draft Constitution also recognises optional, non-binding referendums on other matters. Given the way in which referendums have been abused, various safeguards are introduced: the subject matter of the referendum must be certified by the Attorney-General, and the wording of the question must be approved for clarity and impartiality by the Electoral Commission. Crucially, referendums may only be held on a published draft Bill, not on a general question of policy. In this way, uncertainty as to what is intended by the referendum result is avoided. Referendums may not be held on money Bills or on withdrawal from treaties. It is further specified, for the avoidance of doubt, that such referendums are merely advisory, and it is for Parliament to determine how to respond to the results.

It is necessary for the draft Constitution to reaffirm and restore those rules of parliamentary government and political conduct which were previously dealt with by convention, or left to political self-restraint, but which now call for stricter and clearer constitutional regulation. This would include codifying the rules on the summoning, prorogation, and dissolution of Parliament, Royal Assent to legislation, and the formation and removal of Governments.

Considerations of space in this chapter do not enable a full explanation of all the constitutional design choices in the draft. The overall approach, following the methodology of Jennings and de Smith, is to reflect choices based upon the best practice of modern Westminster Model constitutions. Very little in the draft is truly innovative. All of it is drawn from tried and tested provisions, found in some part or parts of the Commonwealth, which represent the evolution and development of the Westminster Model into its mature form.

This includes, for example, provisions that would permit the King, in situations where the Government has lost its majority, to refuse a prorogation, thus avoiding a rerun of the constitutional crisis of 2019. It also includes the formal nomination of the Prime Minister by a vote of the House of Commons – a rule intended to ensure smooth Government formation, and to reinforce the Prime Minister's democratic legitimacy and authority, in the context of a proportionally elected House and the expectation of coalition government.[16]

The draft Constitution further contains provisions preventing the abuse of emergency and delegated powers, protecting the neutrality and professionalism of the Civil Service, safeguarding the impartiality and resilience of the Electoral Commission, requiring parliamentary approval for military deployments, upholding ethical standards in public life, reforming the honours system, and safeguarding of the roles, duties, and privileges of the Opposition. There are rules in the draft Constitution dealing with the pay and allowances of MPs, the declaration of Members' interests, the openness of parliamentary proceedings, the supervision of the security services, the revision of the Ministerial Code, the standards of police conduct, and much more besides.

Many words in the draft Constitution are dedicated to matters such as the composition and independence of the Electoral Commission, the manner in which the Boundaries Commission is to redraw constituency boundaries, the process for making appointments to public office, and so on. This detail is prosaic, but important. Those not familiar with constitutions might think all this an overkill: prolix detail where a few general principles might suffice. Experience teaches, however, that it is precisely on these dull details that the health and resilience of a constitution depends, and that it is better to be precise than vague. Governments seeking to undermine democratic institutions apply their corroding pressure at precisely these points, and if they are weak, the whole structure crumples.

The Public Service Commission is one example of a so-called 'fourth branch' institution – that is, an independent body that is not executive, legislative, or judicial, but exists in its own space as a 'neutral guardian' of the institutional order.[17] Its function is to protect the permanence, impartiality, and professionalism of the Civil Service from any attempts by the Government to capture or corrupt it.

The Constitutional Offices Selection Commission is a key institution. It would be composed on a cross-party basis: the chair would be chosen by the Prime Minister with the concurrence of the Leader of the Opposition, three members would be chosen by the Prime Minister, two members would be chosen by the Leader of the Opposition, one member would be chosen by the leader of the Third Party in the House of Commons, and one member would be chosen by the Lord Speaker. To these would be added, *ex officio*, the Cabinet Secretary in a non-voting capacity. This *cross-party* institution would then appoint other – *non-partisan* – bodies, such as the Public Service Commission, thus providing a double insulation between party politics and public administration.

This arrangement is not only a passive safeguard against the corroding effects of partisan patronage. It is also an attempt to establish the Public Service Commission as an 'engine room' of the new constitution: an active, positive, institution, with a mandate to recruit, select, train, develop, and promote the cadre of high-quality officials needed to restore competent and effective government in England.[18]

These insulating, 'neutral guardian' institutions support and overlap each other in intricate ways. The Public Service Commission appoints three (out of nine) members of the Electoral Commission, four (out of nine) members of the Boundaries Commission, one (out of five) members of the Commission on Standards in Public Life, and one (out of twelve) members of the Lords Appointments Commission. The Judicial Service Commission appoints one member of the Electoral Commission, one of the members of the Commission on Standards in Public Life, and one member of the Lords Appointments Commission. The Lord Speaker holds another intricately overlapping position: he or she appoints one member of the Constitutional Offices Selection Commission, one member of the Commission on Standards in Public Life, one member of the Lords Appointments Commission, and four (out of nine) members of the Honours Commission.

This is not a strict, artificial, 'separation of powers'. Rather, it is a subtle and interlocking dispersal of power, combining democratic representation and responsibility on the one hand, with permanent, non-partisan public bodies on the other. Democracy and meritocracy, short-term public accountability, and long-term public interest, are thereby joined in a 'mixed constitution'.[19] These institutions reflect the pre-modern idea that the role of a constitution is to create structures that ensure that the best people are put in positions of public responsibility, and that unsuitable people – those without the virtue to rule well – are excluded from power.[20] These public bodies also ensure that, while a Government with a large majority in the House of Commons would be able to govern and to legislate, it would not be able to capture the state-as-such. The publicness – rather than partisanship – of the state, as the common servant of all, would be preserved.[21]

Another small but vital part of the draft Constitution is found in section 166, which deals with public inquiries, royal commissions and citizens' assemblies. The difference between a public inquiry and a royal commission is that the former is set up in order to investigate a particular failure or problem, to look into what went wrong, and to make recommendations for avoiding similar errors in the future. They are important mechanisms of accountability and of institutional learning and memory, which if properly deployed can help improve the quality of government.

Royal commissions, on the other hand, examine a broad area of policy and make recommendations for change in policy or legislation. Royal commissions have historically been a driving force of political, economic, and social reform.[22] They usually consist of several commissioners, with a variety of experiences and expertise, who are appointed to examine an issue, to take evidence upon it, to consider options, and to produce a report on which the Government can then act. Royal commissions enable difficult, complex issues to be considered in a holistic way. As an adjunct to parliamentary politics, they make up for some of the latter's shortcomings, such as lack of expertise, partisanship, and the difficulty of seeing long-term solutions above the din of the news cycle.

Sadly, royal commissions seem to have fallen into disuse: there has been none for a quarter of a century (the last was established by Blair in 1999 to consider reform of the House of Lords).[23] In consequence, many difficult policy issues which would have benefited from a more deliberate, dispassionate, long-term, and evidence-based approach – such as housing and planning, welfare reform, public transport, or energy transition and resilience – have instead, to our detriment, been left to the normal cut and thrust of daily politics.

Citizens' assemblies are deliberative bodies, usually consisting wholly or mainly of randomly selected members of the public, established to consider a particular topic. They are seen by some as an alternative to decision-making by elected Governments and Parliaments. Some people see this as a wonderful democratic innovation, others as a threat to representative democracy, outsourcing to irresponsible and unelected members of the public issues that it is the duty of elected representatives to resolve. Neither of these extreme positions seems convincing. Citizens' assemblies are not an alternative to representative democracy. At best, they are an auxiliary to it. It makes sense to see them as an alternative to royal commissions. They perform the same sort of role: examining a policy area, hearing expert and public evidence, weighing options, and making recommendations. The only real difference is that while royal commissions tend to be quite small, with a membership chosen from among experts or the 'great and good', citizens' assemblies are bigger, with a membership selected to represent ordinary citizens.

## (b) Rights and principles

A constitution is not merely a 'frame of government'. It is also an instrument by which the citizens covenant together to declare the shared principles and values that unite them as members of a polity with a common identity.

Once, there might have been an assumed consensus about who 'we' were – what the United Kingdom was, what it stood for, and what it would not stand for. Those unspoken assumptions no longer hold. Part of the function of a constitution-building process would be to try to reach a new consensus around these issues. Some of the marks of shared identity and common purpose arising from that process might be embedded in the constitution, whether in the preamble, or in those parts of the text dealing with national identity, fundamental principles, or guaranteed rights.

It is in relation to principles, values, and identity that strategic compromise with moderate conservatives might be most fruitful. The centre of this common ground must be the European Convention on Human Rights. The Convention protects those basic rights that are essential for democracy itself (freedom of expression, information, assembly, and association), that are integral to a free society (such as fair trials and the due process of law), or that no decent, humane civilisation should ever violate (such as freedom from torture and slavery). If we abandon this common ground, as some are eager to do, then we are no longer in the realm of liberal-democratic politics, but some sort of more or less explicitly authoritarian state. That explicitly right-wing populists should endorse this authoritarian turn is unsurprising. That many mainstream Conservatives should blithely follow them into that error is unconscionable.

The European Convention on Human Rights was grounded in English history and is best seen as a succinct codified expression of the English tradition of liberty. It is designated as European not because it comes *from Europe*, but because it was applied *to Europe*, when it became clear, after the end of the Second World War, that some basic freedoms were just too fundamental, too essential, for any decent and civilised society to place them at the mercy of the majority of day. This was also recognised by Colonial Office lawyers, who gladly used the European Convention as the basis for Commonwealth Bills of Rights around the world.[24]

Although taking the European Convention as its starting point, the draft Constitution does recommend some small changes and additions to those rights. The European Convention does not, for example, include the right to trial by jury, which is preserved in this draft. Rules on such matters as the employment of prisoners have also been tightened up, so as to recognise things like community service orders, but not to allow the abuse of prison labour.

The Human Rights Act 1998 incorporated European Convention rights into domestic law, but it was hobbled from the start by the principle of parliamentary sovereignty. Unlike in most other democracies, English courts do not have the authority to annul or disapply primary legislation incompatible with Convention rights. They can only issue a Declaration of Incompatibility. It is then up to Parliament – in effect, to the Government – to determine whether and how to respond. The draft Constitution would end that halfway house of weak justiciability, by establishing rights upon a properly entrenched and justiciable basis.

In establishing directly justiciable human rights, the draft Constitution would reject the populist and absolutist view that in a parliamentary democracy, it is for Parliament *alone*, without recourse to the courts, to determine the nature and extent of rights, and to resolve conflicts between rights.

There is a constitutional balance between legislative and judicial functions, between Parliament and courts, and between utilitarian collective policy-making and the rights of individuals.[25] Ultimately, the absence of directly justiciable rights tips everything on to the side of utilitarianism: that which is useful to the Government, in achieving its current policy goals, prevails, even over personal rights. That might sound democratic, but only in the crudest, most majoritarian way. Perhaps it is acceptable for those who have political clout; indeed, we hear the loudest complaints against judicial power from those with the most political and economic power. People at the margins, whose voices are never heard in majoritarian politics, for whom no Government speaks up, are most in danger: refugees, prisoners, outsiders, minorities, the poor. These are the people who are given short shrift by majority rule, for whom justiciable human rights, and the ability to assert those rights in a judicial forum, matter most.

However, the courts are not the *only* interpreter of rights. Courts become involved only as a reviewing body, when someone asserts that the decision of the Government and Parliament, in the limits of rights or the balance between them, was incorrect, and that as a result their constitutional rights have been infringed. Neither are the courts the *final* interpreter. Ultimately, judicial decisions can be overturned by means of a constitutional amendment. Parliament (not by a simple majority, but by a sufficient, constitution-amending consensus) and the people (voting in a referendum on the proposed amendment) would have the final say.

Contrary to the fears of some theorists, constitutional entrenchment does not narrow, but rather broadens, public discussion on rights. It means that rights cannot be taken away by a Government of the day with a working majority. A deeper discussion, and wider consensus, is required before we dare meddle with the fundamentals of a free society.

If we can agree upon European Convention rights as an essential foundation, we shall do well. Some would go further, and seek to constitutionalise social, economic, and cultural rights. Here more caution might be called for, because the common ground is less secure.

In contrast to those rights protected by the European Convention, social, economic, and cultural rights call for more delicate, controversial, policy decisions. They concern matters of taxation, spending, service delivery, and resource allocation. Some might argue that these things should be resolved by ordinary politics: it is legitimate, according to this view, for different parties to have different views about how to define, balance, prioritise, and achieve socio-economic and cultural goals; and therefore, on democratic grounds, policy should be decided by Parliament, not by the courts.

Others, generally on the left, take the view that all rights are interdependent, and that traditional rights such as freedom of speech and assembly are of little value in practice if one is hungry or homeless. The constitution, in seeking to establish a country that is not only democratic, but also decent, has to promote certain egalitarian, uplifting, social, economic, and cultural outcomes if it is to be legitimate.

The sensible moderate compromise between these two positions is to recognise socio-economic and cultural rights in the constitution, but only as 'Directive Principles' which are not directly justiciable. This approach is adopted in many Westminster Model constitutions, having been pioneered by Ireland and India. Directive Principles recognise that the state has a duty to promote flourishing, in policy areas such as health, education, housing, social security, and working conditions, but without specifying, at a constitutional level, how exactly it should fulfil that obligation. Their inclusion is valuable because they create expectations. They make it clear that the state has duties and responsibilities that go beyond just the preservation of 'life, liberty, and property'; the state has active powers that must be used for the public good. Although not directly justiciable, courts may rely upon them when interpreting the other provisions of the constitution or other laws. They speak mostly, however, to the political rather than the legal aspect of the constitution. They remind politicians and voters alike of the terms of a 'social contract' against which the outcomes of public policy can be tested.

## (c) The monarchy

In contrast to some other, more radical, constitutional reform proposals,[26] the draft Constitution presented here would not establish a republic. Insofar as the monarchy remains widely popular in England, it would be wiser – in the interests of continuity and consensus – for it to be retained.

This is more, however, than just a pragmatic act to appease traditionalists. It can be a sensible constitutional design choice in its own right. The potential of the monarchy to promote unity, stability, and legitimacy, even in the midst of constitutional change, should not be underestimated. Visible, tangible links to the past give the ship of state a deep keel. Whenever a country declares a 'year zero' and destroys those links with its own past, it is in danger of capsizing into tyranny. A well functioning democracy under a ceremonial hereditary crown is better than authoritarian misrule under a strutting tyrant titled 'President of the Republic'.

In another sense, the logic of a new constitution could still be republican with a small 'r'. It would establish a state defined by *public government*, where public authority is orientated towards the public good. A democratic written constitution is the people's title deed. It means that state is a 'public thing', literally a *res publica*, while those elected to govern and represent the people are merely the tenants, and not the freeholders, of public power. This substantive republicanism – the orientation of the state to the public good – is far more important than the formal republicanism of having an elected president.

Besides, the monarch reigns only so long as our representatives in Parliament so choose. Even the Royal Family's own website acknowledges this reality: 'the succession to the throne can be regulated by Parliament and [...] a Sovereign can be deprived of his/her title through misgovernment'.[27] Ultimately, the King is but a 'blinged up' public servant, who has a job to do just like the rest of us.

Indeed, paradoxical though it might seem, there is a republican case for constitutional monarchy. Although not elected, constitutional monarchs are in some sense representative: they represent the people, the state, the nation, the whole community.[28] Of course, monarchs do so in a different way from elected politicians; they represent not as chosen and sent emissaries of the people, but as living embodiments of the people – in the same way, perhaps, as a sports team is represented by its mascot.

In representing the people in this different way, constitutional monarchs can help preserve the publicness of the state. Unlike a Prime Minister, or a popularly elected President (who invariably represents a party and a programme), the monarch encompasses all. The monarch symbolically declares, by their very existence and presence, that the state does not belong to one person, one party, or one part of the community; the state is a *res publica* – a public thing – with the constitutional monarch as the representative embodiment of the universal public. Monarchs thereby block the path to others – dictators and tyrants – who would falsely claim such public universality for themselves.[29]

Of course, democratic principles and constitutional clarity demand that the powers and functions of the monarch be tightly prescribed. Monarchs should be bound to act only on the advice of responsible ministers. The circumstances in which they are allowed to exercise a 'reserve power', at their own discretion, should be narrowly specified, such that these powers are used to protect, and not to undermine, the rules of parliamentary democracy. These limited reserve powers include, in the draft, the power: (1) to dismiss a Prime Minister who has lost a vote of confidence, but refuses to resign or to request a dissolution of Parliament; (2) to refuse a dissolution to a Prime Minister who has lost the confidence of the House of Commons if another Government can be formed without a dissolution; (3) to dissolve Parliament if the office of Prime Minister is vacant and no successor enjoying the confidence of the House of Commons can be appointed; (4) to refuse a prorogation, if requested by a Government that appears to have lost the confidence of the House; and (5) to appoint and dismiss, subject to law, staff of the Royal Household.

The draft Constitution retains the Privy Council, too. It would continue to be, in principle, the body by which the monarch is advised. It would be composed of various *ex-officio* members (Cabinet ministers, party leaders, and those who have held certain high offices), as well as members appointed for life by the monarch, on the advice of the Prime Minister, after consultation with the Leader of the Opposition. The executive functions of the Privy Council would continue to be performed by ministers. The Privy Council's wider use is as a body through which informal exchange can take place, on delicate issues, between Government and the leaders of the major opposition parties. It is further envisaged that the Privy Council would provide the pool of experienced and trustworthy personnel from which certain other bodies (the Intelligence and Security Committee, the Commission on Standards in Public Life, the Honours Commission, and the Judicial Committee of the Privy Council) would be formed.

### (d) The Church of England

The established status of the Church of England – that is, the legal connection between Church and state – is often seen as one of those embarrassing legacies from bygone days, long overdue for reform. Many constitutional reformers take this view as axiomatic. We are often reminded that 'the United Kingdom and Iran are the only two countries with clerics in their legislature'. Everyone forgets about Belize, a democratic country with church representation in the Senate, because it does not fit that assumption. The IPPR draft of 1991 and the Political and Constitutional Reform Committee's draft of 2014 both simply disestablish the Church, as if it were an uncontroversial bit of tidying up.

There is another perspective. Far from being a relic or an irrelevance, the constitutional status of the Church of England is in fact vital to the constitutional identity – we might call it the 'metaphysical constitution' of England.[30] England is a country where the Church has, since Anglo-Saxon times, been intimately bound with the state and the nation. We can understand the Kingdom of England as having two mutually supporting elements, the civil and the ecclesiastical, with the monarch as the bridge between them. The constitution has to address both these elements, not just one.

Much of what follows here will be hard to accept for some, religious or not, who have a principled objection to any form of established religion. I ask only that the arguments be given a fair hearing. I present establishment not only as a point on which compromise with moderate conservatives is possible, but also as a positive good in its own right. At any rate, I wish to show the reader that an English constitution does not have to be strictly secular, in the way the American and French constitutions are. It could continue to recognise the role of Christianity, and of the Church of England in particular, in maintaining the faith, values, and culture of the English people. Furthermore, as we become a more diverse society, in which Christianity is no longer a near-universal cultural assumption, some might see this constitutional connection between Church and state as more, not less, important, in under-girding a national community.

Establishment of the Church of England does not limit freedom of religion, nor diminish the equal rights of all citizens regardless of their religion or lack thereof. The liberal principles of religious liberty and non-discrimination, which go back to Catholic Emancipation and to the repeal of the Test and Corporation Acts in the early nineteenth century, would be guaranteed under the draft Constitution. Rather, establishment is simply a constitutional recognition that 'the State has a duty to provide for the moral and spiritual welfare of its citizens and that the Church, supported and recognised by the State, is the means by which the State fulfils that duty'.[31] It recognises the place of Christianity in the nation's heritage, and grounds the English state upon a certain core of shared Christian values, norms, and traditions. If that core is maintained, tolerance and diversity can be built upon it, without undermining the nation's historic character.

In maintaining the established Church, the state also acknowledges, at a constitutional level, that it does not exist in an ethical vacuum, acting as a law unto itself. The state is not the sole arbiter of right or wrong. The powers of those entrusted with public authority, or placed in positions of leadership, are not absolute or despotic, but are constrained by certain values and standards of right, justice, ethics, and natural law, which are binding upon all just societies, but especially on those that dare to call themselves Christian.

The democratic state exists to serve good purposes, and its governors stand in the need of good counsel and moral teaching, and sometimes of faithful exhortation and loving rebuke, to remind them that their duty is to serve the public interest, not their own desires. The Church of England has tried – although not always successfully – to provide that.

William Temple's *Christianity and Social Order*, first published in 1944, provided a Christian moral foundation for the welfare state in the post-war era.[32] On the other hand, the Church failed to resist the rise of the 'permissive society' in the 1960s and 1970s. While the indomitable campaigner Mary Whitehouse led a popular crusade against indecency in broadcasting, most of the bishops and clergy were terrified of appearing out of touch or out of date. They tried hard to move with the times, but came across as weak and indistinct. In the second half of the twentieth century, the weak-armed, flaccidly spoken, woolly-minded English vicar became a stock figure of fun. Subsequently, the Church's own failings, including horrific sexual abuse scandals, have further eroded its moral authority.

Nevertheless, the Church has continued to intervene with a Christian voice on a range of policy issues, including improving ethical standards in public life, ending exploitative pay-day lending, reducing child poverty, caring for the environment, and protecting refugees. It has at times been directly critical of Government policies, in publications such as *Faith in the City* (1985)[33] and *Who Is My Neighbour?* (2015).[34] If, in so doing, it has aroused the ire of populist pundits, this only proves the worth of the Church as a ballasting institution in our society, that marches (thank God) to a different moral beat than that of right-wing tabloid headline writers.

Church establishment therefore acts as a reminder. It reminds the monarch, ministers, parliamentarians, civil servants, judges, magistrates, councillors, police constables, teachers, opinion-formers, and every citizen, that to govern is to serve. Without this reminder, constitutional human rights and civil liberties, which are vital to a free and just society, can easily be misunderstood; if applied as mere abstractions, shorn from the Christian root from which they have sprung, they can produce absurd results, actually harming, rather than protecting, freedoms of conscience and expression.[35]

In the same way, democracy depends upon being reminded of the fact that those who rule are servants, not masters, of the people. The Cross atop the Crown represents the principle that public authority has itself been humbled and crucified; the state exists not to be served but to serve the public. As the Reverend Glen Scrivener puts it, our culture has been 'shaped by the Cross to the point where greatness is expressed in service'.[36] Without such a concept of ethically responsible servant leadership – grounded upon truth, justice, and compassion – democracy can easily deteriorate into cruel, crude, and crass populist perversions of itself.

Church establishment also relates to national identity, heritage, and belonging. It is the line that holds fast both state and nation to their Christian moorings. It upholds and strengthens what might be called England's 'metaphysical constitution', unbroken since the days of Saint Edmund the Martyr. In the 2021 census, Christians, for the first time in modern history, became a nominal minority in England and Wales, with just 46.2% of people calling themselves Christian – down from 59.3% in 2011.[37] Despite this social and demographic change, the Church of England is still one of the few English national institutions to enjoy broad public respect and recognition, rivalled only by the national football team. Multiplying the loaves and fishes of its limited resources, it still does excellent work in parishes up and down the land, running everything from foodbanks and debt advisory services to parent–toddler groups and pensioners' clubs. Even if fewer than half the people actively identify as Christian believers, a sense of Christian cultural heritage, and of Christian values, still has resonance and meaning in England's story. In every cathedral and every parish in the land, the Church is an institutional custodian of the English collective memory, of the buildings and the places that make England what it is; of the words and the songs – and, yes, the faith and the prayers – that have held the nation together over the centuries. As the historian Bijan Omrani writes:

> The origins of English kingship, the very idea of English nationhood, the rule of law, English law generally, education, spirituality, notions of ethics, charity, tolerance and public duty all have their roots in Christian doctrine, and English culture – the arts, landscape, language, literature, music, social life – would be unrecognisable without the Christian leaven.[38]

Cutting the Church totally loose from the state, by disestablishment, would abandon this cultural and social role to a merely private organisation, having no public recognition, patronage, or connection to the national community. That would be a particularly savage form of cultural privatisation.

Having an established Church does not mean that England is, or even claims to be, a universally Christian country. It merely recognises the fact that it is, culturally and historically, a deeply 'Christianised' country. That is valued, in particular, by those who are *not* believing or practising Christians, but who are pleased to belong to a culture that has been shaped by Christianity. In any case, the invisible church of born-again Spirit-filled believers probably never included more than a minority of the population, in England as in any nation. Nevertheless, from the early Middle Ages until just a few generations ago, nominal Christianity was the norm, and Christian ideas held sway over the narratives, ethics, and assumptions of English society. Not everyone conformed to a model of Christian holiness and goodness – far from it – but there was a common view, shaped by the pervasive cultural, social, and educational influence of Christianity, of what holiness and goodness *looked like.*[39]

As English society becomes more diverse, the passing on to new generations of a shared national identity, and of a generously ecumenical set of shared values, cannot be taken for granted. Making a multi-ethnic, multi-faith society work, in freedom, peace, and harmony, while also holding on to an inclusive national culture in which all can share, means we must hold fast to that which is good and cherish those things that bind people together as a nation. Abandoning England's Christian heritage at a constitutional or symbolic level does not make that vital task any easier; recognising it, teaching it, sharing it, preserving it, making its influence on our history and culture accessible and understandable to all people, regardless of their own faith or lack thereof, does.

Recognition of a constitutional connection between the Church of England and the English state does not mean that the Church should be subject to state control, nor that there should be no institutional separation between Church and state. On the contrary, the constitution should preserve the institutional separation between temporal and spiritual authorities, recognising that the *ecclesia* and the *res publica* are separate institutions, each with its own mission, purpose, powers, membership, and system of government.

The new constitution should guarantee the freedom of the Church of England, as long promised in the first article of Magna Carta: 'anglicana ecclesia libera sit'.[40] This includes the right of the Church to govern itself through its own Synods, and the right, free from any political patronage, to choose its own bishops. Bishops used to be appointed by the Crown on the advice of the Prime Minister, and at times this power was exercised on blatantly partisan terms, to the detriment of the health, freedom, and dignity of the Church. In 1976, this was curtailed by the establishment of a Crown Appointments Commission (later, Crown Nominations Commission), which recommended two names to the Prime Minister for each diocesan bishop to be chosen, from which the Prime Minister would then select one. During the premiership of Gordon Brown, it became the established practice for the Crown Nominations Commission to make clear its first choice, and for the Prime Minister to forward that choice to the monarch without any exercise of patronage or discretion.

The draft Constitution builds upon, but clarifies, this practice, removing the last vestigial role of the Prime Minister. It would empower the Church, acting through the Crown Nominations Commission or such other body as the General Synod may designate for that purpose, to propose a candidate directly to the monarch, without going through the Prime Minister. The monarch, as Supreme Governor, would then issue the *congé d'élire* in the name of that candidate, so that the College of Canons could formally elect the candidate under the Appointment of Bishops Act 1533.[41] Ultimately, this would mean that the Church as a body, and not the Crown, has control over episcopal and archepiscopal appointments.[42]

The General Synod would be able to legislate directly on internal ecclesiastical matters. Having been passed by the General Synod, a Church measure would, as at present, be referred to the Ecclesiastical Committee, a joint committee of both Houses. If the Ecclesiastical Committee were satisfied that the measure dealt exclusively with internal ecclesiastical affairs, it would be submitted directly to the monarch for Royal Assent. Parliamentary approval by resolution (currently required for all Church measures) would be necessary only if the Ecclesiastical Committee considered that a Church measure had extra-ecclesiastical effect.

Parliament, no longer absolute over the Church, but constitutionally constrained to respect the Church's freedom over its own affairs, would lose the right to legislate for the Church: it would not be possible for Parliament to force doctrinal, liturgical, or structural changes on the Church, nor to stand in the way of the Church making its own changes.

In short, while preserving the *connection* between the Church and the state, the form of establishment outlined in the draft Constitution undoes the Henrician *subordination* of the former to the latter. It does not treat the Church as a department of the state, but recognises its place in the nation.

Without such freedom from state control, the Church would not be able to fulfil its mission effectively or faithfully. Only at the top – in the dual role of the constitutional monarch as Supreme Governor of the Church – are they institutionally fused, and then only ceremonially and symbolically. The principle is ecclesiastical self-government under the protection, not control, of the Crown.

The aim is neither to create a 'Christian state' (we are constituting twenty-first-century England, not sixteenth-century Geneva), nor to create a tamed 'state church', but to ensure both the freedom of the Church, on the one hand, and the Christian foundations of a pluralist and tolerant democratic state, on the other, are not undermined, but are duly honoured and maintained.

The most compelling arguments against this type of reformed establishment come not from secular progressives, but from orthodox opinion within the Church. Some argue that the worthiness of the Church of England as an *established church* ultimately depends upon it being a *true church*. The only authority with which the Church speaks on public issues, and the only authority that makes the Church worth listening to in public life, over any other well meaning NGO, is the authority of Christian truth itself. If the Church of England does not cling closely to the foundations of that truth, but becomes buffeted and overwhelmed by the ideological trends of the age, such that it falls into gross error or even apostasy, establishment would be useless, or worse.

The theology of that argument must be left to more qualified authors in other places. As a constitutional scholar, not a theologian, I am primarily concerned with the Church's constitutional role in the state, and its social, cultural, and moral influence on society; that is, with the 'outward and visible' Church, which 'functions within the sphere of human law'.[43]

Some might say, and perhaps not wrongly, that this is missing the point. The Church is not a social, civic, cultural, and educational institution, the purpose of which is to turn out well mannered, decently behaved, morally upright, and socially responsible English men and women. It is the body and the bride of Christ. Certainly, it would be wrong to see the Church of England as 'the National Trust at prayer'. The Church of England is nothing if it is not a local branch of the universal church gathered from all nations on the day of Pentecost.

Any regeneration of England worthy of the name must be led and accompanied by a revival of the English Church and by the re-evangelisation of the English people.[44] Changing the constitution can only get us so far, without a change in the culture that comes, ultimately, from the Gospel. In light of the census figures cited above, the clergy of the Church of England have a duty to see their role today as missionaries, sent into their parishes to reconvert the English. However, the Great Commission is not something that a constitution can, nor should attempt, to fulfil.

It is enough, for constitutional purposes, to recognise that the Church of England, in Articles XIX, XX and XXI of its Articles of Religion, denies its own infallibility. It admits that it is, in its visible form, prone to all human error. On the whole, a synodical constitution, recognising a great degree of internal pluralism, has served it well, enabling differences to be managed and self-correction to take place. When one part of the Church has drifted too far in one direction, other parts have challenged it, and eventually pushed it back on course. If it seems that some parts of the Church have fallen into error or lassitude, we may be encouraged by the faithful remnant, through which it may, by the work of the Holy Spirit, and in God's good time, be corrected and revived.

If all this seems a little bit crazy, fear not. In practical terms, if you are not into this religion stuff, it probably will not make any difference to you. This is a long justification for a minimally modified codification of the status quo.

## (e) Devolution and local government

The most challenging part of reconstituting England is the devolution of power from the centre. The establishment of an English Parliament and Government neatly solves the 'English question', but it does nothing, in itself, to disperse power and resources away from Westminster and Whitehall.

As discussed in Chapter 3, England is, in terms of its regional geography, a surprisingly variegated country. The north–south divide, eloquently depicted by J. B. Priestley's *English Journey* in the 1930s, continues to have cultural, social, and economic resonance. Recent works such as *Northerners* by Brian Groom[45] and *The Northumbrians* by Dan Jackson[46] have attempted to honour northern identities and to give recognition to this 'other England', so often airbrushed out of prevailing (southern, Normanised) images of Englishness.

More prosaically, England is a country of extreme regional economic disparities. Deindustrialisation in the 1980s hit the United Kingdom, especially northern England and the Midlands, harder than other advanced economies; this, coupled with the concentration of subsequent growth in London and the South East, meant that on indicators such as GDP per capita, productivity, and disposable income, the United Kingdom had by the 2010s become 'one of the most regionally unequal of the world's industrial economies'.[47] By 2018, the North East of England had just 41% of the GDP per capita of Greater London.[48]

This is not, of course, to deny the poverty that exists in London and the South East. London contains some of the poorest, as well as the richest, neighbourhoods. Yet the fact remains that London receives more than its fair share of public funding; in 2021, £19,231 per person was spent in London, as against an average of £16,223 per person in the North.[49] London also generates more revenue per person, but that is just further evidence of regional imbalance. A poor person in London has access to better public transport infrastructure than a poor person outside of London, is likely to do better in school,[50] and likely to earn a higher salary. By almost every measure, London and the South East have pulled away from the rest of England. One could argue that England is no longer a rich country, but a struggling country containing a rich megapolis in its south-eastern corner.

The problem is not just an economic, infrastructural, or developmental one; it is also, at its root, a constitutional problem. Parliamentary sovereignty – which traps England in a top-down, unitary, centralising, state – has failed. The concentration of power, wealth, and resources in London has drained the productive capacity of the rest of the country and kept everyone poorer. A new constitutional system, entrenching devolution, is necessary to bring about real and sustained regional rebalancing; no other foundation would be secure against attempts by the Government to curtail it.

Central government has a role to play in enabling regional rebalancing but, for both practical and political reasons, Whitehall cannot do it all. In practical terms, different parts of the country have different policy needs and priorities. No doubt Surrey has its fair share of problems, but they are not the same problems as those of, say, Cumbria or Newcastle. A top-down, highly centralised, 'Whitehall-knows-best state' (good and necessary though it is for some purposes) can neither adequately understand these diverse needs nor craft intelligent policy responses to them.

In political terms, there is a huge difference between being a supplicating recipient of central hand-outs, bidding for a project here and grant there, and being an autonomous political authority having democratic initiative, with the ability to decide priorities and to control its own future and resources. Only the latter can give people the sense of civic responsibility necessary to produce good and lasting results.

The empowerment of local democratic institutions, under locally responsible leadership, is the only way to 'take back control', and thereby to properly overcome England's sense of alienation from distant, out-of-touch decision-making. People want more control over their own communities and a closer link between those who make the decisions and those on whose behalf decisions are made. They want to be governed by people who know, share, and understand the needs of their corner of England. Above all, they want the democratic power to revitalise their towns, raise their living standards, repair their public infrastructure, improve their public services, and to restore their lost civic pride. They do not need the central Government to turn up and dump a 'free port' on them, whether they want it or not.

Without that sense of democratic control, we get not only bad policies, but bad politics. Local governments are the schools of democracy, the place where ordinary citizens can be more directly involved.[51] Shorn of autonomy, civic and democratic life atrophies. The result of excessive centralisation is a general demoralisation of the people. People stop caring about things they cannot influence. The aldermanic class (the owners of small businesses and provincial professionals who would normally provide the mainstay of civic leadership) collapses. Citizens lose initiative, becoming resigned, fatalistic, passive, and supplicant.

On the other hand, when local leaders, responsible to local people, have hold of the levers power, the results can be impressive. Energies are unleashed. Initiative abounds. The spirit of liberty is a spirit of transformation. In Frome in Somerset, for example, a group of concerned citizens managed to win a majority on the previously stagnant town council, and were able to use even the modest powers and resources at their disposal to regenerate their town – and, in the process, to restore civic pride and civic identity.[52]

'Levelling up' – the Johnson-era buzz-word for investment in northern and peripheral England – is therefore pointless, and doomed to fail, unless it is accompanied by a genuine shift of both resources and democratic power. The Government's preferred strategy for this has been to offer 'devolution deals' to patchworks of local authorities, allowing them a thin slice of power and resources in return for amalgamating their functions. These arrangements have resulted in some positive changes. There is an elected Mayor of Greater Manchester – an office presently held by a former Cabinet minister and almost a national household name – who can make certain strategic leadership decisions about development and public services in the Greater Manchester area. Similar 'metropolitan mayors' have been established for other conurbations, including Leeds (West Yorkshire Combined Authority), Sheffield (South Yorkshire Combined Authority), Birmingham (West Midlands Combined Authority), and Liverpool (Liverpool City-Region Combined Authority). All this is, perhaps, a good start, but no more than that. The range of devolved powers is limited and the central Government retains tight control over their use.

There are three basic problems with the devolution arrangement as it has been practised so far. First, it is based on *sui generis* arrangements, with each Combined Authority area having different powers. For the most part, these powers are very limited. They are administrative, rather than legislative, in nature. They fall a long way short of the powers that have been devolved to Scotland, Wales, and Northern Ireland (and Northern Ireland, in terms of its population, is not much bigger than a big English county). Moreover, all their powers come with strings attached. They are doled out, or withheld, by the central Government, like carrots and sticks, by the grace and favour of Whitehall: 'Be a good boy with your bus services, and we might let you build a tramway too'. There is no sense in which localities are *entitled* to have and to use these powers. They might exercise certain powers, but do not inherently *possess* them. Parliamentary sovereignty precludes that transfer of power; as long as local authorities are merely creatures of statute, with no constitutional recognition, they can be cut, chopped, amalgamated, and abolished, just as the central Government desires.

Moreover, the central Government does not trust devolved authorities with powers that it does not control. Whitehall and Westminster still have to keep tabs on what the devolved authorities do, and struggle to move beyond the Tudor statecraft of centralised authority. They will sit on and squash anything they do not like. Devolution as it now exists in England is merely a way of getting 'the provinces' to do what the centre wants, not of letting the people who live there do what they decide is in their own best interests. On such a wrong-footed foundation, little that is great or lasting can ever be built.

Second, the governance arrangements accompanying 'devolution deals' are weak and fall short of proper democratic standards. The centre-piece is the elected mayor. This is not a bad development. Having someone who is directly elected by the people, directly accountable to them, and who in consequence is a well known name whose face is recognised in the street – not an anonymous bureaucrat or party-hack councillor – is almost certainly a good thing. It is equally necessary, however, that mayors have some council or assembly with which they share power – a body that can question them, advise them, hold them accountable, and scrutinise and approve (or not) the mayor's decisions. Such a body exists, as a directly elected democratic Assembly, only in Greater London. Elsewhere, they decided not to bother with dedicated institutions of accountability. Instead, the councils of the combined authorities are made up of the representatives of the lower-level local authorities in their areas. The metropolitan mayors float above that existing structure, as a kind of bolt-on extra, but they are not really held accountable by it.

The third problem with the current approach is its patchiness. Some places have these devolution deals, but not all. This *ad hoc* bodging – the opaqueness and incoherence of it all – also means that city-region devolution has not really had an impact on England's political culture and discourse more generally. If you live in Greater Manchester, Liverpool, or Birmingham, then perhaps you see the effect of these metropolitan mayors in the life of your city; if not, English devolution is invisible and irrelevant.

The existence of these mayors has failed to transform national politics. There is no effective integration of the metropolitan mayors with the national Government. The Council of Nations and Regions, which was established by the Government in 2024, might be a good start, but it lacks any statutory basis or effective powers, and its role is confused by the competing dynamics of being a body representing both English local government and the other, non-English, nations of the United Kingdom.

In other words, devolution within England is hampered by the fact that it is treated, in a country that has not yet got to grips with constitutional government, as an administrative, rather than a constitutional, matter. Devolution is handled by Whitehall as a way of parcelling out service delivery. It is not seen in the wider context of democratic renewal and the redistribution of power and resources more equitably across the country. There is no real interest in overcoming the local democratic deficit that is at the root of some of the worst regional disparities in quality of life in the Western world.

Decentralisation of power at a constitutional level is a major plank of the Charter 88 agenda that reformers have demanded for more than thirty years. A new constitution should give practical realisation to that idea. That means it should establish, throughout England, a robust and coherent system of devolved government.

Some previous constitutional proposals, such as the IPPR's 1991 draft, imagine English devolution based on twelve large regions. However, this macro-regionalism has been resisted. However, this has been resisted, especially by those interested in restoring an English national Parliament. This resistance comes partly from the sense that those regions are modern bureaucratic conveniences, and alien to the English tradition. Resistance to regionalism also comes from a concern that macro-regions (such as those based on the NUTS-1 units, previously used for elections to the European Parliament) are too big and diverse to bring government tangibly closer to people. These regions might make sense for purposes of national representation: indeed, as noted above, there is a case for the use of regional lists in elections to the House of Commons. The NUTS-1 regions are also potentially useful for national-level planning in relation to major infrastructure and development projects. However, they are too large to serve as engines of regeneration or as sites of democratic empowerment. The North West Region, to give an example, includes Manchester and Liverpool, as well as parts of rural Lancashire and Cumbria (historically Cumberland and

Westmoreland). As a unit of governance, that makes no sense. There is no close commonality of interest, nor shared civic identity.

Instead, it would be better to have a larger number of smaller units of devolution, based upon counties and city-regions. London, Bristol, Birmingham, Leeds, Sheffield, Liverpool, Newcastle, Sunderland and Gateshead, and Teesside, might all have city-region status, encompassing (perhaps with some modifications) their existing combined authority areas. The rest of the country would be divided into counties. Each of them – with the notable exception of Greater London – would be a very convenient size, having a population somewhere between that of Malta (about half a million people) and Latvia (about two million people). That is big enough to enable the devolution of substantial powers and resources, and to prevent political domination by any locally concentrated group, while still small enough to be responsive.

The aim of these devolution proposals is to give greater voice, power, recognition, and resources to all parts of England, and so to overcome both the political concentration of power in Whitehall and the gross regional economic disparities that result from decades of disempowerment, fund starvation, micromanagement, and neglect. Constitutionally entrenched devolution is a way of giving power to the northern cities, but not *only* to the northern cities. There are folks in Devon who have no desire to be governed from London, when they could just as well, in many matters affecting their daily lives, be governed from Exeter. There are people in Norfolk who would rather trust people of their own county in Norwich than those far away in Whitehall.

Implemented at county and city levels, devolution avoids the stigma associated with the word 'regionalism'. Strong counties and cities were historically part of the English system.[53] To give them constitutionally recognised roles and powers is exactly the sort of reforming restoration England needs. Devolution to counties and cities should therefore be attractive not only to Charter 88-style democratic reformers, who are concerned with the dangers of over-centralised power, but also to Burkean conservatives who see the value in 'little platoons'. If we wish to have a voice in democratic self-government, the county or city is the best training ground. If we wish to hold on to a rooted sense of place and identity – a sense of belonging somewhere, and having some control and agency over decisions affecting our lives and communities, even in a large and globalising world – then our own county or city is not a bad place to start.

Protecting local institutions from the relentless march of centralisation is key to the constitution's role in protecting English liberties and England's way of life. The draft Constitution seeks not merely to protect abstract democratic rights, like freedom of expression and the right to protest (important though these are), but also to establish sites of effective democratic empowerment, in the form of county and city authorities, and – crucially – to protect very particular, localised, traditional rights, such as the right of a community to manage its common land, or the right of lowly landfolk to walk in the woods unharried by the landlords.

This raises a wider point. It is a common assumption that a written constitution should be short and general. In fact, the opposite is often true. A short, general constitution may be too vague to provide protection and too full of easily exploited loopholes. It is in any case far more open to judicial interpretation – if one's concern is about the excess of judicial power, it is better for the constitution to say what it means and to mean what it says. A detailed, specific, even intricate, constitution is usually preferable. This is especially true in terms of decentralisation, where an attempt is being made to wrestle power away from a historically over-strong centre.

Beneath the city and county authorities there would have to be another level of local government – parish, town, district, and borough councils – to deal with micro-local issues. While the counties and cities are busy building integrated transport networks, these lower-tier local authorities would look after the park benches, litter bins, and flower beds.

The draft also preserves certain peculiar local rights. It recognises and confirms the privileges of the City of London Corporation (as distinct from Greater London, which has 'City' status under the Constitution). While the draft includes 'all modern conveniences' – in terms of democratic institutions and human rights – it is by no means an exercise in sweeping modernist minimalism. It is full of interesting, and carefully conserved, nooks and crannies: Courts Leet, Ecclesiastical Courts, Verderers of the New Forest, the Thames Conservancy, and officers of the Household. This is constitution-making in the gothic, not classical, mode.[54]

It also preserves local ceremonial offices such as those of the lord lieutenant and high sheriff. The lord lieutenant represents the monarch, hosts civic events, and has a few miscellaneous, mostly honorific, functions concerned with local military units. High sheriffs have certain residual functions concerned with the administration of justice. The only change proposed in the draft Constitution is to bring lieutenancy areas and shrieval areas into line with the county and city boundaries. The aim is to consolidate the counties and cities not just as administrative areas, nor even as political jurisdictions, but also, through the inclusion of ceremonial representation, as social communities. Just as at the national level the ceremonial office of the monarch is separate from the political office of the Prime Minister, so at the county and city level the lord lieutenant and high sheriff would be separate from the mayor as political head. Their real job is to represent, to unite, to set the right tone, and to help build a community: not only to host official visits by the King, or attend judges on circuit, but also to open the county show, to award the prize for the largest marrow, to visit urban regeneration projects, to host tea parties for volunteers in the county hall gardens, and thereby to help reknit the torn social fabric of England.

## (f) Summary

Constitution-making is like squeezing a balloon. Even good constitutional characteristics have to be balanced against one another; pressing in too hard in one place may cause it – if the whole thing does not burst – to bulge out in another. It is desirable, for example, for the constitution to establish institutions that enable swift, decisive government, which can take bold decisions and respond effectively to crises. It is also desirable to make sure that decisions are not hasty, but well considered and well advised. These two criteria, if not always exact opposites, are at least potentially in tension, and have to be carefully reconciled. In the same way, giving local communities control over their own affairs, so that they can control their own resources, use their own initiative, and develop a sense of local pride and civic virtue, is an admirable and necessary goal; but so is the creation of an effective state that can mobilise resources, overcome deep regional disparities, and drive economic redevelopment across the board. Sometimes, the middling, moderate course is best. Sometimes, it is necessary to pick a side and then try to mitigate the expected disadvantages of that choice in other ways.

A common mistake is to hyper-correct past errors. In post-war Italy, for example, a desire to prevent a return to one-party rule resulted in a constitution so full of veto points and checks and balances that the stability and effectiveness of the state were undermined. France in 1958 made the opposite mistake, hyper-correcting weak 'assembly government' by the establishment of a presidential system that was really a form of 'elective Bonapartism'.[55]

Whatever compromises are struck in the constitution-building process, it is important for the constitution to be considered as a whole system, which maintains a degree of internal coherence. The choice of electoral system for the House of Commons and the composition of the second chamber, for example, must be considered together, and not as unrelated questions. Likewise, the composition and role of the second chamber might depend upon the solution found to the territorial dispersion of power – a federal upper house is probably quite different to that of a unitary but devolved state. The rules on government formation and removal must neatly dovetail with the rules on the dissolution and the summoning of Parliament, and with the powers of the head of state. There are integrated 'package deals', not an infinite *a la carte* menu of design choices. Everything has to fit together. Piecemeal reforms, tackling one constitutional issue at a time without reference to all the others, are bound to fail.

The constitutional package outlined in this chapter would close the perilous gaps in the unwritten constitution, better protect fundamental rights, end the uncertainty caused by the erosion of constitutional conventions, and help restore proper constitutional norms. It is designed – thanks to proportional representation and other institutional reforms – to end narrow, exclusive 'winner takes all' politics, and thereby to improve the quality of governance. It also seeks to guard against corruption, manipulation, and authoritarian backsliding; to strengthen Parliament and ensure that public policies are properly debated and justified; to protect civil liberties; and to reinforce the neutrality, as well as the independence and resilience of both the judiciary the Civil Service, and bodies such as the Electoral Commission. It would strengthen processes of democratic scrutiny and accountability. It would bring government closer to the people through devolution. In short, it would be the biggest reorganisation of England's system of government since the Glorious Revolution.

Nevertheless, such a constitution is not a blueprint for a radical, novel, or alien political system. Rather, it is a prudently reformed, and lovingly restored, development of England's Westminster Model. It does not seek to throw out established institutions, nor to replace them with outlandish, untried, experimental forms of government. The democratic system established by it would be reformed in specifics, but still, in general structure, familiar. It is not a rejection of the English constitutional tradition, but the consummation of it.

The prerogatives of the Crown would be trimmed down and narrowly specified. The major conventional rules governing the exercise of its power would be codified. The power to declare war and to authorise deployments of troops, for example, would be made subject to parliamentary approval. Most of the time, however, in outward appearance, things would seem unchanged, with the King still on the throne, and the Prime Minister still in the Cabinet, still doing what monarchs and Prime Ministers respectively have done since the norms of parliamentary democracy took shape in the reign of Queen Victoria. The reformed House of Lords would no longer contain hereditary peers, but it would function much in the same way as it long has, at least since the Parliament Act 1911 and the Life Peerages Act 1958. The Speaker would be able to recall Parliament into session if petitioned by one-third of the MPs, but would still follow *Erskine May*. The nomination of the Prime Minister would be made by a vote of the House Commons, but the nominee would still go to the Palace to be formally appointed. The devolved county and city authorities would have much mightier and freer hands to do the good work of renewing England, but in ways that build upon historical institutions.

Thanks to proportional representation, there would be a greater likelihood of a coalition Government, but democracy would still chiefly depend upon political parties putting forward manifestos, contesting general elections, trying to form a Government with a majority in the House of Commons, and being ultimately responsible to the people at the next election. A Government with a working majority in the House of Commons could not unilaterally change basic constitutional rules, but it would still be able to govern, to set policy, and expect to get most ordinary legislation through Parliament.

Cumulatively, these reforms are vital, just as the corruptions, abuses, and uncertainties of the present system are cumulatively fatal. Yet there is nothing very radical, and certainly nothing untried or dangerous, in the reform agenda put forward in the draft Constitution. It is not new, original, or daring. It is long-anticipated and very *normal*. It is more in the spirit of 1689 and 1832 than of 1649 or 1789.[56]

Even so, to promote constitutional normality is a bold step in a country that has become abnormal or subnormal. We should not be naïve about the political difficulties of even this moderate constitutional change. The scale of the challenge is immense, the elite opposition to constitutional refoundation strong and deeply embedded. To build an English state that serves the public interest is to take on what R. H. Tawney once called 'the oldest and toughest plutocracy in the world'.[57]

## Notes

1  D. Erdos (2009) 'Charter 88 and the Constitutional Reform Movement: a retrospective', *Parliamentary Affairs*, Vol. 62, No. 4, pp. 537–551.
2  A. Lijphart (1999) *Patterns of Democracy* (Yale University Press).
3  I. Simpson (2022) 'Long running survey finds majority support proportional representation', Electoral Reform Society website (23 September), https://www.electoral-reform.org.uk/long-running-survey-finds-majority-support-for-proportional-representation/, accessed 11 November 2022.
4  S..Butt, E. Clery, and J. Curtice (eds) (2022) *British Social Attitudes: The 39th Report* (National Centre for Social Research), https://bsa.natcen.ac.uk/media/39477/bsa39_constitutional-reform.pdf, accessed 11 November 2022.
5  D. Cowan (2022) 'Labour Party conference backs proportional representation', Electoral Reform Society website (27 September), https://www.electoral-reform.org.uk/labour-party-conference-backs-proportional-representation/, accessed 24 October 2022.
6  House of Commons Reform Committee (2009) *Rebuilding the House* (Report of First Session 2008–9, HC 1117).
7  I. Dunt (2023) *How Westminster Works … and Why It Doesn't* (Weidenfeld and Nicolson).
8  Ibid.
9  Some thought was given to a prescribed regional balance, in the manner of the Canadian Senate, requiring a certain number of peers to be chosen from each region of England. That idea was eventually dismissed on the grounds of unnecessary complication, but three gentler inducements to greater regional representation are incorporated into the draft: (1) the Lords Appointments Commission is mandated to give due consideration to regional balance in making appointments; (2) the Chair of the National Council of Local Authorities is a member of the Commission; and (3) having held senior local government office is one of the specified qualifying criteria for appointment to the House of Lords (section 75(3)(f) of the draft Constitution in the annex).
10  House of Lords (Peerage Nominations) Bill [HL], 2023. The Bill had not been passed at the prorogation of Parliament in 2024, immediately preceding the 2024 dissolution, and made no further progress.
11  Since ministers have to be a member of one or other of the two Houses of Parliament, appointments to the Lords might continue to be a useful means of bringing external talent to the ministerial team. The Prime Minister would, in such cases, be able to nominate a person to a vacancy in the Lords, submitting their name to the Lords Appointments Commission. However, the Prime Minister would no longer be able to insist on the appointment. The Commission would have a veto, and so there would be a filter, a check, against the abuse of this power.
12  For more on constitutional amendment procedures, see: M. Böckenförde (2017) Constitutional Amendment Procedures (Constitution-Building Primer No. 10) (Stockholm: International IDEA).
13  Constitution of the Solomon Islands, section 61.
14  Constitution of Malta, article 66.
15  Constitution of Jamaica, section 49(3).
16  This means that an outgoing Prime Minister might hold on to office for a few weeks, in a caretaker capacity (see section 150 of the draft Constitution), before the coalition talks are complete, Parliament meets, and a Prime Minister is nominated by a resolution of the House of Commons. Unless the parties commit to pre-electoral coalitions, or the election result is a clear majority for one party, removal vans in Downing Street on the day after a general election would probably be a rarity. At the same time, the very long periods of government formation experienced in places like Belgium and the Netherlands would be avoided by a provision (section 107) enabling a dissolution of Parliament and another election if a Prime Minister cannot be appointed within thirty days.
17  The term 'neutral guardian', for these independent state commissions, was coined, as far as I have been able to tell, by S. A. de Smith, who identified them as a distinctly

Westminster Model contribution to constitutional design. See S. A. de Smith (1964) *The New Commonwealth and Its Constitutions* (Stevens).

18  Under Margaret Thatcher, in 1981 the Treasury was given control of Civil Service pay and promotion, as well as control over the appointment of Permanent Secretaries across Whitehall. Since the Treasury has always been 'more traditionally aligned with the City and finance than with domestic industry', this 'would prove a powerful device to spread neoclassical orthodoxy and its methods' – A. Innes (2023) *Late Soviet Britain: Why Materialist Utopias Fail* (Cambridge University Press), p. 120. The Public Service Commission is intended to be a driver of a different sort, towards a state that can *do good things*, like construct infrastructure.

19  The concept of the 'mixed constitution', combining rule of the people with rule of the best, is of ancient origin and was a staple idea of Western political thought for centuries. The Westminster Model in its mature form, marrying parliamentary democracy to meritocratic public administration, can be understood as a modern instance of this ancient idea. See J. Milbank and A. Pabst (2016) *The Politics of Virtue: Post-Liberalism and the Human Future* (Rowman and Littlefield).

20  On the concept of a constitution as a means of institutionalising public virtue, see J. Hankins (2023) *Political Meritocracy in Renaissance Italy: The Virtuous Republic of Francesco Patrizi of Siena* (Harvard University Press).

21  On the principle of preserving the publicness of the state from political capture, see S. E. Bagg (2024) *The Dispersion of Power: A Critical Realist Theory of Democracy* (Oxford University Press).

22  T. J. Cartwright (1975) *Royal Commissions and Departmental Committees in Britain: A Case-Study in Institutional Adaptiveness and Public Participation in Government* (London: Hodder and Stoughton).

23  C. Talbot (2023) Royal Commissions Part One – 'A subject wrapped in a haze of common knowledge'?, Constitution Society website (28 July), https://consoc.org.uk/royal-commissions-part-one/, accessed 6 May 2025.

24  C. Parkinson (2007) *Bills of Rights and Decolonisation: The Emergence of Domestic Human Rights Instruments in Britain's Overseas Territories* (Oxford University Press).

25  J. Laws (2021) *The Constitutional Balance* (Hart).

26  See: T. Benn and A. Hood (1993) *Common Sense: A New Constitution for Britain* (Hutchinson); I. McLean (2009) *What's Wrong with the British Constitution?* (Oxford University Press); and I. Ward (2004) *The English Constitution: Myths and Realities* (Hart).

27  https://www.royal.uk/succession, accessed 1 February 2023.

28  P. Manow (2010) *In the King's Shadow: The Political Anatomy of Democratic Representation* (Polity Press), pp. 32–33.

29  This idea of the monarch as the keystone of the arch of a republican state is no novelty. It has roots in English constitutional history. The first Statute of Westminster (1275) opened with, 'The King wills and commands, That the Peace of holy Church and of the Land, be well kept and maintained in all Points, and that common Right be done to all, as well Poor as rich, without respect of Persons.' In other words, the king's official will was not to be the master of the people, but to be protector of the peace, and upholder of the law.

30  On the 'metaphysical constitution' of England, and its distinction from the 'mechanical constitution', see W. E. Bulmer (2025) 'Could a constitution capture the essence of Englishness?, *Seen and Unseen*, 21 April, available at https://www.seenandunseen.com/could-constitution-capture-essence-englishness, accessed 13 May 2025.

31  C. Smith (2005) 'The Church of England: some historical reflections on a constitutional conundrum', *Northern Ireland Legal Quarterly*, Vol. 56, No. 3, pp. 394–420, quote at p. 395.

32  W. Temple (1984) *Christianity and Social Order* (Shepheard-Walwyn).

33  Church of England Commission for Urban Priority Areas (1985) *Faith in the City* (Church House Publishing).

34  House of Bishops (2015) *Who Is My Neighbour? A Letter from the House of Bishops to the People and Parishes of the Church of England for the General Election 2015* (Church House Publishing).

35 C. Cox, et al. (2015) *Magna Carta Unravelled: The Case for Christian Freedoms Today* (Wilberforce Publications).

36 G. Scrivener (2022) 'Compassion – how Christianity made our moral world', Unapologetic 2/4, YouTube, posted 17 October 2022, https://www.youtube.com/watch?v=vp4i6SOd8XI, accessed 3 November 2022.

37 P. Duncan, C. Aguilar García, and L. Swan (2022) 'Census 2021 in charts: Christianity now minority religion in England and Wales', *The Guardian*, 29 November 2022, https://www.theguardian.com/uk-news/2022/nov/29/census-2021-in-charts-christianity-now-minority-religion-in-england-and-wales, accessed 26 January 2023.

38 B. Omrani (2025) *God is an Englishman: Christianity and the Creation of England* (Forum).

39 T. Holland (2020) *Dominion: The Making of the Western World* (Abacus); G. Scrivener (2022) *The Air We Breathe: How We All Came to Believe in Freedom, Kindness, Progress, and Equality* (Good Book Company); R. McLaughlin (2021) *The Secular Creed: Engaging Five Contemporary Claims* (Gospel Coalition).

40 'The English church shall be free.'

41 The Crown Nominations Commission, for the appointment of diocesan bishops, consists of the two archbishops, six members elected by the clergy and laity of the diocese (chosen by its Vacancy in See committee), and six members elected by the General Synod. For the appointment of the Archbishop of Canterbury, the Commission has a slightly broader basis, including five representatives from the global Anglican communion; the Prime Minister appoints the chair, and the Prime Minister's Appointments Secretary is a non-voting member. As long as the principle of representation of the clergy and laity of the is maintained, the precise composition of the nominating body is a matter of prudence and expedience. These details are not, therefore, written into the draft Constitution, but are left for the General Synod to determine, and to revise from time to time.

42 My personal preference would be to go one step further: to repeal the Appointment of Bishops Act 1533, and to restore the ancient constitution of the Church, according to which bishops should be freely elected by the clergy and laity of each diocese. In practical terms, that would mean election by the Diocesan Synod, by the College of Canons of the cathedral of the relevant episcopal see, or by some electoral body combining both of these. I am not, however, sufficiently sure of my ground to write this into the draft Constitution. The proviso to subsection (3) of section 165 is broad enough to enable such reform in future, but without imposing it.

43 W. B. Littlejohn (2015) *Richard Hooker: A Companion to His Life and Work* (Cascade Books), pp. 158–159.

44 There are some signs that this might already be happening, with a resurgence of Christianity among 'Gen-Z'. See R. McAleer and R. Barwood-Symmons (2025) *The Quiet Revival* (Bible Society).

45 B. Groom (2023) *Northerners: A History, from the Ice Age to the Present Day* (Harper North).

46 D. Jackson (2021) *The Northumbrians: North-East England and Its People: A New History* (C. Hurst and Co.).

47 A. Stansbury, D. Turner, and E. Balls (2023) 'How to tackle the UK's regional economic inequality: focus on STEM, transport, and innovation', Centre for Economic Policy Research, https://cepr.org/voxeu/columns/how-tackle-uks-regional-economic-inequality-focus-stem-transport-and-innovation, last accessed 22 April 2025.

48 OECD (2020) *OECD Regions and Cities at a Glance 2020* (OECD Publishing), https://doi.org/10.1787/959d5bao-en, last accessed 22 April 2025.

49 M. Johns and H. Hutt (2023) *The State of the North 2023: Looking Out to Level Up* (Institute for Public Policy Research (IPPR) North).

50 A. Fazackerly and T. Helm (2023) 'Children without a bed aren't going to be interested in school: can Britain's north–south education divide be repaired?', *The Guardian*, 27 August.

51 J. S. Mill (1861) *Considerations on Representative Government*.

52 P. Macfadyen (2017) *Flatpack Democracy: A DIY Guide to Creating Independent Politics* (Eco-Logic Books).

53 M. Loughlin (2003) 'The demise of local government', in V. Bogdanor (ed.), *The British Constitution* (Oxford University Press), pp. 521–556.

54 Conservators are a little-known institution, except perhaps by the those familiar with the up-river Thames, but they are vital in certain pockets of England like Dartmoor or the Malvern Hills. Often consisting of a mixture of elected, co-opted, *ex-officio* and nominated members, representing various local interests and stakeholders, conservators manage common land and rivers for the public benefit. Verders' courts have jurisdiction over royal forests, dealing with such matters as grazing rights.

55 On the contrasting experiences of constitutional 'over-correction' in Italy and France, see R. Hague, M. Harrop, and S. Breslin (1992) *Comparative Government and Politics: An Introduction* (3rd edn) (Macmillan), p. 267.

56 The 1689 Glorious Revolution and the 1832 Reform Act were moderate, reformist, settlements. The 1649 execution of King Charles I and the 1789 French Revolution were violent breaks with the past, which attempted to overthrow, rather than to reform and improve, the established order.

57 E. M. Passes (1994) *The Christian Socialism of R. H. Tawney* (PhD thesis: London School of Economics), p. 123.

# 6

# Constitution-building and the way forward

## (a) Design of constitution-building processes

Democratic constitutions do not come down on tablets of stone. Most are produced through a process of discussion and negotiation – 'arguing and bargaining' – that enables an acceptable constitutional settlement to be reached.[1] The text of the constitution is but the record – the icon in writing – of that settlement. It is no coincidence that the first proper draft of a written constitution for England, arising from the Leveller movement during the Civil Wars, styled itself 'An Agreement of the People' – because that is precisely what a constitution is and should be: a statement of what has been agreed, among the people or their representatives, as the common foundation of the state.

The lack of a written constitution is a consequence of our never having reached such an agreement. There was an inter-elite settlement after the Glorious Revolution, but at no point have the people – not just the men of many acres and those in the Funds – agreed to the foundational rules of how we are to govern ourselves. As Thomas Paine put it more than two centuries ago, 'the people have yet a constitution to form'.[2]

'The people' is an over-loaded term. Capitalised for constitutional purposes as 'We the People', it conveys the idea of a single, unitary, undifferentiated mass, with one united will. In reality, however, 'the people' is made up of you, me, and millions of other persons, all with their own identities and relationships. All nations are complex and composite, made up of people from different regions, religions, sexes, classes, and occupations, with diverse outlooks and desires. These diversities may be represented through different parties, as well as by the various civil society groups – trades unions, professional associations, religious organisations, and so on – which together make up the warp and weft of the nation's fabric. Enduring and effective constitutions incorporate that complexity; they accommodate it, recognise it, and protect it.

Constitutions cannot therefore represent only one voice or ideology, when democracy necessarily speaks in polyphony. Universal assent is not realistic, but there should be a sufficient consensus around the constitution – a broad agreement and a general consent, among the main parties and major social groups – such that the constitution reflects the nation's common ground, its centre of gravity.

This process of consensus-finding and consent-seeking cannot be by-passed: a constitution is not viable unless it is acceptable. At the same time, however, we cannot wait for consensus and consent to emerge spontaneously. They must be sought, encouraged, and built. That usually calls for a deliberate and structured constitution-building process, and dedicated institutions where the hard work of hammering out a constitutional settlement can take place.

Countries around the world have deployed a variety of mechanisms and processes for the purpose of reaching a constitutional settlement. These can include directly elected, indirectly elected, appointed, and randomly selected bodies. There can be parliamentary committees, expert commissions, public consultations, and referendums. Two or more of these different elements may be combined, each being deployed at a different stage of the process in order to achieve the right balance of necessary characteristics: inclusion, legitimation, expertise, participation, deliberation, decision, and efficiency. A brief sketch of a few historical cases will illustrate some ways in which these mechanisms and processes can be interwoven to reach a democratic constitutional settlement.

In Kenya, the drafting of the 2010 constitution began (or rather, it might be more accurate to say, resumed, since it followed on from an earlier, failed process) with the passage by Kenya's Parliament of the Constitution of Kenya Review Act. This give a statutory foundation to the process and meant that the momentum of reform was kept up. The main constitution-making body was small, appointed, and expert: the Committee of Experts had just nine members, one-third of whom were international advisors. The Committee did not work from a blank piece of paper; it built upon drafts which had been extensively discussed in the previous failed process. It was further guided by an extensive process of public consultation on contentious issues. However, since the Committee of Experts lacked the political inclusion and legitimacy needed to make final decisions, its draft was – as required by the Constitution of Kenya Review Act – handed over to the politicians, in the form of a par-liamentary select committee. That committee dealt with the draft in secret, engaging in tense inter-elite political bargaining, even going so far as to exclude the Committee of Experts from its meetings. Many of the changes made by the select committee sought to undo the Committee of Experts' proposals, and to weaken proposed restraints on power. To get a final draft required some hard bargaining, and at times acrimonious exchanges, between the parliamentarians and the experts. Participation was broadened again at the end of the process, when the final draft was submitted to the people in a referendum.[3] The fact that there would be a referendum provided a constraint to the whole process: the Committee of Experts and the parliamentary select committee knew that they had to come up with a solution acceptable to the public.

In Spain, for the constitution of 1978, the first major step was to adopt the Law of Political Reform, which set the structure and trajectory of the process. To achieve legitimacy and defeat spoilers, this law was submitted to a referendum. Then followed the direct election of a Constituent Congress. The Constituent Congress delegated much of the drafting work to a parliamentary committee of just seven MPs. Crucially, however, those MPs represented a balance of the political movements in the country; although small in number, the committee reflected a broad range of political support. The result of this committee's work was then put to a second referendum, by which the new constitution was approved. In other words, while a handful of people ultimately held the pen, they held it only by virtue of an election, and only at the specific prior authorisation, and subject to the final approbation, of the people.[4]

The process must be designed to succeed. So many constitutional change processes just run out of steam, or else they go through all the preliminary motions – appointing a commission, conducting education and outreach activities to raise awareness and encourage engagement, holding public consultations, hearing evidence, and writing a report – only for the recommendations of that report to be ignored by the Government. That has been the fate of many constitutional reform processes in the Caribbean. That is why mooring the process in an enabling statute is so important: it can place a statutory duty on the Government to put recommendations to a vote, rather than allowing them to be filed away and forgotten. Quite often, constitution-making bodies confront Governments with unwelcome recommendations that would limit the Government's abuses of power, or close loopholes that the Government enjoys exploiting. In these situations, it is very tempting for the Government just to drag its feet and try to run down the clock to the next election. Timelines set down in the legislation can help to avoid that, and instead to keep the momentum up, and the pressure on.

It is also wise to avoid processes that are too complicated, or that include so many different voices and stages that it is hard to reach agreement. For example, some countries try to balance expertise and inclusion by creating a small, expert Constitutional Commission, with responsibility for drafting a new constitution, and a larger, more inclusive Constitutional Conference, with responsibility for debating and approving it. That can be a recipe for disaster. Members of the second body, having not drafted the constitution, can turn against it. They want to get their oar in. Since they were not involved in the negotiations and compromises that are embodied in the draft, they try to reopen questions that should have been settled, and the whole thing can fall apart.

This also applies when Parliament, having been excluded from the early stages of the process, is brought in near the end to approve a draft that has been negotiated elsewhere. At that point, Parliament can only either endorse what has been done by others, or else wreck it. The way around this is to ensure that the parliamentary leaders, ideally from both sides of the House, are brought in to the process from the beginning; if they have been involved in negotiating and producing the draft, they are less likely to want to kill it.

## (b) Constitution-building in England

It is well to think about constitution-building in the abstract, or in comparative terms, but can we really imagine such a thing in an English context? If so, what sort of process might be suitable?

Received wisdom is that constitutional change comes only after independence from colonial rule, defeat in a war, the end of a civil war, or some similarly cataclysmic collapse of former institutions.[5] However, states can – and often do – engage in constitutional change in less than catastrophic circumstances.[6] In 2023 and 2024, I was called upon to assist, however marginally, with constitutional change processes in Barbados, Belize, Saint Lucia, and Trinidad and Tobago, all of which are relatively stable and functioning democracies, but in need of constitutional reform to improve their institutions. If those Caribbean nations – and many more besides, from Luxembourg to Sweden – can undertake constitutional reform in relatively favourable circumstances, why can't we?

Given the general lack of public knowledge about constitutional matters, and the lingering reluctance of the main parties and much of officialdom even to consider a written constitution, we would have to start at the beginning – creating a momentum for change with a campaign, led by a civil society coalition, making the case for a new constitution.

Existing civil society and campaigning groups with an interest in political and constitutional reform should, as far as possible, be brought into that coalition, but it would probably take a new campaigning body, with a core mandate to secure a written constitution, to drive it. The aim of this campaign would be to put a written constitution onto the agenda, setting out the case and vision for constitutional refoundation. Its primary goal would be to make one, at least, of the major parties sign up, in its manifesto, to a Constitutional Transition Act. If that can be achieved, then Horace's dictum applies: 'He who has begun is half finished'. From there, it is mostly a matter of sustaining the political will to drive the change through once that party is in Government.

Between the constitutional vandalism of the recent Conservative Party and the constitutional complacency of the Labour Party,[7] getting such a commitment from one of the major parties will be the biggest hurdle. Nevertheless, it is not necessarily insurmountable. After extensive discussion in academia, in civil society, and within political parties, a sufficient consensus on the agenda for reform was achieved, at least across the broad centre-left, in the mid-1990s. This enabled the Labour Party to make substantial (if vague) commitments to constitutional change in its 1997 general election manifesto, and to achieve some, although by no means all, of that agenda once in office. That experience gives us some hope, if a similar unity and momentum can be built, for a future constitutional refoundation movement that will be able to finish the job.

The publication of *A New Britain* by the Labour Party in 2022 shows that there is some chance to engage Labour on constitutional issues, but also confirms the difficulty of convincing the party to rise above piecemeal tinkering – and British nationalism – in favour of a more coherent settlement. The Liberal Democrats, the Greens, the Scottish National Party, and Plaid Cymru are likely to be more receptive, but they must not be allowed to claim it as their exclusive domain. Being a cross-party campaign, the reform movement must try to cultivate support among moderate Conservatives who see that things cannot go on as they are, and who wish to distance themselves from, and defeat, the authoritarian populist right.

Constitution-building is tricky. More often than not, it fails. Pro-reform alliances can be strained by the day-to-day reality of Government, and the momentum and unity needed to sustain a constitution-building process can be lost. Differences over small points can be played up for partisan or personal advantage. The experience of Sri Lanka after 2015, where momentum for constitutional reform was squandered in bickering between coalition partners, provides a salutary warning.[8] So it is vital to be ready to seize the moment with a clear plan of action, to act fast, and then to keep going without being sidetracked.

This calls for effective leadership – someone who can mobilise public support for the process, and lead people gently but firmly through it, while being a consensus-builder and a reconciler. If constitution-making is a process, then it needs to be project managed and needs a project leader. There is no avoiding the fact that the first requirement is a Prime Minister who has a commitment to, and mandate for, reform. The absence of such a Prime Minister from the political scene at the moment should not dissuade people, however, from taking initial steps. Publishing a draft Constitution for public debate, to help distil and present the issues, and to show how it might be done, is one such initial step. Lord Norton argued that three conditions must be met if constitutional reform is to succeed: leadership, a window of opportunity, and coherent set of proposals.[9] We must wait for leadership to find its window of opportunity, but in the meantime we can develop, and build consensus around, a coherent set of proposals.

A Government seeking to bring about constitutional renovation should proceed by introducing a Constitutional Transition Bill. If passed, the resulting Act would provide a statutory basis for the constitution-building process, setting its scope, direction, and timing. It would establish the constitution-making body, and would determine its composition, its powers, the terms of office and remuneration of its members, how its chair is to be chosen, and so forth. That constitution-making body would be able to drive the process, keeping up the momentum because it has its own statutory duties to fulfil, independently of shifting Government priorities.

The Constitutional Transition Act might also prescribe the terms of reference for that body, and thereby set the agenda – and perhaps the boundaries – for reform early in the process. If a political consensus on the desired substance of the new constitution has already been reached in the pre-legislative stage, then that can be incorporated into the Act, making the process of decision-making so much easier.

### (c) The constitution-making body

One central issue to be resolved at an early stage of planning the process is the type and composition of the constitution-making body to be employed. Some countries, such as India after independence, South Africa after the end of apartheid, and France and Italy after the Second World War,[10] have used elected Constitutional Assemblies for this purpose.

A directly elected Constitutional Assembly would be the most radically democratic option, especially if elected by means of proportional representation, which would break the residual two-party duopoly and enable a broad range of interests and options to be heard. Elections to a Constitutional Assembly would give parties an opportunity to set out their pitch on a range of constitutional issues, and would allow the public to debate, and to give their support to, these proposals. It would then be the function of the Constitutional Assembly to reach agreement on, and to adopt, the new constitution on behalf of the people.

While not unheard of in Commonwealth countries, elected Constitutional Assemblies are relatively rare. It is hard to imagine that a newly elected Government, fresh from a victory at the polls and with a majority in the House of Commons, would risk throwing that position away by calling for the election of a Constitutional Assembly that would, even temporarily, replace Parliament. It is also hard to imagine a directly elected body, created solely for constitution-making, sitting alongside Parliament, such that parliamentary leaders are forced to share the glory and the limelight with another set of elected representatives. Aside from these practical and political barriers, Constitutional Assemblies reflect a theory of 'constituent power', rooted in popular sovereignty, that has always been stronger in the French than the British tradition.[11]

Fortunately, there exists in the Westminster system of government a type of body perfectly adapted to constitution-building: the royal commission. As already noted, a royal commission is a body appointed to investigate a problem, to consider evidence from the public or from certain interested parties, and to issue a report with recommendations that can form the basis for legislation. Royal commissions have already been used to consider stand-alone elements of constitutional change – such as the Wakeham Commission on reform of the House of Lords, which reported in 2000.

A Constitutional Commission would be a sort of 'super royal commission'. It might differ from other royal commissions in three respects. First, as mentioned above, it should have a statutory basis in the Constitutional Transition Act – an Act regulating the whole constitution-making process. Second, its membership should be not merely expert, but also sufficiently politically inclusive, on the one hand, to drive the project forward, and, on the other, to give legitimacy to its result. Third, rather than merely issuing a report and making general recommendations, the Commission should be required to produce a complete draft Constitution, which can then be debated and adopted. Otherwise, it is too easy for the Government to ignore its recommendations. Everything must be designed to keep up the focus and the momentum, and to prevent inertia from thwarting necessary reforms.

In terms of composition, it is not easy to prescribe an exact list of groups to be represented in the membership of the Constitutional Commission, or the proportion of seats to be allocated to them. Such details would have to be laid down by the Constitutional Transition Act, based on the Government's analysis of the political situation at the time, and perhaps on inter-party negotiations when during the drafting and passage of the Constitutional Transition Bill.

In general terms, however, it might include senior Members of Parliament from all sides of the House, including a critical mass of front-benchers who are able to make deals and carry their supporters with them. Thus, although not elected – and not in opposition to, or competition with, Parliament – the Constitutional Commission should reflect, at least, the breadth of the pro-reform coalition. To these might be added a sturdy cohort of academic and other experts (who will form the basis of the drafting and technical committees, to be discussed below), as well as a sprinkling of suitable persons representing local government, and of the economic, professional, religious, and civil society groups that make up the fabric of the nation, to broaden the base of participation, support, and legitimacy.[12]

If Scotland, Wales, and Northern Ireland are still in the Union, their representatives must also be included in the Constitutional Commission, even if permitted to vote only on those matters directly affecting their own status. Similar consideration might be given, if the Commission's terms of reference envisage a United Kingdom on the lines proposed in this book, to the Crown Dependencies and self-governing British Overseas Territories.

The selection of expert members of the Commission is of vital importance. It would be supremely beneficial to choose people who are familiar with written constitutions in other Westminster Model contexts, not those used only to working in the absence of a written constitution. Experts on the constitutions of Ireland, the Indian subcontinent, the Anglophone Caribbean, and other Commonwealth countries would be particularly valuable. Some of these might serve as members of the Commission, others as technical advisors in support of the Commission's work.

No less important is the selection of the chair. Here there are two main approaches. First, the chair can be a worthy figurehead, who fronts the project, but does not take much of an active role in its deliberations. Such a person might be a respected elder statesperson, with cross-party appeal, who is very good at smiling, shaking hands, and patting on backs. Their role is to bring people together, to keep the goodwill flowing, and smooth over difficulties by well timed dinner invitations. Second, the chair could be the minister responsible for constitutional affairs, giving the Government a very involved, hands-on role in the work of the Commission. The role of the latter type of chair is to drive the constitutional process to a successful conclusion.

I have seen both these approaches in Commonwealth countries. Either approach can work, provided that the chair understands how to play their role, and provided that the other crucial parts of the organisation – such as the head of the secretariat, discussed below – are able to fill the gaps. On balance, however, letting the minister responsible for the constitutional reform process serve as chair of the Commission is probably the better option. Reflecting on recent Caribbean processes, I have argued elsewhere for 'a government-led process, in which the constitutional review body is a small body of experts and advisors whose leadership is fused with the government, ultimately under government direction and used to inform and canvass support for government policies in the form of a constitutional amendment bill'.[13] This way of proceeding 'seems best calculated to get the reform passed, if the government's will remains steadfast'.[14] It is important to remember, however, that a Government-led process is not the same as a Government-dominated process, and that a real and sincere attempt should be made both to consult widely and to build a cross-party consensus.

The Constitutional Transition Act should set out the terms of reference of the Constitutional Commission. The more clarity, precision, and agreement there is at that early stage, the better. For example, if a Government has fore-made plans for a constitutional refoundation project, which have been set out in its manifesto, and if those plans are backed by public opinion and major interest groups, and endorsed by Parliament in setting the Constitutional Commission's terms of reference, then the main role of the Commission would be to turn these political agreements into a constitutional draft. It would also enable the Constitutional Commission to have a leaner composition. This was the case, for example, when Malaya (later Malaysia) adopted its constitution in 1956. The Constitutional Commission for Malaya was a technical body, headed by Lord Reid and made up of Commonwealth constitutional experts. The Commission did not need to be politically representative, because its only duty was to give effect, in legal form, to arrangements which had already been agreed in substance by the Malayan political actors.[15]

That will be the neatest and quickest way of proceeding, and – if the political will behind it is there – the way most likely to succeed in getting a new constitution. The problem, however, is that it really does depend on those pre-agreements being made, and genuinely so. Ramming it through without such prior agreement might end up with a constitution on paper, but it might suffer from a lack of legitimacy, political acceptance, and public endorsement, which increases the risk of failure in the longer term.

If it is not possible to reach such detailed agreement before its terms of reference are set, then the Commission will have to do more political work, finding and sealing such agreements, before it gets down to drafting – and either the composition of the Commission must reflect this, or else there must be other means for the Commission to get a political decision on contentious issues.

The Constitutional Commission should have the ability to delegate initial drafting to a drafting committee, which might consist of its political leaders and the expert members, assisted by the technical advisors. This committee would prepare an initial draft for discussion and modification by the body as a whole. Getting to a draft – giving the body something solid to chew on, rather than going around in circles with generalities – is vital to driving the process forward and producing a satisfactory outcome.

The Constitutional Commission would need a well staffed secretariat. The choice of the head of the secretariat is a crucial one. As noted above, there is a kind of double-act between the chair of the Commission and the head of the secretariat. If the chair is a gentle shepherd of consensus, the head of the secretariat must crack the whip and see that the work is done before momentum dissipates. If the chair is the driver, the head of the secretariat must act as a balance and a restraint, and ensure that consensus is maintained.

Finally, it would help if some respected celebrities with the status of 'national treasures' could be involved as public spokespersons for the Commission. A well respected actor or comedian might be worth more, in terms of reaching the public, than any number of front-bench politicians.[16]

England is a constitutionally illiterate country. Most people, having never lived in a properly constituted state, have little idea of what a constitution is or does. There is a massive civic education task to undertake. To remedy this, the Constitutional Transition Act should place a statutory duty upon the Constitutional Commission, through its secretariat, to conduct civic education activities at every stage of the process. Crucially, the conversation should be two-way. Besides its duty to educate the public, the Constitutional Commission should also be required to consult the public, either in general, or at least in respect of specific contentious issues. The substantive value of public consultation is debatable, and its need and scope vary depending on the degree of political consensus already existing at the start of the process, and on the extent of popular mobilisation around specific constitutional issues. Most people do not have well developed views on, say, the exact mechanism for the dissolution of Parliament. The general public are better able to describe the symptoms than to prescribe the cure. Yet, as the Constitutional Commission would be a physician to the body-politic, it needs to listen well to the patient's ailments, and know the patient's history, if it is to find a cure that will be accepted, not rejected.

There is also often some intangible benefit to be gained from the process of public consultation, regardless of the result. It brings people into the constitutional discussion and takes that discussion out to the people, which all helps to build a sense of public ownership over the resulting constitution. Think of it as the Constitutional Commission's 'bedside manner', putting the country at ease.

There is, in a broader context, some interest in using citizens' assemblies, with randomly selected memberships, as a means of gathering and processing public views on constitutional issues. Citizens' assemblies are a democratic innovation with a lot of potential. They have shown their worth when they have been able to focus on the consideration of specific, thorny, constitutional issues, such as the review of constitutional rules on abortion and same-sex marriage in Ireland.

Citizens' assemblies are not, however, a magic bullet. It is doubtful whether a citizens' assembly with a randomly selected membership would be able to function as the primary constitution-making body. The problem is one of negotiating ability: a citizens' assembly speaks for itself and its randomly selected members, who, though supposed to reflect society, have no mandate, no responsibility to constituents, and no ability to bind others to their conclusions. It is not a forum in which the complicated trade-offs and decisions necessary to draft a complete constitution can be hammered out.

Furthermore, the demand for a body made up of randomly selected 'ordinary citizens' often comes from a desire to exclude the tainted and discredited established elites – politicians, political parties, stuffy old duffers with plummy accents – from the process. While perhaps laudable, this is impracticable. As the experience of Iceland shows, attempts to exclude the existing elite or establishment only succeed in turning them against the process. It is much better to include them in it, and to encourage them – by their involvement in it – to reach compromises by which they are then bound.

Of course, public consultation does not absolve the Government and the Constitutional Commission from doing the hard work of reaching a constitutional settlement and turning it into a draft. Difficult political compromises will have to be made, sometimes behind closed doors. There will be moments when the results of public consultations, particularly if they point to unworkable

155

or irreconcilable conclusions, will have to be set aside. The Constitutional Commission might have to balance the findings of public consultation, or the findings of a citizens' assembly, against their own judgment and the expert advice available to them.

### (d) Approval and adoption of the constitution

The Constitutional Transition Act, in addition to establishing the Constitutional Commission, setting its terms of reference, its budget and its timelines, and creating its secretariat, also needs to prescribe the process by which the new constitution is to be approved and adopted. It is good to reach agreement on these mechanisms at an early stage, so that there is less scope for procedural wrangling and derailment later on.

If there were to be an elected Constitutional Assembly, it might be sufficient, from the point of view of legitimacy, for that body to enact the new constitution without any further ado. That is how the Indian and South African constitutions were adopted. South Africa had an interesting provision whereby enacting the constitution required a two-thirds majority in the Constitutional Assembly, but if a two-thirds majority could not be reached, a referendum would have been held to approve the constitution. There was therefore an incentive to reach a sufficient consensus, in order to avoid the uncertain prospect of a referendum; at the same time, however, a minority could not veto things forever, because the referendum is a potential tie-breaker.

In the more likely context of a smaller, appointed, Constitutional Commission, it might make sense to require a two-thirds majority of the Commission to endorse the draft Constitution. If the composition of the Commission is well designed, such that known 'spoilers', likely to object for the sake of it, are minimised, and if its terms of reference are clear, it should not be impossible to reach such a sufficient consensus.

However, such a Constitutional Commission would not have the public legitimacy to actually enact the draft. For that, the approval of Parliament would be needed. It is vital, therefore, that Parliament be kept on board during the process – hence the need for front-benchers to be members of the Commission, ideally for the responsible minister to chair it, and for the terms of reference of the Commission to have been approved by Parliament in advance.

It is also necessary to prevent Parliament, at this late stage in the process, from duplicating the Constitutional Commission's work, or from picking apart finely negotiated solutions that the Commission has already found. To this end, the Constitutional Transition Act should either require the draft to be voted upon by Parliament *in toto*, or at least to set high procedural thresholds (e.g. a two-thirds majority) for any change introduced at the parliamentary stage. If Parliament does not approve the Constitution within the time, or by the majority, required by the Constitutional Transition Act, then under the terms of that Act it might be put directly to the people. The Constitutional Transition Act would provide the legal authority needed to bring the Constitution into effect, but it is worth remembering that the new Constitution itself would not be an Act of Parliament. It would be above all Acts of Parliament. Once the Constitution has come into effect, Diceyan parliamentary sovereignty would be abolished. The old pre-constitutional sovereign Parliament would be no more. The new Parliament, created by the Constitution, would be bound by that Constitution, except to the extent that the Constitution may be amended.

If there is a chance of the constitutional draft going to a referendum, the drafters must carefully weed out 'killer clauses'. 'Killer clauses' are particular provisions that might be relatively insignificant in themselves, and which are only a small part of the overall constitutional settlement, but nevertheless risk discrediting the whole draft and can become a pretext for mobilising voters against it. In Kenya, abortion was very nearly a killer clause: the Roman Catholic Church, having supported the constitution-making process up to that point, came close to using its influence to defeat the new constitution over that issue. It is generally better, if possible, for the drafters to reach a compromise that Parliament can accept on all such matters, rather than run the risk of a referendum.

The process thus outlined – civil society mobilisation, political leadership, a Constitutional Transition Act, detailed terms of reference, a balanced and credible Constitutional Commission that includes front-bench political leadership, public education and public consultation, the development of a draft, and the adoption of that draft either by Parliament or, if need be, by the people – is not perfect or flawless. Other ways of achieving the same goals could also be imagined. It does, nevertheless, seem to be the best, most practical and reliable, means of getting a proper constitution.

This process would give the English people the right to frame a constitution for themselves, through fairly robust democratic processes. It would respond to the concerns of those, like Professor Jeff King, who make the democratic case for constitutionalism – namely, that the ground rules by which we are governed should be framed by the people.[17] Symbolically and psychologically, as well as institutionally, the constitution-making process would be an opportunity for an old country to have the conversations about itself that it has not had for a very long time, and to make a fresh start.

Even if the content of the resulting constitution is Burkean – preserving much of the inherited Westminster Model, the monarchy, the House of Lords, and the Church of England, and owing more to the Whig spirit of 1689 than the radical spirit of 1649 – the *process* would fulfil the dream of the Levellers and Thomas Paine. It would be an exercise of popular, sovereign, constituent power that casts off the despised 'Norman yoke' and makes the English a free people, living under their own constitutional law, at last.[18]

## Notes

1 Elster, J. (1995) 'Forces and mechanisms in constitution making', *Duke Law Journal*, Vol. 45. pp. 364–396, https://scholarship.law.duke.edu/cgi/viewcontent.cgi?article=3297&context=dlj, accessed 11 November 2022.

2 T. Paine (1791) *The Rights of Man*, https://www.gutenberg.org/files/3742/3742-h/3742-h. htm, accessed 25 October 2022.

3 C. Murray (2022) 'Making and remaking Kenya's constitution', in T. Ginsburg and S. Bisarya (eds), *Constitution Makers on Constitution Making* (Cambridge University Press), pp. 37–76.

4 V. Ferreres Comella (2013) *The Constitution of Spain: A Contextual Analysis* (Hart).

5 J. Elster (1995) 'Forces and mechanisms in the constitution-making process', *Duke Law Journal*, Vol. 45, No. 2, pp. 364–396.

6 S. Bisarya and A. K. Abebe (forthcoming) 'Fixing the roof while the sun is shining: constitutional reform for democratic resilience of the judiciary', in *Annual Review of Constitution Building 2024* (International IDEA).

7 I have friends who might put it the other way around, accusing Labour of constitutional vandalism, and the Conservatives of constitutional complacency. Perhaps the difference between us is that they think that Blair–Brown reforms were the beginning of the end because they went too far, whereas I think those reforms were the beginning of the end because they did not go far enough.

8 A. Cats-Baril (2020) 'Coalitions for constitutional change: Sri Lanka's constitutional crisis and the Maldives' 2018 elections', in *Annual Review of Constitution Building: 2018* (International IDEA).

9 P. Norton (2000) 'Reforming Parliament in the United Kingdom', *Journal of Legislative Studies*, Vol. 6, No. 3, pp. 1–14.

10 J. C. Adams and P. Barile (1966) *The Government of Republican Italy* (2nd edn) (Houghton Mifflin); P. Williams (1958) *Politics in Post-war France* (2nd edn) (Longmans, Green and Co.).

11 W. E. Bulmer (2024) 'The constitution of liberties: polycentric constitutionalism and the Westminster Export Model', in D. Thunder and D. Paniagua (eds), *Polycentric Governance and the Good Society: A Normative and Philosophical Investigation* (Lexington Books).

12 The Scottish Constitutional Convention, which developed the devolution settlement in the 1990s, consisted of partisan representatives from the parties that chose to participate – Labour, the Liberal Democrats, and the Scottish Green Party – but also included representatives of so-called 'civic Scotland', such as local authorities, the Scottish churches, the Scottish Trades Union Congress, and FSB Scotland (the Federation of Small Businesses).

13 W. E. Bulmer (2024) 'Constitutional reform in the Commonwealth Caribbean', in *Annual Review of Constitution Building 2023* (International IDEA), p. 17.

14 Ibid.

15 A. Harding (2022) *The Constitution of Malaysia: A Contextual Analysis* (2nd edn) (Hart).

16 The two names that came first to my mind – merely as illustrative of their public standing and 'national treasure' status, without making any assumptions about the willingness of these particular individuals – were Dame Judy Dench and Sir Stephen Fry. Someone of that calibre, anyway.

17 J. King (2019) 'The democratic case for a written constitution', *Current Legal Problems*, Vol. 72, No. 1, pp. 1–36.

18 While the Norman yoke was indeed heavy, it is important not to get too far into the myth of Anglo-Saxon freedom. As Marc Morris points out, Anglo-Saxon society was also 'unequal, patriarchal, persecuting and theocratic' – M. Morris (2021) *The Anglo-Saxons: A History of the Beginnings of England* (Penguin), pp. 5–6. So although I use the term 'Normans' to refer to the public-school-educated British ruling class, and to all those who own the land and run the country, I hope the reader recognises that this Norman versus Saxon imagery is being used only metaphorically, as a rhetorical device to critique England's persistent class-based inequalities of wealth, power, status, and opportunity. Even so, Rudyard Kipling's words read true: 'The Saxon is not like us Normans. His manners are not so polite. / But he never means anything serious till he talks about justice and right' ('Norman and Saxon A.D. 1100').

# 7

# Good government and political culture

## (a) How constitutions support good government

Constitution-building is not a decorative exercise. The aim of adopting a constitution is not to have a document that looks impressive on paper; it is to set the state upon solid ground, so that it can better serve the common good and advance the public interest. As Sir Ivor Jennings put it, 'A constitution is but a means to an end, and the end is good government'.[1]

The basic Aristotelean distinction between good and bad government is that good government governs in the public interest, for the common good, while bad government governs in the private interests of the rulers, perverting public power for personal gain.[2] The various reasons for England to adopt a new written constitution – to reinvigorate and strengthen democracy, to restore and protect civil liberties, to guard against corruption and misrule, take power away from Whitehall and bring decision-making closer to the people, to improve the mechanisms of both political and legal accountability, to reaffirm an inclusive, civic English national identity – all connect, whether directly or indirectly, with the aim of promoting good government in the public interest.[3]

All this is not for the sake of a constitution itself, but for the fruits of good government that a good constitution is likely to bring forth. The intention is that England should be a normal, decent, constitutional democracy, with a well functioning state that serves the public interest, as that interest is discerned by inclusive democratic processes. The 'fruits of good government' are to be found in an England that is sufficiently prosperous and reasonably fair (even for those who did not go to an expensive school, or do not have generational wealth to carry them through life). The result of good government is a country able once again to hold its head up alongside other leading European countries, based not upon past glories, but upon its current achievements in practical things like reducing child poverty, building decent infrastructure, and improving the quality of the National Health Service.

These are modest, moderate, and mature ambitions. Yet they are ambitions that seem very far off, beyond the scope of what the current constitutional order and political system seems able to deliver. A constitutionally decrepit state lacks the institutional ability to overcome England's crippling socio-economic disparities between classes, generations, and regions. Over-centralised, crudely majoritarian, increasingly corrupt, and barely democratic institutions will inevitably produce erratic, reactive, narrowly based, disjointed, government, no matter who is Prime Minister or which party is in power.

That is why overcoming the constitutional malaise is crucial to reversing England's chronic socio-economic under-performance. We need to tackle to problems of low growth and low productivity. Unleashing more free market, supply-side economics, with entrepreneurs set free from taxes and regulations, which was the neoliberal solution to stagnation, is not going to solve the problem anymore. We had maxed out the benefits of that approach by the late 1980s. Persisting in it today is going to make thing worse for the vast majority. The solution has to be a state-led national development strategy: infrastructure, research and development, planning reform, technical and vocational education, and an active industrial policy to attract public and private investment. All that will take, at least, ten years to start to filter through, even in the best case. We have already lost more than fifteen years of growth since the financial crisis of 2008 – and Brexit has just compounded the problem. It is going to be really hard to pull out of this. British politics has not yet looked reality in the face. We need to start from about where Spain was in the 1970s, or Poland in the 1990s, and build from there. A national development strategy needs broad buy-in, cross-party support, deep collaboration from finance, industry, and universities – and we need to stick at it for at least a generation to have a hope of turning things around. Yet our political system is incapable of delivering that. Long-term planning, evidence-based decision-making, cross-party cooperation, and so on, are beyond what our political system can currently deliver. So there is no hope of economic revival without major political reform, and fixing the constitution, far from being a distraction from the bread-and-butter issues of everyday life, is the precondition of being able to address those issues effectively. The key to success is a functioning, inclusive, and resilient democratic state that is orientated to the public interest. To quote Tom Paine again:

> When it shall be said in any country in the world, my poor are happy; neither ignorance nor distress is to be found among them; my jails are empty of prisoners, my streets of beggars; the aged are not in want, the taxes are not oppressive; the rational world is my friend, because I am the friend of its happiness: when these things can be said, then may that country boast its constitution and its government.[4]

As the constitutional order has strained, stretched, and snapped, so has the underlying social contract – the unspoken rule of harmony that says all citizens are, in the final analysis, on the same side. It is that social contract which makes people willing to pool risks and resources through public institutions, because those institutions are seen as legitimate, competent, reliable actors, whose policies, in general, are orientated to the public interest and the common good. This is what makes possible a decent and civilised life, in a free, flourishing, and functioning society. Without such willingness, without such trust, without such an undergirding social contract, without a reliable and dependable constitutional order, there can only be tyranny or anarchy.

Two common features of under-performing countries are *low state capacity* and *high levels of corruption*. The state functions as a private fiefdom – a source of patronage and plunder for those in charge – and as an instrument of repression to keep that fiefdom from being shared with those who do not have a place at the table. Poverty, squalor, disease, idleness, and ignorance are the signs of a weak, privatised, fractured state, that milks the public for the benefit of a few rich or well connected insiders. The remedy is a competent, just, and inclusive state that is willing and able to serve the public good. Look around you, in the blighted, worn-out, and struggling parts of England, and use your own eyes to see what sort of state governs us.

A visible indication of an ill-constituted state is the juxtaposition of private wealth and public poverty. The millionaire's mansion overlooks a potholed street. People pay, if they can, for private healthcare and schools, because nothing in the public sector works. For example, an under-performing state cannot effectively keep down energy prices or prevent the discharge of untreated sewage into rivers and onto beaches, because the key infrastructure is in private, not public, hands, and the state's regulatory and enforcement mechanisms are too weak or too compromised to bring them to heel. So those with shares in energy companies or water companies profit, while the public suffer.

In a flourishing country, it is the opposite. People pay their taxes (even rich people pay their fair share), and a well functioning, capable, and non-corrupt state means they get a lot back in terms of public services and infrastructure. The municipal play-parks in Luxembourg are works of art. The state schools gleam. The village halls shine. A high-productivity economy, sustained by active investment in education and infrastructure, means that, in percentage terms, tax burdens are actually lighter. The United Kingdom has relatively high taxes on working- and middle-class people, but not a lot to show for it, because the productive base of our economy has deliberately been destroyed. A country cannot sustain a proper, well functioning public sector when the private sector consists mostly of low-grade retail parks and call centres.

The United Kingdom has long been hobbled by a fundamental ideological mistake made in 1979. That mistake was to deindustrialise, and to destroy the productive power of the economy, allowing the gap between rich and poor to widen, while undermining the state's ability to run, control, develop, regulate, and fund a proper public sector. The problem was not so much Conservatism, as the *wrong kind* of Conservatism. If the main centre-right party had been a Gaullist party committed to state-led development, as in France, or a German-style economically moderate Christian Democratic party, we would all be better off today. Instead, we got slash-n-burn, cut-n-privatise, neoliberal Thatcherites, who stripped everything, and built nothing. Real value was sucked out of the economy, leaving only low-wage, low-skill jobs, while speculators in the City of London were able to gamble with people's lives. State capacity, public ethics, and democracy itself were all hollowed out – privatised away, farmed out to for-profit companies – by an ideology that was paradoxically opposed to government, yet authoritarian.

The neoliberal destruction of the public realm and of the real economy was, however, possible only because the unwritten and unreformed system of government, which Labour had left in place, enabled it. After the Second World War, Labour carefully maintained the absolute sovereignty of Parliament, with its concentration of centralised and unconstrained power. The party was wary of reforms that might have moderated the power of the state machine now in its hands. Labour's constitutional conservatism ultimately had the opposite effect. Majoritarian rule and parliamentary sovereignty did not pave the way to socialism; they allowed Thatcher and her successors to impose neoliberalism without limit, moderation, or restraint. 'Left Diceyanism' is a dead-end.

The apparent irony is that excessive concentration of power in the hands of a Government with a majority in a sovereign Parliament has weakened, not strengthened, the state's ability to serve the public interest. First-past-the-post elections, centralisation in Whitehall, and the lack of entrenched constitutional fundamentals have meant that policy can be made without discussion, compromise, agreement, or proper long-term planning. Instead, we got ideological assaults upon all public institutions, driven by intensely motivated minorities and a small coterie of special interests. In contrast, an inclusive and resilient constitutional state produces more inclusive and resilient policies – policies that, when they emerge from the political process, have broader backing, greater coherence, and less volatility over time.[5] Moderating restraints on the government, of the sort envisaged in the Charter 88 agenda, would help strengthen the capacity – and willingness – of the state to serve the public good.

It is a mistake, then, to think of the constitution only as sharing and restraining power. It also legitimates power. It guides it and sustains it. It broadens its foundation. Without a constitution the Government might be near-absolute, but the state – the common weal, or *res publica* – is desperately weak. The lack of a constitution frees the Government from restraints, but, paradoxically, it makes the absolutist state fragile and cowardly. It has no sure foundation. It has no firm principles upon which to stand. It cannot hold the line against existential threats, such as those posed by Islamic fundamentalism or right-wing populism.[6] As Benjamin Constant put it,[7] two centuries ago:

> Those institutions which act as barriers against power simultaneously support it. They guide it in its progress; they sustain its efforts; they moderate its excesses of violence and stimulate it in its moments of apathy. They rally around it the interests of the various classes. Even when it fights them, they impose upon it certain considerations which makes its mistakes less dangerous. But when these institutions are destroyed, power, lacking anything to contain it, begins to march haphazardly; its step becomes uneven and erratic. As it no longer follows a fixed rule, it now advances, now recoils, now becomes agitated, now restless; it never knows whether it is doing enough, or too much. Sometimes it is carried away and nothing can stop it; sometimes it subsides and nothing can revive it. It rids itself of allies while thinking to be rid of enemies.[8]

We may well ask, in relation to constitutions, 'Do men not gather figs of thorns, or grapes of briers?' To this we might answer, if such a paraphrase of Luke 6:43–45 is not misconstrued as impious, 'Every good constitution bringeth forth good government; but a corrupt constitution bringeth forth evil government. A good constitution cannot bring forth evil government, neither can a corrupt constitution bring forth good government.' With this comes a salutary warning, 'Every constitution that bringeth not forth good government is hewn down, and cast into the fire'.

So, when it comes to mending a country in decline or crisis, the first thing to do is to make sure the constitution is sound, and that democracy and governance work as they should. Tend the tree, and the fruits will follow in due course.

A 'good tree' would incorporate such moderate and overdue reforms as experience has shown to be necessary. As noted in Chapter 5, this would include the full Charter 88 agenda: proportional representation for the House of Commons, devolution of power to counties and cities, the codification and limitation of the Crown prerogatives, and a reformed House of Lords, all wrapped up in a resilient written constitution that can be amended only by a sufficiently broad consensus. A judicially enforced Bill of Rights, based upon the European Convention, would protect hard-won and time-honoured English liberties. Other proposed reforms – regulations on standards in public life, the Ministerial Code, the Honours Commission, safeguards to protect the neutrality and professionalism of the Civil Service, and rules on the appointment and tenure of the members of the Electoral Commission and Boundaries Commission – would uphold the integrity of the democratic political system, and of its administrative and electoral procedures. They would prevent those in public office from manipulating the ground rules for partisan advantage. They would help protect the *public* nature of the state, keeping the state as a public entity that serves public interests, not a private fiefdom to be exploited for private gain.

The proposed Constitution would broaden, ground, and stabilise the state, dragging power down from the ungovernable pinnacle of Downing Street and returning it to lower, safer, ground, whether that is in Cabinet, Parliament, or county hall. This more equal distribution of power between regions, institutions, and classes would stand against the dominant British political tradition – a closed, centralised, executive-dominated, elitist, top-down system of government which serves the interests of political and economic elites, but which lets everyone else down.[9] The effect of these reforms would be to encourage a different type of politics, one that is more deliberate, serious, and collaborative – moderating the use and abuse of power, dampening excesses, and restraining the kind of unilateral, seat-of-the-pants policy-making that so often results in bad decisions, hasty and ill-considered policies, and destabilising U-turns. To get things done in such a system needs serious and collaborative leadership, with more room for people who know their business and less room for showy charlatans. To quote Kipling again, '*And this the Dutchmen know!*'[10]

A particular weakness exists at the ministerial level. Ministers are appointed as a reward not for competence but for loyalty; they have little to no background in the policy issues affecting their departments, and have no chance to master their briefs, even if they wanted to, before being moved on in the next reshuffle.[11] This constant ministerial churn makes for breaking headlines but broken government. Everything is hurried and yet immovable; chaotic, yet sclerotic. Policy is made by press statement, without flowing through proper channels.

These constitutional reforms, by moderating and broadening the exercise of power, would restore good order to the policy-making process. If we stop making things up as we go along, and instead try to agree strategic objectives through a wider process of inclusion, turn them into sensible plans, and work through them more methodically, there will be fewer expensive mistakes, less waste, better long-term planning, more dependable outcomes – and ultimately better government, leading to a better quality of life. It all amounts to a kinder, gentler democracy, which better integrates diverse needs and perspectives into policy-making and legislation, and so better serves the common good.[12]

It should be noted that this constitutional orientation to the public interest does not necessarily favour any policy agenda or particular ideology. The proposed constitution would regulate *how* politics and government should be done – how *we the people*, through the democratic processes of ordinary parliamentary and electoral politics, discern and achieve the common good. It would not, beyond a few general 'Directive Principles', make substantive commitments to *what* the nature of the common good is. Rather, it recognises that reasonable people might disagree about many things, and that healthy democratic politics, sustained and enabled by the constitutional structure, is the mechanism by which such disagreements are transformed, in a peaceful and orderly way, into public policy decisions. Left, centre, and right, if they adhere to democratic and good governance principles, and if they are sincere in their motivation to serve the public interest rather than their own private interests, should be able to unite around these constitutional proposals.

### (b) Beyond the constitution

Although a good constitution is necessary to the health of a democratic state, it is only the beginning, not the end, of the quest for good government. A constitution is like the foundation of a house: without a solid foundation, the house will never be sound, but the foundation alone will not keep the roof in good condition. The whole fabric of the state – not just the constitution, but also the political parties, the public administration, the judiciary, the Armed Forces – must be in good shape. Much depends on the qualities of leadership, character, and integrity to be found in public life at every level. The *moral* as well as *material* conditions of the country must be considered. So, while getting the constitution right matters, it would be folly to imagine that constitutional refoundation alone, unaccompanied by a wider cultural and ethical regeneration, will produce the hoped-for outcome.

As discussed above, the institutional structure of power can change how power is exercised, and thereby influence policy outcomes. Beyond such mechanical approaches, a new constitution can also be a catalyst for the broader moral regeneration of public life. Such regeneration is no easy task. Neither is it quick. Bad habits are hard to shake, while good habits take time and patience to acquire. A country, by adopting a new constitution, can repair its democratic institutions, at least in outward form, in the space of just a few years; to deeply embed democratic values and a strong public service ethos can take generations. It is easier to rebuild a constitution than to rebuild a governing class.[13]

This book has argued that many of the problems England faces can be attributed to constitutional malaise, and has set out proposed constitutional solutions in response. Some problems, however, cannot be solely blamed on the lack of a written constitution. Some are a result of the ideology or incompetence of recent governments, or of a decline in public ethics, and are only partly or indirectly a consequence of constitutional failure. A new constitution is undoubtedly part of the solution to these problems too, but not always in a direct or immediate way.

One of those near-universal problems is the influence of money in politics – or, bluntly put, the rise of an oligarchic political system where wealth is the route to power, and where theoretical political equality is undermined by vast concentrations of private power. This is inherently corrupt, in that it inevitably distributes power according to wealth rather than virtue, and so puts private interests above the public good. This is not a new problem. As Cicero, the Roman statesman and philosopher, expressed it, 'There is, indeed, no uglier kind of state than one in which the richest men are thought to be the best'.[14]

The influence of wealth – 'oligarchic distortion' – works in many ways, visible and invisible. It is manifest in the over-representation of the rich in government and in Parliament. Two-thirds of David Cameron's first Cabinet were millionaires, which means that the 95% of the population who are not millionaires were represented by only a third of the Cabinet.[15] That form of exclusion is less visible, perhaps, than the under-representation of women or ethnic minorities, but no less important. Oligarchic distortion is also evident in explicit acts of bribery and corruption, loosely regulated campaign finance and party donations, the revolving door between lobbyists and government, and the shadowy network of covertly funded think tanks that shape public discourse in the interests of the rich. It is evident, too, in the private ownership of the mass media – print, broadcast, and digital – by rich individuals with an agenda to pursue.

Oligarchic distortion is doubly corrosive in its effects. Firstly, it corrodes governance capacity. Public policies are skewed and public resources squandered. Decisions are taken that suit rich donors and not the general public. As just one instance of this, one might point to the links between certain politicians in the pay of the private healthcare industry and the crisis of the National Health Service. Is that not a conflict of interest? Secondly, oligarchic distortion corrodes moral and democratic capacity, as trust in the system dissipates and belief in its legitimacy are undermined. The sense that 'they are all as bad as each other', and that voting does not matter because the rich always win in the end, becomes dangerously self-fulfilling as it alienates people from democratic engagement.

Oligarchic distortion is a problem, to some degree, almost everywhere. It seems to afflict other Western democracies as well, including some countries with basically sound constitutions. However, some countries do contain it better than others, and there are some things that suitably robust constitutions can do to limit or mitigate it (including, for example, regulating party and campaign financing, and having strict conflict-of-interest rules).

Another widespread problem is the polarisation of civic discourse, caused in part by the loss of shared public spaces, and by the segmentation of opinion into self-contained 'thought bubbles', increasingly conditioned by the algorithms of social media platforms. This is exacerbated by a news media driven by sound bites and obsessed with the political game – the ins and outs, the gaffes and U-turns – rather than addressing the substantive issues behind them.

When, owing to the lack of a proper constitution, the foundations and core principles of the democratic system are contested and unprotected, and when, therefore, a majority in the House of Commons gives a party near absolute power, the stakes of winning are so high that civil debate and civilised disagreement are hard to hold on to. Instead, there is an unseemly, unrestrained, no-holds-barred contest for power; no trick is too dirty, no lie too low. Democracy is built to harness the power of principled disagreement and to turn it to the public good; if principled disagreement (and its counterpart, pragmatic cooperation) turns into point-scoring and a struggle for power at any cost, democracy degenerates into mere 'competitive authoritarianism'.

Take, for example, the unwritten rule that one party ought not to stage high-profile media events in the middle of their opponent's party conference, just to hog the limelight. No constitution can enforce that rule. Yet it might help, over time, indirectly, to create the conditions in which such a rule is respected. A good constitution lowers both the reward of winning and the cost of losing; winners do not get absolute power, losers are not cast into oblivion. That means there is less incentive to play 'hardball'. Rather, both sides gain, over time, from respecting the constitutional system and its norms of democratic civility. However, the effect of the constitution in that case is indirect. The constitution is valuable to the extent that it encourages a spirit of decency and fair play.

A further concern is the decline of political parties. Political parties are supposed to play several crucial roles in a democracy: the recruitment and selection of political leaders, the aggregation and representation of interests, the formation and transmission of political ideas, the civic education of the people, and the mobilisation of voters. Political parties have declined from their heyday as mass-membership institutions in the mid-twentieth century, when they integrated large numbers of ordinary voters into the policy-making and political process. In the early twenty-first century, the major parties have become relatively small, tightly managed, top-down cliques. They function mainly as electoral organisations, to the detriment of their other historical functions as institutions that integrate people into political life, that mediate and moderate political demands, and that transform those demands into credible programmes of government.

Part of the problem is one of political recruitment and training. Recent works by Iain Dunt, Simon Kuper, and Isabel Hardman all point to the persistent problem of under-qualified or otherwise unsuitable MPs.[16] The parties tend to choose loyal activists who are good campaigners, not people who will necessarily make good parliamentarians, and eventually good ministers. The frustrating impotence of being a backbench MP tends to encourage them to focus on constituency business, fielding complaints about potholes and drains that should really be directed to local authorities, rather than developing expertise in policy. In consequence, the pool from which future ministers are drawn is too shallow, and they rarely possess the right skills, knowledge, or experience. Ministers may be good at playing the political game, but are often unsuited to the hard work of governing.

We are increasingly governed by people who have never worked in the real economy. Many follow a path from one of a tiny handful of elite schools to Oxford (occasionally, but rarely, Cambridge), and then into one of a very narrow range of jobs: researcher for an MP, staff of one of the many ideologically aligned think tanks that surround the political clique, public relations or journalism, or perhaps into a City firm if they need first to make money. The best of them might become lawyers, but that is a slow track for those who want to get to the top. Then they become an MP, and in the fulness of time a minister, without ever having learned to manage a complex organisation. They are very good at turning out a pithy 800-word opinion piece and at parrying criticism with humorous Oxford Union-style quips, but have never overseen a multi-million pound development project. They do not have the ability to make good decisions based on weighing evidence and understanding facts. They think they can 'lead people' – they are trained for that – but in the absence of technical competence, the skills they acquired as a prefect, or as captain of the first XI, carry them only so far.

England has long been governed by those formed in the great public schools, but never by such terrible examples of that breed. A century ago, an officer in the Colonial Service, himself a product of that educational system, argued that the public schools 'have produced an English gentleman with an almost passionate conception of fair play', who is not prone to 'that subtle moral deterioration' that otherwise results from the exercise of power.[17] Of course, not all lived up to that ideal – but, crucially, there was a shared ideal and a strong expectation that people ought to live up to it. That ideal is no longer being reliably inculcated. In a 2023 letter to *The Times*, a former Eton master, reflecting on the character of a certain recent occupant of the Tory front bench, publicly apologised for having failed to purge from his pupils that 'sense of privilege, entitlement and omniscience' that can 'damage a country's very fabric'.[18]

The ruling class today (judging its culture as a whole, recognising there are always individual exceptions) seem to have inherited all the vices that beset the worst of their ancestors, but to have lost the virtues once exhibited by the best of them. They have the wealth, swagger, and entitlement of Victorian gentlemen – some even ape the sartorial style – but it counts for nothing if they have not the character of gentlemen. The Conservative Government from 2019 to 2024 was a carnival of Byronic licentiousness: Downing Street parties, while the rest of us took refuge from the plague, were a form of performative transgression that exclaimed, in a language Byron would have understood, '*vaffanculo*' to everyone not in their charmed circle, placed high above mere mortal rules. Meanwhile, Gladstonian qualities – public service, earnestness, responsibility, moral courage, honesty, integrity, self-sacrifice – seemed to have departed. Starmer might, on a personal level, honour these qualities, but he is only human; and in any case it is necessary to institutionalise virtue in laws, norms, cultures, and systems, if human vice and frailty are to be held in check for more than a moment.

The abandonment of what was once termed 'muscular Christianity' may be partly responsible for this decline in the quality of our leaders; in contrast to their nineteenth- or twentieth-century forebears, today's Old Boys are a godless lot. It is hard to instil a sense of ethical responsibility, public duty, or personal integrity into a ruling class that has not learned the lesson of Luke 12:48, 'For unto whomsoever much is given, of him shall be much required'.

A lack of suffering, danger, and discomfort might be another cause. We used to take young men of the upper classes, put them in trenches to suffer and sweat alongside the common soldiery, and let the Pashtuns, Zulus, Germans, or Japanese take pot-shots at them. For those who survived – and many did not – it did them a world of good. If nothing else, it taught them that rank brings obligations and well as privileges, and that the decisions they would make, when they found themselves placed in positions of authority over others, would have life-or-death consequences.[19]

Alongside this degeneration of the ruling class, we have also seen in recent decades the virtual exclusion of the working class from entry into politics – although the current Deputy Prime Minister, Angela Rayner, is a rare exception. The door to political office is narrow and high: even to enter the fray, a potential parliamentary candidate usually needs to have enough independent wealth to be able to spend tens of thousands of their own money on campaigning, and to take months away from paid employment in order to concentrate on nursing a constituency.[20]

One path to public life once open to ordinary people, that provided by the trade unions and mass parties, has closed. As parties have become smaller, more tightly controlled, and professionalised electoral machines, the most reliable way in now lies through a political researcher job at Westminster – thus favouring well connected metropolitans (who are able to work for several years for nominal wages in order to build their political connections) over working-class or even lower-middle-class provincials.

The decline of mass parties and the rise of oligarchy are closely related phenomena. Without rooted mass-membership organisations to give ordinary people a collective voice, and a route up the ladder, the influence of big money flows unchecked. This is not an argument against parties. It is a plea for better parties – for parties that can actually perform their textbook functions.

The behaviour of political parties inside Parliament leaves a lot to be desired, too. Party loyalty and discipline have their place in a democracy. They make the mechanism of delegation and accountability work, and enable voters to choose not only between individuals but between coherent programmes of government. In a parliamentary democracy, parties need leaders, and those leaders need the support of their MPs.[21] Voting against the party whip should remain the exception rather than the rule. However, the culture of unthinking party loyalty has gone too far. There are issues of principle, or occasionally of vital constituency interest, on which MPs *should* vote with their conscience. Free votes, on a range of social and cultural issues, should be more, not less, common. Three-line whips – the strongest form of whipping, to vote against which can have career-limiting consequences – ought normally to be reserved for matters of confidence and supply, or specific manifesto commitments (or, in a coalition, commitments in the coalition agreement). Above all, ministers should be selected with greater regard to their ability rather than loyalty. All this, however, is rather beyond what a constitution can hope to achieve. It is in the realm of constitutional ethics, rather than constitutional law.

A further obstacle to good government is that we are now said to be living in an era of so-called 'post-truth' politics, where spin, propaganda, and deception create virtual realities.[22] If so, then we are in a sore spot indeed. The 'disintegration of truth leads to disintegration of trust';[23] it is impossible to make or keep any promises, and not only the representative system of government, but any form of decent and civilised public life, collapses. So, without a belief in truth – a belief that truth exists and that truth matters – there can be no freedom, no responsibility, no accountability, no justice, no society, no debate, no democracy. As Miroslav Volf put it, 'A post-truth world is post-justice world, and post-justice world looks either like North Korea or Syria'.[24]

The genius of the English system has always been to avoid these disastrous extremes of tyranny and anarchy, and to cling to well tempered liberty under the rule of law. All that depends upon a moral character shaped by a shared set of values that regards truth as sacred.[25] If England wishes to be well governed again, if its people would enjoy freedom and flourishing, the English must learn to become – in the words of Volf again – 'post-post-truth people, seek-to-speak-and-do-the-truth people, the anti-post-truth people'.[26]

A functioning society depends upon institutional trust. We must trust that everyone involved in making our society work will do their duty with honesty, impartiality, integrity, competence, and dedication, and will, each in their own sphere of responsibility, obey the law and be faithful stewards of the public good. We must trust, too, that those few individuals of bad character who breach these rules will be discovered and held to account, so that the peace, order, and good government of the realm be not disturbed.[27]

This trust is not blind, neither is it endless. It depends upon the faith we have in the rules, in public institutions, and in governance processes, and in our fellow citizens. Once taken for granted, this trust is now severely strained in England.[28] It is set to collapse if the process of rebuilding public institutions and public life fails. We may rightly strive for liberty, justice, equality, the common good, and the 'free and civic way of life', as Maurizio Viroli so elegantly expressed it,[29] but all those high-sounding words ultimately require people at all levels of society, from a Minister of the Crown to an ordinary voter, to do the right thing – and to do the right thing instinctively, not because they are forced to do so, but because they know the right thing must be done. In other words, good governance depends upon trust, which depends on civic virtue. Civic virtue cannot be assumed, but its presence or absence is the real difference between those countries that are flourishing and those that are perishing.

### (c) Overcoming the crisis of democracy

All these problems together amount to a crisis of democracy: a failure of our existing models of politics to adequately meet the wants and needs of citizens. It requires a constitutional solution. As has been shown, constitutions can help establish responsive and responsible systems of government. They can help keep the exercise of power genuinely *public*, and so limit domination by a self-serving ruling class or clique. They can protect the right to vote and to protest, can ensure inclusion in decision-making, can devolve power away from the centre to give life to local communities, and even regulate campaign spending or political donations. They can protect the neutral guardian institutions that promote good governance, ensure public accountability, and prevent corruption.

A constitution can create these mechanisms by which democracy operates, but it cannot create the operator. The crisis of democracy goes deeper than any constitution, alone, can fathom. Democracy is based upon certain assumptions about the attributes and values of the *demos*: (1) that people are competent to make decisions about government; (2) that people care about public affairs and have a sense of public duty; (3) that people can get relevant, accurate information on public affairs; (4) that people can discover truth and discern good values through discussion, and that they care enough about truth and decency to do so; (5) that people have relatively equal moral worth, so as to be deserving of equal rights and equal citizenship; (6) that people can create and maintain institutions that limit and constrain power; (7) that political leaders and public officials will generally act responsibly, and respect the norms and values of a democratic system; and (8) that the state has the capacity to administer itself. Where these conditions are not generally met, democracy will fail, or at least be degraded to the point at which it fails to live up to its expectations.

If an absolute monarchy depends on the quality and character of the monarch, a constitutional democracy depends on the quality and character of the people, and of their leaders and representatives. The inescapable fact is that a country needs not only the letter of a good constitution, but also the spirit: good people as well as good laws. We need, even under the best constitution, those whom Lord Hastings of Scarisbrick described as 'people of truth and integrity, of clarity and certainty, of service, commitment and distinction'.[30] Reform of England's constitution and public institutions must be matched by a reform of the heart, of the character of public leaders, and of the culture of public life.[31]

So, if England would flourish, people would do well to remember Nelson's signal at Trafalgar, 'England expects that every man [and, we should add, every woman] will do their duty'.[32] It is for the political parties to select candidates with the right skills to govern well.[33] It is for MPs to discern when their public duty is to follow the party line, and when it is their duty to vote the other way and let the whips be dashed. It is, likewise, for the media to recognise their duty to report what really matters, not just what entertains or sells. It is for voters to demand integrity, competence, and decent policies, and to punish at the ballot box parties and candidates who let them down. It is for educators to train people in the ways of civic virtue. It is for the clergy to bring people to a lively sense of their moral duties and to reconnect local communities. It is for people in leadership roles at all levels to create a healthy culture of responsibility, honesty, service, care, and trust. It is for every person to pay heed to the promptings of love and truth in our hearts, and to do our best, according to the light we are given to see by.

If democracy reflects who we are, it behoves us to be as good as we can be, and, in particular, to cultivate the civic virtues on which freedom and good government depend: moderation, tolerance, common sense, respect for the rule of law, deference to authority within proper limits, dogged resistance when that authority is abused or those limits are exceeded, quiet devotion to duty, responsibility, compassion, regard for proper conduct and human decency, earnestness, seriousness, studiousness, industriousness, and, above all, a humble spirit of public service.

These are deeply unfashionable qualities, which are no longer instilled in England's ruling class, but without which the nation is ill-equipped to face the challenges before it. The flippant, ironic, shallow cleverness that is so dazzling in an Oxford Union debate has been tried and found wanting. England's future must not be defined by that narrow ('*stretto*') self-serving few; their unseriousness, charm, and confident incompetence has brought us to this state of distress. Perhaps the ground has being so churned up that it is now more sand than rock. Without being a Cassandra, there is every chance, if things continue on their present course, that they will get worse before they get any better.

Again, we must face the consequences of the collapse of the previously widely shared Christian ethical framework. The secularisation of society, accelerating apace in the last half century, especially when combined with immigration of people from non-Christian cultures, is one of the most rapid, profound, and risky social changes in history. It is nothing short of a cultural revolution, reversing, in the space of just a few generations, the great 'Jesus revolution' that Christianity wrought upon the Western world and the Western mind.[34] As we are cut off from that vine, so the fruit wilts. We see a return to pagan values – the elevation of wealth, sex, power, and the unanchored self, as the idolatrous gods of our age. The result is a collapse of both values and identity.[35] In place of a common framework of ethics ordered by Christian virtues, we have built a brittle, unstable morality based solely on the notions of the rational egoist *Homo economicus* – a person whose relationships are transactional and whose subjective preferences must be satisfied regardless of their objective merits.[36] There is no universal scale of ethical judgment which enables us to distinguish, except as a matter of personal preference, a life spent in faithful service to the public and to the community from one devoted to cocaine and orgies. It is impossible for such a society to function well. As Wang Huning asked in *America Against America* (1991), 'If the value system

171

collapses, how can the social system be sustained?'[37] How can we say what is good policy, if we do not have some broadly shared notion of what is 'good'?

Refoundation of the English state must therefore be accompanied by a reformation of heart, mind, and culture. In the absence of some grounding and orientating values in society, good government under a democratic system is impossible. As the theologian John Milbank put it, 'An egalitarian democracy actually requires a hierarchy both of values and of persons of excellence. Otherwise, money and sophistry co-conspire to destroy it.' 'Democracy', Milbank argues, requires a parallel concern for 'the formation of good character', for which he uses the Greek word *paideia*.[38]

That is why institutions that promote civic virtue are necessary, and why, in a reformed constitution, there is still room for things like the monarchy, the established Church, the honours system, and a public service broadcaster. These 'institutions of *paideia*', with a clear constitutional foundation on which to base themselves, can have a positive influence on our civic culture, encouraging civic virtue, and forming our notion of the Good.

I do not wish this to be misunderstood in any kind of absolutist or perfectionist terms. This concern for *paideia* does not mean that there should be any totalitarian imposition of values. There must be no attempt to create the 'New Soviet Man', nor anything of that horrific kind. It will be noted that, in the draft Constitution, these institutions of *paideia* are independent from the Government, insulated from partisan politics, and from each other. Their influenced is exerted only within a free society, characterised by freedom of religion, conscience, association, assembly, and expression.

Indeed, freedom is an essential precondition of civic virtue – and civic virtue sustains freedom. They are mutually reinforcing. Duty, honesty, and public responsibility can exist only where citizens have a share in public decisions. Only the free and enfranchised can be frank. Meanwhile, those living under despotic rule are trained to the most debased servility. They are conditioned to be obsequious and devious in order to survive. They learn to live for pleasure – because nothing is secure – and to take nothing seriously, as if life were a futile game, not an earnest mission. The corruption of the state corrupts character.

One corrupted view of the human character against which the institutions of *paideia* should strive is the narrowly economic view of human nature asserted by neoliberalism. For more than forty years, neoliberalism has driven out public service ethics and civic virtue, and has reproduced in capitalist form all the pathologies of the late Soviet system: inefficiency, incoherence, contradiction, duplicity, corruption, and hypocrisy.[39] We must rediscover the values and virtues that can sustain good government and a free and civic way of life – forged not necessarily on the playing fields of Eton, but in provincial grammar schools, Nonconformist chapels, trade unions, friendly societies, and the engineering departments of redbrick universities.

Of course, constitutions do not sustain freedom and good government as if by magic, but by the moral force they possess in the hearts and minds of the citizens. Constitutions declare legitimate expectations and proclaim public norms: they say what is, and is not, acceptable. They act as signposts pointing to shared goals and as yardsticks by which shared standards are measured. Without such a constitution, a state is lost, map-less and route-less, on the moorlands of anomie.

Perhaps the true value of reconstituting England is to be found, therefore, not only in the result (a new written constitution, and the institutional arrangements and rights that flow from it), but also in the process itself, and in the way that the process helps to rebuild trust, to excite civic virtue, and to help people imagine a better country. Coming together through the constitution-building process, to share different perspectives, and to find through and despite those differences our commonalities, can be a transformative, re-unitive, healing, experience; in rebuilding our institutions, it can also repair the shared fabric of common understanding.

In a diverse society, a good constitution can be a rallying point of unity. The unconstituted state of the United Kingdom is a barrier to effective citizenship. We are asked to belong to the rump of an imperial state, without a clear foundation or agreed principles. That makes it hard for outsiders to join. We might have less racism, and better integration, if we had a firmer constitutional order. A good constitution proclaims the civic-democratic values on which our common life is based, giving them prominence, authority, and visibility. A reconstituted English state would actually stand for something. It would, at a constitutional level, answer the question 'What is England called to be?' In response to, and flowing from, that teleological question, there would be agreed rules, standards, and expectations. There would be conditions, too: corrupt things we will not allow or accept. Citizenship would mean something. When all around us we see *disintegration* – of identities, institutions, values, trust, and virtue – constitution-building is a means of *reintegration*.

After having adopted a constitution by which we are covenanted together, we might rightly say:

> There is neither black nor white, neither immigrant nor indigenous, nor is there minority or majority, for we are all one under the constitution. Before, we were not a people, but now we are the people of the constitution; once we had not constituted a common weal, but now we have constituted a common weal.

Those who are familiar with the cadences of those two sentences might dismiss this as an over-realised eschatology, or as an over-sacralisation of secular things.[40] Some might even call it 'constitutional idolatry'.[41] I would put it another way: the Apostles were using the already existing language of the ancient polity, in which citizenship meant something. Restoring this community-of-covenant language to a civil use reaffirms a commitment to constitutional unity, combining freedom with peace, order, and good government in a way that is rooted deeply within the English tradition of political thought, from the Mayflower Compact and beyond.

## (d) Conclusion

The draft Constitution presented in the annex lays out what should be done. We must now come back, in conclusion, to the core argument of this book: the reason why all this matters.

The daily reality in which all but a small, privileged class of people live has worsened over recent decades. We need not recite the catastrophic statistics of homelessness and food bank use, nor repeat stories of babies dying because of mould in damp houses, or children unable to concentrate on their lessons for want of breakfast, or shivering pensioners squashed between low pensions and weakly regulated energy companies, or deadly queues at accident and emergency, or sewage in the rivers, or a thousand and one other signs of the failure of the state, as currently constituted, to serve the common good. Economic pressures have impoverished sections of the population that would previously have considered themselves relatively comfortable. A generation of people – no longer so young – still despair, if they have not inherited wealth, of ever being able to own a home, put down roots, and raise a family in economic security. Public services are stripped to the bone. Infrastructure is crumbling, while major projects are delayed and mismanaged. The economic foundations of the country – its manufacturing base, the skilled jobs that sustained not only homes and families but also dignity and self-respect – have all been allowed to collapse, or deliberately destroyed. England's trade with mainland Europe – the biggest, richest, and best-regulated free trade zone in the world – has been pointlessly impeded; one cannot eat 'British sovereignty', as if it were a Spanish tomato. Absolute poverty, on a scale that was abolished in the mid-twentieth century, has returned.

It is important, in this situation, to remember that this proposal for constitutional renewal aims to strengthen the state, not to weaken it. A new democratic constitution is necessary to restore confidence in the state – both at home and abroad – to increase resilience, to inspire loyalty, and to rebuild public legitimacy. At stake is the ability of the state to manage, mobilise, coordinate, and deliver for the public good, to overcome economic travails, to develop the economy and infrastructure, to reintegrate an increasingly divided society, and thereby to enable a better life for all our people. If this is not done, and the slide continues – an inexorable decline, punctuated by turmoil – then freedom, the English nation, the heritage of ages, all we love, will be in very grave peril.

Constitutional reform cannot therefore be a hobby for geeks who obsess over the niceties of electoral systems. It is not – nor it should ever be – the exclusive concern of leafy-lawned, avocado-eating Liberal Democrats with nothing else to worry about. The constitution, even if its effects are mostly unseen, is of crucial importance to every fretful mother who cannot get a doctor's appointment for her sick child, and to every unemployed person mercilessly 'sanctioned' because an unreliable bus service did not get them to an interview on time. What is at stake is nothing less that the nature of the state and the relationship between the state and its citizens.

A new Prime Minister or new Government with different policies will not be enough. The problem is the nature of the state: the fact that the state is not constituted upon the basis of democratic citizenship for the common good. Constitutional refoundation is about restoring what has been broken, but it is also about reforms that will achieve what England has never yet really had: Gucciardini's *governo largo* – an open, broad-based, 'public state' that is established upon the principles of government of, by, and for the people. While the institutions of the new state would be familiar, its constitutional character would be transformed. The English state would no longer descend from the Norman Conquest and serve only the interests of a narrow elite. It would be reconstituted, upon a solemn covenant, or an Agreement of the People, to serve the common good of its citizens. It is from this change in the character and foundation of the state that all other changes must flow. It is by this means that we build a land of hope and glory for all our people, not just the few.

It must be reiterated that the Constitution proposed in this book, which makes detailed prescriptions on all such matters, is merely an illustrative example, based on my own judgment. In any real process, a different deal might emerge. For example, I have argued that the House of Commons should be elected by proportional representation, while the Lords should be retained, with moderate reforms, as an appointed House of experience and expertise. If, on the other hand, proportional representation for the Commons is politically impossible, the so-called 'Australian compromise' (a majoritarian House of Commons and a proportionally elected Senate) would be the next best solution, moderating the majoritarian principle of Government selection with a more inclusive and representative second chamber.[42]

One might also imagine different outcomes in relation to other matters. In particular, while making the case for the preservation of what might be called the 'metaphysical constitution' of England as a Christian kingdom, with a reformed monarchy and a reformed Church establishment, I do not presume that these arguments will necessarily prevail. While monarchy and Anglicanism are ingrained in the English tradition, they are not essential to the Westminster Model of parliamentary democracy. It is equally possible to have a secular republic, as in India or Fiji, if that is where national consensus lies.

As noted in the Introduction, this book is written for the future. There is increasing appreciation of the need for constitutional change, but it is acknowledged that there is little *effective* appetite, at the time of writing, for the vision here put forward. While it was briefly cheering that the 2022 Labour Party conference passed a resolution in favour of proportional representation, Labour's leadership remains lukewarm at best on a broad constitutional refoundation, and the 2024 manifesto offered nothing of note. Most of the English political class and commentariat are not yet ready to recast the Union, nor to find a way for England to move on, culturally as well as constitutionally, from its British imperial past. So we might all be locked for some time yet in a broken constitutional order, stumbling on in a stagnating – or, rather, deteriorating – state. The aim of this book is simply to sketch out, in practical terms, what a solution to the constitutional question and the English question might look like, and thereby to prepare the way in the wilderness, so that when the opportunity arises, people can be ready.

Being ready takes time. Deep below the constitution and the institutions of the state lie the land and the people, their past and their stories, the folk tales and folk ways of an old nation. Before there can be an English democracy, there must be an English demos, but England is still on the verge of coming to terms with itself. Events recently advertised on the village notice board of Chiselborough included 'a night of sea shanties, a talk on local Anglo-Saxon history, the story of the peasants' struggle for land delivered in folk song' – which was described as a 'wonderful English Valhalla'.⁴³ Such peaceful grassroots revivals of English culture – unashamedly embracing an English national identity – are to be celebrated and encouraged, but these are the signs of a nation still in the foothills of self-discovery and self-acceptance. No one has yet been able to turn this from nostalgic cultural nationalism into a democratic, inclusive, and forward-looking vision of England where the future could be better than the past.⁴⁴ This book, putting a draft Constitution for England on the table for public discussion, might at least spur that conversation.

## Notes

1 W. I. Jennings (1963) *Democracy in Africa* (Cambridge University Press), p. 82.
2 Aristotle, *The Politics*, trans. T. A. Sinclair (1962) (Penguin Classics).
3 'Good government' and 'good governance' are often used interchangeably, but here it is necessary to be a little more precise. 'Good government' and 'good governance' are both needed, and are often closely linked, but they are not quite the same. 'Good governance' is perhaps the more neutral term, which is why it has become more widespread in recent use. It focuses on the rules, institutions, and processes of decision-making at all levels: having fair rules for how decisions are taken, robust procedures, and sound structures. In the United Kingdom, the archetypical 'good governance' institutions include, but are not limited to, the Auditor-General, the Public Accounts Committee, the Parliamentary and Health Service Ombudsman, the Public Service Commission, and so on. 'Good government' is a more expansive and demanding concept; it includes good governance, but goes beyond it. Good government is about making wise, just, prudent, and courageous leadership decisions that serve the common good. Briefly put, good governance concerns the means and the process, while good government also concerns the ends and the results. We hope that the former will help attain the latter.
4 T. Paine (1791) *The Rights of Man*, https://www.gutenberg.org/files/3742/3742-h/3742-h.htm, accessed 3 February 2023.
5 A. Lijphart (2011) *Patterns of Democracy: Government Forms and Performance in Thirty-Six Democracies* (2nd edn) (Yale University Press).
6 B. Ryan (2020) *How the West Was Lost: The Decline of a Myth and the Search for New Stories* (Hurst), pp. 203, 242.
7 Benjamin Constant was a Franco-Swiss Protestant, educated at the University of Edinburgh, and a great Anglophone admirer of the British constitution, as opposed to Napoleon's authoritarian populist regime. His political essays bear re-reading today.
8 B. Constant (1988) 'The spirit of conquest and usurpation and their relation to European civilisation', in B. Fontana (ed.), *Constant: Political Writings* (Cambridge University Press), p. 133.
9 M. Hall (2009) *Political Traditions and Scottish Devolution* (PhD thesis, University of Birmingham), pp. 84–85.
10 Rudyard Kipling, 'The Dutch in the Medway' (original emphasis). The Dutch political system requires policy to be made by negotiation. The need for cross-party agreement

within broad coalitions means that the pros, cons, and potential problems arising from policy decisions have to be explored and resolved before policy is made, not afterwards. Policy-making is slower, but more inclusive and more stable, with better outcomes. See H. Ramkema (2008) *The Dutch Political System in a Nutshell* (Netherlands Institute for Multi-Party Democracy); R. B. Andeweg, G. A. Irwin, and T. Louwerse (2020) *The Governance and Politics of the Netherlands* (5th edn) (Bloomsbury).

11 A. King and I. Crewe (2014) *The Blunders of Our Governments* (2nd edn) (Oneworld Publications).

12 Lijphart, *Patterns of Democracy*.

13 N. Bobbio and M. Viroli (2003) *The Idea of the Republic* (Polity).

14 M. T. Cicero, *On the Commonwealth*, trans. G. Holland Sabine and S. Barney Smith (1976) (Macmillan), p. 139.

15 J. Beattie (2012) 'Millionaire ministers: combined wealth of Cabinet is more than £70M', *The Mirror*, 29 May, https://www.mirror.co.uk/news/uk-news/millionaire-ministers-combined-wealth-of-cabinet-851909, accessed 25 January 2023.

16 I. Dunt (2023) *How Westminster Works ... and Why It Doesn't* (Weidenfeld and Nicolson); S. Kuper (2023) *Chums: How a Tiny Caste of Oxford Tories Took Over the UK* (Profile Books); I. Hardman (2022) *Why We Get the Wrong Politicians* (Atlantic Books).

17 C. Cross (1970) *The Fall of the British Empire* (Paladin), p. 158.

18 J. Claughton (2023) 'Eton's failure', letter to *The Times*, 13 June.

19 It is perhaps no coincidence that one of the few examples of a contemporary Eton-and-Oxford politician has who exhibited anything like the values and character once expected of the imperial ruling class also happens to be the only one who knows his way around Afghanistan and Iraq. The moral decline of the ruling class is nowhere better illustrated than by Rory Stewart having been hounded out of the Conservative Party in 2019. A century ago, he might have made an excellent Prime Minister.

20 Hardman, *Why We Get the Wrong Politicians*, pp. 18–27.

21 This is one reason why the election of party leaders by the membership at large, rather than by MPs, was a mistake – at least when a party is in government. Liz Truss was elected as Tory leader in 2022, and so was appointed as Prime Minister, based not upon the confidence of the parliamentary party, but upon the votes of about 81,000 party members in the country: about 0.1% of the population. That tiny 'selectorate' is of course highly disproportional, being much older, richer, whiter, and more southern – and much more right wing – than the median voter. Not only is that a *democratic* affront, it is also a major *constitutional* problem. In a parliamentary system, where government depends upon the confidence of a majority of MPs, a party leader installed against the wishes of their own MPs is likely to be in a constitutionally impossible position.

22 W. Davies (2016) 'The age of post-truth politics', *New York Times*, 24 August, https://nyti.ms/2c7zwfA, accessed 26 October 2022.

23 K. Mair (2019) *More Truth: Searching for Certainty in an Uncertain World* (IVP Books).

24 M. Volf (2017) Tweet, 2::29 pm, 24 March, https://x.com/MiroslavVolf/status/845281407836585984, last accessed 21 April 2025.

25 R. H. Malden (1952) *The English Church and Nation* (SPCK), p. 58.

26 M. Volf, Tweet, 1120 PM, 9 February 2017, at https://x.com/MiroslavVolf/status/829787066930180098, accessed 9 May 2025.

27 Jennings, *Democracy in Africa*, pp. 43–50.

28 A. Seldon (2010) *Trust: How We Lost It and How to Get It Back* (2nd edn) (Biteback Books).

29 M. Viroli (1999) (*Republicanism*, trans. A. Shugaar (Hill and Wang).

30 M. Hastings (2023) 'Re-enchanting public life' (interview with Lord Hastings of Scarisbrick), Seen and Unseen podcast (17 May), https://www.seenandunseen.com/podcast, accessed 17 May 2023.

31 Italy after the Second World War is an example of a country in which a thorough process of constitutional refoundation produced a fine written constitution, but where no moral reformation accompanied it. Despite a sound constitution, politics and public

administration remained corrupt and inefficient. This is not to say the constitution is irrelevant (no doubt things would have been much worse had the constitution of the Italian Republic not been in place), only that it is insufficient. Reform of the law alone, without a revival of the spirit, cannot save a nation. See: J. C. Adams and P. Barile (1966) *The Government of Republican Italy* (Houghton Mifflin); N. Bobbio and M. Viroli (2003) *The Idea of the Republic* (Polity Press).

32 Jennings, *Democracy in Africa*, p. 46.

33 Pre-modern city-state republics, and the political theorists who defended and expounded their constitutions, put great emphasis on rules and institutions that would encourage good, virtuous, public-spirited people to fill public office, while keeping the roguish, the ambitious, the venial, vicious, and corrupt, as far as possible, out of office. Francesco Patrizi (1413–1494), for example, in his plan for the reconstitution of Siena, proposed a complex system of lot and election designed to ensure that only the most virtuous and accomplished citizens would gain high office. See J. Hankins (2023) *Political Meritocracy in Renaissance Italy: The Virtuous Republic of Francesco Patrizi of Siena* (Harvard University Press). Modern democracies neglect such institutions, essentially privatising the process of candidate selection by leaving it entirely in the hands of political parties. It is not be difficult to imagine quite different arrangements. For example, any person seeking election to a public office would have to go before a scrutiny committee of citizens, selected by random lot from the electoral register of their constituency. Without enquiring into the political opinions of principles of the prospective candidates, it would examine their virtues, education, career trajectory, character, and experience. It would enquire into how they run their household, how they treat their staff, and whether they have any notorious vices. Only those deemed suitable by the scrutiny committee would then be able to apply to the parties for nomination. This seemingly small change to the candidate-nominating process would nevertheless be a radical innovation. Drawing more upon 'ancient' than 'gothic' prudence, it would go far beyond the scope of a neo-Burkean Westminster Model constitution. So it is left to an endnote, and instead we must trust the political parties to act as the guardians of political virtue.

34 G. Scrivener (2022) *The Air We Breathe: How We All Came to Believe in Freedom, Kindness, Progress, and Equality* (Good Book Company).

35 Q. Hogg (Lord Hailsham) (1994) *Values: Collapse and Cure* (HarperCollins).

36 A. Innes (2023) *Late Soviet Britain: Why Materialist Utopias Fail* (Cambridge University Press).

37 See the review by C. Che (2022) 'How a book about America's history foretold China's future', *New Yorker*, 21 March, https://www.newyorker.com/books/second-read/how-a-book-about-americas-history-foretold-chinas-future, accessed 1 November 2022.

38 N. Schneider (2010) 'Orthodox paradox: an interview with John Milbank', The Immanent Frame forum Social Science Research Council website (17 March), https://tif.ssrc.org/2010/03/17/orthodox-paradox-an-interview-with-john-milbank/, accessed 9 September 2024.

39 Innes, *Late Soviet Britain*.

40 If the cadence of these sentences does not ring any bells, see Galatians 3: 27–28 and 1 Peter 2: 10.

41 B. C. Jones (2020) *Constitutional Idolatry and Democracy: Challenging the Infatuation with Writtenness* (Elgar).

42 S. Ganghof (2018) 'A new political system model: semi-parliamentary government', *European Journal of Political Research*, Vol. 57, No. 2, pp. 261–281; T. Khaitan (2021) 'Balancing accountability and effectiveness: a case for moderated parliamentarism', *Canadian Journal of Comparative and Contemporary Law* (University of Melbourne Legal Studies Research Paper No. 941).

43 George Waterhouse (@wasserhouse), Tweet, 10:39 AM, 13 September 2023, at https://x.com/wasserhouse/status/1701893236908806348, accessed 14 May 2025.

44 Incidentally, this is one of the differences between the constitutional debates in England and Scotland. Scotland has moved on from its 'kailyard' phase of national rediscovery.

That is not to say Scotland does not have history, mythology, folk culture, old wounds in the burned-out clachans, and wraiths in the bloody glens. Neither it is to dismiss the importance of these things in shaping and sustaining a sense of national identity. Nevertheless, Scotland seems to have processed that and come to terms with it. It is debating government and governance. It is ready to be a young, modern, forward-looking country. In Scotland, although the ways and means are still very much politically contested, there is definitely a sense that a better future is possible and can be built, if people try.

# Annex

# Draft Constitution

This annex sets out a draft Constitution in accordance with the principles and institutional design choices recommended in this book. By way of a preliminary outline, the main provisions and principles of the proposed draft Constitution are summarised below.

## 1. Restructuring the Union

- Establishment of an English State with its own national institutions, flag, anthem, and Constitution, within a United Kingdom that is reconstituted as a voluntary union of England with: (a) Scotland, Wales, and Northern Ireland (as Associated States); (b) Jersey, Guernsey, and the Isle of Man (as Crown Dependencies); and (c) the Overseas Territories.
- All Associated States, Crown Dependencies, and self-governing Overseas Territories, would have: (a) autonomy over all policy areas except foreign affairs, defence, and citizenship, although with scope for mutual cooperation in other areas; (b) the option to become independent at the time of their own choosing.
- English *nationality* to be recognised along with British *citizenship*: all British citizens born or resident in England to have English nationality.
- Northern Ireland to retain the right, under the Good Friday Agreement, to hold a border poll to unite it with the Republic of Ireland.

## 2. Reform of Parliament

- The Westminster Parliament is to become an English Parliament, consisting of the House of Commons and House of Lords.
- The House of Commons is to consist of 500 members, elected by the mixed-member proportional system (250 elected from single-member constituencies, 250 elected from compensatory regional party lists).
- The House of Lords is to consist of 400 'Parliamentary Peers', appointed on merit by an independent Lords Appointments Commission, according to their expertise, experience, or their ability to represent socio-economic interests and cultural and religious communities. Peers serve until the end of the session of Parliament following their eightieth birthday.
- The powers of the House of Lords – as a chamber of review and restraint – would be similar to those it has now, except that it would also have a veto over constitutional amendments.

- Recognising the role of the Leader of the Opposition and of other opposition parties, and protecting the privileges of opposition parties, including rights to parliamentary time.
- Strengthening the ability of parliamentary committees to hold Government to account.
- Enabling one-third of MPs to call urgent sittings of Parliament when it is adjourned or prorogued.
- Limiting the size of the 'payroll vote' (i.e. the number of MPs in Government office and so bound by collective responsibility).
- Providing a stronger role for Parliament in decisions on the ratification of treaties and in the approval of military action.

### 3. Limiting royal prerogatives and codifying the conventions of parliamentary government

- Monarchy to be retained but reformed: the Crown prerogatives to be strictly limited, and remaining reserve powers narrowly defined.
- Codification of the constitutional conventions on which parliamentary democracy relies (e.g. government formation, dismissal, dissolution, prorogation, Royal Assent).
- The Prime Minister is to be nominated, if there is no obvious majority leader, by a vote of the House of Commons.

### 4. Devolving power within England

- Extensive devolution of power and fiscal resources to English counties and cities as the primary units of local government.
- Protecting lower levels of authority, down to the parish.

### 5. Protecting rights

- Justiciable fundamental rights based on the European Convention on Human Rights.
- Socio-economic rights to be recognised, but only as non-justiciable Directive Principles.

### 6. Upholding institutional integrity

- Protecting professionalism, impartiality, and credibility of the Civil Service.
- Stronger constitutional safeguards to ensure neutrality, independence, and competence of 'fourth branch' institutions, including the Human Rights Commission, Electoral Commission, Boundaries Commission, Public Service Commission, and Judicial Service Commission.

- Constitutional recognition of the 'Nolan' principles for standards in public life.
- Reform of the honours system to restrict partisan patronage.
- Strengthening the Ministerial Code.

### 7. Reforming the Church establishment

- Keeping the establishment of the Church of England, but on a clearer constitutional basis that protects ecclesiastical autonomy (including the selection of its own bishops and the right to legislate for its own affairs with minimal parliamentary interference).

### 8. Protecting the foundations

- All the above to be incorporated into a written, codified Constitution, which would have the status of supreme law.
- The Constitution could be amended only by a two-thirds majority in the Commons and an absolute majority vote in the Lords; in the case of its 'basic structure' provisions, this hurdle must be followed by majority approval in a referendum.

In presenting this draft Constitution, there is no claim to speak *for* England, only *to* England. This document is not intended to be prescriptive, but merely educative and illustrative. It does not purport to be the only, best, or final answer to any of the particular questions of constitutional design that might arise. There is, crucially, no attempt to sidestep the process of consensus-building and constitution-making that must be undertaken if a lasting and legitimate Constitution is to be produced. Rather, it is presented in order to help, encourage and facilitate that process, by presenting the public with a 'worked example'.

As discussed in Chapters 4 and 5 of the book, all lasting constitutions embody a settlement – a national compromise – rather than a victory for any one party. This draft is presented as a proposed compromise between reform and restoration, or between the best principles of Whig parliamentarism and those of Tory reverence for historic institutions. It offers real change, but change within the tradition of the Westminster Model, not contrary to it. For some, the draft might go too far. Its most radical proposals – justiciable fundamental rights, devolution, proportional representation – might not sit well with those still wedded to the idea of a sovereign Parliament and majoritarian rule. For others, the draft might not go far enough. Its treatment of the House of Lords, the Church of England, and the monarchy is so mild and conciliatory, with reform rather than abolition the refrain, that many on the left will be unsatisfied.

In the same way, the draft incorporates almost all of the European Convention on Human Rights with only minor modifications. For some, this will be seen as the epitome of soft liberalism. For others, who might compare the rather minimal 'first generation' rights of the European Convention with the more expansive and ambitious provisions of more recent constitutions, such as those of South Africa (1996) and Fiji (2013), this will seem like the very least we should do. It is important to remember that the European Convention is a floor, not a ceiling; it is designed to prevent tyranny, not to bring about utopia, and it leaves plenty of room – the wide 'margin of appreciation' – for parliaments to set policy.

So be it. This Constitution is neither radical nor reactionary. It is moderate, reformist, and restorative. It seeks to honour the past and to build upon it, neither to throw it away, nor to live stuck in it. It is not 'woke'. It is not 'anti-woke'. It is not left. It is not right. It does not represent a particular side in some of the big cultural and social debates of the day, but it does recognise that people hold a range of views that can coexist under a free constitution. At the same time, it acknowledges the need for effective English democracy, development, and good government, and seeks to provide a sturdy legal and institutional foundation for public government.

The draft Constitution is written in what Professor Tom Ginsburg described to me as 'ancient British legalese'. It does not embrace modern 'plain language' drafting. In part, this is because plain language drafting is often less plain, in practice, than the tortuously precise prose of traditional drafting. Constitutions are legal, as well as social and political, documents, and courts have to make sense of them. Deviation from terms of art, and from the usual turns of phrase in Westminster Model constitutions, can introduce more confusion, not less. In part, this drafting style is an aesthetic preference, just as I prefer a Parliament building in the gothic style to one that looks like it belongs on an industrial estate. A constitution, like a house or a town, should be beautiful as well as functional. If functionality demands that all things must be made new, it is even more important, to English tastes, that it looks reassuringly old-fashioned.

The most difficult thing is to specify exactly what is being constituted: is this a constitution for England, or for the United Kingdom? The answer is that it is both. It creates a 'Kingdom of England', existing within, and as the cardinal centre of, a 'United Kingdom'. The United Kingdom ceases to be 'The United Kingdom of Great Britain and Northern Ireland' and becomes 'The United Kingdom of England and its Associated States, Crown Dependencies, and Overseas Territories'. Most of the Constitution would apply only to England, while certain provisions, dealing with the Associated States, Crown Dependencies, and Overseas Territories, or with United Kingdom-wide institutions, would apply across the United Kingdom. The King would be the 'King of England', reigning in England 'in right of England', but would also be 'King of the United Kingdom', reigning in Scotland as 'King of Scots', in Jersey as 'Duke of Normandy' or 'King in right of the Bailiwick of Jersey', and in Gibraltar as 'King of the United Kingdom'.

This is, admittedly, a constitutional solution of gothic intricacy, not classical simplicity. Yet that is, perhaps, no bad thing. It builds pragmatically upon history, rather than logically upon abstract ideas, in a way that is in keeping with English taste and genius.

# THE CONSTITUTION OF THE UNITED KINGDOM OF ENGLAND AND ITS ASSOCIATED STATES, CROWN DEPENDENCIES, AND OVERSEAS TERRITORIES

# PREAMBLE

Whereas a Constitutional Commission was established, in accordance with the Constitutional Transition Act [DATE], for the purpose of drafting and agreeing a written Constitution;

And whereas the objectives of the Constitution are to establish English statehood within the United Kingdom; to improve and consolidate democratic institutions; to promote good government, freedom, justice, and the common good; to defend the rule of law and protect human rights and civil liberties; to protect the autonomy of the Associated States, Crown Dependencies, and self-governing Overseas Territories; and to provide for the effective devolution of power within England;

And whereas the people of England hereby –

(a) acknowledge the supremacy of God, the dignity of the human person, and the need for freedom to be founded upon the rule of law and respect for moral and spiritual values;

(b) affirm our commitment to the principles of the Commonwealth Charter and to the fundamental rights declared in the United Nations Universal Declaration of Human Rights and the European Convention on Human Rights;

(c) declare our intention to establish and maintain an open society and democratic State in which all persons may, to the full extent of their capacity, play a due part in public and civic life, and where power shall be accountable to the people;

(d) pledge to uphold the solidarity of the United Kingdom in matters of mutual interest, while safeguarding the autonomy of the Associated States, Crown Dependencies, and Overseas Territories;

(e) resolve that the economic system should serve the common good by ensuring humane conditions of labour, protecting the weak, vulnerable and needy, providing quality public services, promoting the equitable distribution of wealth and resources, and ensuring good stewardship of the environment.

And whereas the text of the draft Constitution prepared by the Constitutional Commission has been approved in accordance with the terms required by the Constitutional Transition Act;

And whereas we, the people of England, loyal subjects of our sovereign lord King Charles, by the Grace of God, of England, and of his other realms and territories, King, Defender of the Faith, do by this Constitution, solemnly and mutually covenant and combine ourselves together into a civil body politic, for our better ordering and preservation, and furtherance of the objectives aforesaid;

And whereas the King wills and commands that the peace of the Church and of the Land be well kept and maintained in all points, and that common right be done to all, as well poor as rich, without respect of persons;

Now, therefore, be it ordered by the King's Most Excellent Majesty that the following shall have effect as the Constitution of the United Kingdom of England and its Associated States, Crown Dependencies, and Overseas Territories.

God Save the King

# CHAPTER I. THE STATE AND THE CONSTITUTION

**1.    Foundational Principles**

(1) ENGLAND shall be a self-governing Free State within the United Kingdom, to be known as the 'Kingdom of England'.

(2) England's form of government is a constitutional parliamentary democracy, founded upon Christian values and upon the principles of representative and responsible government, social justice, the common good, decentralisation, and respect for human rights, civil liberties, and the rule of law.

**2.    Supreme Law**

(1) Except as provided in subsection (2), this Constitution shall apply only to England.

(2) The following provisions of this Constitution shall apply throughout the United Kingdom –
   (a)  this section;
   (b)  section 3;
   (c)  Chapter XIV;
   (d)  the Sixth Schedule; and
   (e)  any other provision specifically referring or relating to the Associated States, Crown Dependencies, or Overseas Territories; and
   (f)  any other provision specifically referring or relating to United Kingdom institutions.

(3) This Constitution is the supreme law of England and, in so far as it applies to them under subsection (2), of the other parts of the United Kingdom.

(4) If any Act of Parliament or other law is inconsistent with this Constitution, this Constitution shall prevail and the Act of Parliament or other law shall, to the extent of inconsistency, be void.

### 3. Territorial Waters and Maritime Jurisdiction

(1) The United Kingdom claims its territorial waters, exclusive economic zone, and all other maritime rights, under international law.

(2) Except as otherwise agreed between the Government of England and the Government of the Associated State, Crown Dependency, or self-governing Overseas Territory concerned –

    (a) the Parliament of England may legislate for the territorial waters, the exclusive economic zone, and other maritime rights, under the jurisdiction of England, and all revenues arising therefrom shall accrue to the Government of England;

    (b) the legislature of each Associated State, Crown Dependency, and self-governing Overseas Territory may legislate for the territorial waters, the exclusive economic zone, and other maritime rights, under the jurisdiction of that Associated State, a Crown Dependency, or a self-governing Overseas Territory, and all revenues arising therefrom shall accrue to the Government thereof.

### 4. English Nationality

(1) Subject to subsection (2), all citizens of the United Kingdom ('British citizens') who were born in England, or who are permanently resident in England, shall have English nationality.

(2) An Act of Parliament may provide that a person to whom subsection (1) applies, who acquires 'belonger' status or nationality in some part of the United Kingdom other than England, shall thereby cease to have English nationality.

Provided that such person shall re-acquire English nationality upon returning to permanent residence in England or upon losing or renouncing 'belonger' status or nationality in another part of the United Kingdom.

### 5. National Symbols

(1) England's national flag shall be the Cross of St George.

(2) The English national anthem shall be 'Jerusalem'.

(3) The national emblem of England shall be the red and white English Rose.

(4) The royal banner of arms of England shall be the three lions emblem, blazoned: *Gules, three lions passant guardant in pale or armed and langued azure.*

(5) St George's Day and St Edmund's Day shall be recognised in honour of England's patron saints.

## 6. Official Languages

(1) English is the official language of England, and subject to this section is the working language of the English Parliament, public administration in England, and English courts and local authorities.

(2) It shall be the duty of the English Parliament, the English courts, and all other public bodies in England, to make adequate provision for –

(a) the use of Braille and British Sign Language as auxiliary languages in England for the benefit of persons who are blind, partially sighted, deaf, or hard of hearing; and

(b) the use of translators and interpreters for those not proficient in English –

(i) in relation to law enforcement and the judiciary in England, to the extent necessary in the interests of justice for the protection of their rights as guaranteed by this Constitution; and

(ii) in relation to public services in England, to the extent reasonably practicable to ensure adequate access to those services.

# CHAPTER II. FUNDAMENTAL RIGHTS AND FREEDOMS

7. **Right to Life**

(1) Everyone's right to life shall be protected by law.

(2) No one shall be sentenced to death or executed.

(3) No one shall be regarded as having been deprived of his or her life in contravention of this section if he or she dies as a result of a lawful act of war or from the use, to such extent and in such circumstances as are permitted by law, of such force as is absolutely necessary –
   (a) for the defence of any person from violence or for the defence of property;
   (b) in order to effect a lawful arrest or to prevent the escape of a person lawfully detained; or
   (c) for the purpose of suppressing a riot, insurrection, or mutiny.

8. **Prohibition of Torture**

No one shall be subjected to torture or to inhuman or degrading treatment or punishment.

9. **Prohibition of Slavery and Forced Labour**

(1) No one shall be held in slavery or servitude.

(2) No one shall be required to perform forced or compulsory labour.

(3) For the purpose of this section the term "forced or compulsory labour" shall not include:
   (a) any work, not of a hazardous, demeaning, or exploitative nature, required to be done by order of a court –
      (i) as a punishment for a criminal offence,
      (ii) in lieu of a sentence of fine or imprisonment, or any part thereof, or
      (iii) during conditional release from detention;
   (b) any service of a military character imposed by Act of Parliament during time of war or threat of invasion, or, in case of conscientious

objectors, civilian service exacted instead of compulsory military service;

(c) any service lawfully exacted in case of an emergency or calamity threatening the life or well-being of the community;

(d) any work or service which forms part of normal civic obligations.

## 10. Right to Personal Liberty and Security

(1) No one shall be seized, imprisoned, dispossessed, outlawed, exiled, or ruined in any way, nor in any way proceeded against, except by the lawful judgment of his or her peers and the law of the land.

(2) Everyone has the right to liberty and security of person. No one shall be deprived of his or her liberty save in the following cases and in accordance with a procedure prescribed by law:

(a) the lawful detention of a person after conviction by a competent court;

(b) the lawful arrest or detention of a person for non-compliance with the lawful order of a court or in order to secure the fulfilment of any obligation prescribed by law;

(c) the lawful arrest or detention of a person effected for the purpose of bringing him or her before the competent legal authority on reasonable suspicion of having committed an offence or when it is reasonably considered necessary to prevent his or her committing an offence or fleeing after having done so;

(d) the detention of a minor by lawful order for the purpose of educational supervision or his or her lawful detention for the purpose of bringing him or her before the competent legal authority;

(e) the enforcement of reasonably justifiable quarantine rules for the prevention of the spreading of infectious diseases;

(f) the lawful detention of persons of unsound mind, or persons whose cognitive capacity is severely impaired by alcohol or drugs, for the purposes of their self-protection;

(g) the lawful arrest or detention of a person to prevent his or her effecting an unauthorised entry into the country or of a person against whom action is being taken with a view to deportation or extradition.

(3) Everyone who is arrested shall be informed promptly, in a language which he or she understands, of the reasons for his or her arrest and of any charge against him or her.

(4) Everyone arrested or detained in accordance with the provisions of paragraph (c) of subsection (2) shall be brought promptly before a judge or magistrate and shall be entitled to trial within a reasonable time or to release pending trial. Release may be conditioned by guarantees to appear for trial.

(5) Everyone who is deprived of his or her liberty by arrest or detention shall be entitled to take proceedings by which the lawfulness of his or her detention shall be decided speedily by a court and his or her release ordered if the detention is not lawful.

(6) Everyone who has been the victim of arrest or detention in contravention of the provisions of this article shall have an enforceable right to compensation.

(7) No one shall be deprived of his or her liberty merely on the ground of inability to fulfil a contractual obligation.

11. **Right to a Fair Trial**

(1) To no one shall right or justice be sold, delayed, or denied. In the determination of his or her civil rights and obligations or of any criminal charge against him or her, everyone is entitled to a fair and public hearing within a reasonable time by an independent and impartial tribunal established by law. Judgment shall be pronounced publicly, but the press and public may be excluded from all or part of the trial in the interest of morals, public order, or national security as accepted in a democratic society, where the interests of juveniles or the protection of the private life of the parties so require, or to the extent strictly necessary in the opinion of the court in special circumstances where publicity would prejudice the interests of justice.

(2) Everyone charged with a criminal offence shall be presumed innocent until proven guilty according to law.

(3) Everyone charged with a criminal offence shall have the following minimum rights:
   (a) to be informed promptly, in a language which he or she understands and in detail, of the nature and cause of the accusation against him or her;
   (b) to have adequate time and the facilities for the preparation of his or her defence;
   (c) to defend himself or herself in person or through legal assistance of his or her own choosing or, if he or she has not sufficient means to pay for legal assistance, to be given it free of charge when the interests of justice so require;
   (d) to examine or have examined witnesses against him or her and to obtain the attendance and examination of witnesses on his or her behalf under the same conditions as witnesses against him or her;
   (e) to have the free assistance of an interpreter if he or she cannot understand or speak the language used in court; and
   (f) to be tried by jury in any case where trial by jury would have been allowed under the law of England in effect on the appointed day.

**12.   No Punishment without Law**

(1) No one shall be held guilty of any criminal offence on account of any act or omission which did not constitute a criminal offence at the time when it was committed, nor shall a heavier penalty be imposed than the one that was applicable at the time the criminal offence was committed.

(2) Subsection (1) shall not prejudice the trial and punishment of any person for any act or omission which, at the time when it was committed, was a crime against humanity according to the general principles of law recognised by civilised nations.

**13.   Right of Appeal in Criminal Matters**

(1) Everyone convicted of a criminal offence by a tribunal shall have the right to have his or her conviction or sentence reviewed by a higher tribunal. The exercise of this right, including the grounds on which it may be exercised, shall be governed by law.

(2) This right may be subject to exceptions in regard to offences of a minor character, as prescribed by law, or in cases in which the person concerned was tried in the first instance by the highest tribunal or was convicted following an appeal against acquittal.

**14.   Compensation for Wrongful Conviction**

When a person has by a final decision been convicted of a criminal offence and when subsequently his or her conviction has been reversed, or he or she has been pardoned, on the ground that a new or newly discovered fact shows conclusively that there has been a miscarriage of justice, the person who has suffered punishment as a result of such conviction shall be compensated according to law, unless it is proved that the nondisclosure of the unknown fact in time is wholly or partly attributable to him or her.

**15.   Right not to be Tried or Punished Twice**

(1) No one shall be liable to be tried or punished again in criminal proceedings for an offence for which he or she has already been finally acquitted or convicted in accordance with the law.

(2) The provisions of subsection (1) shall not prevent the reopening of the case in accordance with the law and penal procedure, if there is evidence of new or newly discovered facts, or if there has been a fundamental defect in the previous proceedings, which could affect the outcome of the case.

16. **Right to Respect for Private and Family Life**

(1) Everyone has the right to respect for his or her private and family life, home and correspondence.

(2) There shall be no interference by a public authority with the exercise of this right except such as is in accordance with the law and is necessary in a democratic society in the interests of national security, public safety, or the economic well-being of the country, for the prevention of disorder or crime, for the protection of public health, or for the protection of the rights and freedoms of others.

17. **Freedom of Thought, Conscience, and Religion**

(1) Everyone has the right to freedom of thought, conscience, and religion. This shall include –
   (a) freedom to change his or her religion or belief;
   (b) freedom, either alone or in community with others, and in public or private, to manifest his or her religion or belief, in worship, teaching, practice, and observance; and
   (c) freedom to deny, denounce, criticise, or ridicule, any religion, belief, or religious practice or institution.

(2) Freedom to manifest one's religion or beliefs shall be subject only to such limitations as are prescribed by law and are necessary in a democratic society in the interests of public safety, for the protection of public order, public health or acceptable standards of public morality, or for the protection of the rights and freedoms of others.

(3) In the exercise of any functions which they assume in relation to education and to teaching, the public authorities shall respect the right of parents to ensure such education and teaching in conformity with their own religious and philosophical convictions.

18. **Freedom of Expression**

(1) Everyone has the right to freedom of expression. This right shall include freedom to hold opinions and to receive and impart information and ideas without interference.

(2) The exercise of these freedoms, since it carries with it duties and responsibilities, may be subject to such formalities, conditions, restrictions, or penalties as are prescribed by law and are necessary in a democratic society, in the interests of national security, territorial integrity, or public safety, for the prevention of disorder or crime, for the protection of health or morals, for the protection of the reputation or rights of others, for preventing the disclosure of information received in confidence, or for maintaining the authority and impartiality of the judiciary.

(3) Subsection (1) shall not prevent the public authorities from requiring the licensing of broadcasting, television, or cinema enterprises according to law.

## 19. Freedom of Assembly and Association

(1) Everyone has the right to freedom of peaceful assembly and to freedom of association with others, including the right to form and to join trade unions for the protection of his or her interests.

(2) No restrictions shall be placed on the exercise of these rights other than such as are prescribed by law and are necessary in a democratic society in the interests of national security or public safety, for the prevention of disorder or crime, for the protection of health or morals, or for the protection of the rights and freedoms of others.

## 20. Right to Vote

(1) Subject to this section, every person who is a British citizen or a citizen of the Republic of Ireland and is at least eighteen years of age on the date of the poll, shall, if resident in England, be entitled to be registered as an elector and to vote in referendums, elections to the House of Commons, and elections to local authorities of the area in which he or she resides.

(2) Parliament may by law restrict the right of a person to be registered as an elector, to the extent justifiable in a free and democratic society, only on the grounds that he or she –
   (a) is under legal guardianship on grounds of insanity or severe mental incapacity;
   (b) is under a custodial sentence for a term of or exceeding twelve months; or
   (c) is a member of the Royal Family.

(3) An English national who is not resident in England at the time of a referendum or election may nevertheless be registered, and cast a vote, as an overseas voter, unless he or she is eligible to vote in an Associated State, Crown Dependency, or self-governing Overseas Territory.

(4) Parliament may provide by law for the granting of the right to be registered as an elector for local elections to non-citizens who are permanently resident in England.

## 21. Marriage Rights

(1) Men and women of marriageable age have the right to marry and to found a family, according to the laws governing the exercise of this right.

(2) Spouses shall enjoy equality of rights and responsibilities of a private law character between them, and in their relations with their children, as to marriage, during marriage and in the event of its dissolution.

(3) This section shall not prevent such laws being enacted as are necessary in the interests of children.

## 22.  Protection of Property

(1) Every natural or legal person is entitled to the peaceful enjoyment of possessions. No person shall be deprived of possessions except in the public interest and subject to the conditions provided for by law and by the general principles of international law.

(2) Subsection (1) shall not, however, impair the right of the Parliament, a County or City Assembly, or a local authority, within its competence –
   (a) to enact such laws as it may deem necessary to control the use of property in accordance with the general interest;
   (b) to secure the payment of taxes or other contributions or penalties; or
   (c) to bring utilities, infrastructure, public services, or strategic industries into public ownership, provided that compensation is paid in advance at prevailing market rates.

## 23.  Freedom of Movement

(1) Everyone lawfully within England shall, within that territory, have freedom of movement and the freedom to choose his or her residence.

(2) Everyone shall be free to leave the territory of England.

(3) No restrictions shall be placed on the exercise of the rights set forth in subsections (1) or (2) other than such as are in accordance with law and are necessary in a democratic society in the interests of national security or public safety, for the maintenance of public order, for the prevention of crime, for the protection of health or morals, or for the protection of the rights and freedoms of others.

## 24.  Right of Abode

(1) All British citizens, whether or not they are English nationals, and all citizens of the Republic of Ireland, have the right of abode in England; and no British or Irish citizen shall be expelled, by means either of an individual or of a collective measure, from the territory of England.

(2) No British or Irish citizen, or lawful resident of England, shall be deprived of the right to enter the territory of England.

## 25. Procedural Safeguards Relating to the Expulsion of Aliens

(1) Collective expulsion of aliens is prohibited.

(2) An alien lawfully resident in the territory of England shall not be expelled therefrom except in pursuance of a decision reached in accordance with law and shall be allowed:
   (a) to submit reasons against his or her expulsion;
   (b) to have his or her case reviewed; and
   (c) to be represented for these purposes before the competent authority or a person or persons designated by that authority.

(3) An alien may be expelled before the exercise of his or her rights under paragraphs (a), (b), and (c) of subsection (2), when such expulsion is necessary in the interests of public order or is grounded on reasons of national security.

## 26. Freedom of Information

(1) Everyone has the right to freedom of information, including –
   (a) access to official files, documents, reports, statistics, and other information, in whatever form; and
   (b) access to any information held on them by the public authorities or by any private person or corporation under contract to or on behalf of any public authority.

(2) No restrictions shall be placed on the right declared and recognised by subsection (1), other than such restrictions prescribed by law as are necessary in a democratic society, in the interests of national security, territorial integrity, or public safety, for the prevention of disorder or crime, for the protection of health or morals and of the reputation or the rights of others, privacy, prevention of contempt of court, protection of parliamentary privilege, for preventing the disclosure of information communicated in confidence, or for maintaining the authority and impartiality of the judiciary.

## 27. Prohibition of Discrimination

(1) Every individual is equal before and under the law, and has the right to the equal protection and equal benefit of the law without discrimination, and, in particular, without discrimination based on race, national or ethnic origin, colour, religion, sex, sexual orientation, age, or mental or physical disability.

(2) Subsection (1) does not preclude any law, programme, or activity that has as its object the amelioration of conditions of disadvantaged individuals or groups, including those that are disadvantaged because of race, national or ethnic origin, colour, religion, sex, age, or mental or physical disability.

### 28. Limitations and Restriction on Rights

(1) Nothing in this Chapter may be interpreted as implying for any public authority, group, or person any right to engage in any activity or perform any act aimed at the destruction of any of the rights and freedoms set forth herein or at their limitation to a greater extent than is provided for in this Chapter.

(2) The restrictions permitted under this Chapter to the said rights and freedoms shall not be applied for any purpose other than those for which they have been prescribed.

### 29. Right to an Effective Remedy

(1) Anyone whose rights or freedoms, as guaranteed by this Constitution, have been infringed or denied may apply to a court of competent jurisdiction to obtain such effective remedy as the court considers appropriate and just in the circumstances, notwithstanding that the violation has been committed by persons acting in an official capacity.

(2) Where, in proceedings under subsection (1), a court concludes that evidence was obtained in a manner that infringed or denied any rights or freedoms guaranteed by this Constitution, the evidence shall be excluded if it is established that, having regard to all the circumstances, the admission of it in the proceedings would bring the administration of justice into disrepute.

### 30. Existing Rights

The guarantee in this Constitution of certain rights, freedoms, or liberties shall not be construed as denying the existence of any other rights, freedoms, or liberties that exist by virtue of any statute, charter, royal warrant, letters patent, or by common law; but in case of any incompatibility between rights, freedoms, or liberties, those expressly guaranteed by this Constitution shall prevail over any other right, freedom, or liberty.

### 31. Derogation of Rights in Emergencies

(1) His Majesty, on the advice of the Prime Minister, may by proclamation declare that a state of emergency exists in England for the purposes of this section.

Provided that in so far as the circumstances allow, the Prime Minister should consult with the Leader of the Opposition before tendering such advice to His Majesty; and in any case, the Prime Minister should inform the Leader of the Opposition as soon as reasonably practicable after such advice has been tendered.

(2) A state of emergency may be declared under subsection (1) only on the grounds –

    (a) that the United Kingdom is at war, or a state of war is imminent, or any part of the territory of England, or of an Associated State, Crown Dependency, or Overseas Territory, is under threat of invasion or attack; or

    (b) that a public emergency has arisen as a result of natural disaster, flood, fire, outbreak of pestilence, outbreak of infectious disease, uprising or unrest, or other calamity, on such a scale as to be likely to endanger the public safety or to deprive the community, or any substantial portion of the community, of supplies or services essential to life.

(3) Every declaration of emergency shall, unless it has in the meantime been approved by a resolution of both Houses of Parliament supported by the votes of an absolute majority of the members of each House, expire –

    (a) in the case of a declaration made when Parliament is sitting, at the expiration of a period of seven days beginning with the date of publication of the declaration; and

    (b) in any other case, at the expiration of a period of twenty-one days beginning with the date of publication of the declaration.

Provided that Parliament shall without delay, and in any case within twenty-one days, be summoned to vote upon the declaration of emergency.

(4) A declaration of emergency that has been approved by a resolution of both Houses in pursuance of subsection (3) shall, subject to subsection (5), remain in force for six months or such shorter period as may be specified in the resolution, and that period may be renewed, by means of a resolution of both Houses supported by the votes of two-thirds of the members of each House, for further periods of not more than six months.

(5) A declaration of emergency may at any time be revoked –

    (a) by His Majesty acting on the advice of the Prime Minister; or

    (b) by a resolution of the House of Commons or House of Lords supported by the votes of a majority of the members of that House.

(6) Parliament may provide by law, during any period when a declaration of emergency is in effect and to the extent reasonably justifiable for the purpose of dealing with the emergency, for the limitation of the rights guaranteed by sections 10 (personal liberty and security), 16 (respect for private and family life), 19 (freedom of association and assembly), and 23 (freedom of movement).

(7) Orders and regulations made under any law enacted under subsection (6) shall be laid before both Houses as soon as may be practicable after coming into effect, and may be suspended or revoked by either House, by means of a resolution passed by an absolute majority of the members thereof.

(8) Laws enacted under subsection (6), and all orders and regulations made under any such law, shall unless sooner repealed or revoked cease to have effect upon the expiration or revocation of a declaration of emergency, and any person detained under any such law, regulation, or order shall thereupon be released, unless there are other lawful grounds for his or her continued detention.

## 32.   Human Rights Commission

(1) There shall be a Human Rights Commission which shall consist of a Chair and at least four other members, appointed by His Majesty on the advice of the Constitutional Offices Selection Commission in accordance with section 130.

(2) Subject to this Constitution and in accordance with any provisions prescribed by Act of Parliament, the Human Rights Commission shall have responsibility for –
  (a) promoting the protection and observance of, and respect for, human rights;
  (b) providing or supporting civic education about the rights and freedoms recognised in this Constitution, as well as in international treaties or conventions which have been incorporated into English law;
  (c) monitoring and reporting on the observance of human rights;
  (d) making recommendations to Ministers concerning any matter affecting the rights and freedoms recognised in this Constitution;
  (e) receiving and investigating complaints about alleged abuses of human rights, and taking steps to secure appropriate redress if human rights have been violated, including making applications to the courts for redress or for other forms of relief or remedies;
  (f) making recommendations to Parliament, or to local authorities, to improve the protection of human rights; and
  (g) performing any other functions or exercising any powers as are conferred on the Commission by law.

(3) The term of office of a member of the Human Rights Commission shall be –
  (a) in the case of the Chair, six years;
  (b) in the case of other members, five years.

# CHAPTER III. DIRECTIVE PRINCIPLES

**33. Applicability of Directive Principles**

(1) The Directive Principles enumerated by this Chapter are declaratory and are intended for the direction of the Government, Parliament, and other public authorities.

(2) Except as provided in subsection (3), sections 34 to 42 inclusive are non-justiciable, and do not give rise to any directly enforceable legal right or duty.

(3) The courts shall have due regard to the Directive Principles in the interpretation of the Constitution and other laws; and, in so far as it is possible to do so, courts shall read and give effect to primary and subordinate legislation in a way which is not incompatible with these Directive Principles.

(4) 'The State' in this Chapter means the Government, Parliament, local authorities, and other public bodies, in their respective spheres of authority.

**34. Protection of the Family**

(1) The State shall recognise and protect the family as a natural and fundamental unit of society.

(2) In particular, the State shall adopt measures to support marriage and to promote the material and moral well-being of families, including policies to achieve the eradication of child poverty.

**35. Conservation and Countryside**

(1) The State shall endeavour to conserve and restore the natural environment, and to safeguard and protect England's nature for future generations.

(2) The State shall take measures to protect natural habitats; prevent pollution and to maintain the purity of the air and water; sustainably manage

natural resources; promote bio-diversity and encourage soil health and wildlife; and prevent, reduce, and mitigate the effects of climate change.

(3) The State shall establish and maintain national parks, and shall promote public access to the countryside, including recognition of a 'right to roam' on mountains, coastal paths, open moors, and public land.

(4) The principles of this section shall be applied in ways that recognise the principles of sections 37 and 42.

### 36. Culture

(1) The State shall protect the cultural traditions and heritage of the English people, and promote the development and enrichment of English culture.

(2) In particular, the State shall preserve historic sites, monuments, and memorials, and shall maintain and support libraries, archives, museums, art galleries, theatres, orchestras, and other cultural amenities.

### 37. Housing

(1) The State shall be responsible for improving housing conditions.

(2) In particular, it shall be the responsibility of the State to ensure that everyone has a right to decent housing and that no person is involuntarily made homeless.

### 38. Healthcare

(1) The State shall be responsible for the promotion of public health and accessible, quality, healthcare.

(2) In particular, it shall be the duty of the State to provide for the maintenance of a high-quality National Health Service, freely accessible to all.

### 39. Education

(1) While respecting the rights of families to choose private, church, or home schooling, the State shall promote and support education.

(2) In particular, the State shall provide by law for publicly funded preschool, primary, and secondary education, and shall provide financial support to enable access to further and higher education.

### 40. Employment Rights

(1) The State shall protect the rights of workers, including the right to form and join trade unions for the promotion of their interests, the right to

collectively bargain, and the right to conditions of work which are fair and which respect the dignity of the person.

(2) In particular, it shall be the duty of the State to ensure by law that everyone has the right to safe and healthy conditions of work, to a decent living wage, and to adequate opportunities for rest and leisure.

### 41. Social Security and Pensions

It is the duty of the State to ensure that persons who are unable to work by reason of physical or mental disability or infirmity, or because of family caring responsibilities, or because they are unable to find suitable employment, or because they have reached the age of retirement, have a right to adequate means of financial support, including by public payments if required, to maintain their health, dignity, and independence.

### 42. Promotion of National Development

(1) The Government shall develop and implement a National Development Plan, the aims of which shall be to promote the sustainable, inclusive and equitable development of England, to support economic, industrial, and infrastructural growth, to increase national prosperity, to improve the quality of life of the people, and to eradicate poverty.

(2) Parliament may enact legislation to regulate economic activity for the common good, which may include, but shall not be limited to, regulation for the protection of workers, consumers, and the environment.

(3) Parliament may enact legislation to nationalise utilities, services, and infrastructure, as well as industries of national economic or strategic importance, and to provide for their operation by publicly owned corporations for the national interest.

### 43. Reports to Parliament

(1) The Government shall report annually to both Houses of Parliament on progress made towards the implementation of the National Development Plan and towards the realisation of these Directive Principles.

(2) The report made under subsection (1) shall be the subject of a debate on a substantive motion in each House.

# CHAPTER IV. HEAD OF STATE

### 44. His Majesty to be Head of State

(1) His Majesty King Charles III, and His heirs and successors according to law, shall be the Head of State.

(2) Every reference to His Majesty in this Constitution shall be deemed to also include a reference to His Majesty's heirs and successors to the Crown according to law.

(3) Subject to the proviso to subsection (1) of section 171, the royal styles and titles of His Majesty and his heirs and successors, and of the Royal Family, shall be prescribed by Act of Parliament.

### 45. Parliament to Regulate Succession

(1) The law of succession shall be determined by Act of Parliament.

(2) In recognition of the conventions established by the Statute of Westminster 1931 and the Perth Agreement 2011 no Bill to alter the succession shall be introduced to Parliament unless the Prime Minister has consulted the Heads of Government of His Majesty's other Realms and Territories.

### 46. Powers and Functions of Head of State

(1) The only lawful powers and functions of His Majesty are those prescribed by this Constitution or by any law in effect under this Constitution, and such powers and functions shall be exercised solely in accordance with this Constitution and the law.

(2) Subsection (1) shall not be construed as preventing His Majesty, in his own deliberate judgment, from performing –
    (a) ceremonial, civic, social, or charitable functions, of a non-partisan nature, in accordance with the customs and traditions of parliamentary monarchy; or
    (b) functions in relation to the office of Head of the Commonwealth, if occupying that office.

### 47. Head of State to Act on Advice

(1) All powers, functions, and duties of His Majesty under this Constitution shall be exercised in accordance with the advice of the Cabinet, or of the Prime Minister, or of a responsible Minister acting under the general authority of the Cabinet.

(2) Subsection (1) shall not apply where His Majesty is –
   (a) required by this Constitution to act on the advice of any other person or authority;
   (b) required by this Constitution to act in a situation without a need for advice; or
   (c) authorised by this Constitution to act in accordance with his own deliberate judgment.

(3) The question of whether His Majesty has received or acted in accordance with advice under this section shall not be enquired into in any court of law; but the validity and lawfulness of any act arising from such advice may nevertheless be subject to judicial review according to law.

(4) If His Majesty is required to exercise any power or to perform any function in accordance with the advice of any person or authority, and he does not so act within seven days after the advice is received by His Majesty, or within such period as the person or authority tendering that advice shall specify, then His Majesty shall at the end of that period be deemed to have acted in accordance with the advice.

### 48. Head of State to be Informed

The Prime Minister shall keep His Majesty informed concerning the general conduct of the Government and shall furnish His Majesty with such information as he may from time to time request with respect to any particular matter relating to the Government of England.

### 49. Coronation Oath

(1) Subject to subsection (2), each successor to the Crown shall take and subscribe the Coronation Oath in the form set out in the First Schedule within ninety days after his or her accession.

(2) A person who is a minor upon accession to the Crown shall take the Coronation Oath within ninety days after he or she ceases to be a minor.

### 50. Regency and Counsellors of State

(1) Parliament may make provision by law for the appointment of a Regent to act as Head of State during the minority or prolonged incapacity of the King (or Queen regnant).

(2) Parliament may make provision by law for the appointment of one or more Counsellors of State to perform such functions of the Head of State as may be delegated to them during any period in which His Majesty is temporarily absent or incapacitated.

(3) Any reference in this Constitution to His Majesty shall be taken to include a Regent or a Counsellor of State authorised to perform the functions of Head of State under this section.

## 51. Royal Finances

(1) There shall be payable out of the Consolidated Fund such monies, to be known as the 'Sovereign Grant', as may from time to time be prescribed by Act of Parliament for the maintenance of the Head of State, the Royal Family, and the Royal Household.

(2) The Keeper of the Privy Purse shall be responsible for publishing the annual accounts of the Royal Household. Those accounts shall be subject to auditing by the National Audit Office.

## 52. Household Officers and Staff

(1) Subject to any provisions prescribed by Act of Parliament, the authority to appoint the Lord Steward, Lord Chamberlain, Private Secretary to the Sovereign, Keeper of the Privy Purse, Master of the Household, and other officers and staff of the Royal Household, and to remove and to exercise disciplinary control over these officers and staff, is vested in His Majesty acting in accordance with his own deliberate judgment.

(2) Subsection (1) does not apply to those officers of the Household acting as Government party whips, who shall be appointed and dismissed by His Majesty on the advice of the Prime Minister.

## 53. Privy Council

(1) There shall be a Privy Council of England, which shall consist of –
    (a) all persons who hold, or have held, under this Constitution, the offices of –
        (i) Prime Minister,
        (ii) Minister of Cabinet rank,
        (iii) Speaker of the House of Commons,
        (iv) Lord Speaker,
        (v) Leader of the Opposition,
        (vi) Leader of the Third Party,
        (vii) President, Deputy President, or Justice of the Supreme Court,
        (viii) Lord Chief Justice, or Master of the Rolls, and
        (ix) Archbishop of Canterbury or Archbishop of York.

(b) such persons, being English nationals and at least forty years of age, as His Majesty on the advice of the Prime Minister, after consultation with the Leader of the Opposition, may appoint to the Privy Council.

(2) For the transaction of routine business only Privy Councillors who are Ministers shall attend the Privy Council, and three Ministers shall constitute a quorum for an official act of the Privy Council.

(3) His Majesty acting on the advice of the Prime Minister may summon meetings of the Privy Council for the consideration of any matter of State of fundamental importance.

(4) A member of the Privy Council shall hold office as such for life, unless he or she –
   (a) resigns from the Privy Council;
   (b) is removed from the Privy Council by His Majesty, acting on the advice of the Prime Minister, after consultation with the Leader of the Opposition, on the grounds of gross misconduct;
   (c) is disqualified from membership of the Privy Council under any Act of Parliament.

(5) Privy Councillors shall be administered the Privy Council Oath as prescribed in the First Schedule.

# CHAPTER V. EXECUTIVE

### 54. Executive Power

(1) The executive authority of England shall be vested in His Majesty, and subject to the provisions of this Constitution shall be exercised by His Majesty's Government, or by any Minister thereof, either directly or through officers subordinate to them.

(2) Nothing in this section shall prevent Parliament from conferring functions of an executive or administrative nature on other persons or authorities.

### 55. Government and Cabinet

(1) The English Government shall consist of the Prime Minister, the Deputy Prime Minister, the Great Officers of State, the Secretaries of State, and other Ministers of Cabinet rank, and the Ministers of State and junior Ministers (however designated).

(2) There shall be a Cabinet which shall consist of the Prime Minister, the Deputy Prime Minister, the Great Officers of State, and such Secretaries of State and other Ministers as His Majesty acting upon the advice of the Prime Minister may from time to time summon and appoint to the Cabinet.

(3) The Cabinet shall be the principal instrument of policy, and shall be charged with the general direction and control of the English Government, for which it shall be collectively responsible to the House of Commons.

### 56. Appointment of Ministers

(1) The Prime Minister of England shall be appointed by His Majesty in accordance with this section.

(2) Whenever the office of Prime Minister is vacant, His Majesty shall appoint as Prime Minister the member of the House of Commons who is leader of the party or coalition having a majority of seats in that House.

(3) If a Prime Minister cannot be appointed under subsection (2), whether because no one party or coalition has a majority of seats, or because the

party or coalition having a majority of seats does not have an undisputed leader who is willing to serve as Prime Minister, or for other cause, His Majesty shall appoint as Prime Minister the member of the House of Commons who is nominated by a resolution of that House.

(4) Subject to this Constitution, the House of Commons may, by Standing Orders, make provision for the proposal of candidates and for the conduct of voting upon resolutions for the nomination of a Prime Minister under subsection (3), but any such resolution shall be voted upon by open voting and shall be passed if approved by a simple majority of the members present and voting.

(5) His Majesty, acting on the advice of the Prime Minister, shall appoint Ministers other than the Prime Minister.

### 57. Removal of Ministers

(1) If following a general election it shall appear that the Prime Minister, as a result of that election, does not command the confidence of a majority in the House of Commons, and the Prime Minister does not resign, His Majesty may in his own deliberate judgment remove the Prime Minister from office.

(2) If the House of Commons passes a resolution supported by the votes of a majority of all the members of the House declaring that it has no confidence in the Government and the Prime Minister does not resign within five days after the passing of that resolution, His Majesty shall, subject to subsection (3), remove the Prime Minister from office.

(3) His Majesty shall not remove the Prime Minister from office under subsection (2) if, within five days following a vote of no confidence –
   (a) the House of Commons passes a resolution that it has confidence in the Government; or
   (b) Parliament is dissolved by His Majesty upon the advice of the Prime Minister.

(4) The Prime Minister shall also cease to hold office –
   (a) upon his or her death;
   (b) if he or she tenders his or her resignation in writing to His Majesty;
   (c) if he or she ceases to be a member of the House of Commons otherwise than by reason of the dissolution of Parliament.

(5) A Minister other than the Prime Minister shall cease to hold office –
   (a) upon his or her death;
   (b) if he or she tenders his or her resignation in writing to the Prime Minister;
   (c) if His Majesty, on the advice of the Prime Minister, dismisses him or her;

(d) if he or she ceases to be a member of either House of Parliament otherwise than by reason of the dissolution of Parliament; or

(e) if the Prime Minister resigns, is removed, or otherwise ceases to hold office.

(6) A Minister who ceases to hold office under paragraph (e) of subsection (5) shall continue to serve in a caretaker capacity until he or she is re-appointed, or until his or her successor is appointed, in accordance with this Constitution.

## 58.   Number of Ministers

(1) The total number of Cabinet Ministers (including the Prime Minister) shall not at any time exceed twenty.

(2) The total number of persons holding ministerial office shall not at any time exceed one-sixth of the total membership of the House of Commons.

## 59.   Ministers to be Members of Parliament

(1) Subject to the provisions of this section –
    (a) a person may hold ministerial office only if he or she is a member of the House of Commons or of the House of Lords; and
    (b) the Prime Minister, Deputy Prime Minister, Chancellor of the Exchequer, and a majority of the Ministers of Cabinet rank must be appointed from among the members of the House of Commons.

(2) If Parliament is dissolved, a person who was a member of the House of Commons or the House of Lords immediately before the dissolution may be appointed to, or may continue to hold, ministerial office, for up to sixty days after the day on which Parliament meets following the general election after such dissolution, after which period he or she shall cease to hold ministerial office unless he or she is a member of the House of Commons, or of the Lords, as required by subsection (1).

## 60.   Absence, Incapacity, or Vacancy of the Prime Minister

(1) Whenever the Prime Minister is absent from England, or is by reason of illness or other cause unable to perform the functions of his or her office, His Majesty, on the advice of the Prime Minister, if there is a Prime Minister in office and if the Prime Minister is capable of tendering such advice, or otherwise on the advice of the Cabinet, may authorise the Deputy Prime Minister or some other member of the Cabinet to perform those functions, until that authorisation is in like manner revoked.

(2) If the office of Prime Minister is vacant because of the death or resignation of the incumbent, and until such time as a Prime Minister is appointed in accordance with section 56, His Majesty on the advice of the Cabinet shall authorise the Deputy Prime Minister or some other member of the Cabinet to perform the duties of Prime Minister.

## 61. Allocation of Portfolios

(1) His Majesty, acting on the advice of the Prime Minister, may, by directions in writing, charge the Prime Minister or any other Minister with responsibility for any business of the Government, including the administration of any department thereof.

(2) Each Minister shall be individually responsible for his or her personal conduct and for the policy and administration of the department under his or her charge.

## 62. Leave of Absence and Acting Ministers

(1) His Majesty, acting in accordance with the advice of the Prime Minister, may grant leave of absence from his or her duties to any Minister other than the Prime Minister.

(2) Whenever any Minister is for any cause unable to perform any of the functions of his or her office, whether or not leave of absence has been requested or granted, His Majesty on the advice of the Prime Minister may appoint any other person qualified to hold ministerial office to act in the said Minister's stead, either generally or in the performance of any particular function.

## 63. Oaths to be Taken by Ministers

No person shall enter upon the duties of any ministerial office unless he or she has taken and subscribed the Oath of Allegiance and Oath of Office (and, in the case of a Minister newly appointed to the Privy Council, the Privy Council Oath), as prescribed by the First Schedule.

## 64. Permanent Secretaries and Cabinet Secretary

(1) Where any Minister has been charged with responsibility for any department of the Government of England, he or she shall exercise general direction and control over that department; and, subject to such direction and control, the department shall be under the supervision of a senior public officer (in this Constitution referred to as a Permanent Secretary) appointed for that purpose.

(2) There shall be a Cabinet Secretary, who shall be a senior public officer, and who shall –

    (a) have charge of the Cabinet Office;

    (b) be responsible, in accordance with such instructions as may be given to him or her by the Prime Minister, for arranging the business for, and keeping the minutes of, the Cabinet, and for conveying the decisions of the Cabinet to the appropriate authority; and

    (c) have such other functions as the Prime Minister may lawfully direct.

## 65. Ministerial Code and Cabinet Manual

(1) The Cabinet Secretary, under the general direction of the Prime Minister, and after consultation with the Leader of the Opposition and Leader of the Third Party, shall draft and lay before Parliament –

    (a) a Ministerial Code, which shall *inter alia* provide authoritative official guidance on the procedures and practices of the Cabinet, the duties and responsibilities of Ministers, the relationship between Ministers and civil servants, the conduct of Ministers in relation to Parliament, and the standards of ethics, conduct, professional behaviour, and integrity expected of Minsters; and

    (b) a Cabinet Manual, which shall provide authoritative official guidance on the operation of constitutional conventions and practices under this Constitution.

(2) Any revisions to the Ministerial Code or Cabinet Manual shall come into effect only after having been scrutinised by the Privileges Committee of the House of Commons and then approved by a resolution of that House.

## 66. Law Officers

(1) The Law Officers are senior Crown officials, of ministerial rank, appointed under this section to provide legal advice to the Government or to perform such other duties of a legal character as may be conferred upon them in accordance with this Constitution.

(2) The Law Officers include –

    (a) the Attorney-General, who shall be the principal legal advisor to the Government; and

    (b) the Solicitor-General, who shall deputise for and assist the Attorney-General as required, and to whom any function vested in the Attorney-General may, by order of the Attorney-General, be delegated.

(3) Notwithstanding sections 56 and 57, the Law Officers shall be appointed and removed by His Majesty on the advice of the Prime Minister after consultation with the Judicial Service Commission.

(4) No person shall be appointed as a Law Officer unless he or she has right of audience in the superior courts and possesses such other legal qualifications and experience as may be prescribed by Act of Parliament.

(5) A Law Officer may be a member of either House of Parliament and may attend sittings of either House of Parliament, but may vote only in the House of which he or she is a member.

(6) The Law Officers shall not be members of the Cabinet, but may be summoned by the Prime Minister to attend Cabinet meetings as required to give advice on legal matters.

(7) If a Law Officer resigns or is removed from office, the Prime Minister shall cause the circumstances of the resignation or removal to be communicated by statement to the House of Commons within one week after removal, if the Parliament be sitting, or, if it be not sitting, within one week after the opening of the next session of Parliament.

(8) The specification of certain duties or functions to be performed by a Law Officer in this Constitution shall not prevent additional duties, functions, or powers being conferred upon that Law Officer by or in accordance with the law.

(9) If a Law Officer is for any reason unable to perform the duties and functions of his or her office, those duties and functions may be performed by such other suitably qualified person as may be prescribed by law.

(10) In the exercise of any powers conferred on a Law Officer by any law requiring the Law Officer to act in accordance with his or her individual judgment, the Law Officer shall not be subject to the direction or control of any other person or authority.

## 67. Director of Public Prosecutions

(1) There shall be a Director of Public Prosecutions who shall be a public officer.

(2) The Director of Public Prosecutions shall be appointed by His Majesty on the advice of the Prime Minister given after consultation with the Judicial Service Commission.

(3) No person shall be appointed as Director of Public Prosecutions unless he or she has right of audience in the superior courts and possesses such legal qualifications and experience as may be prescribed by or in accordance with an Act of Parliament.

(4) The Director of Public Prosecutions shall not be a member of either House of Parliament.

(5) The Director of Public Prosecutions shall serve for a term of four years and may be reappointed, but may be removed by His Majesty on

the advice of the Prime Minister, after consultation with the Judicial Service Commission, on grounds of incapacity, neglect of duty, or gross misconduct.

Provided that if a Director of Public Prosecutions is removed from office the Prime Minister shall cause the circumstances of the removal to be communicated by statement to the House of Commons within one week after removal, if the Parliament be sitting, or, if the Parliament be not sitting, within one week after the opening of the next session of Parliament.

(6) The Director of Public Prosecutions shall have the power in any case in which he or she considers it desirable so to do –

(a) to institute criminal proceedings against any person before any court of law (other than a court-martial) in respect of any offence alleged to have been committed by that person;

(b) to take over and continue any such criminal proceedings that have been instituted or undertaken by any other person or authority; and

(c) to discontinue at any stage before judgment is delivered any such criminal proceedings instituted or undertaken by himself or herself, or by any other person or authority.

(7) Subject to subsection (9), the powers conferred on the Director of Public Prosecutions by paragraphs (b) and (c) of subsection (6) shall be vested in him or her to the exclusion of any other person or authority.

Provided that where any other person or authority has instituted criminal proceedings, nothing in this section shall prevent the withdrawal of those proceedings by or at the instance of that person or authority, and with the leave of the court.

(8) For the purposes of this section, any appeal from a judgment in criminal proceedings before any court or any case stated or question of law reserved for the purpose of any such proceedings to any other court shall be deemed to be part of those proceedings.

Provided that the power conferred on the Director of Public Prosecutions by paragraph (c) of subsection (6) shall not be exercised in relation to any appeal by a person convicted in any criminal proceedings or to any case stated or question of law reserved at the instance of such a person.

(9) The powers of the Director of Public Prosecutions may be exercised by him or her in person, or through other suitably qualified persons deputised to act under the delegated authority of the Director of Public Prosecutions and in accordance with his or her general or special instructions.

## 68.   Prerogative of Mercy

(1)  His Majesty may –
  (a)  grant to any person convicted of any offence a pardon, either free of conditions or subject to lawful conditions;
  (b)  grant to any person a respite, either indefinite or for a specified period, from the execution of any punishment imposed on that person for such an offence;
  (c)  substitute a less severe form of punishment for that imposed on any person for such an offence; or
  (d)  remit the whole or part of any punishment imposed on any person for such an offence or any penalty or forfeiture otherwise due to the Crown on account of such an offence.

(2)  The powers of His Majesty under subsection (1) shall be exercised on the advice of the Advisory Committee on the Prerogative of Mercy.

(3)  The Advisory Committee on the Prerogative of Mercy shall consist of –
  (a)  the Minister responsible for Justice, as Chair;
  (b)  the Attorney-General, or in the absence thereof the Solicitor-General;
  (c)  three other persons appointed by His Majesty on the advice of the Prime Minister, at least one of whom shall be a probation officer or social worker and at least one of whom shall be a medical practitioner.

(4)  Further provision on the composition, tenure, organisation, and functioning of the Advisory Committee on the Prerogative of Mercy may be made by Act of Parliament.

# CHAPTER VI. PARLIAMENT

## *Division 1. Establishment of Parliament*

### 69.  Composition of Parliament

There shall be a Parliament of England, which shall consist of His Majesty, the House of Commons, and the House of Lords.

## *Division 2. The House of Commons*

### 70.  Composition of the House of Commons

The House of Commons shall consist of five hundred members, styled 'Members of Parliament', who shall be elected by the registered electors using the Additional Member System of proportional representation, such that –

(a) two hundred and fifty members (styled 'constituency members') shall be elected from single-member constituencies; and

(b) two hundred and fifty members (styled 'list members') shall be elected from regional lists on a compensatory basis so as to ensure overall proportional representation by party.

### 71.  Qualifications for Membership of House of Commons

(1) Subject to subsection (2), a person shall be qualified for election as a member of the House of Commons, and shall not be so qualified unless, at the date of his or her nomination for election —

(a) he or she has attained the age of eighteen years;

(b) he or she is an English national;

(c) he or she is registered as an elector in elections of the House of Commons; and

(d) he or she is resident in the constituency or region for which he or she is a candidate.

(2) No person shall be qualified to be a member of, or to be nominated for election to, the House of Commons if he or she —

(a) is, by virtue of his or her own act, under any acknowledgement of allegiance, obedience, or adherence to any foreign power or State;

(b) is under any law adjudged or otherwise declared to be of unsound mind;

(c) is an undischarged bankrupt, having been adjudged or otherwise declared bankrupt under any law;

(d) is under a custodial sentence for a term of or exceeding twelve months;

(e) has at any time in the previous five years been convicted by any court of any offence that is connected with corrupt or illicit electoral practices and is prescribed by Act of Parliament as a disqualifying offence;

(f) is a member of the Electoral Commission or the Boundaries Commission, or the holder of any other office, specified by law, the functions of which involve responsibility for, or in connection with, the conduct of any election to the House of Commons, County or City Authorities, or other local authorities;

(g) is a public officer, a judge, a police officer, a member of the Armed Forces, or the holder of any other office of profit in the service of the Crown (other than a ministerial office) or other public employment which disqualifies him or her from membership of the House of Commons under any Act of Parliament; or

(h) has an interest in any contract with the Government of England that is proscribed by or in accordance with an Act of Parliament.

(3) For the purposes of this section –

(a) 'member of the Armed Forces' means a member of the Royal Navy, Army, Royal Air Force, or other Armed Forces of the Crown, but does not include retired members or reservists not on active service;

(b) a person in receipt of a pension from the Crown shall not solely by reason of that pension be deemed to hold an 'office of profit in the service of the Crown';

(c) two or more terms of imprisonment that are required to be served consecutively shall be regarded as a single term of imprisonment for the aggregate period of those terms.

(4) No person may at any election be a candidate for more than one constituency or list.

## 72. Tenure of Office of Members of the House of Commons

(1) Subject to this section, a member of the House of Commons shall serve until the next dissolution of Parliament following his or her election.

(2) A member of the House of Commons shall also cease to hold office as such if he or she –

(a) becomes a member of the House of Lords;

(b) ceases to be qualified for election to the House of Commons, or becomes disqualified for election to the House of Commons, under section 71 or under any law made in pursuance of that section;

(c) fails to attend sittings of the House of Commons for three consecutive months of any session of the Parliament, except in so far as permission for reasonable absence (on the grounds of sick leave, compassionate leave, parental leave, or otherwise) may be granted according to the Standing Orders of the House;

(d) resigns his or her seat in writing to the Speaker; or

(e) is recalled from office in accordance with any Act of Parliament providing for the recall of members by their electors on the grounds of gross misconduct.

(3) A member of the House of Commons who has been adjudged or declared to be of unsound mind, adjudged or declared bankrupt, sentenced to imprisonment, or convicted of any offence prescribed under paragraph (d) or (e) of subsection (2) of section 71 of this Constitution shall be suspended from the sittings of the House, but shall not cease, on that ground, to be a member of the House of Commons until such time as any rights of appeal against that decision have been exhausted.

## 73. Vacancies in the House of Commons

(1) Whenever the seat of any member of the House of Commons becomes vacant by reason of death, resignation, or otherwise –

(a) in the case of a constituency member, His Majesty acting on the advice of the Speaker of the House of Commons shall issue writs for a by-election to take place in the appropriate constituency within ninety days of the vacancy arising; or

(b) in the case of a list member, the Speaker of the House of Commons shall inform the Electoral Commission, which shall assign the seat to the next-ranking person on the party list, in the appropriate region, of the former member, who is qualified and willing to serve as a member.

(2) This section shall not apply if Parliament is dissolved, or if it is due to be dissolved under subsection (1) of section 107 during the ninety days after the vacancy arising.

## 74. Speaker and Deputy Speakers of the House of Commons

(1) There shall be a Speaker and one or more Deputy Speakers of the House of Commons who shall be elected by the House from among its members.

(2) The election of the Speaker and the Deputy Speakers shall be by secret ballot and by majority vote; if no candidate for the office of Speaker or Deputy Speaker receives a majority of the votes cast, subsequent rounds of voting shall take place, and the candidate who receives the lowest number of votes shall be eliminated after each round of voting.

(3) The election of a Speaker, or Deputy Speakers, shall take place –
(a) as soon as may be practicable after Parliament first meets following a general election; and
(b) whenever the office of Speaker, or Deputy Speaker, is vacant.

(4) A person shall not be qualified to be elected as Speaker or Deputy Speaker if he or she holds ministerial office.

(5) The Speaker or a Deputy Speaker shall vacate his or her office—
(a) if he or she ceases to be a member of the House of Commons;
(b) if he or she is appointed to any ministerial office or as a shadow Minister;
(c) when Parliament first meets following a general election;
(d) if he or she is removed from office by resolution of the House of Commons supported by the votes of two-thirds of all the voting members; or
(e) if he or she resigns the office of Speaker or Deputy Speaker in writing to His Majesty.

(6) If the office of Speaker is vacant, no business shall be transacted in the House of Commons other than –
(a) the election of a Speaker; and
(b) the swearing-in of new members of the House.

(7) The Speaker and Deputy Speakers shall –
(a) perform their duties impartially, on behalf the House as a whole, with particular regard to the rights of all members to be fairly heard;
(b) cease, while in that office, to be an active member of any political party; and
(c) vote only to exercise a casting vote, according to convention, in case of a tie.

(8) In the absence of the Speaker and Deputy Speakers, the House of Commons may elect any member of that House (not holding ministerial office or being a shadow Minister) to preside.

## Division 3. The House of Lords

### 75. Composition of the House of Lords

(1) The House of Lords shall consist of four hundred Peers of the Realm, styled 'Parliamentary Peers'.

(2) The Parliamentary Peers shall be appointed by His Majesty on the advice of the Lords Appointments Commission established by section 76.

(3) The Parliamentary Peers shall be appointed from among persons who are qualified in accordance with section 77, from the following categories –
(a) persons who have held ministerial office or other high political or parliamentary office;

(b) persons who have served with merit and distinction in high administrative, military, diplomatic, or judicial office;

(c) persons who represent trade unions, manufacturers, chambers of commerce, professional associations, agriculturalists, or other relevant economic or social interests;

(d) serving or former archbishops or bishops of the Church of England, or leaders of other Christian churches, or of other religious bodies recognised by law;

(e) persons who have made outstanding contributions to academia, the arts, culture, philosophy, jurisprudence, science, industry, technology, philanthropy, or charitable work; or

(f) persons who have held office as Mayor or Chief Executive Officer of a County or City, or as the Leader or Chair of a borough or district council, or have otherwise held senior local government office.

(4) The Lords Appointments Commission shall establish an open and transparent process by which nominees for appointment as Parliamentary Peers may be proposed by Ministers, public entities, trade unions, professional associations, churches and other religious bodies, academic institutions, other civil society organisations, and the public.

(5) In making nominations for the appointment of Parliamentary Peers, the Lords Appointments Commission shall endeavour to ensure that all nominations are made –

(a) on merit, according to the qualifications, expertise, experience, wisdom, character, integrity, and virtue of the candidates;

(b) in such a way as to maintain a balance of representation in the House of Lords between the six qualifying categories enumerated in subsection (3); and

(c) with due consideration to the need for the Lords to represent the diversity of English society in terms of sex or gender, socio-economic class, ethnicity, religion, region of origin or residence, and political affiliation.

## 76. Lords Appointments Commission

(1) There shall be a Lords Appointments Commission which shall consist of –

(a) the Lord Speaker, who shall be *ex-officio* Chair of the Commission;

(b) two members, at least one of whom shall have held ministerial office, appointed by His Majesty on the advice of the Prime Minister;

(c) one member appointed by His Majesty on the advice of the Leader of the Opposition;

(d) one member appointed by His Majesty on the advice of the Leader of the Third Party;

(e) one member, being a person who has held senior judicial office, appointed by His Majesty on the advice of the Judicial Service Commission;

(f) one member, being a person who has held senior local government office, appointed by His Majesty on the advice of the National Council of Local Authorities;

(g) one member, being a serving or retired bishop of the Church of England, appointed by His Majesty on the advice of the Archbishop of Canterbury, given after consultation with the Archbishop of York;

(h) one member, being a former senior civil servant of Permanent Secretary grade or equivalent, appointed by His Majesty on the advice of the Public Service Commission;

(i) two members appointed by His Majesty on the advice of the Convenor of Crossbench Peers, given after consultation with the President of the Royal Society and the President of the British Academy; and

(j) one member, being a former senior officer of the Armed Forces, appointed by His Majesty on the advice of the Defence Council.

(2) In making appointments under subsection (1), consideration shall be given to the gender balance, regional balance, and political balance of the Lords Appointments Commission.

(3) The members of the Lords Appointments Commission shall be appointed as soon as possible, and in any case within ninety days, after the first meeting of Parliament following a general election and, subject to this Constitution, they shall serve until the next dissolution of Parliament.

## 77. Qualifications for Membership of the House of Lords

(1) Subject to this section, a person shall be qualified for membership of the Lords if, and shall not be so qualified unless, he or she is an English national and has attained the age of forty years at least.

(2) The provisions of subsections (2) and (3) of section 71 shall apply, *mutatis mutandis*, to the Lords.

(3) A Parliamentary Peer may not be a member of the House of Commons nor be a candidate for election to that House, but for the avoidance of doubt it is hereby declared that a member of a local authority may simultaneously serve in the House of Lords.

(4) A serving member of the Lords Appointments Commission, who is not already a Parliamentary Peer, shall not, while continuing in that office, be eligible for appointment to the House of Lords.

### 78. Tenure of Office of Parliamentary Peers

(1) Subject to subsection (2), a Parliamentary Peer shall hold office in the House of Lords until the end of the session of Parliament immediately following their eightieth birthday.

(2) A person shall also cease to be a member of the House of Lords if he or she –
  (a) ceases to be qualified for membership of the House of Lords, or becomes disqualified for membership of the House of Lords;
  (b) fails to attend sittings of the Lords for three consecutive months of any session of the Parliament, except in so far as permission for reasonable absence (on the grounds of sick leave, compassionate leave, parental leave, or otherwise) may be granted according to the Standing Orders of the House of Lords;
  (c) is removed for gross misconduct by means of a resolution of the House of Lords passed by a three-fourths majority of members; or
  (d) resigns his or her seat in writing to the Lord Speaker.

### 79. Vacancies in the House of Lords

Whenever the seat in the House of Lords becomes vacant, the Lord Speaker shall without delay inform the Lords Appointments Commission, which shall, as soon as may be practicable and in any case within ninety days after notice has been given, nominate to His Majesty a suitably qualified person for appointment as a Parliamentary Peer.

### 80. Lord Speaker and Deputy Lord Speakers

(1) There shall be a Lord Speaker and at least one Deputy Lord Speaker, who shall be elected by the House of Lords from among its members.

(2) The election of the Lord Speaker and Deputies shall be by secret ballot and by majority vote; if no candidate receives a majority of the votes cast, subsequent rounds of voting shall take place, with the candidate who receives the lowest number of votes being eliminated after each round of voting.

(3) The election of the Lord Speaker and Deputies shall take place –
  (a) as soon as may be practicable after Parliament first meets following a general election; and
  (b) whenever the office of Lord Speaker, or Deputy, is vacant.

(4) A person shall not be qualified to be elected as the Lord Speaker or as a Deputy Lord Speaker if he or she holds ministerial office.

(5) The Lord Speaker, or a Deputy Lord Speaker, shall vacate his or her office—
  (a) if he or she ceases to be a member of the House of Lords;

(b) if he or she is appointed to any ministerial office or as a shadow Minister;

(c) when the House of Lords first meets after a general election;

(d) if he or she is removed from office by resolution of the House of Lords supported by the votes of two-thirds of all the voting members; or

(e) if he or she resigns the office of Lord Speaker, or Deputy, in writing to His Majesty.

(6) If the office of Lord Speaker is vacant, no business shall be transacted in the House of Lords, except –

(a) the election of a Lord Speaker; and

(b) the installation of new Parliamentary Peers.

(7) The Lord Speaker and Deputies shall –

(a) perform their duties impartially, on behalf the House of Lords as a whole, with particular regard to the rights of all members to be fairly heard;

(b) cease, while in that office, to be an active member of any political party; and

(c) vote only to exercise a casting vote, according to convention, in case of a tie.

(8) In the absence of the Lord Speaker and all Deputy Lord Speakers, the House of Lords may elect any Parliamentary Peer (not holding ministerial office or being a shadow Minister) to preside.

## Division 4. Provisions Applicable to both Houses

### 81. Oath to be Taken by MPs and Peers

No member of either House of Parliament shall sit or vote in the House of Commons or Lords until he or she shall have taken and subscribed the Oath of Allegiance and the Oath of Office as prescribed by the First Schedule.

### 82. Questions on Membership of Parliament

(1) The Supreme Court shall have jurisdiction to hear and determine any question whether –

(a) any person has been validly elected as a member of the House of Commons;

(b) the seat of any member of the House of Commons has become vacant;

(c) any person has been validly appointed as a member of the House of Lords; or

(d) the seat of any member of the House of Lords has become vacant.

(2) An application to the Supreme Court for the determination of any question under paragraph (a) or (b) of subsection (1) may be made by –
(a) any registered elector in the constituency of the member concerned;
(b) any member of the House of Commons; or
(c) the Attorney-General.

(3) An application to the Supreme Court for the determination of any question under paragraph (c) or (d) of subsection (1) of this section may be made by –
(a) any member of the House of Lords; or
(b) the Attorney-General.

(4) If an application to the Supreme Court is made by a person other than the Attorney-General, the Attorney-General may intervene and may then appear or be represented in the proceedings.

(5) Parliament may make provision with respect to –
(a) the circumstances and manner in which and the imposition of reasonable conditions upon which any application may be made to the Supreme Court for the determination of any question under this section; and
(b) the powers, practice, and procedure of the Supreme Court in relation to any such application.

(6) The determination by the Supreme Court of any question under this section shall not be subject to appeal.

(7) In the exercise of his or her functions under this section, the Attorney-General shall act in a non-partisan manner and shall not be subject to the direction or control of any other person or authority.

**83.    Unqualified Persons Sitting or Voting**

(1) Any person who sits or votes in either House of Parliament, knowing or having reasonable grounds for knowing that he or she is not entitled to do so, shall be guilty of an offence and liable to a fine as prescribed by Act of Parliament for each day on which he or she so sits or votes.

(2) No person shall be prosecuted for an offence under this section except by, or with the permission of, the Attorney-General, who shall before prosecuting or granting permission to prosecute consult with the Speaker of the House of Commons or the Lord Speaker, as the case may be.

**84.    Voting and Quorum**

(1) Except where a greater majority is prescribed by –
(a) this Constitution; or
(b) the Standing Orders of either House;

any question proposed for decision in the House of Commons or House of Lords shall be determined by a majority of the votes of the members present and voting.

(2) No business shall be transacted at any sitting of either House if objection is taken by any member present that the number of members present (besides the member presiding) is smaller than one-fourth of the total number of members of that House (excluding vacancies).

## 85. Effect of Vacancies

The House of Commons and the House of Lords may each act notwithstanding any vacancy in its membership (including any vacancy not filled when either House first meets after a general election), and the presence or participation of any person not entitled to be present at or to participate in the proceedings of either House shall not invalidate those proceedings.

## 86. Sessions to be Public

(1) Subject to subsection (2), the proceedings of the House of Commons and the House of Lords, and of any committee thereof, shall be open to the public and the press.

(2) Either House of Parliament may, by a two-thirds majority vote, exclude the public and press from any meeting of that House, or a committee thereof, on the grounds of military or diplomatic secrecy.

Provided that a House shall not exclude the public or press from any meeting unless the Leader of the Opposition, after having been briefed by the Prime Minister on Privy Council terms, consents thereto.

(3) There shall be an official record of parliamentary proceedings which shall be published and made available for public inspection.

## 87. Remuneration of Members

(1) Members of Parliament and Parliamentary Peers shall be entitled to such salaries and allowances, including pensions, from public funds as may from time to time be determined by Act of Parliament.

(2) No Bill for an Act of Parliament to alter the salaries and allowances of Members of Parliament or Peers shall be introduced into either House of Parliament except on the recommendation of an independent and non-partisan review board to be established by Act of Parliament.

(3) No Act of Parliament to increase the salaries and allowances of Members of Parliament or Peers shall come into effect until after a general election to the House of Commons has taken place.

### 88. Register of Interests

(1) There shall be a register of interests, in which the members of the House of Commons and House of Lords must disclose their pecuniary interests.

(2) The register of interests shall be published at least quarterly and made available for public inspection.

(3) Any member of the House of Commons or House of Lords who has a financial interest (including benefits in kind) in any matter –

    (a) must declare that interest before taking part in any proceedings of the House of which he or she is a member, or any committee relating to that matter; and

    (b) may not vote in the House of Commons or House of Lords, or any committee on any question relating to that matter.

(4) Each House shall make further provision by Standing Orders for the enforcement of this section, which may include the exclusion of any member of that House who fails to comply with, or acts in contravention to, subsections (1) or (3) or any provisions so made for the enforcement thereof.

### 89. Clerks and Parliamentary Staff

(1) There shall be –

    (a) a Clerk of the Parliaments, who shall be the chief clerk of the House of Lords, and who shall be appointed by the House of Lords on the nomination of the Lord Speaker; and

    (b) an Under-Clerk of the Parliaments, who shall be the chief clerk to the House of Commons, and who shall be appointed by the House of Commons on the nomination of the Speaker.

(2) The Clerk or Under-Clerk of the Parliaments shall not be removed except on the grounds of misconduct, neglect of duty, or incapacity, by means of a resolution passed by the House of Lords (in the case of the Clerk) or House of Commons (in the case of the Under-Clerk), approved by not less than two-thirds of all the members of the House concerned.

(3) The Clerk and Under-Clerk of the Parliaments, subject to the law and to the Standing Orders of each House, shall have responsibility for –

    (a) advising each House on parliamentary law, practice, privilege, and procedure;

    (b) acquiring, holding, managing, and disposing of land and other property of each House;

    (c) entering into contracts for the purposes of each House; and

    (d) supervising, under the general direction of the Speaker of the House of Commons or the Lord Speaker, the management of the staff and facilities of each House.

(4) The salaries, allowances, and conditions of service of the Clerk and Under-Clerk of the Parliaments and other parliamentary staff shall be determined by or in accordance with an Act of Parliament.

## Division 5. Privileges and Procedures of both Houses

### 90. Privileges of the Two Houses

(1) Subject to this Constitution, the powers, privileges, and immunities of the House of Commons and the House of Lords, and the members and committees thereof, shall be such as may from time to time be defined by Act of Parliament, or subject to any such Act by the Standing Orders of the House concerned.

(2) Subject to this Constitution, each House of Parliament shall have the power to adopt Rules and Standing Orders for the regulation of its proceedings, with power to attach penalties for their infringement, and each House shall have power to ensure freedom of debate, to protect its official documents and the private papers of its members, and to protect itself and its members against any person or persons interfering with, molesting, or attempting to corrupt its members in the exercise of their duties.

(3) No Member of either House of Parliament shall be liable to proceedings in any court in respect of anything said or any vote given by him or her in the House of which they are a member or any committee thereof, and no person shall be so liable in respect of the publication by or under the authority of that House, or committee, of any report, paper, votes, or proceedings.

(4) Each House of Parliament, and its committees, shall have the power to summon any person to appear before it for the purpose of giving evidence or providing information, for which purposes each House and its committees shall have the same power as the High Court to enforce the attendance of witnesses and examine them on oath, affirmation, or otherwise, and to compel the production of documents or other materials or information as required for its proceedings.

### 91. Order of Business in House of Commons

(1) Subject to this section, the Standing Orders of the House of Commons may provide that Government business shall normally have priority in the House.

(2) At least one-fourth of sitting days shall be reserved for Opposition, backbench, and Private Members' business.

(3) Opposition Days shall be divided between the official Opposition and other opposition parties in proportion to their share of the seats in the House.

(4) There shall continue be an all-party committee of backbench members, to be known as the Backbench Business Committee, which shall have responsibility for scheduling backbench business.

(5) It shall be the responsibility of the Speaker, in consultation with the Leader of the House, the Leader of the Opposition, the Leader of the Third Party, and the Chair of the Backbench Business Committee, to ensure a balanced allocation of Opposition Days, Backbench Business Days, and days for consideration Private Members' Bills, during each month of the session.

(6) Regardless of any priority otherwise given to Government business, a motion of no confidence tabled by the Leader of the Opposition shall, if no other motion of no confidence tabled by the Leader of the Opposition has been voted upon in the last ninety days, be voted upon within three days.

(7) Subsection (6) shall not prevent members other than the Leader of the Opposition from tabling a motion of no confidence when they control the order paper, or else with the leave of the House.

## 92. Parliamentary Committees

(1) Each House shall establish such committees as may be required to scrutinise the Government, to examine Bills and secondary legislation, and to perform such other functions as are specified from time to time by law or by the Standing Orders, or any resolution, of either House.

(2) Except as provided in subsection (3), no person holding any ministerial office may be a member of any committee established under this section.

(3) The Minister serving as Leader of the House of Commons or Leader of Government Business in the House of Lords may be an *ex-officio* member of any committee concerning the privileges, procedures, or administration of that House.

(4) The Standing Orders of the House of Commons and House of Lords shall include provisions to ensure that the composition of each committee of that House established under this section, or any joint committee of both Houses, shall, to the extent reasonably practicable –
  (a) reflect the partisan composition of the House;
  (b) have due regard to gender balance and regional representation; and
  (c) consider any other factor, including the experience and expertise of members, relevant to the work of the committee.

(5) The Standing Orders of the House of Commons and the House of Lords shall make provision for the free election of the Chairs of committees by a secret ballot of the House, in such a way as to ensure the proportional distribution of Chairs between the parties.

Provided, the Chair of the Public Accounts Committee shall always be an Opposition member.

## 93. Intelligence and Security Committee

(1) There shall be an Intelligence and Security Committee which shall be responsible for scrutinising and reporting on the expenditure, administration, operations, and policies of the intelligence and scrutiny services.

(2) The Intelligence and Security Committee shall consist of nine members, of whom –
   (a) five shall be appointed by the Speaker of the House of Commons from among the members of the House of Commons who are Privy Councillors; and
   (b) four shall be appointed by the Lord Speaker from among the Parliamentary Peers who are Privy Councillors.

(3) No person shall be appointed to the Intelligence and Security Committee if he or she holds a ministerial office or the office of Speaker, Deputy Speaker, Lord Speaker, or Deputy Lord Speaker.

(4) The provisions of subsection (4) of section 92 shall apply to the composition of the Intelligence and Security Committee.

(5) The Chair and the Deputy Chair of the Intelligence and Security Committee shall be chosen by and from among its members by secret ballot.

(6) Further provision for the constitution, organisation, and functions of the Intelligence and Security Committee may be made by or in accordance with an Act of Parliament.

## 94. Speech from the Throne

(1) At the opening of each session of Parliament, His Majesty shall address both Houses of Parliament, in terms prescribed by the Prime Minister, to inform Parliament of the Government's legislative agenda and its policy priorities for the coming session.

(2) An address under subsection (1) shall be followed by a debate in the House of Commons after the withdrawal of His Majesty on a motion proposed by the Prime Minister; and if that motion is rejected by the House of Commons, or passed by the House with any amendment with which the Government does not concur, it shall be regarded as a vote of no confidence for the purposes of subsection (1) of section 57.

## 95.  Ministerial Statements

(1) It is declared that when Parliament is in session important announcements of Government policy should normally be made, in the first instance, by means of a ministerial statement in Parliament.

(2) Subsection (1) shall not apply if, owing to urgent circumstances, making an immediate statement is impracticable; but it shall nevertheless be the duty of the Minister to make a statement to Parliament as soon as may be practicable thereafter.

(3) This section shall not be enforced in any court of law, but it shall be the responsibility of each House to give effect to this section by its Standing Orders.

## Division 6. Legislation and other Powers

## 96.  Legislative Authority of Parliament

(1) Subject to this Constitution, Parliament shall have the authority to enact, amend, and repeal any laws for the peace, order, and good government of the whole or any part of England, including laws of extra-territorial effect.

(2) Parliament shall have exclusive authority to legislate in respect of matters coming within the classes of subjects enumerated in Part I of the Third Schedule ('List of Reserved Powers').

(3) Without prejudice to the generality of subsection (1), it is recognised that Parliament should not normally legislate in respect of matter coming within the classes of subjects enumerated in Part II of the Third Schedule ('List of Devolved Powers') unless the Minister responsible for a Government Bill to that effect, after having consulted the National Council of Local Authorities, declares that there is a compelling public interest to do so.

(4) The power of Parliament to make laws shall be exercisable by Bills passed by both Houses of Parliament (or, as provided by sections 99 and 100, by the House of Commons alone) and assented to by His Majesty.

## 97.  Delegated Legislation

(1) Subject to subsections (2) and (3), Parliament may provide by law for the delegation to any person or authority other than Parliament of power to make regulations, orders, statutory instruments, and other secondary legislation having the force of law.

(2) Where a power is delegated under subsection (1), Parliament shall provide in the principal Act for the parliamentary control of the use of any power so delegated, by means of –

(a) a requirement for the delegated legislation to be approved by a resolution of both Houses before it comes into effect;

(b) a requirement to lay the delegated legislation before both Houses of Parliament for at least twenty-eight days before it comes into effect, during which time either House of Parliament may by resolution disallow the delegated legislation; or

(c) a requirement to lay the delegated legislation before both Houses of Parliament as soon as may be practicable after it has come into effect, and for the delegated legislation to be repealed if so resolved by either House of Parliament.

(3) Delegated legislation under this section may not amend, suspend, or repeal Acts of Parliament.

## 98.  Introduction of Bills

(1) Subject to the provisions of this Constitution and to the Standing Orders of each House, any member of either House may introduce any Bill or propose any motion for debate in, or may present any petition to, that House, and the same shall be debated and disposed of according to the Standing Orders of that House.

(2) For the avoidance of doubt, it is hereby declared that there shall be no requirement to secure the consent of His Majesty or of any member of the Royal Family to the introduction of a Bill, even if the Bill concerns the prerogatives of the Crown or the personal property or interests of His Majesty or of any member of the Royal Family.

(3) Parliament may establish an expedited procedure for enacting private or hybrid Acts of Parliament, so long as any person, authority or corporate body specially and directly affected by a private or hybrid Bill shall have an adequate right to petition against the Bill in both Houses.

## 99.  Provisions Relating to Money Bills

(1) 'Money Bill' means a public Bill which, in the opinion of the Speaker of the House of Commons, contains only provisions dealing with any of the following matters –

(a) the imposition, repeal, remission, alteration, or regulation of taxation;

(b) the imposition, for the payment of debt or other financial purposes, of charges on the Consolidated Fund or any other public funds or on monies provided by Parliament, or the variation or repeal of any such charges;

(c) the grant of money to the Crown or to any authority or person, or the variation or revocation of any such grant;

(d) the appropriation, receipt, custody, investment, issue, or audit of accounts of public money;

(e) the raising or guarantee of any loan or the repayment thereof, or the establishment, alteration, administration, or abolition of any sinking fund provided in connection with any such loan; or

(f) other fiscal matters incidental to any of the matters aforesaid.

(2) A Money Bill shall not be introduced, nor shall any amendment to a Money Bill be accepted, except upon the recommendation of the Crown certified by a responsible Minister.

(3) A Money Bill shall be introduced only in the House of Commons; and the House of Lords shall not proceed with any Money Bill that has not first been passed by the House of Commons and sent by that House to the House of Lords.

(4) If a Money Bill passed by the House of Commons and sent to the Lords at least thirty days before the end of the session is not passed by the Lords within thirty days, or is passed only with amendments to which the House of Commons does not agree, that Bill shall, if the House of Commons so resolves, be deemed to have been passed by both Houses and shall be presented to His Majesty for Royal Assent.

**100. Relations between the Two Houses**

(1) This section applies to any Bill other than a Money Bill or a Bill for amendment of this Constitution.

(2) If any Bill to which this section applies is passed by the House of Commons in two successive sessions (whether or not Parliament is dissolved between those sessions) and, having been sent to the Lords in each of those sessions at least one month before the end of the session, is rejected by the Lords in each of those sessions, that Bill shall, if the House of Commons so resolves, be deemed to have been passed by both Houses and shall be presented to His Majesty for Royal Assent.

Provided that the foregoing provisions of this subsection shall not have effect unless at least six months have elapsed between the date on which the Bill is passed by the House of Commons in the first session and the date on which it is passed by that House in the second session.

(3) For the purposes of this section, a Bill shall be deemed to be rejected by the Lords if it is not passed by the House of Lords without amendment, or it is passed by the Lords with any amendment which is not agreed to by the House of Commons.

(4) For the purposes of this section, a Bill that is sent to the Lords in any session shall be deemed to be the same Bill as a former Bill sent to the Lords in the preceding session if, when it is sent to the Lords, it is identical with the former Bill or contains only such alterations as are certified by the Speaker to be necessary owing to the time that has elapsed since

the date of the former Bill or to represent any amendments which have been made by the Lords in the former Bill in the preceding session and agreed to by the House of Commons.

(5) Without limiting its powers or duties under this Constitution, the House of Lords shall, in the performance of its legislative and scrutinising functions, have particular regard to –

  (a) improving the technical quality, coherence, and practicality of legislation;

  (b) giving consideration to future generations and to long-term public interests;

  (c) protecting the rights and interests of minorities, and those not other-wise adequately represented;

  (d) preventing hasty or ill-considered legislation; and

  (e) protecting the powers, rights, and autonomy of local authorities.

## 101. Amendment of the Constitution

(1) This Constitution may be amended by means of an Act of Parliament enacted in accordance with the provision of this section, and shall not otherwise be amended.

(2) No Act of Parliament shall be construed as amending this Constitution unless it is explicitly stated in the long and short titles of the Bill that it is an Act for that purpose.

(3) A Bill for the amendment of this Constitution shall not be submitted to His Majesty for Royal Assent unless at least six months has elapsed between the first reading of the Bill in the House of Commons and the passing of that Bill by that House on its final reading.

(4) A Bill for the amendment of this Constitution shall not be deemed to have been passed by Parliament unless it has been approved on its final reading –

  (a) in the House of Commons by not less than two-thirds of the total number of members of that House; and

  (b) in the House of Lords by an absolute majority of the Parliamentary Peers.

(5) In so far as it concerns any 'entrenched provision' specified in Part I of the Fourth Schedule, a Bill for the amendment of this Constitution shall not be submitted for Royal Assent unless it has been referred to the people of England in a referendum held under section 149 and has been approved by a majority of the votes cast (i.e. fifty per centum plus one of the valid votes cast) in that referendum.

(6) In so far as it concerns any 'specially entrenched provision' specified in Part II of the Fourth Schedule, a Bill for the amendment of this

Constitution shall not be submitted for Royal Assent unless it has been referred to each of the Associated States, Crown Dependencies, and self-governing Overseas Territories to which it shall apply, and has been approved, by resolution, by a two-thirds majority of the elected members (excluding vacancies) of the legislature of each of the said Associated States, Crown Dependencies, and self-governing Overseas Territories.

(7) For the purposes of this section, an amendment includes any alteration, repeal, or addition to any part of this Constitution, including its Preamble and Schedules.

(8) Whenever the Constitution has been amended, it shall be the duty of the Attorney-General to publish the revised consolidated text of the Constitution.

## 102. Royal Assent

(1) It shall be the duty of the Speaker of the House of Commons and the Lord Speaker jointly to certify, before submitting a Bill for Royal Assent, that the provisions of this division of the Constitution have been complied with, and such certificate shall be final and conclusive for the purpose of granting Royal Assent to legislation.

(2) When a Bill is submitted to His Majesty for Royal Assent in accordance with this Constitution His Majesty shall, within thirty days of the date of submission, signify Royal Assent to the Bill.

(3) Parliament may by law regulate the manner in which Royal Assent to a Bill shall be signified.

(4) If Royal Assent has not been signified within the period specified in subsection (2), the Bill shall, if the House of Commons so resolves, be deemed to have received Royal Assent at the expiry of that period.

(5) When a Bill receives or is deemed to have received Royal Assent it shall be published in the Gazette; and, unless some other date of commencement is provided by law, the Act shall come into effect upon the date of such publication.

(6) Parliament may, subject to section 12, make laws with retrospective effect.

(7) All laws made by Parliament shall be styled 'Acts of Parliament'. The words of enactment shall be –
(a) for constitutional amendments, 'Be it enacted by The King's Most Excellent Majesty, by and with the advice and consent of the Lords and Commons of England, in Parliament assembled, according to the provisions for constitutional amendment –'
(b) for legislation passed in accordance with section 100, 'Be it enacted by The King's Most Excellent Majesty, by and with the advice and

236

consent of the Commons of England, in accordance with section 100 of the Constitution, in Parliament assembled –';

(c) for Bills levying taxes, customs, duties or granting supply, 'We, Your Majesty's most dutiful and loyal subjects, the Commons of England in Parliament assembled, towards raising the necessary supplies to defray Your Majesty's public expenses, and making an addition to the public revenue, have freely and voluntarily resolved to give and to grant unto Your Majesty the several duties hereinafter mentioned; and do therefore most humbly beseech Your Majesty that it may be enacted, and be it enacted –';

(d) for all other legislation, 'Be it enacted by The King's Most Excellent Majesty, by and with the advice and consent of the Lords and Commons of England, in Parliament assembled –'.

### 103. Parliamentary Control of the Armed Forces

(1) His Majesty shall be Commander-in-Chief of the Armed Forces of the United Kingdom and shall exercise command on the advice of the Prime Minister, or the Secretary of State for Defence acting under the direction of the Prime Minister.

(2) The recruitment, pay, organisation, discipline, and administration of the Armed Forces shall be regulated by or in accordance with Acts of Parliament; such Acts shall remain in effect for not more than five years from their date of enactment, but may be renewed.

(3) Subject to any Act of Parliament, His Majesty on the advice of the Prime Minister may establish –
(a) a National Security Council to advise and assist the Prime Minister in the coordination of the defence of the realm; and
(b) a Defence Council to exercise administrative control over the Armed Forces.

(4) Subject to subsection (5), war shall not be declared, nor shall any army or land forces be deployed on combat operations outside of the United Kingdom, except as expressly authorised by a resolution of the House of Commons.

(5) His Majesty, on the advice of the Prime Minister, may order such urgent military action, without the prior approval of the House of Commons, as the Prime Minister may deem necessary for –
(a) the territorial defence of England, or any of other part of the United Kingdom; or
(b) the fulfilment of any obligation under a treaty of collective defence.

(6) If an action is taken under subsection (5), the Prime Minister shall, as soon as may be practicable thereafter, make a statement to the House of Commons, which shall be the subject of a debate and vote on a substantive motion to grant approval retrospectively.

## 104. Approval of Treaties

(1) Every proposed international treaty, convention, or international agreement, having been signed by the responsible Minister or plenipotentiary on behalf of the Crown, shall be laid before both Houses of Parliament for a scrutiny period of twenty-one days, or such longer or shorter period as may be prescribed, in relation to that proposed treaty, convention, or international agreement, by a resolution of the House of Commons.

(2) Every proposed international treaty, convention, or international agreement, shall, after the expiry of the scrutiny period, be the subject of a debate on a substantive motion in the House of Commons; and no treaty, convention, or international agreement shall be ratified by or in the name of His Majesty unless the House of Commons passes a resolution authorising and requesting its ratification.

(3) All treaties, conventions, and international agreements duly ratified shall bind the United Kingdom in international law; but no treaty, convention, or international agreement shall have direct effect as part of the law of England, except by authority of an Act of Parliament.

(4) Nothing in this Constitution shall prohibit the ratification and implementation by law of any treaty, convention, or international agreement for the purpose of –
   (a) joining any international organisation or intergovernmental organisation, union of States, military alliance, or other mechanism for the promotion of peace, defence, security, trade, environmental protection, or other common interests;
   (b) delegating legislative, executive, or judicial powers to such organisation, union, or alliance, in accordance with such treaty, convention, or agreement, to the extent necessary or reasonable to realise its objectives; and
   (c) accepting, in accordance with the terms of such treaty, convention, or agreement, the superiority and direct applicability of the law of such organisation, union, or alliance, and the jurisdiction of the courts thereof.

(5) A treaty, convention, or agreement duly ratified, shall not be withdrawn from, nor denounced, unless so authorised by an Act of Parliament.

## Division 7. Sessions, Prorogation, and Dissolution

## 105. Sessions of Parliament

(1) Each session of Parliament shall be held at such place within England and shall begin at such time as His Majesty on the advice of the Prime Minister shall appoint.

Provided that –
(a) if Parliament has been dissolved, a session of Parliament shall begin no later than fourteen days after the date of the general election following that dissolution;
(b) there shall be at least one session of Parliament in each calendar year, and no session may continue for more than one year; and
(c) a period of three months shall not elapse between the last sitting of Parliament in one session and its first sitting in the next session.

(2) If at any time when Parliament is prorogued or the House of Commons is adjourned not less than one-third of the members of the House of Commons, by means of a written petition to the Speaker, request a sitting of Parliament for the consideration of urgent and important matters, the Speaker shall advise His Majesty to summon Parliament to sit as soon as may be practicable, and in any case within ten days of the receipt of the petition by the Speaker, and His Majesty shall act in accordance with that advice.

(3) Subject to subsections (1) and (2) of this section, the sittings of the House of Commons and the House of Lords shall be held at such time and place as each House may, by its Standing Orders or otherwise, determine.

## 106. Prorogation of Parliament

(1) Subject to this section, His Majesty, acting on the advice of the Prime Minister, may at any time prorogue Parliament.

(2) His Majesty shall not prorogue Parliament on the advice of a Prime Minister who does not command the confidence of a majority of the members of the House of Commons.

(3) His Majesty may, in his own deliberate judgment, refuse to prorogue Parliament until the House of Commons, by resolution, declares that it has confidence in His Majesty's Government.

(4) The effect of prorogation is to terminate the current session of Parliament and to end all business of that session, but it shall nevertheless be lawful for each House to make provision for –
(a) the carrying over of business into the next session; and
(b) committees of that House to continue to meet while Parliament is prorogued.

## 107. Dissolution of Parliament

(1) Subject to this section, Parliament shall continue for five years from the date of the first sitting of the House of Commons after any general election and shall then stand dissolved.

(2) During time of war, or when a state of public emergency is in effect, Parliament may, by means of a resolution passed by a majority of not less than two-thirds of the total membership of both Houses, extend the period of five years specified in subsection (1) for not more than six months.

(3) A resolution under subsection (2) may be renewed for further periods of not more than six months by a subsequent resolution passed by a majority of not less than two-thirds of the total membership of both Houses.

Provided that the life of Parliament shall not be extended under this subsection for a total period of more than twenty-four months.

(4) Subject to subsections (5) and (6) Parliament may be dissolved at any time by His Majesty, acting on the advice of the Prime Minister.

(5) His Majesty may, in his own deliberate judgment, refuse the Prime Minister's advice to dissolve Parliament if it shall appear to His Majesty that –
   (a) the Prime Minister does not command the confidence of a majority of members of the House of Commons; and
   (b) it is possible for the Government to be carried on for a reasonable time and with a working majority in the House of Commons (whether under a new Prime Minister or otherwise) without a dissolution.

(6) If the office of Prime Minister has been vacant for not less than thirty days and it shall appear to His Majesty that a Prime Minister commanding the confidence of the House of Commons is unlikely to be appointed within a reasonable time, then His Majesty, in his own deliberate judgment, may dissolve Parliament.

(7) If between a dissolution of Parliament and the next ensuing general election of members of the House of Commons an emergency arises of such a nature that, in the opinion of the Prime Minister, it is necessary for Parliament to be summoned before that general election can be held, His Majesty, acting on the advice of the Prime Minister may, by proclamation, summon both Houses of the preceding Parliament; and the preceding Parliament shall thereupon be deemed (except for the purposes of section 108) not to have been dissolved, but shall be deemed (except as aforesaid) to be dissolved on the date on which the polls are held in the next ensuing general election.

## 108. General Elections

Whenever Parliament is dissolved, writs shall forthwith be issued for a general election to the House of Commons to be held on a date appointed by His Majesty acting on the advice of the Chair of the Electoral Commission, being a date no sooner than thirty days, and no later than sixty days, after the date of the dissolution.

## *Division 8. The Opposition*

**109. Opposition Leaders**

(1) The Speaker of the House of Commons shall designate as Leader of the Opposition –
   (a) the member of the House of Commons who is parliamentary leader of the largest opposition party in that House; or
   (b) if there is no member of the House of Commons who can be appointed under paragraph (a), the member of the House of Commons who appears to the Speaker to command the support of the largest single group of members of the House who do not support the Government.

(2) The office of Leader of the Opposition shall become vacant –
   (a) if the Leader of the Opposition ceases to be a member of the House of Commons otherwise than by reason of a dissolution;
   (b) if the Leader of the Opposition is appointed to ministerial office, joins a coalition, enters into a 'confidence and supply' agreement with the Government, or otherwise ceases to be in Opposition to the Government; or
   (c) if, following a change in the composition of the House of Commons or a change in the leadership of the largest opposition party in that House, a new appointment to the office of Leader of the Opposition is to be made under subsection (1).

(3) During any period in which there is a vacancy in the office of Leader of the Opposition, the provisions of this Constitution containing the requirement that actions shall be taken by, in accordance with the advice of, or after consultation with, or with the concurrence of, the Leader of the Opposition shall have effect as if the current *de facto*, interim, or acting leader of the largest opposition party in the House of Commons were the Leader of the Opposition.

(4) The Leader of the Opposition shall be entitled to a salary chargeable upon the Consolidated Fund equivalent to that of a Minister of Cabinet rank.

(5) The Leader of the Third Party in the House of Commons, and the leaders of other opposition parties each having at least ten members of the House of Commons, shall be entitled to an official salary chargeable upon the Consolidated Fund equivalent to that of a Minister not of Cabinet rank.

(6) Provision shall be made by Act of Parliament for the payment of adequate public funds to all opposition parties represented in the House of Commons, on the basis of an equal share of the total fund for each vote received by the candidates of that party at the most recent general election, in order to support their party activities and policy development.

(7) The Leader of the Opposition and the leaders of the other opposition parties in the House of Commons shall, in addition to any powers, functions, or privileges accorded to them by this Constitution, by any Act of Parliament, or by parliamentary Standing Orders, enjoy such powers, functions, or privileges as are recognised by the custom and tradition of Parliament.

# CHAPTER VII. JUDICIARY

**110. Judicial Authorities**

(1) The judicial authority of England shall be vested in –
   (a) the Supreme Court of England;
   (b) the Senior Courts of England, namely –
       (i) the Court of Appeal;
       (ii) the High Court of Justice;
       (iii) the Crown Court;
   (c) the County Court and the Family Court; and
   (d) such other courts and tribunals as may from time to time be established in and for England, or any part thereof, by Act of Parliament.

(2) Subject to this Constitution, Parliament shall by law determine the composition, jurisdiction, powers, and authority of courts and tribunals.

**111. Supreme Court of England**

(1) The Supreme Court of England shall consist of –
   (a) the President of the Supreme Court;
   (b) the Deputy President of the Supreme Court;
   (c) at least seven but not more than thirteen other Justices of the Supreme Court.

(2) In addition to any other jurisdiction conferred upon it by any Act of Parliament, the Supreme Court shall have final appellate authority over any case concerning –
   (a) any question as to the interpretation, operation, or application of this Constitution, including questions as to the compatibility with this Constitution of any Act of Parliament, or any other instrument having the force of law;
   (b) the enforcement of constitutionally protected fundamental rights and liberties; or
   (c) a question of law of general public interest.

(3) Notwithstanding anything in this section, the Supreme Court may, in its discretion, grant special leave to appeal from any judgment, decree, determination, sentence, or order in any cause or matter passed or made by any court or tribunal in England.

(4) An Act of Parliament may confer upon the Supreme Court such supplemental powers not inconsistent with any of the provisions of this Constitution as may appear to be necessary or desirable for the purpose of enabling the Court more effectively to exercise the jurisdiction conferred upon it by or under this Constitution.

(5) If at any time it appears to the Attorney-General that a question of law has arisen, or is likely to arise, which is of such a nature and of such public importance that it is expedient to obtain the opinion of the Supreme Court upon it, he or she may refer the question to the Supreme Court for consideration, and the Supreme Court may, after such hearing as it thinks fit, report its opinion thereon.

(6) The Supreme Court shall have power to issue directions, orders, or writs, including writs of habeas corpus, quashing orders, mandatory orders, and prohibiting orders, as required for the enforcement of this Constitution and the protection of constitutional rights and liberties.

(7) All courts in England shall be bound to follow the precedents of the Supreme Court on questions of law.

## 112. Appointment of Judges

(1) All judges shall be appointed by His Majesty acting on the advice of the Judicial Service Commission established by section 113.

(2) The transfer or promotion of a judge shall be considered to be a new appointment and the provisions of this section shall be applied accordingly.

(3) No person shall be appointed to the Supreme Court unless he or she has served as a judge in one of the Senior Courts for not less than two years or been a qualified legal practitioner for not less than fifteen years; and no person shall be appointed to any other judicial office unless he or she possesses such legal qualifications and has such experience in legal practice, or previous service in judicial office, as may be prescribed by law.

(4) In the performance of its functions, the Judicial Service Commission shall –
   (a) establish a fair, open, and transparent process for the recruitment and selection of judges;
   (b) recommend candidates for appointment solely on merit, according to their –
      (i) legal expertise and experience;
      (ii) skills necessary for judicial office; and
      (iii) personal integrity and suitability of character.
   (c) promote equal opportunities, specifically but not exclusively with respect to sex, ethnicity, and social class.

### 113.   Judicial Service Commission

(1) The Judicial Service Commission shall consist of –
   (a) six lay members, one of whom shall be Chair of the Commission, appointed under subsection (2), and
   (b) seven judicial members, one who whom shall be Deputy Chair, appointed under subsection (3),
   (c) two legal members appointed under subsection (4).

(2) The lay members shall be appointed by His Majesty on the advice of the Constitutional Offices Selection Commission in accordance with section 130, from among persons who are not, and have never been, qualified legal practitioners, in order to represent the general public interest.

(3) The judicial members shall be appointed by His Majesty, from among those who have held judicial office for at least five years, on the advice of the Judges' Council or such other body or bodies representing judges as may be appointed for that purpose by or under any Act of Parliament.

(4) The legal members shall be appointed by His Majesty on the advice of the Chair of the Judicial Service Commission, after consultation with the organisations representing the legal profession.

(5) The term of office of a member of the Judicial Service Commission shall be –
   (a) in the case of the lay members, five years;
   (b) in the case of the judicial members, three years;
   (c) in the case of the legal members, four years.

### 114.   Tenure and Removal of Judges

(1) Subject to the provisions of this section, a member of the judiciary shall vacate his or her office when he or she attains the age of retirement prescribed by law, but the age of retirement applicable to a particular member of the judiciary shall not be altered after his or her appointment, except with his or her consent.

(2) A member of the judiciary may resign from office by submitting his or her resignation in writing addressed to His Majesty, copied to the Chair of the Judicial Service Commission.

(3) A member of the judiciary shall not be removed from office except by means of a resolution supported by the votes of not less than two-thirds of the total membership of both Houses of Parliament; and no such resolution shall be passed by either House unless the Judicial Service Commission has conducted an enquiry into the conduct or capacity of the judge, and has recommended to both Houses that the judge ought to be removed on the grounds of misbehaviour, incapacity, or neglect of duty.

(4) No discussion shall take place in either House of Parliament with respect to the conduct of any member of the judiciary in the discharge of his or her judicial duties except upon a motion for removal under the terms of this section.

(5) A judicial office shall not be abolished while there is a substantive office holder.

**115. Magistrates**

(1) Magistrates (known as Lay Justices or Justices of the Peace) shall be appointed by the Lord Chief Justice in the name and on behalf of His Majesty.

(2) The qualifications of magistrates, the procedures for their appointment under subsection (1), and provisions relating to their training, conduct and conditions of service, terms of office, and age of retirement, shall, subject to any Act of Parliament, be prescribed by the Judicial Service Commission.

(3) Magistrates shall not be removed from office during the term of their appointment, except by a decision of the Judicial Service Commission, on the grounds of incapacity, neglect of duty, misconduct, or legal disqualification.

**116. Coroners**

(1) There shall be a Chief Coroner of England who shall be appointed by the Lord Chief Justice after consultation with the Judicial Service Commission.

(2) Each County and City shall be a Coroner's Area, to which shall be appointed -
(a) a Senior Coroner; and
(b) one or more Area Coroners and Assistant Coroners, the number of which shall be determined by the Chief Coroner after consultation with the Senior Coroner.

(3) The provisions of section 114 (Tenure and Removal of Judges) shall apply to Coroners.

(4) Subject to this section, further provision may be made by Act of Parliament for –
(a) the powers and functions of Coroners, in relation to –
(i) the holding of Coroner's Courts,
(ii) the conduct of inquests into suspicious deaths and deaths in custody,
(iii) treasure trove, and

(iv) any other matters properly belonging to the office of Coroner; and

(b) the legal qualifications and experience required of Coroners; and

(c) the appointment, tenure, removal, and remuneration, and conditions of service, of Coroners.

## 117. Judicial Independence and Neutrality

(1) The courts and tribunals, and all judges, magistrates, and coroners, shall be independent of the legislature and executive, and shall be subject only to this Constitution and the law.

(2) All persons with responsibility for matters relating to the judiciary or the administration of justice must uphold the continued independence of the judiciary and must not seek to influence particular judicial decisions through any special access to the judiciary.

(3) A person holding office as a judge, magistrate or coroner shall not –
(a) be a member of, a candidate for election to, the House of Commons, or a local authority;
(b) be a member of the House of Lords;
(c) be an active member of, or advisor to, any political party; or
(d) act in such a way as to call his or her political neutrality into question.

(4) Judges, magistrates, and coroners shall receive such salaries and allowances and shall be subject to such other terms and conditions of service as may from time to time be prescribed by Act of Parliament.

Provided that the salary, allowances, and terms and conditions of service of a judge, magistrate, or coroner shall not be altered to his or her disadvantage during his or her continuance in office.

(5) A judge, magistrate, or coroner shall not enter upon the duties of his or her office unless he or she has taken and subscribed the Oath of Allegiance and Judicial Oath as prescribed by the First Schedule.

# CHAPTER VIII. FINANCE

**118. Consolidated Fund**

(1) There shall be a Consolidated Fund, into which, subject to this Constitution and the provisions of any law for the time being in effect, all public revenues shall be paid.

(2) No sum shall be paid out of the Consolidated Fund except on the authority of a warrant under the hand of the Minister responsible for finance or under the hand of some person authorised by him or her in writing; and sums so issued shall be disposed of for meeting public expenditure authorised under section 120 or 121 of this Constitution or, in the case of statutory expenditure, as authorised by law.

**119. Estimates**

(1) The Minister responsible for finance shall, before the end of each financial year, cause to be prepared annual estimates of revenue and expenditure for public services during the succeeding financial year, which shall be laid before the House of Commons.

(2) The estimates of expenditure shall show separately the sums required to meet statutory expenditure and the sums required to meet other expenditure proposed to be paid out of the Consolidated Fund.

(3) For the purposes of this Chapter, 'statutory expenditure' means –
  (a) expenditure charged on the Consolidated Fund or on the general revenues and assets of the State by virtue of any provisions of this Constitution or by virtue of the provisions of any other law for the time being in force; and
  (b) the interest on the public debt, sinking fund payments, redemption monies, and costs, charges, and expenses incidental to the management of the public debt.

**120. Authorisation of Expenditures**

(1) The Minister responsible for finance shall, in respect of each financial year, at the earliest convenient moment, introduce in the House of Commons an Appropriation Bill containing, under appropriate heads for the several services required, the estimated aggregate sums which are

proposed to be expended (otherwise than by way of statutory expenditure) during that financial year.

(2) Whenever –
   (a) any monies are expended or are likely to be expended in any financial year on any services which are in excess of the sum provided for that service by the Appropriation Act relating to that year; or
   (b) any monies are expended or are likely to be expended (otherwise than by way of statutory expenditure) in any financial year upon any new service not provided for by the Appropriation Act relating to that year, statements of excess or, as the case may be, supplementary estimates shall be prepared by the Minister responsible for finance and then laid before and voted on by the House.

(3) In respect of all supplementary expenditure voted under subsection (2), the Minister responsible for finance may, at any time before the end of the financial year, introduce into the House a Supplementary Appropriation Bill containing, under appropriate heads, the estimated aggregate sums so voted, and shall, as soon as possible after the end of each financial year, introduce into the House a final Appropriation Bill containing any such sums which have not yet been included in any Appropriation Bill.

(4) That part of any estimate of expenditure laid before the House of Commons which shows statutory expenditure shall not be voted on by the House, and such expenditure shall, without further authority of Parliament, be paid out of the Consolidated Fund.

## 121. Withdrawal in Advance of Appropriations

(1) The House of Commons may, by resolution approving estimates containing a vote on account, authorise expenditure for part of any financial year before the passing of the Appropriation Act for that year, but the aggregate sums so voted shall be included, under the appropriate heads, in the Appropriation Bill for that year.

(2) Where at any time Parliament has been dissolved before any provision or any sufficient provision is made under this Chapter for the carrying on of the government, the Minister responsible for finance may issue a warrant for the payment out of the Consolidated Fund of such sums as he or she may consider necessary for the continuance of the public services until the expiry of a period of six months commencing with the date on which the House of Commons is dissolved.

(3) A statement of the sums authorised under subsection (2) shall, as soon as practicable, be laid before and voted on by the House of Commons and the aggregate sums so voted shall be included, under the appropriate heads, in the next Appropriation Bill.

### 122. Contingencies Fund

(1) Subject to subsection (2), Parliament may by law authorise the creation of a Contingencies Fund and may authorise the Minister responsible for finance to make advances from that Fund if he or she is satisfied that there is an unforeseen need for expenditure for which no provision or no sufficient provision has been made by an Appropriation law.

(2) Where any advance is made by virtue of an authorisation conferred under subsection (1), a supplementary estimate of the sum required to replace the amount so advanced shall, as soon as practicable, be laid before and voted on by the House of Commons, and the sum so voted shall be included in a Supplementary Appropriation Bill or a Final Appropriation Bill.

### 123. Salaries and Budgets of Constitutional Officers

(1) Subject to subsection (4), there shall be paid to the officers to whom this section applies such salaries and allowances as may be prescribed by or under any Act of Parliament, which are hereby charged on the Consolidated Fund.

(2) The salary and allowances payable to any officer to which this section applies, and his or her other terms of service, shall not be altered to his or her disadvantage after his or her appointment.

(3) This section applies to –
    (a) the President, Deputy President, and Justices of the Supreme Court;
    (b) all Judges (however designated) of the Senior Courts of England;
    (c) the Chair and other members of –
        (i) the Human Rights Commission,
        (ii) the Judicial Service Commission,
        (iii) the Public Service Commission,
        (iv) the Electoral Commission,
        (v) the Boundaries Commission,
        (vi) the Lords Appointments Commission,
        (vii) the Constitutional Offices Selection Commission,
        (viii) the Honours Commission, and
        (ix) the Commission on Standards in Public Life;
    (d) the Ombudsman;
    (e) the Auditor-General,
    (f) the Cabinet Secretary,
    (g) Permanent Secretaries;
    (h) the Leader of the Opposition; and
    (i) the Leader of the Third Party.

(4) An *ex-officio* member of an Independent Commission who receives a salary in respect of the office which entitles him or her to be a member of that Commission shall not receive any salary as a member of that

Commission, but shall receive such allowances as may be payable in respect of his or her service on the Commission.

### 124. Public Debt

The Public Debt of England, including the interest on the debt, sinking fund payments, and redemption monies in respect of that debt and costs, charges, and expenses incidental to the management of that debt, shall be charged on the Consolidated Fund.

### 125. Auditor-General

(1) There shall be an Auditor-General, who shall be appointed by His Majesty upon a resolution of the House of Commons.

(2) A motion for a resolution under subsection (1) shall be moved by the Chair of the Public Accounts Committee on the basis of a recommendation made by the Public Accounts Committee following an open, fair, and meritorious selection process.

(3) The Auditor-General shall have overall charge and direction of the National Audit Office, which shall be responsible for auditing and reporting upon the accounts of the Government, the County and City Authorities, local authorities, and statutory public bodies.

(4) The Auditor-General and any person authorised by him or her for the purpose of carrying out inspections shall have access to all records, books, vouchers, documents, cash, stamps, securities, stores, or other government property in the possession of any person in the service of a public authority.

(5) The Auditor-General shall serve for a term of ten years and shall continue to hold office, subject to subsections (6) and (7), until his or her successor is appointed.

(6) The Auditor-General may resign from office by submitting his or her resignation in writing to His Majesty.

(7) The Auditor-General may be removed from office only by means of a resolution passed by a majority of not less than two-thirds of all the members of the House of Commons praying for his or her removal on grounds of incapacity, neglect of duty, or gross misconduct.

(8) The Auditor-General shall not be subject to the direction or control of any other authority in the performance of his or her duties.

(9) The Auditor-General shall report annually to the House of Commons with a statement of audits and investigations undertaken and of such recommendations, if any, for improving the economy and efficiency of public bodies as he or she shall see fit.

# CHAPTER IX. PUBLIC SERVICE

**126. The Civil Service**

There shall be a permanent, professional, and non-partisan Civil Service for the competent, efficient, and impartial public administration of England under the direction of responsible Ministers.

**127. Public Service Commission**

(1) There shall be a Public Service Commission which shall consist of a Chair and at least four other Commissioners, appointed by His Majesty on the advice of the Constitutional Offices Selection Commission in accordance with section 130.

(2) A majority of the members of the Public Service Commission shall be appointed from among persons who are former senior Civil Servants or otherwise qualified and experienced in the management of public bodies.

(3) The term of office of the Chair and other members of the Public Service Commission shall be five years.

(4) A member of the Public Service Commission shall not, within a period of three years commencing with the date on which he or she last held or acted in that office, be eligible for any appointment which is made by, on the advice of, or after consultation with, the Public Service Commission.

**128. Powers and Functions of the Public Service Commission**

(1) The Public Service Commission shall have a duty to uphold the integrity and impartiality of the Civil Service and to promote the efficiency, competence and professionalism of Civil Servants.

(2) The Public Service Commission shall have the authority to recruit, select, and appoint all Civil Servants and public officers, except those to which sections 129, 130, or 131 apply; this includes the power to make appointments by promotion and transfer, to confirm acting or temporary appointments, and to remove and otherwise exercise lawful disciplinary control over members of the Civil Service.

(3) The Public Service Commission shall keep under review all matters relating to the salaries, benefits, allowances, and other conditions of service

in the Civil Service, and shall give advice thereon to the responsible Minister.

(4) The Public Service Commission shall, in the manner it considers best calculated to promote the efficiency and effectiveness of the Civil Service, perform the functions conferred by this section with the object of maintaining the principle of selection and promotion on merit in relation to public appointments.

(5) Subject to any Act of Parliament, the Public Service Commission may establish a Senior Appointments Board having responsibility for appointments to the Senior Civil Service.

(6) The Public Service Commission may –
   (a) subject to any Act of Parliament, designate any officer of the Commission or any public officer as an 'appointing authority'; and
   (b) delegate in writing, subject to such lawful conditions as the Commission may prescribe, any of power vested in the Commission to an appointing authority.

(7) The Public Service Commission shall, subject to any Act of Parliament, adopt a Code of Practice for appointing authorities and may publish from time to time such additional guidance to appointing authorities as the Commission shall see fit.

(8) The Public Service Commission shall inspect and audit public appointment policies and practices pursued by all appointing authorities to ensure that the Code of Practice is being observed by them.

(9) The appointing authorities shall provide the Public Service Commission with such information as the Public Service Commission may require.

(10) The Public Service Commission shall be responsible for setting and administering Civil Service and Foreign Service Examinations.

(11) Subject to any Act of Parliament, the Public Service Commission may, at the request of a Minister, carry out such additional functions as may be agreed between the Minister and the Public Service Commission.

### 129. Appointments Subject to Prime Minister's Approval

(1) The power to appoint persons to hold or to act in the offices of Cabinet Secretary, Permanent Secretary, Director-General of the Security Service, Chief of the Secret Intelligence Service, and Ambassador, High Commissioner, or other principal diplomatic representative of His Majesty's Government, including the power to confirm appointments, and the power to exercise disciplinary control over persons holding or acting in such offices, shall vest in His Majesty acting on the advice of Public Service Commission given with the concurrence of the Prime Minister.

(2) If the Prime Minister objects to any candidate for appointment to an office to which this section applies, the Prime Minister may require the Public Service Commission to propose another candidate.

## 130. Appointments on Advice of the Constitutional Offices Selection Commission

(1) This section applies when His Majesty is required by this Constitution to make an appointment on the advice of the Constitutional Offices Selection Commission.

(2) The Constitutional Offices Selection Commission shall consist of –
   (a) a Chair of the Commission, who shall be appointed by His Majesty on the advice of the Prime Minister with the concurrence of the Leader of the Opposition;
   (b) three members appointed by His Majesty on the advice of the Prime Minister;
   (c) two members appointed by His Majesty on the advice of the Leader of the Opposition;
   (d) one member appointed by His Majesty on the advice of the Leader of the Third Party in the House of Commons;
   (e) one member appointed by His Majesty on the advice of the Lord Speaker; and
   (f) the Cabinet Secretary, as an *ex-officio* non-voting member.

(3) Whenever an appointment to which this section applies is to be made, the Constitutional Offices Selection Commission shall openly advertise positions and conduct a meritorious selection process, having regard to the following criteria –
   (a) the integrity, independence, and personal qualities of the candidates;
   (b) the candidates' competence, including relevant qualifications and experience; and
   (c) the need to reflect English society, especially but not exclusively in terms of sex, socio-economic class, ethnicity, religion, and political perspective.

(4) The Constitutional Offices Selection Commission shall nominate one candidate and one substitute candidate for each vacancy.

(5) The nominated candidate shall be appointed by His Majesty acting on the advice of the Chair of the Constitutional Offices Selection Commission.

Provided that if there is any impediment to the appointment of that candidate, the Chair of the Constitutional Offices Selection Commission shall advise His Majesty to appoint the substitute.

(6) If more than one vacancy arises at the same time in an institution to which appointments must be made, the Constitutional Offices Selection

Commission may recruit to all those vacancies simultaneously and may nominate a slate of candidates, and an appropriate number of substitutes, to fill the vacancies.

(7) The Constitutional Offices Selection Commission shall, after consultation with the Commission on Standards in Public Life, adopt regulations for situations in which a member of the Commission, other than an *ex-officio* member, is required to recuse themselves from a selection process on grounds of conflict of interest or for other cause.

(8) Subject to this Constitution, the term of office of members of the Constitutional Offices Selection Commission appointed under paragraphs (a) to (e) of subsection (2) shall end upon the dissolution of Parliament.

## 131. Ministerial and Statutory Appointments

(1) This section applies to –
   (a) directors, governors, board members, trustees, councillors, and other persons (howsoever designated) being members of, or having direction or supervisory control over, any publicly owned corporation, statutory body, or other public body established by any Act of Parliament, Royal Charter, or otherwise;
   (b) special advisors to Ministers; and
   (c) all other public appointments, not being part of the Civil Service or the Armed Forces, whose appointment is not otherwise provided for by this Constitution.

(2) The power to appoint persons to hold or to act in offices to which this section applies (including the power to confirm appointments), and the power to exercise disciplinary control over persons holding or acting in such offices and the power to remove such persons from office, shall, unless otherwise provided by or in accordance with an Act of Parliament, be vested in a responsible Minister.

(3) An appointment to any office to which this section applies shall be made according to the principles of merit, fairness, and openness, and subject to the code of practice to be issued by the Public Service Commission.

## 132. Ombudsman

(1) There shall be an Ombudsman who shall be appointed by His Majesty on the advice of the Constitutional Offices Selection Commission in accordance with section 130.

(2) The Ombudsman shall serve for a term of six years and shall continue to hold office, subject to subsections (3) and (4), until his or her successor is appointed.

(3) The Ombudsman may resign from office by submitting his or her resignation in writing to His Majesty.

(4) The Ombudsman may be removed from office only by means of a resolution passed by a majority of not less than two-thirds of all the members of the House of Commons praying for his or her removal on grounds of incapacity, neglect of duty, or gross misconduct.

(5) The Ombudsman shall not be subject to the direction or control of any other authority in the performance of his or her duties.

### 133. Functions of the Ombudsman

(1) The principal functions of the Ombudsman shall be to provide citizens with a means of redress against maladministration, to prevent and rectify arbitrary or unfair administrative decisions, to promote good governance, and to make recommendations for the improvement of the practices and procedures of public bodies.

(2) The Ombudsman shall have the authority –
   (a) to enquire into the conduct of any person to whom this section applies in the exercise of his or her office or authority; and
   (b) to enquire into any decision or recommendation made, including any advice given or recommendation made to a Minister, or any act done or omitted by any department of Government or any other authority to which this section applies, or by officers or members of such a department or authority, being action taken in exercise of the administrative functions of that department or authority.

(3) The Ombudsman may conduct enquires in the following circumstances –
   (a) where a complaint is duly made to the Ombudsman by any person alleging that the complainant has sustained an injustice as a result of a fault in administration;
   (b) where a member of either House of Parliament requests the Ombudsman to investigate the matter on the ground that one or more persons, or a class of persons, specified in the request has or may have sustained such injustice; or
   (c) in any other circumstances in which the Ombudsman considers that he or she ought to investigate the matter on the ground that some person or body of persons has or may have sustained such injustice.

(4) Subject to subsection (5), the Ombudsman's investigatory authority shall extend to –
   (a) all departments, ministries, and agencies of the Government;
   (b) all offices, commissions, corporate bodies, and public agencies established by or under any Act of Parliament;
   (c) local authorities;
   (d) all private persons, businesses, or corporations acting on behalf of, or

under contract with, the Government or any department, Ministry, or agency thereof, or any local authority, in so far as it relates to their contractual obligations for the provision, distribution, or management of goods or services for or on behalf of the public.

(5) The Ombudsman's investigatory authority shall not extend to –
   (a) His Majesty;
   (b) any judge or magistrate in the exercise of his or her judicial functions; or
   (c) the Armed Forces.

(6) In determining whether to initiate, continue, or discontinue an enquiry, the Ombudsman shall act in his or her discretion and, in particular and without prejudice to the generality of this discretion, the Ombudsman may refuse to initiate or may discontinue an enquiry where it appears to him or her that –
   (a) the subject matter of the complaint is trivial;
   (b) the complaint is frivolous, vexatious, or not made in good faith; or
   (c) the complainant has not a sufficient interest in the substance of the complaint.

(7) Where in the course of an enquiry it appears to the Ombudsman that there is evidence of any corrupt act by any person in connection with the public service, the Ombudsman shall report the matter to the appropriate authority with his or her recommendation as to any further investigation he or she may consider proper.

(8) The Ombudsman may bring to the attention of the responsible Minister any defects which appear to him or her to exist in the administration or in any law.

(9) Parliament may by law confer further functions or powers on the Ombudsman and may make further provision for the exercise of his or her functions and powers.

(10) Where, after making an enquiry, the Ombudsman is of the opinion that the action that was the subject matter of enquiry was contrary to law, based wholly or partly on a mistake of law or fact, unreasonably delayed, or otherwise unjust or manifestly unreasonable the Ombudsman shall –
   (a) report his or her opinion, and his or her reasons, to the principal officer of any department or authority concerned, or other authority responsible for the action, and may make such recommendations as he or she thinks fit; and
   (b) request that officer to notify him or her, within a specified time, of any steps that it is proposed to take to give effect to such recommendations.

(11) Where after a report under subsection (10) is submitted no action is taken which seems to the Ombudsman to be adequate and appropriate within

such period as the Ombudsman may prescribe, the Ombudsman, if he or
she thinks fit, after considering any comments made by or on behalf of
any department, authority, body, or person affected, may send a copy of
the report and any further recommendations to the Prime Minister and
to any Minister concerned, and may thereafter make such further report
to the House of Commons on the matter as he or she thinks fit.

# CHAPTER X. LOCAL GOVERNMENT

### 134. Local Government

(1) For the purposes of devolved self-government, England shall be divided into Counties and Cities.

(2) The principal local authority of each County and City shall be the County or City Authority, which shall be a body corporate in the name of the County or City, and which shall consist of –

    (a) a County or City Assembly, which shall be the representative, legislative, deliberative, and scrutinising body of the Authority; and

    (b) a Mayor, who shall be the head of the Authority and leader of its executive.

(3) Each County and City Authority shall have a Chief Executive Officer, who shall be appointed by the Mayor, with the approval of the Assembly, to act as the administrative manager of the Authority.

(4) Each County or City may be divided into districts, boroughs, towns, and parishes, each of which shall be governed by a Council, and by such other local government officials as may be prescribed by law.

(5) Local authorities shall have such powers, functions, and duties, including regulatory and administrative powers, as may from time to time be conferred upon them by or in accordance with this Constitution or any Act of Parliament.

### 135. Local Government Boundaries

(1) Until and unless otherwise provided by an Act of Parliament enacted in accordance with subsection (2), the number, names, and boundaries of Counties and Cities shall, with effect from the appointed day, be as prescribed in the Second Schedule.

(2) No Bill for an Act of Parliament to amend the number, names, and boundaries of Counties and Cities as specified in the Second Schedule shall be introduced to either House of Parliament unless the County or City Assembly of each County or City to be affected by any proposed change has passed a resolution certifying its consent to the Bill.

(3) The number, names, and boundaries of boroughs, towns, districts, and parishes shall be determined, subject to any Act of Parliament, by an Act of the Assembly of the County or City in which it lies.

### 136. Local Government Elections

(1) The members of a local authority shall be elected according to law by the registered electors resident in the area of the local authority's jurisdiction.

(2) The members of County and City Assemblies shall be elected by the Additional Member System of proportional representation.

(3) The Mayor of each County and City, and the Mayors of such districts, boroughs and towns as have directly elected Mayors, shall be elected by the registered electors resident in the jurisdiction thereof by the Alternative Vote system.

(4) Except when a state of emergency is in effect, elections to local authorities shall take place not later than the end of the fourth calendar year after the year in which they were last held, and casual vacancies in the membership of local authorities shall be filled in accordance with law.

### 137. Legislative Powers of Counties and Cities

(1) Subject to this Constitution, each County and City Assembly shall have the authority to enact legislation (to be known as 'Acts of Assembly') having the force of law in the County or City in respect of any matter –
  (a) enumerated in Part II of the Third Schedule ('List of Devolved Powers'), or
  (b) delegated to the County or City by or in accordance with any Act of Parliament.

(2) An Act of Assembly shall have effect in and for the County or City as long and as far only as it is not repugnant to any Act of Parliament, and in case of incompatibility between an Act of Assembly and an Act of Parliament, the Act of Parliament shall prevail.

### 138. Disallowance of Acts of Assembly

(1) Every Act of Assembly shall without delay be transmitted by the Clerk of the County or City Assembly concerned to the Secretary of State.

(2) The Secretary of State may, within sixty days after receipt of the Act of Assembly, disallow the Act of Assembly, or any part thereof, on the grounds that the Act of Assembly, or disallowed part thereof –
  (a) is repugnant to this Constitution;
  (b) is beyond the legislative powers of the County or City Assembly;
  (c) substantially concerns or affects any matter on the List of Reserved Powers;

(d) is incompatible with the obligations of England under international law;

(e) is detrimental to the interests of any other County or City; or

(f) is detrimental to the peace, order, and good government of England.

(3) If an Act of Assembly is disallowed under subsection (2), the Secretary of State shall without delay, in writing, inform the Mayor of the County or City concerned of the disallowance and of the reasons for the Secretary of State's decision.

(4) A County or City Authority may, at the request of the Mayor thereof, and with the consent of an absolute majority of the County or City Assembly, seek judicial review, according to law, of the Secretary of State's decision disallow an Act of Assembly enacted by that County or City.

(5) In this Chapter, 'Secretary of State' means the principal Secretary of State having responsibility, for the time being, for local government, however designated.

## 139. Local Government Finance

(1) A Revenue Fund shall be formed for every local authority, into which shall be paid all revenues raised by or accruing to the local authority, and all monies paid over to the local authority by His Majesty's Government or by any department thereof.

(2) The Revenue Fund shall be appropriated by the local authority for such lawful purposes as the local authority may prescribe, or, in the case of monies granted or loaned to the local authority for particular purposes, then for such purposes as may be prescribed in that grant or loan.

(3) Each local authority shall, subject to this Constitution, any Act of Parliament, and any applicable County or City Act of Assembly, provide for its funding by means of local taxation, precepts, grants-in-aid, or otherwise.

(4) Each local authority shall annually publish its closed accounts for the previous year and its financial projections for the year ahead.

## 140. National Council of Local Authorities

(1) There shall be a National Council of Local Authorities which shall consist of –

(a) the Mayor of each County or City, or a member of the County or City Assembly delegated by the Mayor to act on their behalf; and

(b) one delegate elected by the borough, district, town, and parish authorities within each County or City, chosen in such manner as the County or City Authority shall, subject to any Act of Parliament, prescribe.

(2) The National Council of Local Authorities shall annually elect a Chair and a Deputy Chair from among its members.

(3) The National Council of Local Authorities shall act as a forum for coordination and cooperation among the local authorities, and between the local authorities and His Majesty's Government.

(4) The National Council of Local Authorities shall meet in plenary at least twice each financial year, such that six months shall not elapse between one meeting of the Council and the next.

Provided that a meeting of the Council shall be held within ten days if so ordered by the Prime Minister, or by the Chair or Deputy Chair of the Council.

(5) The National Council of Local Authorities may appoint and direct working committees to develop and implement common policies, procedures, or frameworks of cooperation for –
   (a) the joint or reciprocal provision of public services across local authority boundaries; and
   (b) the sharing or coordination of resources and assets between local authorities.

(6) The National Council of Local Authorities may make recommendations to the Prime Minister or the Chancellor of the Exchequer concerning –
   (a) the distribution of public revenues between the Government and local authorities, and the principles or formulas upon which such distribution shall be based;
   (b) the making of grants-in-aid to local authorities;
   (c) the exercise by local authorities of borrowing powers; and
   (d) any other financial matter referred to the National Council of Local Authorities by the Prime Minister or the Chancellor of the Exchequer.

(7) Before introducing the budget or any Bill concerning any of the matters specified in subsection (6), the Chancellor of the Exchequer must consider any recommendations made by the National Council of Local Authorities; and, if the Bill deviates from such recommendations, the Chancellor of the Exchequer shall, before the Bill is introduced, make a statement to the House of Commons explaining the reasons for that deviation.

(8) The National Council of Local Authorities may establish Regional Committees, consisting of the representatives of all local authorities in each region, to consider matters of regional policy and coordination. Regional Committees may meet at a convenient place in their own region, as determined by each Regional Committee.

(9) Additional functions and powers may be vested in the National Council of Local Authorities by Act of Parliament.

# X. Local Government

### 141. Power to Intervene in Local Authorities

(1) If at any time it shall appear to the Prime Minister, after having consulted the National Council of Local Authorities, that a local authority cannot adequately perform its functions, or that the government of any local authority cannot be properly carried on in accordance with this Constitution and the law, the Prime Minister may request both Houses of Parliament to pass a resolution under this section.

(2) When a resolution under this section is in effect, His Majesty's Government may, subject to any Act of Parliament further regulating the exercise of this power, intervene in the local authority to which the resolution applies to the extent reasonably necessary to restore peace, order, and good government, which may include –
   (a) issuing instructions to the local authority, concerning the exercise of any function;
   (b) appropriating any monies from the local authority's Revenue Fund, or prohibiting such appropriation;
   (c) suspending any elected member of the local authority from the performance of his or her functions;
   (d) transferring any power vested in the local authority to an Administrator designated for that purpose by His Majesty on the advice of the Public Service Commission.

(3) A resolution under this section must specify the reasons for the intervention.

(4) A resolution under this section shall have effect if passed by an absolute majority of the total membership of both Houses of Parliament, and shall remain in effect for a period of not more than ninety days; but it may be extended, for another period of not more than ninety days, by another resolution passed in like manner.

(5) Any intervention in a County or City under this section shall have as its object the restoration, as soon as may be reasonably practicable, of the self-government of the local authority in accordance with this Constitution.

### 142. Lieutenancy and Shrieval Areas

(1) Each County and City shall be a Lieutenancy Area, to which His Majesty, after consultation with the Mayor thereof, shall appoint a Lord Lieutenant, assisted by a Vice Lieutenant and one or more Deputy Lieutenants, to be His Majesty's personal representatives therein and to perform such ceremonial, civic and representational duties as may be required by any law or custom.

(2) Each County and City shall be a Shrieval Area, to which a High Sheriff and one or more Under-Sheriffs shall continue to be appointed in accordance with the Sheriffs Act 1887.

(3) Subject to this Constitution, and unless subsequently altered by an Act of Parliament, the functions, duties, and privileges of Lords Lieutenant, Vice Lieutenants, and Deputy Lieutenants, and of High Sheriffs and Under-Sheriffs, shall continue as they were immediately before the appointed day.

### 143. Preserved Local and Particular Rights

(1) The City of London is to have all its ancient liberties and free customs, both on land and water, and nothing in this Constitution shall affect any right, liberty, custom, or privilege enjoyed by the City of London Corporation before the appointed day.

(2) The following institutions shall continue as before the appointed day, and shall not be abolished, amalgamated, reformed, nor have their rights or privileges infringed, except by their own consent –
   (a) Courts Leet, Courts Baron, Manor Courts, and other local courts preserved by the Administration of Justice Act 1977 for the purposes of taking presentments with respect to matters of local concern, for the management of commons and village greens, for the appointment of certain local officers, and for other local purposes of a non-judicial nature; and
   (b) Conservators of rivers, forests, commons, levels, or other lands or resources held in trust by them, or otherwise managed by them for the public benefit, established by, or under any law in effect before 24 June 2016.

(3) The existing rights of Charter Trusts, including the election of ceremonial mayors and deputy mayors and the continuation of mayoral and civic traditions, shall be preserved under this Constitution, and shall not be abolished nor infringed.

Provided that where any former city, borough or other local authority having a Charter Trust is restored (whether having the same boundaries or otherwise), the rights of the Charter Trust may, in accordance with an Act of Parliament, be returned to that local authority.

(4) Any local authority which immediately before the appointed day was entitled to the name and style of a city shall retain the name and style of a city, notwithstanding the fact that it is not designated as a City in accordance with the Second Schedule.

(5) Subject to any Act of Parliament, His Majesty, on ministerial advice, may award the name and style of city, by royal charter, to any borough, district, town, or parish authority.

(6) In every civil parish there shall be an annual Parish Meeting, which shall all electors of the Parish shall be entitled to attend, for the purpose of discussing parish affairs and exercising any functions conferred on such meetings by law.

(7) Public footpaths, bridleways, and byways are the common heritage of the people forever, and no ancient public footpath, bridleway, or byway, whether officially recorded upon a definitive map or otherwise, may be permanently closed to the public; nor may any such footpath, bridleway, or byway be temporarily closed to the public, except for some reasonable public purpose (including, but not limited to, maintenance), according to law.

(8) Village greens, commons, and other public land held in trust for the community, shall be protected and managed by the responsible local authority, or other trustees appointed for that purpose according to law, and shall not be sold, privatised, or otherwise alienated or removed from common use, unless authorised by a private Act of Parliament.

(9) All rights of forest commoners shall faithfully be preserved; and the composition and jurisdiction of the existing Verderers Courts shall not be altered, except by means of a private Act of Parliament.

(10) In recognition of the distinct identity and character of Cornwall, the County Assembly of Cornwall shall be styled the 'Cornish Assembly', and shall, in addition to the powers and functions granted to County Assemblies by or under this Constitution, have the authority to enact Acts of Assembly in relation to –
   (a) the rights, duties, powers, functions, and regulation of the Duchy of Cornwall estate;
   (b) the regulation and taxation of short-term lets, holiday homes, and second homes;
   (c) Cornish language and culture; and
   (d) such other matters as may be agreed in a devolution agreement reached between the Cornish Assembly and the Secretary of State.

# CHAPTER XI. ELECTIONS, REFERENDUMS, AND PARTIES

### 144. Conduct of Elections and Referendums

(1) In a referendum, or any election to the House of Commons, or to any local authority, the votes shall be given by secret ballot.

(2) Notwithstanding subsection (1), provision shall be made by law for postal or proxy voting in the case of persons of who are unable to cast a ballot in person or are unable without unreasonable inconvenience to attend a polling place.

(3) Persons shall be registered to vote only in the constituency or local authority ward in which they usually reside; or, in the case of citizens not currently resident in England, in the constituency or ward in which they usually resided immediately before taking up residence outside of England.

(4) In elections using the Additional Member System, the following rules apply to the nomination of candidates –
   (a) each registered political party may nominate –
      (i) one constituency candidate for each constituency for which an election is being held, and
      (ii) a number of list candidates up to the number of list seats to be filled;
   (b) independents may be nominated only for constituency seats;
   (c) a candidate may be nominated for both a constituency seat and a list seat in the same region (or, in the case of a local authority election, for both a constituency seat and a list seat in the same local authority);
   (d) each registered political party nominating list candidates for any election shall declare to the Electoral Commission, in accordance with such procedures as the Electoral Commission shall require, the order of the ranking of list candidates.

(5) In elections using the Additional Member System, the following rules apply to the casting and counting of votes –
   (a) each registered elector, in respect of any election, may cast only one vote, which may be cast for only one constituency candidate nominated for the constituency in which the elector is registered;

(b) if a vote is cast for a constituency candidate who is nominated by a registered political party, and if that party has also nominated a list of candidates for the regional list (in the case of elections to the House of Commons) or authority-wide list (in the case of elections to a local authority), that vote shall also count as a vote for that party's list;

(c) if a vote is cast for a constituency candidate who is an independent, or who is nominated by a registered political party that has not also nominated a list of candidates for the regional list (or authority-wide list, as the case may be), then that vote shall not count as a vote for any party's list.

(6) In elections using the Additional Member System, the following rules apply to the allocation of seats –

(a) the candidate receiving the greatest number of votes in each constituency, if qualified and not disqualified from election, shall be elected; and

(b) a number of candidates shall be elected from each registered party's regional list (or authority-wide list, as the case may be), such that the total number of candidates of that party to be elected (including the constituency members and the list members) shall be proportional to the share of votes cast for the candidates of that party, according to the D'Hondt electoral formula;

(c) candidates shall be drawn from each party's list, in order of the initial ranking submitted to the Electoral Commission under paragraph (d) of subsection (4), to fill each party's allocation of list seats in accordance with paragraph (b) of this subsection.

Provided that where a candidate on the party's list is also a constituency candidate, and is elected by a constituency, that candidate shall be excluded from the party's list of candidates, and their place shall be given to the next-ranking list candidate who has not been elected by a constituency.

(7) Subject to this Constitution, Parliament shall provide by law for the registration of voters, the conduct of elections, nomination of candidates, appointment of returning officers, election deposits, spending limits in campaigns, restrictions on sources of financing, requirements to declare sources of financing, the suppression of corrupt or illicit electoral practices, and for any other purpose connected with the holding of elections and referendums.

(8) Subject to this Constitution, Parliament shall provide by law for the regulation and registration of political parties, including rules on party financing and rules for the election of the leaders of parliamentary parties by their members of Parliament.

(9) Any law enacted under subsections (7) or (8), and any regulation, administrative rule, instruction, code of practice, or official guidance, issued

under any such law, must have as its purpose the promotion of free, fair, and credible elections, and must not have the effect of unfairly advantaging or disadvantaging any particular candidate or party.

(10) Every Bill for an Act of Parliament under subsection (7) and (8) shall be submitted to the Electoral Commission for comment between its first and second readings in the House of Commons, and such a Bill shall not proceed to its second reading unless the Electoral Commission has had a period of at least ninety days during which to study the Bill and to report its analysis of the Bill to both Houses.

## 145. Electoral Commission

(1) There shall be an Electoral Commission consisting of nine members, of whom—

    (a) the Chair of the Electoral Commission shall be appointed by His Majesty on the advice of the Constitutional Offices Selection Commission in accordance with section 130;

    (b) the Deputy Chair of the Electoral Commission, who must be a serving or retired judge having knowledge and experience of electoral law, shall be appointed by His Majesty on the advice of the Judicial Service Commission;

    (c) three voting Commissioners shall be appointed by His Majesty on the advice of the Public Service Commission; and

    (d) four non-voting Commissioners shall be appointed as follows –

        (i) one shall be appointed by His Majesty on the advice of the Prime Minister;

        (ii) one shall be appointed by His Majesty on the advice of the Leader of the Opposition; and

        (iii) one shall be appointed by His Majesty on the advice of the Leader of the Third Party; and

        (iv) one shall be appointed by His Majesty on the advice of the Speaker of the House of Commons, given after consultation with the leaders of any other registered political parties.

(2) The term of office of a member of the Electoral Commission shall be –

    (a) in the case of the members appointed under paragraphs (a), (b) and (c) of subsection (1), six years; and

    (b) in the case of the members appointed under paragraph (d) of subsection (1), four years.

Provided, that if the term of office of any member of the Electoral Commission is due to expire when Parliament is dissolved, that term of office shall continue until the first meeting of Parliament following the next general election.

**146. Powers and Functions of the Electoral Commission**

(1) Subject to this Constitution and in accordance with any provisions prescribed by Act of Parliament, the Electoral Commission shall have responsibility for –

(a) supervising the administration of elections and referendums at all levels of government, and supervising the conduct of election and referendum campaigns, in order to ensure that elections and referendums are conducted freely, fairly, credibly, and lawfully;

(b) supervising the compilation of electoral rolls and facilitating the registration of voters;

(c) ensuring compliance with such laws as may be in effect to regulate the registration of political parties and campaigns, the nomination of candidates, and donations and expenditures for political purposes;

(d) such other functions, relating to ensuring the free, fair, credible, and lawful conduct of elections and referendums, as may be vested in the Commission by law.

(2) For the purpose of the exercise of any of its functions, the Electoral Commission may confer powers or impose duties on any authority of the Government or any County, City, or local authority.

**147. Boundaries Commission**

(1) There shall be a Boundaries Commission which shall consist of nine members, of which –

(a) the Chair of the Boundaries Commission shall be appointed by His Majesty on the advice of the Constitutional Offices Selection Commission in accordance with section 130;

(b) four voting Commissioners shall be appointed by His Majesty on the advice of the Public Service Commission; and

(c) four non-voting Commissioners shall be appointed as follows –

(i) one shall be appointed by His Majesty on the advice of the Prime Minister;

(ii) one shall be appointed by His Majesty on the advice of the Leader of the Opposition; and

(iii) one shall be appointed by His Majesty on the advice of the Leader of the Third Party; and

(iv) one shall be appointed by His Majesty on the advice of the Speaker of the House of Commons, given after consultation with the leaders of any other registered political parties.

(2) The term of office of a member of the Boundaries Commission shall be –

(a) in the case of the members appointed under paragraphs (a), (b), and (c) of subsection (1), six years;

(b) in the case of the members appointed under paragraph (d) of subsection (1), four years.

### 148. Delimitation of Constituencies

(1) The Boundaries Commission shall keep under review the constituencies for elections to the House of Commons and to each local authority, including –

   (a) the number of constituencies;

   (b) the names of constituencies;

   (c) the boundaries of constituencies; and

   (d) the number of compensatory list members to be returned from each region (in the case of the House of Commons) or on an authority-wide basis (in the case of local authorities).

(2) Each constituency for the House of Commons, and each ward constituency within a local authority, shall contain, as nearly as may be reasonably practicable, an equal number of resident qualified electors.

   Provided that in determining the boundaries of parliamentary or local government constituencies the Boundaries Commission may deviate from strict proportionality to the extent reasonably justifiable so as to give due consideration to –

   (a) community or diversity of interests;

   (b) physical features and natural boundaries;

   (c) historical identity;

   (d) alignment of parliamentary constituencies with local government boundaries; and

   (e) sparsity or density of population.

(3) The total number of members of the House of Commons to be elected from each region, including both the constituency members from constituencies in the region and the compensatory list members of the region, shall be, as nearly as may be practicable, proportional to the number of resident qualified electors in the region.

(4) The Boundaries Commission shall conclude a review under subsection (1) at intervals of not less than every ten years and shall on completion report its recommendations to Parliament.

(5) As soon as may be practicable after the Boundaries Commission has submitted a report under subsection (4), the Prime Minister shall lay before the House of Commons a draft Order, prepared by the Boundaries Commission, for giving effect to the recommendations contained in the report.

(6) If the motion for the approval of any draft Order laid before the House of Commons is approved by resolution, the Prime Minister shall submit it to His Majesty who shall make an Order accordingly.

(7) If the motion for the approval of any draft Order under this section is rejected by the House of Commons, or not passed by that House within

ninety days of being submitted to it, the Prime Minister shall invite the Boundaries Commission to reconsider and revise the draft Order.

(8) If after reconsideration of the draft Order the Boundaries Commission submits the draft Order again, with or without modifications, the Prime Minister shall lay it before the House of Commons; and that draft Order shall be deemed to have been approved by the House of Commons after three months have elapsed from the date of its submission, unless during that time the draft Order is rejected by a resolution of the House of Commons passed by a majority of not less than two-thirds of all its members.

(9) An Order made under this section shall come into force upon the next dissolution of Parliament (or the next election to any local authority to which the Order applies) after the Order has been made.

Provided that an Order shall not apply to any election held within twelve months of the date on which the Order has been made, if the Electoral Commission determines that it is impracticable to give effect to the new constituency boundaries in time for that election to be properly conducted.

(10) The question of the validity of any Order made under this section shall not be enquired into in any court of law.

## 149. Referendums

(1) Two types of England-wide referendum are recognised as lawful under this Constitution –

(a) a 'constitutional referendum' on an amendment to an entrenched provision of this Constitution, to be held in accordance with subsection (5) of section 101; and

(b) an 'advisory referendum', held under the authority of an Act of Parliament.

(2) A constitutional referendum shall be held, on a date to be determined by the Prime Minister after consultation with the Electoral Commission, no later than twelve months, and no sooner than three months, after the Bill for the amendment of an entrenched provision of the Constitution has been passed by Parliament under subsection (4) of section 101; and if a referendum has not been held before the expiry of twelve months, the amendment Bill shall be deemed to have lapsed.

(3) The outcome of a constitutional referendum shall be binding: if approved by a majority of votes cast in the referendum, the Bill shall be submitted for Royal Assent without delay; but if it is not so approved, the Bill shall be deemed to have lapsed and shall not be submitted for Royal Assent.

(4) Subject to this section, an advisory referendum may be held, under any Act of Parliament, to ascertain the views of the people of England on any Bill, other than a Money Bill or a Bill to amend any entrenched provision of this Constitution (for which a constitutional referendum is necessary).

(5) A referendum may not be held on a general or specific question of policy not expressed in the form of a published draft Bill.

(6) No referendum shall be held unless–
   (a) the subject matter of the referendum has been certified by the Attorney-General as allowable under the terms of this section; and
   (b) the Electoral Commission has certified that the wording of the question to be put to the people in the referendum is accurate, unbiased, and unambiguous.

(7) An advisory referendum shall be non-binding and shall have no effect in law. It is for Parliament to decide whether, when, and how to give effect in law to the result of an advisory referendum.

(8) A local authority may, subject to any Act of Parliament, hold a local advisory referendum within the local authority area, on any matter within the competence of that local authority.

## 150. Caretaker Convention

(1) The caretaker convention shall come into effect when any of the following conditions are met –
   (a) Parliament is dissolved;
   (b) the House of Commons has passed a vote of no confidence in the Government;
   (c) the office of Prime Minister becomes vacant for any cause; or
   (d) the Prime Minister ceases to be the leader of his or her party, or coalition.

(2) The caretaker convention shall cease to have effect when either of the following conditions are met –
   (a) a vote of confidence in the Government has been passed; or
   (b) a new Prime Minister has been appointed, or a Prime Minister has been re-appointed, under section 56.

(3) Whenever the caretaker convention is in effect –
   (a) the Government should conduct only –
      (i) routine business that is unlikely to give rise to political controversy, or
      (ii) such urgent business as cannot be delayed;
   (b) the Government should not, except in emergencies, announce any new policy initiatives, new spending estimates, or new legislative Bills, nor enter into any new contracts; and

(c) Ministers should, so far as possible, maintain a clear distinction between their political roles and their official positions, and if a general election is to be held, must not use their public office in any way to influence the election result.

(4) The provisions of subsection (3) shall not be enforceable in any court, and the effect of any action taken by the Government or any Minister shall not be invalided solely by reason of the fact that the caretaker convention was in effect; but it shall be the moral duty of all in public life to ensure compliance with the caretaker convention.

# CHAPTER XII. INDEPENDENT COMMISSIONS

**151. Definition of Independent Commissions**

(1) Independent Commissions are independent, non-partisan bodies, established to preserve the integrity of public institutions, to support constitutional democracy, and to uphold good government in accordance with this Constitution.

(2) The term 'Independent Commissions' includes –
  (a) the Human Rights Commission;
  (b) the Lords Appointments Commission;
  (c) the Judicial Service Commission;
  (d) the Public Service Commission;
  (e) the Electoral Commission;
  (f) the Boundaries Commission;
  (g) the Constitutional Offices Selection Commission;
  (h) the Honours Commission; and
  (i) the Commission on Standards in Public Life.

**152. Appointment of Independent Commissions**

(1) A person shall not be qualified to be appointed as a member of an Independent Commission if –
  (a) he or she is, or has at any time during the five years immediately preceding his or her appointment been, a member of ether House of Parliament, or of a local authority;
  (b) he or she is, or has at any time during the said five years been, nominated as a candidate for election as a member of the House of Commons or a local authority;
  (c) he or she is, or has at any time during the said five years been, the holder of an office in, or the employee of, any registered political party; or
  (d) he or she is not an English national.

(2) Subsection (1) shall not apply in the case of an *ex-officio* member of an Independent Commission.

(3) In making appointments to an Independent Commission, the person or authority making or advising upon the appointment shall –

    (a) ensure appointments are made on merit, according to the qualifications, expertise, experience, wisdom, character, integrity, and virtue of the candidates; and

    (b) give due consideration to representing English society in terms of sex, socio-economic class, ethnicity, religion, and region of origin or residence.

### 153. Oath

A member of an Independent Commission shall not enter upon the duties of his or her office until he or she has taken and subscribed the Oath of Allegiance and the Oath of Office in the form set out in the First Schedule to this Constitution.

### 154. Tenure and Removal of Commissioners

(1) Subject to subsection (2), a member, other than an *ex-officio* member, of an Independent Commission shall –

    (a) serve for such term as may be prescribed, in respect of any Independent Commission, by this Constitution;

    (b) if otherwise qualified, be eligible for reappointment to the same office once; and

    (c) cease to hold office at the end of his or her term, but continue to perform the duties of that office until his or her successor is duly appointed.

(2) Where no term of office for a member of an Independent Commission is otherwise prescribed by this Constitution, that term shall be six years from the date of appointment.

(3) A member of an Independent Commission, other than an *ex-officio* member, shall also cease to hold office –

    (a) upon death;

    (b) if he or she submits his or her resignation in writing to His Majesty;

    (c) if any circumstances arise that, if he or she were not a member of the Commission, would cause him or her to be disqualified to be appointed as such;

    (d) if under a custodial sentence for a term of or exceeding twelve months;

    (e) is deemed to have vacated office under subsection (4); or

    (f) if he or she is removed from office in accordance with subsection (5).

(4) A member of an Independent Commission, other than an *ex-officio* member, who without reasonable excuse or the leave of the Commission,

absents himself or herself from four consecutive meetings of the Commission, shall be deemed to have vacated office with effect from the date of the fourth such meeting.

(5) A member of an Independent Commission, other than an *ex-officio* member, shall be removed from office during his or her term of office only upon a resolution passed by two-thirds majority in both Houses of Parliament, praying for his or her removal on the grounds of incapacity, neglect of duty, or gross misconduct.

(6) An *ex-officio* member of an Independent Commission shall cease to be a member of that Commission if he or she ceases for any reason to hold the office which entitles him or her to serve as a member of that Independent Commission.

## 155. Vacancies in Independent Commissions

(1) A vacancy in an Independent Commission shall be filled as soon as may be practicable, and in any case within ninety days of the vacancy arising, by means of a new appointment made in the manner, and by the person or authority, prescribed by this Constitution.

(2) A person who is for the time being performing the duties of an officer who is entitled to *ex-officio* membership of an Independent Commission shall serve as a temporary member of the appropriate Independent Commission, until such time as an appointment is made to the position carrying *ex-officio* membership.

(3) An Independent Commission shall continue to perform its functions notwithstanding any vacancy in its membership; and no act, proceeding, or decision of a Commission shall be invalid by reason only of such vacancy, or of any defect in the appointment of a member of the Commission.

## 156. Chairs of Independent Commissions

(1) The Chair of an Independent Commission shall be –
(a) that member of the Commission who is designated as Chair by this Constitution; or
(b) if no such designation is made, by the member of the Commission elected by the members of that Commission to serve as Chair.

(2) The Chair of each Independent Commission shall have the right to summon and to preside at all meetings of the Commission, but in the absence of the Chair from any meeting, another member elected by the members present, from among themselves, shall preside at such meeting.

(3) Any power or function vested in the Chair of an Independent Commission by this Constitution or any law may, if the office of Chair is vacant or if the Chair is unable for any reason to perform his or her duties, be lawfully exercised by another voting member of the Commission duly elected by its members.

## 157. Meetings of Independent Commissions

(1) The quorum for any meeting of an Independent Commission shall be three-fifths of the total membership of the Commission, excluding any vacancies.

(2) Each Independent Commission shall endeavour to make decisions by consensus.

Provided that in the absence of consensus, decisions of an Independent Commission shall be taken by a majority of the members present and voting, and in the event of an equality of votes, the Chair or the member presiding at the meeting shall have a casting vote.

(3) Each Independent Commission may appoint committees for the discharge of any functions or powers vested in the Commission and may, subject to any Act of Parliament, delegate any powers vested in the Commission to any such committee.

(4) Subject to this section, each Independent Commission may determine its own rules of procedure and order of business.

## 158. Staff of Independent Commissions

(1) Subject to this Constitution and to any Act of Parliament, each Independent Commission shall have the authority to appoint such officers of the Commission as the Commission may require.

(2) The salary and allowances of the officers of each Independent Commission, and their terms and conditions of service, shall, subject to any Act of Parliament, be determined by the Commission and shall be charged on the Consolidated Fund.

(3) Subject to any Act of Parliament, an Independent Commission, or a committee thereof, may delegate the exercise of any of its powers or functions to any officer of the Commission, subject to such lawful conditions and procedure as may be determined by the Commission.

(4) An officer of an Independent Commission to whom the exercise of any function or power is delegated shall exercise, perform, and discharge such function or power in accordance with such rules as may be prescribed by the Commission, and subject to the Commission's direction and control.

## 159. Autonomy

In the exercise of its functions and powers under this Constitution or any other law, an Independent Commission shall not be subject to the direction or control of any other person or authority.

## 160. Reporting

(1) Each Independent Commission shall make an annual report to both Houses of Parliament, and may make additional reports to both Houses of Parliament as it deems necessary or expedient.

(2) The reports of each Independent Commission shall be published and made available to the public.

## 161. Further Provisions

Parliament may by law make further provision for the constitution, organisation, funding, functions, and powers of any Independent Commission.

# CHAPTER XIII. MISCELLANEOUS PROVISIONS

**162.** **Principles of Public Life**

(1) This section shall apply to –
- (a) The Prime Minister and all Ministers;
- (b) members of the House of Commons or the House of Lords;
- (c) public officers;
- (d) judges, magistrates, and coroners;
- (e) Law Officers;
- (f) members and officers of County or City Authorities or any other local authority;
- (g) holders of an office under section 142;
- (h) police officers;
- (i) staff of non-departmental public bodies;
- (j) the Chair, other members, and staff of all Independent Commissions;
- (k) the members of the Advisory Committee on the Prerogative of Mercy;
- (l) the Auditor-General;
- (m) the Ombudsman;
- (n) members and officers of statutory public bodies or public corporations; and
- (o) all other persons in a position of public trust and responsibility to whom this section shall be applied by Act of Parliament.

(2) All persons to whom this section applies have a duty to conduct themselves in accordance with the 'Nolan' Principles of Public Life set out in the Fifth Schedule.

(3) The Ministerial Code and Cabinet Manual, the Standing Orders of each House, the rules of County and City Authorities and other local authorities, and any Code of Conduct or Practice adopted by the Public Service Commission, Judicial Service Commission, or any other Commission or public body, to guide their practices, official guidance, and disciplinary decisions, shall be intended to give effect to the 'Nolan' Principles specified in subsection (2).

### 163. Commission on Standards in Public Life

(1) There shall be a Commission on Standards in Public Life, which shall consist of –
   (a) a Chair, appointed by His Majesty on the advice of the Constitutional Offices Selection Commission; and
   (b) one member appointed by His Majesty on the advice of the Judicial Service Commission;
   (c) one member appointed by His Majesty on the advice of the Public Service Commission;
   (d) one member appointed by His Majesty on the advice of the Speaker of the House of Commons; and
   (e) one member appointed by His Majesty on the advice of the Lord Speaker.

(2) The members of the Commission on Standards in Public Life appointed under paragraphs (a) and (b) of subsection (1) shall be appointed from among persons who have held high judicial office.

(3) The member of the Commission on Standards in Public Life appointed under paragraph (c) of subsection (1) shall be appointed from among persons who have served as a Permanent Secretary or equivalent grade in the Civil Service.

(4) The members of the Commission on Standards in Public Life appointed under paragraphs (d) and (e) of subsection (1) shall be appointed, on a non-partisan basis, from amongst members of the Privy Council.

(5) The Commission on Standard in Public Life shall, in accordance with any further provisions made by Act of Parliament, be responsible for –
   (a) advising on ethical issues relating to standards in public life;
   (b) conducting inquiries into standards of conduct, with a view to making recommendations and improving practice;
   (c) promoting compliance with, and knowledge and awareness of, the principles of public life enumerated in the Fifth Schedule; and
   (d) such other matters relating to standards in public life, not of a judicial nature, as may be conferred upon it by Act of Parliament.

### 164. Public Honours

(1) There shall be an Honours Commission, which shall consist of –
   (a) the Lord Chamberlain, as Chair; and
   (b) two members appointed by His Majesty on the advice of the Prime Minister;
   (c) one member appointed by His Majesty on the advice of the Leader of the Opposition;
   (d) one member appointed by His Majesty on the advice of the Leader of the Third Party;

(e) four members appointed by His Majesty on the advice of the Lord Speaker, given after consultation with the Convenor of Crossbench Peers, on a non-partisan basis, from among Privy Councillors who have served in high judicial, civil service, diplomatic, military, or ecclesiastical office.

(2) The term of office of members of the Honours Commission appointed under paragraphs (b) to (e) of subsection (1) shall expire at the dissolution of Parliament.

(3) Knighthoods and all other public honours shall be awarded by His Majesty only on the advice, and with the consent, of the Honours Commission.

(4) Subsection (3) does not apply to –
  (a) medals for military service, valour, or gallantry, which may be awarded by His Majesty on the recommendation of the Secretary of State for Defence;
  (b) honours which by law or custom are within the personal gift of the monarch; and
  (c) life peerages, which are to be awarded on the advice of the Lords Appointments Commission according to section 76.

(5) The Honours Commission shall be responsible for ensuring that the honours to which this section applies are awarded only in accordance with the principles of merit, fairness, and openness, in recognition of genuine public or humanitarian service or other meritorious achievements, and that no partisan or personal consideration is permitted to influence the award of honours.

(6) Further provision for the forms, grades, or orders of honours may be made by or in accordance with an Act of Parliament.

(7) Subject to any Act of Parliament, an honour may be revoked by His Majesty, on the advice of the Honours Commission, on grounds of misconduct.

**165.  The Church of England**

(1) The English Church shall be free, and shall have its rights undiminished, and its liberties unimpaired.

(2) The Church of England shall be synodically governed by Deanery Synods, Diocesan Synods, and a General Synod consisting of the House of Bishops, House of Clergy, and House of Laity.

(3) His Majesty shall continue, subject to this Constitution, to be Supreme Governor of the Church of England.

Provided that any episcopal appointment, or any other appointment to an ecclesiastical office that immediately before the appointed day was in the gift of the Crown, shall be made by His Majesty upon the nomination of the Crown Nominations Commission, or such other selection or electoral body of the Church as the General Synod may by Church Measure prescribe for that purpose.

(4) The General Synod shall have sole and exclusive legislative power over the Church of England, including authority to adopt its own Canons and Church Measures, in relation to matters of church doctrine, liturgy, administration, organisation, ministry, and other internal ecclesiastical affairs.

(5) Church Measures, having been adopted by the General Synod, shall be presented to the Ecclesiastical Committee of Parliament; if the Ecclesiastical Committee is satisfied that a Church Measure solely concerns internal ecclesiastical matters, the Committee shall present it directly to His Majesty with a recommendation for Royal Assent.

(6) If the Ecclesiastical Committee determines that a Church Measure, or any part thereof, concerns any extra-ecclesiastical matter, the same shall not form part of the law of England unless it has been approved by Parliament as prescribed by the Church Assembly (Powers) Act 1919.

(7) A Canon or Church Measure passed in accordance with this section and assented to by His Majesty, shall, from the date of its commencement, have force of law in England.

(8) Nothing in this Constitution shall have the effect of invalidating –
(a) any law or custom for the Christian coronation and anointing of the monarch;
(b) any law or custom for the holding of Church of England or ecumenical Christian services of commemoration, dedication, or thanksgiving on public occasions;
(c) any Act of Parliament or other law –
(i) providing for the employment of chaplains in the Armed Forces, schools, hospitals, prisons, and other publicly funded institutions,
(ii) recognising Christian holidays as public holidays,
(iii) regulating trading on Christian holidays and days of rest,
(iv) providing for the public funding of Church of England schools,
(v) allocating public funds to support the stipends of Church of England clergy,
(vi) allocating public funds for the upkeep of church buildings of aesthetic, cultural, or historical importance, or
(vii) permitting the ringing of church bells and excepting church bells from regulations which would otherwise regulate noise or public nuisance.

(9) His Majesty and his heirs and successors must be Protestants and in communion with the Church of England in accordance with the Act of Settlement 1701.

(10) The composition, constitution, powers, and duties of the Church Commissioners, the Board of Governors, the Church Estates Commissioners, the Archbishops' Council, ecclesiastical courts, Churchwardens, and all other ecclesiastical offices, clerical and lay, shall, until and unless otherwise provided by any Church Measure, or by an Act of Parliament enacted at the request of the General Synod, continue in accordance with the law in effect immediately before the appointed day.

### 166. Royal Commissions and Public Inquiries

(1) His Majesty, acting on ministerial advice, may in accordance with this section –
   (a) establish by Royal Warrant a Royal Commission to inquire into and report upon –
      (i) the working of any existing law or policy,
      (ii) the necessity or expediency of any legislation or policy,
      (iii) any other matter of public importance where a question of legislation or policy is to be considered; and
   (b) establish by Order-in-Council a Public Inquiry to inquire into and report upon –
      (i) the administration of the Government or any department thereof,
      (ii) the conduct of any public officer,
      (iii) any disaster or accident (whether due to natural causes or otherwise) in which members of the public were killed or injured or were or might have been exposed to risk of death or injury, or
      (iv) any other matter of public importance where a question of fact is to be determined.

(2) The instrument establishing a Royal Commission or Public Inquiry under subsection (1) shall prescribe –
   (a) the title of the Royal Commission or Public Inquiry;
   (b) the names of the persons nominated as its Chair and members;
   (c) its terms of reference;
   (d) any special provisions respecting the manner in which the Royal Commission or Public Inquiry is to proceed;
   (e) the date for the commencement of its work; and
   (f) the date for delivery of its report.

(3) Subject to subsections (4) and (5), His Majesty on ministerial advice may –

(a) remove for incapacity, gross misconduct, or other stated cause –
    (i) the Chair of any Royal Commission or Public Inquiry,
    (ii) any other member of a Royal Commission or Public Inquiry;
(b) appoint any other person as the Chair or as a member of the Royal Commission or Public Inquiry, whether to fill a vacancy arising from the death, resignation, or removal of the Chair or any member, or otherwise;
(c) appoint any other person as an assessor to assist any Royal Commission or Public Inquiry;
(d) alter the terms of reference of a Royal Commission or Public Inquiry;
(e) alter the date of commencement of a Royal Commission or Public Inquiry; or
(f) alter the date for the delivery of its report.

(4) An instrument for establishing a Royal Commission, or Public Inquiry under subsection (2) or altering any of the particulars in accordance with subsection (3) shall, before coming into effect –
(a) be presented to Parliament by a responsible Minister; and
(b) be the subject of a debate on a substantive motion in the House of Commons.

(5) An instrument under paragraph (a)(ii) or (b) to (f) inclusive of subsection (3) shall not be issued except with the concurrence of the Chair of the Royal Commission or Public Inquiry concerned.

(6) A person shall not be appointed as a Chair or member of a Royal Commission or Public Inquiry unless the responsible Minister is reasonably satisfied that the person to be appointed –
(a) is suitably qualified and experienced; and
(b) has no conflict of interest likely to impair his or her neutrality or independence.

(7) Whenever it is proposed to appoint a public officer as the Chair or a member of a Royal Commission or Public Inquiry, the responsible Minister shall consult the Public Service Commission before nominating that person.

(8) Whenever it is proposed to appoint a serving or retired judge as the Chair or a member of a Royal Commission or Public Inquiry, the responsible Minister shall consult the Judicial Service Commission before nominating that person.

(9) A Royal Commission or Public Inquiry shall have the power to summon any person to appear before it for the purpose of giving evidence or providing information, for which purposes each Royal Commission or Public Inquiry shall have the power to enforce the attendance of witnesses and examine them on oath, affirmation, or otherwise, and to compel the production of documents or other materials or information as required for its proceedings.

(10) Each Royal Commission or Public Inquiry –
    (a) shall, subject to any rules prescribed by the instrument of its establishment, regulate its own procedure; and
    (b) shall not be subject to the direction or control of any other person or authority.

(11) A Royal Commission or Public Inquiry shall, on or before the date prescribed for the delivery of its report, report its findings, together with any recommendations, to both Houses of Parliament.

(12) Further provision relating to the organisation, conduct, powers and duties, and financial arrangements, of Royal Commissions and Public Inquiries, and for connected purposes, may be made by Act of Parliament.

### 167. Citizens' Assemblies

(1) Parliament may provide by law for the selection of a Citizens' Assembly to consider and report on any matter of legislation or policy.

(2) An Act enacted under subsection (1) shall make provision for –
    (a) the selection of the members of the Citizens' Assembly from among the registered voters of England on a randomly selected or otherwise representative and inclusive basis;
    (b) the appointment of a suitably qualified and experienced person as Chair of the Citizens' Assembly;
    (c) a process for the assignment of independent experts to assist the Citizens' Assembly in its deliberations;
    (d) such secretarial and clerical support to the Citizens' Assembly as may be required;
    (e) the adequate compensation of members of the Citizens' Assembly, including such travel, subsistence, loss of earnings, and other allowances as may be required; and
    (f) any other matters relevant to the proper functioning of the Citizens' Assembly.

(3) Each Citizens' Assembly shall, within twelve months of its date of appointment or such other time as may be prescribed by law, submit its report, with recommendations, to Parliament.

(4) A Citizens' Assembly shall have the power to summon any person to appear before it for the purpose of giving evidence or providing information, for which purposes each Citizen's Assembly shall have the power to enforce the attendance of witnesses and examine them on oath, affirmation, or otherwise, and to compel the production of documents or other materials or information as required for its proceedings.

(5) Each Citizen's Assembly –
    (a) shall, subject to any rules prescribed by Act of Parliament, regulate its own procedure; and

(b) shall not be subject to the direction or control of any other person or authority.

### 168. Organisation of Police Services

(1) Except as otherwise provided by this Constitution or by law, policing in England is a principally a devolved responsibility of Counties and Cities.

(2) Each County and City Authority shall be responsible according to law for the maintenance of an efficient and effective territorial Police Service, which shall be under the command of a Chief Constable.

(3) Subject to subsection (4), Chief Constables and other senior police officers shall be appointed by County and City Authorities, in accordance with such provisions as to their qualifications, training, promotion, tenure, and discipline, as may be prescribed by or under any Act of Parliament.

(4) The Minister responsible for policing shall have the authority –
  (a) to veto the appointment of a County or City Chief Constable on grounds of unsuitability, conflict of interest, or any irregularity in the manner of their appointment; and
  (b) to remove any Chief Constable from office on grounds of incapacity, neglect of duty or misconduct.

Provided that the Minister shall consult with His Majesty's Inspectorate of Constabulary and obtain the approval of the Cabinet before exercising any such authority, and that any exercise of authority by a Minister under this subsection shall without delay be reported to both Houses of Parliament.

(5) Policing must be conducted lawfully, impartially, professionally, and in accordance with Sir Robert Peel's Nine Principles of Policing (1829).

(6) All police officers shall be required to take the Constable's Oath as prescribed by the First Schedule.

(7) Parliament shall provide by law for the establishment, maintenance, and operation, at national level, of –
  (a) His Majesty's Inspectorate of Constabulary, to monitor and report on the efficiency and effectiveness of Police Services;
  (b) an independent authority to investigate complaints against the police; and
  (c) institutions to support the training and professionalism of Police Services;
  (d) a National Police Service for the prevention of terrorism and serious and organised crime; and
  (e) Transport Police, and any other specialist or non-territorial police service.

### 169. Public Broadcasting Corporation

(1) There shall be a Public Broadcasting Corporation (PBC) which shall be a corporate body responsible for the provision of public service broadcasting.

(2) The mandate of the PBC shall be to provide free-to-access public-interest programming, across a range of media, to –
  (a) inform, educate, and entertain;
  (b) provide impartial news and balanced coverage of public affairs; and
  (c) promote civic, educational, and cultural life.

(3) The PBC shall be under the strategic direction of a Board of Governors, which shall consist of nine members, who shall be appointed by His Majesty acting on the advice of the Constitutional Offices Selection Commission according to section 130.

(4) A majority of the members of the Board of Governors of the PBC shall be appointed from among persons who are suitably qualified and experienced in media, culture, or the arts.

(5) Further provision for public broadcasting and the organisation, powers, and functions of the PBC shall be made by Act of Parliament.

# CHAPTER XIV. THE UNITED KINGDOM

**170. Foundation of the United Kingdom**

(1) The jurisdictions of the United Kingdom, other than England, are specified in the Sixth Schedule.

(2) The United Kingdom is a voluntary Union, which exists for the mutual benefit, protection, security, and prosperity of its constituent parts, and for the preservation of their autonomous democratic self-government in internal affairs.

(3) The Union Flag shall continue to be the flag of the United Kingdom; it shall be used by the Council of the United Kingdom and shall be flown by the Armed Forces, the diplomatic service, and other public bodies of the United Kingdom, or of any part thereof when acting for or on behalf of the United Kingdom.

(4) 'God Save the King' shall be the anthem of the United Kingdom.

(5) Notwithstanding subsection (3) and (4) each Associated State, Crown Dependency, and British Overseas Territory may adopt by law its own flag, coat of arms, anthem, and other national symbols.

**171. Unity of the Crown**

(1) The Associated States, Crown Dependencies and Overseas Territories, unless otherwise determined in accordance with section 180 or 181, shall remain parts of His Britannic Majesty's Dominions; and the King (or Queen, if Queen Regnant) of England, shall also be the King (or Queen, if Queen Regnant) of the United Kingdom.

Provided that where another title is borne by the Head of State in an Associated State or Crown Dependency, that title shall be used in and for that jurisdiction.

(2) The rights and powers of the Crown in each Associated State, Crown Dependency, and self-governing Overseas Territory shall be determined by the Constitution and laws thereof.

### 172. United Kingdom Powers

(1) Subject to this section, the Parliament of England shall have the authority to enact laws for the peace, order, and good government of the whole or any part of the United Kingdom, in relation to any of the following matters—

(a) armed forces and defence;

(b) foreign affairs;

(c) citizenship and passports;

(d) visas and immigration, and consular services;

(e) international aid and development;

(f) currency;

(g) internal market and customs;

(h) the provision of cross-border services;

(i) disaster relief, emergency planning, and aid to civil power; and

(j) any other matter, including financial matters, mutually agreed by the English Government and the Government of the Associated State, Crown Dependency, or self-governing Overseas Territory, concerned.

(2) An Act of Parliament enacted under this section shall not extend to any Associated State, Crown Dependency, or Overseas Territory, unless it is stated in the Act that it so applies.

(3) Before introducing a Bill for Act of Parliament under paragraphs (a) or (c) of subsection (1), the English Government shall, so far as reasonably practicable, consult with the Government of each Associated State, Crown Dependency, and self-governing Overseas Territory, to which the Act shall extend.

(4) An Act of the English Parliament enacted under paragraphs (d) to (j) of subsection (1) shall not extend to an Associated State, Crown Dependency, or self-governing Overseas Territory, unless its enactment has been requested and consented to by the Government of each jurisdiction to which it shall apply.

### 173. Council of the United Kingdom

(1) There shall be a Council of the United Kingdom, which shall be the principal body for making and coordinating policy across the United Kingdom in relation to the matters specified in section 172.

(2) Subject to subsections (3) and (4), the Council of the United Kingdom shall consist of –

(a) the Prime Minister, who shall be Chair of the Council of the United Kingdom; and

(b) the First Minister, Chief Minister, or Premier, of each Associated State, Crown Dependency, and self-governing Overseas Territory.

(3) In the absence of the Prime Minister, the English Government may be represented in the Council of the United Kingdom by a Minister of Cabinet rank.

(4) In the absence of its First Minister, Chief Minister, or Premier, the Government of an Associated State, Crown Dependency, or self-governing Overseas Territory, the same shall be represented in the Council of the United Kingdom by a Minister of Cabinet rank in the Government concerned.

(5) The Prime Minister shall summon the Council of the United Kingdom from time to time, such that –
(a) a period of six months shall not elapse between meetings of the Council of the United Kingdom;
(b) the Council of the United Kingdom shall be summoned without delay in the event of war, or threat of invasion concerning any part of the United Kingdom; and
(c) the Council of the United Kingdom shall be summoned as soon as may be reasonably practicable, and in any case within ten days, if so requested, on a matter of urgency, by not less than one-third of the members of the Council.

(6) The Council of the United Kingdom shall elect two Deputy Chairs from among its members, one of whom shall represent an Associated State or Crown Dependency, and one of whom shall represent an Overseas Territory.

## 174. Secretariat of the Council of the United Kingdom

(1) There shall be a Secretariat staff to support the functions of the Council of the United Kingdom.

(2) The Secretary General and other Secretariat staff shall be seconded from the Civil Services of England, the Associated States, the Crown Dependencies, and the self-governing British Overseas Territories, in accordance with such regulations as the Council of the United Kingdom may prescribe.

## 175. Financial Agreements

(1) Except as provided in this section, England, and each Associated State, Crown Dependency, and self-governing Overseas Territory, shall be self financing and shall have full fiscal autonomy.

(2) Each Associated State, Crown Dependency, and self-governing Overseas Territory shall contribute to the costs of the common defence, security,

diplomatic, consular services, and common institutions of the United Kingdom, in accordance with bilateral agreements made with the Government of England.

(3) Nothing in this section shall prevent agreements being made, through the Council of the United Kingdom, to harmonise certain taxes and duties between England and the Associated States, the Crown Dependencies, and Overseas Territories.

## 176. British Citizenship

(1) There shall continue to be a citizenship of the United Kingdom known as 'British citizenship'.

(2) All persons who immediately before the appointed day had British citizenship shall, with effect from the appointed day, continue to be British citizens under this Constitution.

(3) Every person who is born on or after the appointed day shall have British citizenship if –
(a) they were born in the United Kingdom;
(b) they are born outside of the United Kingdom, to –
(i) at least one parent who is a British citizen, or
(ii) at least one deceased parent who would, otherwise than by their death, have been a British citizen at the time of that person's birth.

(4) For the purposes of subsection (2) a person under eighteen years of age who is adopted by a British citizen shall be entitled to British citizenship as if they had been born to that adoptive parent.

(5) Parliament may make further provision by law for the acquisition of British citizenship by birth, marriage, and naturalisation.

Provided that such provision shall not unfairly discriminate on the grounds of race, ethnic origin, colour, religion, sex, age, or mental or physical disability.

(6) No British citizen may ever be deprived of that citizenship except by means of an act of voluntary renunciation.

(7) Any person who has had their British citizenship revoked before the appointed day, and who would, if not for that revocation, have been entitled to be a British citizen, shall hereby have their British citizenship restored, in like manner as if that revocation had never had effect.

(8) Parliament may make provision by law for the voluntary renunciation of British citizenship, but the renunciation of British citizenship shall apply only to the person making the renunciation and shall not affect the rights of the spouse, or any child, or any other dependent, of that person.

(9) A British citizen, or a person who has the right to acquire British citizenship, and who is also a citizen of another country, or is entitled to acquire citizenship of another country, shall not, solely on the ground that he or she is or becomes a citizen of that other country, be deprived of his or her British citizenship, nor be refused the right to acquire British citizenship, nor be required to renounce citizenship of that other country, nor be denied a British passport.

(10) Subject to subsection (3) of section 172, laws enacted under this section concerning British citizenship apply throughout the United Kingdom.

Provided that this shall not limit the authority of the legislature of any Associated State, Crown Dependency, or self-governing Overseas Territory, to make laws for its own nationality, residency, or 'belonger' status.

## 177. Institutions of Self-Government

(1) Each Associated State, Crown Dependency, and self-governing Overseas Territory shall enjoy the right to democratic self-government, according to its own Constitution, laws, and customs, over all domestic and local matters, saving only –
   (a) the legislative powers of the English Parliament as specified in section 172;
   (b) the executive powers of His Majesty, or of the Governor, Lieutenant-Governor, or other principal representative of His Majesty, over foreign affairs, defence, and such other matters as may expressly be reserved to them by the Constitution or laws of each jurisdiction; and
   (c) the judicial powers of the Judicial Committee of the Privy Council.

(2) Subject to subsection (3), each Associated State, Crown Dependency, and self-governing Overseas Territory shall have the right to adopt or amend its own Constitution, by means of a Constitution Act passed by a two-thirds majority of the members of its legislature, confirmed by the people of the Associated State, Crown Dependency, or self-governing Overseas Territory in a referendum, and assented to by His Majesty.

(3) The Constitution of an Associated State, Crown Dependency, or self-governing Overseas Territory shall be based upon the principles of parliamentary democracy, the rule of law, and human rights, and shall not be incompatible with this Constitution.

(4) The Overseas Territories without self-governing status shall be governed according to such rules as may be enacted, subject to any Act of Parliament, by Order-in-Council.

(5) An Associated State, Crown Dependency, or self-governing Overseas Territory in which one or more languages other than English are

widely spoken or have cultural salience shall make provision, by its own Constitution and law, for the recognition, protection, and use of such languages for public purposes in that Associated State, Crown Dependency, or self-governing Overseas Territory.

## 178. Judicial Committee of the Privy Council

(1) There shall continue to be a Judicial Committee of the Privy Council which shall have final appellate jurisdiction in relation to appeals from Associated States, Crown Dependencies, Overseas Territories, and certain Commonwealth countries, according to their several Constitutions and laws.

(2) Appeals which immediately before the appointed day would lie to the Judicial Committee of the Privy Council, other than appeals under subsection (1), shall lie to the Supreme Court of England.

(3) The Judicial Committee of the Privy Council shall consist of those Privy Councillors who hold or have held high judicial office, or are otherwise entitled to membership of the Judicial Committee by virtue of any Act of Parliament.

## 179. Conduct of Foreign Relations

(1) The English Government shall have the authority to act, in the name of the United Kingdom, for and on behalf of any Associated State, Crown Dependency, or Overseas Territory, in relation to foreign affairs and defence.

Provided that, so far as reasonably practicable, the English Government shall act under this subsection only in consultation with the Government of each Associated State, Crown Dependency, or self-governing Overseas Territory concerned.

(2) The Government of England may, through its duly appointed representatives, act for and on behalf of the United Kingdom in the United Nations and in any other international organisation of which the United Kingdom is a member; but it may, when a matter especially concerning an Associated State, Crown Dependency, or self-governing Overseas Territory is being discussed, appoint a representative of that jurisdiction to act instead.

(3) Treaties and international agreements may be negotiated by England on behalf of the whole United Kingdom.

Provided, a treaty or international agreement shall not apply to any Associated State, Crown Dependency, or self-governing Overseas Territory, as part of the domestic law thereof, unless adopted by an Act of its legislature.

(4) Nothing in this Constitution shall prohibit any Associated State, Crown Dependency, or self-governing Overseas Territory from having its own intergovernmental representation, in matters within its competency, subject to such protocols as may be agreed with the Government of England.

### 180. Northern Ireland

(1) Nothing in this Constitution shall restrict the right of the Northern Ireland Executive, in accordance with the Belfast (Good Friday) Agreement 1999, to hold a border poll (referendum) on the question of the reunification of Ireland at any time.

(2) If Irish reunification is approved in a referendum held under subsection (1) –

    (a) Northern Ireland shall on a day agreed between the Governments of England and the Republic of Ireland cease to be an Associated State and become part of the Republic of Ireland;

    (b) the Government of England shall work in good faith, in cooperation with the Government of the Republic of Ireland and the Northern Ireland Executive for an orderly and peaceful transition to Irish unification, and for continuing cooperation in the spirit and in accordance with the Belfast (Good Friday) Agreement.

### 181. Transition to Independence

(1) An Associated State, Crown Dependency, or self-governing Overseas Territory shall have the right, at any time, to become an independent country, by the means prescribed by this section.

(2) The intention to become independent shall be signified by a resolution to that effect passed by a three-fifths majority vote of the elected members of the legislature of the Associated State, Crown Dependency, or Overseas Territory.

(3) Upon a resolution being passed in accordance with subsection (2), the Government of the Associated State, Crown Dependency, or Overseas Territory, and the English Government, shall in good faith, and within twelve months from the date of the resolution, negotiate the terms of an independence agreement, which shall provide for an orderly, peaceful transition to independence, for the division of assets and liabilities, and for continuing cooperation in such matters of mutual interest as may be agreed.

(4) At the end of the period specified in subsection (3), the Government of the Associated State, Crown Dependency, or Overseas Territory concerned shall put the draft independence agreement, and a draft Constitution

for the independent State, to the people thereof in a referendum, to be held in accordance with an Act of the legislature of that Associated State, Crown Dependency, or Overseas Territory; and if a majority of votes cast are in favour of terms of independence, then the Associated State, Crown Dependency, or Overseas Territory, shall become independent under the terms of that agreement and Constitution.

(5) In any referendum on independence, the English Government and the Council of the United Kingdom shall maintain a strict impartiality.

# CHAPTER XV. FINAL AND TRANSITIONAL PROVISIONS

### 182. Interpretation

(1) In this Constitution, unless otherwise specified or the circumstances otherwise necessarily imply –

   (a) 'absolute majority vote' means a vote passed by more than one-half of the membership of a body, excluding any vacancies;

   (b) 'alien' means a person who is not a British citizen or a citizen of the Republic of Ireland;

   (c) 'appointed day' means the day, being not later than three months after the Constitution Act has received Royal Assent, appointed by His Majesty in Council for the commencement of this Constitution;

   (d) 'appointing authority' means any person or authority to whom the power to make public appointments is granted by delegation from the Public Service Commission or to which such authority is granted by any other law;

   (e) 'Act of Assembly' means an Act of a County or City Assembly;

   (f) 'Assembly Bill' means a Bill for an Act of Assembly;

   (g) 'British Academy' means the British Academy for the Promotion of Historical, Philosophical and Philological Studies;

   (h) 'the Crown' means –

      (i) the Crown in right of England, in relation to English affairs,

      (ii) the Crown in right of an Associated State or Crown Dependency, in relation to the affairs of that Associated State or Crown Dependency;

      (iii) the Crown in right of the United Kingdom, in relation to the affairs of Overseas Territories or of the United Kingdom as a whole.

   (i) 'Cabinet' means the Cabinet of England established under section 55;

   (j) 'City' means a City as defined by or in accordance with the Second Schedule, and unless the context otherwise demands excludes any other local authority which enjoys the name and style of a city under any Royal Charter or otherwise in accordance with subsection (4) of section 143;

   (k) 'Charter Trust' means a trust established under the Local Government Act 1972 to preserve the chartered rights and corporate identity of a city or borough which does not constitute a local government area;

(l) 'Chief Constable' includes the Commissioner of the Metropolitan Police Service;

(m) 'Convenor of Crossbench Peers' means the Peer, not being a member of any political party, who is elected by the Peers who are not members of any political party to represent their interests in the Lords;

(n) 'Coroner' includes the Chief Coroner, senior coroners, area coroners, and assistant coroners;

(o) 'County' means a County as defined by or in accordance with the Second Schedule, and unless the context otherwise demands excludes any other territorial division which has otherwise been designated as a county;

(p) 'English national' means a person who has English nationality under this Constitution;

(q) 'existing law' means the law in effect immediately before the appointed day;

(r) 'Great Officers of State' means the persons for the time being holding the offices of Chancellor of the Exchequer, Lord Chancellor, Home Secretary, Foreign Secretary, and Secretary of State for Defence;

(s) 'the Government' means His Majesty's Government in and for England;

(t) 'High Court' means the High Court of Justice;

(u) 'His Majesty's Inspectorate of Constabulary' includes His Majesty's Inspectorate of Constabulary and Fire and Rescue Services or any other body, howsoever designated, performing the functions of an inspectorate of policing;

(v) 'judicial office' means the office of a judge, and unless otherwise stated does not include the office of a magistrate;

(w) except where otherwise stated, 'law' includes any instrument having the force of law and any unwritten rule of law, and 'lawful' and 'lawfully' shall be construed accordingly;

(x) 'Leader of the Third Party' means the leader in the House of Commons of the largest opposition party other than that of the Leader of the Opposition;

(y) 'local authority' means any County, City, parish, town, borough or district authority;

(z) 'Lord Chancellor' means the Cabinet Minister responsible for Justice;

(aa) 'magistrate' means a 'lay justice' and does not include a district judge (magistrates' courts)' as defined by the Crime and Courts Act 2013;

(ab) 'military office' means any draft, post, or appointment held as an officer, warrant officer, senior rating, or non-commissioned officer in any of His Majesty's English Armed Forces;

(ac) 'Minister' means a Minister in the Government of England and, unless the context otherwise requires, includes the Prime Minister, the Deputy Prime Minister, the Chancellor of the Exchequer, Secretaries of State, Ministers of State, Ministers without Portfolio,

Parliamentary Under-Secretaries, the Attorney-General and Solicitor-General; and 'ministerial office' shall be construed accordingly,

(ad) 'ministerial advice' means the formal advice of a responsible Minister acting under the general authority of the Cabinet;

(ae) 'Minister responsible for finance' means the Chancellor of the Exchequer, or, to the extent authorised and delegated by the Chancellor of the Exchequer, the Chief Secretary to the Treasury;

(af) 'opposition party' means any political party represented in Parliament which –

(ag) is not in government, whether as a sole party of government or as member of a governing coalition, and

(ah) does not have a confidence-and-supply arrangement with any party in government;

(ai) 'Parliament' means the English Parliament, or Parliament of England, established by this Constitution;

(aj) 'Peer' means, unless the context otherwise demands, a 'Parliamentary Peer' (that is, a person who is a member of the House of Lords under this Constitution) and excludes a holder of a peerage who is not so appointed, or who has ceased to be a member of the House of Lords;

(ak) 'police officer' means a person who holds the office of constable and has taken the Constable's Oath in the form set out in the First Schedule (or any previous form of the oath);

(al) 'private Act' means an Act of Parliament (including a personal Act or a local Act), conferring particular powers or benefits on any person or body of persons (including, but not limited to individuals, local authorities, companies, or corporations) in excess of or in conflict with the general law;

(am) 'private Bill' means a Bill for a private Act of Parliament;

(an) 'public office' includes any office of emolument in the Civil Service of the Crown in the service of the Government of England, including diplomatic offices, but does not include ministerial office, judicial office, military office, the office of constable, or offices in the service of any local authority, any office in a statutory board, corporation, or non-departmental public body;

(ao) 'qualified and experienced' means having such qualifications and experience as may be prescribed by law, or, subject to any provisions prescribed by law, as the appointing body shall determine to be necessary;

(ap) 'Register of Interests' means the Register of the Interests of Members of both Houses or any equivalent register for members of local authorities;

(aq) 'region' means a region as defined by or in accordance with the Second Schedule;

(ar) 'Royal Society' means the Royal Society of London for Improving Natural Knowledge;

(as) 'Royal Family' includes the monarch, the monarch's consort, the siblings of the monarch and their spouses, and the six people next in the line of succession to the throne and their spouses, but excludes any person who has declared that they have ceased to perform royal duties;

(at) 'sentence of imprisonment' means a custodial sentence imposed by a court of law for a criminal offence, but does not include any period of remand, probation, or parole;

(au) 'session', in relation to the Parliament, means the sittings of the Parliament concerned commencing when it first meets after this Constitution comes into force or after the most recent prorogation or dissolution of Parliament, and terminating when that Parliament is prorogued or dissolved;

(av) 'sitting', in relation to either House of Parliament, means a period during which the House is sitting continuously without adjournment and includes any period during which the House is in committee;

(aw) 'spouse' includes a civil partner;

(ax) 'Supreme Court' means the Supreme Court of England; and

(ay) 'two-thirds majority' or 'majority of two-thirds' means the affirmative votes of two-thirds of the total membership, excluding vacancies.

(2) Unless stated otherwise or unless the context otherwise requires –

(a) references in this Constitution to 'he', 'him', 'his', shall be taken to include 'she' and 'her', and vice versa;

(b) references to 'he' or 'she', 'he or she', 'him or her', or 'his and her(s)' shall be taken to include 'they', 'them', and 'their(s)', and any other pronouns, regardless of a person's gender or gender identity;

(c) words in this Constitution in the singular shall include the plural, and words in the plural shall include the singular, as the case may require;

(d) references in this Constitution to a section or schedule shall be construed as a reference to that section of, or that schedule to, this Constitution;

(e) references in this Constitution to a subsection shall be construed as a reference to that subsection of the section in which the reference occurs; and

(f) if the reigning monarch is female, the words 'King', 'His Majesty', and masculine pronouns in relation the King, shall be read as 'Queen' and 'Her Majesty', and the corresponding feminine pronouns.

(3) Any power is conferred by this Constitution to make any order, proclamation, rules, or regulations or to give any directions or make any designation, shall be construed, unless stated otherwise, as including a power, exercisable in like manner, to amend or revoke any such order, proclamation, rules, regulations, directions, or designation.

(4) No provision specifying that a person or authority shall 'not be subject to the direction or control of any other person or authority' shall be construed as precluding a court from exercising jurisdiction in relation to any question whether that person or authority has performed the functions of his, her, or its office in accordance with this Constitution or any other law.

(5) A person shall not be regarded as holding an office by reason only of the fact that he or she is in receipt of a pension or other like allowance in respect of his or her former holding of office.

(6) Unless the context otherwise requires, a reference in this Constitution to the holder of an office by the term designating his or her office shall include, to the extent of his or her authority, a reference to any person for the time being authorised to exercise the functions of that office.

(7) Except in the case where this Constitution provides for the holder of any office thereunder to be such person holding or acting in any other office as may for the time being be designated in that behalf by some other specified person or authority, no person may, without his or her consent, be nominated for election to any such office or be appointed to or to act therein or otherwise be selected therefor.

(8) An oath required by this Constitution or by any law, other than the Coronation Oath, may also validly be taken in the form of an affirmation, and the religious invocation may be omitted

(9) Nothing in this Constitution shall be construed as preventing Parliament from enacting legislation to provide for general amnesties, or to quash any convictions in order to rectify injustices.

### 183. Peerages and Honours (Further Provisions)

(1) A person appointed to serve as a Parliamentary Peer in the House of Lords, if he or she does not already hold a peerage, shall be made a Baron in terms of the Life Peerages Act 1958.

Provided that an Archbishop or Bishop of the Church of England appointed as a Parliamentary Peer shall not be made a Baron, but shall sit as a Lord Spiritual.

(2) Nothing in this Constitution shall limit the right of any person to inherit a hereditary peerage created before the appointed day; but no new hereditary peerage may be created after the appointed day.

(3) For the avoidance of doubt, a member of the peerage who is not a Parliamentary Peer shall nevertheless keep their peerage rank and title.

(4) Nothing in this Constitution shall prevent a peerage or other honour being awarded by the Crown to a British citizen who is not an English

national, in accordance with the Constitution and laws of the Associated State, Crown Dependency, or Overseas Territory in which he or she resides, but a peerage under this subsection shall not confer any right to sit or vote in the House of Lords.

## 184. Transitional Provisions

The Seventh Schedule shall have effect.

## 185. Short Title

This Constitution may be cited as 'The Constitution of England' [DATE].

# FIRST SCHEDULE – OATHS

### Coronation Oath

The form of the coronation oath, and the administration thereof, shall be as prescribed by the Coronation Oath Act 1688, or as subsequently provided by Act of Parliament.

### Oath of Allegiance

I, [A.B.], do swear [or affirm] that I will be faithful and bear true allegiance to His [or Her] Majesty [name of the King or Queen of England for the time being] and Her [or His] heirs and successors according to law. [So help me God.]

### Oath of Office

I, [A.B.], will uphold the Constitution of England, and will discharge the duties of the office of [...] faithfully, with integrity and to the best of my ability. [So help me God.]

### Privy Council Oath

You do swear by Almighty God [or affirm] that you will to the best of your judgment freely give your honest counsel and advice to His Majesty, and that in all things you will be a true and faithful counsellor; and you do further swear [or affirm] that you will not on any account, at any time whatsoever, disclose the counsel, advice, opinion, or vote of any particular Minister, Counsellor, or other person, and that you will not, except as authorised or required by law, directly or indirectly reveal the business or proceedings of any His Majesty's Council, or the nature or contents of any documents communicated you in an official capacity or any matter coming to your knowledge in such capacity. [So help you God.]

## Judicial Oath

I, [A.B.], do swear [or affirm] that I will uphold and defend the Constitution and laws of the England, and that I will administer justice to all persons alike in accordance with the Constitution, laws, and usages of England without fear or favour, affection or ill-will. [So help me God.]

## Constable's Oath

I, [A.B.] do solemnly and sincerely swear [or affirm] that I will well and truly serve His [or Her] Majesty in the office of constable, with fairness, integrity, diligence, and impartiality, upholding fundamental human rights and according equal respect to all people; and that I will, to the best of my power, cause the peace to be kept and preserved, and prevent all offences against people and property; and that while I continue to hold the said office I will to the best of my skill and knowledge discharge all the duties thereof faithfully according to the Constitution and the law. [So help me God].

# SECOND SCHEDULE –
# REGIONS, COUNTIES, AND CITIES

**Region: GREATER LONDON**

City:     1. Greater London

**Region: WESSEX**

City:     2. Greater Bristol
(Greater Bristol to include the existing West of England Combined Authority Area)

Counties:  3. Cornwall (including the Isles of Scilly)
4. Devon
5. Dorset
6. Gloucestershire
7. Somerset
8. Wiltshire

**Region: SOUTH EAST**

Counties  9. Berkshire
10. Buckinghamshire
11. East Sussex
12. Hampshire
13. Kent
14. Isle of Wight
15. Oxfordshire
16. Surrey
17. West Sussex

**Region: WEST MERCIA**

City:     18. Greater Birmingham
(Greater Birmingham to include the existing West Midlands Combined Authority Area)

Counties:  19. Herefordshire
20. Shropshire
21. Staffordshire
22. Warwickshire
23. Worcestershire

## Region: EAST MERCIA

Counties:  24. Derbyshire
25. Leicestershire
26. Lincolnshire
(Lincolnshire to include the existing Greater Lincolnshire Combined County Authority Area).
27. Northamptonshire
28. Nottinghamshire
30. Rutland

## Region: ANGLIA

Counties:  31. Bedfordshire
32. Cambridgeshire
(Cambridgeshire to include the existing Cambridgeshire and Peterborough Combined Authority Area)
33. Essex
34. Hertfordshire
35. Norfolk
36. Suffolk

## Region: YORKSHIRE

Cities:  37. Greater Leeds
(Greater Leeds to include the existing West Yorkshire Combined Authority Area)
38. Greater Sheffield
(Greater Sheffield to include the existing South Yorkshire Combined Authority Area)

Counties:  39. North Yorkshire
40. East Yorkshire
(East Yorkshire to include the existing Hull and East Yorkshire Combined Authority Area)

## Region: NORTH WEST

Cities:    41. Greater Manchester
(Greater Manchester to include the existing Liverpool City-Region
Combined Authority Area)
42. Greater Liverpool
(Greater Liverpool to include the existing Liverpool City-Region
Combined Authority Area)

Counties:  43. Cheshire
44. Cumbria
45. Lancashire

## Region: NORTHUMBRIA

Cities     46. Greater Newcastle
(Greater Newcastle to include the North of Tyne Combined
Authority Area, excluding Northumberland)
47. Sunderland and Gateshead
(Sunderland and Gateshead to include the North East Combined
Authority Area, excluding County Durham)
48. Teesside
(Teesside to include the Tees Valley Combined Authority Area)

Counties:  49. County Durham
50. Northumberland

# THIRD SCHEDULE – RESERVED AND DEVOLVED POWERS

**Part I. List of Reserved Powers**

(1) Agriculture and food generally, including national standards and policies relating to –
  (a) animal health and welfare;
  (b) plant health, plant varieties and seeds;
  (c) use and sale of genetically modified organisms;
  (d) public health and hygiene in the food industry;
  (e) food security;
  (f) food standards, labelling, and prevention of adulteration;
  (g) regulation and licensing of slaughterhouses.

(2) Census and statistics for national purposes.

(3) Civil and criminal law generally, including –
  (a) civil procedure;
  (b) criminal procedure;
  (c) law of evidence;
  (d) courts, the judicial system, and judicial administration;
  (e) prisons, the prison service, and the probation service;
  (f) rehabilitation of offenders;
  (g) legal aid;
  (h) regulation of the legal professions.

(4) Commercial law generally, including –
  (a) bankruptcy and insolvency;
  (b) arbitration;
  (c) registration and incorporation of businesses;
  (d) corporate ethics and social obligations;
  (e) banking and building societies, insurance, investments, and financial services.

(5) Constitution, institutions, and machinery of national government, including –
  (a) the Crown, succession to the Crown and regencies;
  (b) Crown Estate;
  (c) Royal Household and Sovereign Grant;
  (d) the Parliament and the Parliamentary estate;

    (e)  the Civil Service;
    (f)  regulation of elections, political parties, campaign finance, and related matters;
    (g)  the judiciary;
    (h)  the Privy Council;
    (i)  Freedom of Information;
    (j)  National Archives;
    (k)  Royal Commissions and Public Inquiries;
    (l)  Citizens' Assemblies.

(6)  Defence, including –
    (a)  naval, military, and air forces, and other armed forces;
    (b)  any armed forces attached to or operating with any of the armed forces; visiting forces;
    (c)  defence works; military and protected areas; naval, military, and air force bases, barracks, aerodromes, and other works;
    (d)  war and peace; alien enemies and enemy aliens; enemy property; trading with an enemy; war damage; war risk insurance; national service;
    (e)  control of nuclear, biological, and chemical weapons, and other weapons of mass destruction.

(7)  Ecclesiastical law and relations between Church and State, subject to section 165.

(8)  Education, in so far as it concerns –
    (a)  the National Curriculum;
    (b)  school-leaving age;
    (c)  qualification and registration of teachers and other educational workers;
    (d)  universities and institutions of higher education, including student bursaries, grants, and loans;
    (e)  national qualifications and examination boards.

(9)  Employment law generally, including –
    (a)  minimum wage;
    (b)  protection of health and safety in the workplace;
    (c)  regulation of working hours, public holidays, days of rest, and holidays;
    (d)  employment tribunals;
    (e)  trade union rights and industrial relations;
    (f)  prohibition of the employment of minors;
    (g)  equal opportunities legislation in the workplace.

(10)  External affairs, including –
    (a)  treaties, agreements, and conventions;
    (b)  Commonwealth affairs;
    (c)  diplomatic and consular representation;
    (d)  participation in international bodies and organisations;

    (e) foreign and extra-territorial jurisdiction;
    (f) foreign aid and international development.

(11) Firearms, ammunition, and explosives.

(12) Fishing within territorial waters and the Exclusive Economic Zone.

(13) Forestry.

(14) Health generally, including –
    (a) the National Health Service and the provision of universal public healthcare;
    (b) vaccination schemes;
    (c) quarantine, and the prevention and control of epidemics;
    (d) medical and pharmaceutical research;
    (e) regulation and licensing of medicines and associated products;
    (f) regulation and registration of doctors, nurses, midwives, dentists, opticians, and other healthcare professionals;
    (g) medical ethics;
    (h) regulation of abortion and euthanasia;
    (i) regulation of private medical services and medical insurance;
    (j) the funding and supervision of the training of medical professionals;
    (k) specialist care and medical facilities serving needs of more than one County or City;
    (l) clinical governance, and inspecting and regulating standards of healthcare.

(15) Home affairs, in so far as it concerns –
    (a) English nationality;
    (b) visas, immigration, and asylum;
    (c) passports and national identity documents;
    (d) control and security of borders, ports, and airports;
    (e) extradition to or from England;
    (f) fugitive offenders.

(16) Housing, in so far as it concerns –
    (a) national building codes and building safety standards;
    (b) national frameworks for housing and planning policy.

(17) Infrastructure and public utilities affecting more than one County or City, including –
    (a) power generation and supply;
    (b) the National Grid;
    (c) internet, telephones, telecommunications, and other like services;
    (d) regulation of radio frequencies and the electromagnetic spectrum.

(18) Marriage, divorce, and matrimonial causes, including –
    (a) parental rights;
    (b) the custody and guardianship of children;
    (c) adoption law.

(19) National Lottery.

(20) National Parks.

(21) National security, including –
   (a) the Security Service;
   (b) the Secret Intelligence Service;
   (c) Government Communications Headquarters.

(22) Nuclear energy and control of radioactive substances.

(23) Offshore oil and gas; use of territorial waters, the seabed, and Exclusive Economic Zone.

(24) Policing, in so far as it concerns –
   (a) national minimum policing standards, including standards of recruitment and training;
   (b) cooperation between County and City police services; or
   (c) the matters specified in subsection (6) of section 168.

(25) Poisons, dangerous drugs, and hazardous substances.

(26) Postal services and the Royal Mail.

(27) Public broadcasting services, except local and public-access broadcasting.

(28) Public holidays (except local holidays) and days of national celebration, mourning, or commemoration.

(29) Race relations, gender equality, and prohibition of unlawful discrimination.

(30) Science and research, including –
   (a) astronomical, meteorological, and cartographic services;
   (b) space, arctic, and oceanic exploration and research;
   (c) learned societies founded by Royal Charter, Royal Warrant, Letters-Patent, or Act of Parliament;
   (d) funding of research and innovation by the English Government;
   (e) conservation and research in Sites of Special Scientific Interest.

(31) Shipping and navigation generally, including-
   (a) shipping and navigation on the high seas and in tidal and estuarine waters;
   (b) lighthouses and other provisions for the safety of navigation;
   (c) wrecks and salvage;
   (d) admiralty jurisdiction;
   (e) sea ports and harbours;
   (f) His Majesty's Coast Guard.

(32) Social security and welfare benefits generally, including –
   (a) old age pensions, unemployment benefits, and National Insurance;
   (b) parental allowances and child benefits;
   (c) sickness benefits and payment to persons with disabilities;

310

    (d) pensions or other benefits payable to veterans or their dependants;

    (e) any other benefit declared by Act of Parliament to apply to England as a whole.

(33) Taxation, in so far as it concerns –
    (a) income or payroll taxes;
    (b) corporation taxes;
    (c) value added taxes;
    (d) revenues from oil, gas, mines, and minerals;
    (e) customs and excise duties;
    (f) inheritance taxes (death duties);
    (g) any other taxes declared by Act of Parliament to be exclusively levied by the national Government.

(34) Titles of honour and dignities, including peerages, knighthoods, military medals, and awards for public service or bravery.

(35) Trade and commerce, including –
    (a) currency, coinage, and legal tender;
    (b) bills of exchange and promissory notes;
    (c) weights and measures;
    (d) intellectual property, patents, trademarks, and copyrights;
    (e) foreign trade, imports, and exports.
    (f) consumer protection, product safety, and trading standards.
    (g) competition policy and state-aid rules;
    (h) the Bank of England.

(36) Transport affecting more than one County or City, including –
    (a) driver and vehicle licensing;
    (b) the Highway Code;
    (c) motorways and trunk roads;
    (d) regulation of road haulage and vehicle safety;
    (e) railways (other than local railways, light railways, and tramways);
    (f) air travel, air traffic control, and civil aviation;
    (g) canals, inland waterways, and navigable rivers;
    (h) any transportation project declared by Act of Parliament to be of strategic importance.

(37) Water supply and water management, in so far as it concerns –
    (a) the inspection, regulation, and ownership of water companies;
    (b) ensuring acceptable standards of water supply and quality;
    (c) water catchments, reservoirs, and water conservation;
    (d) the regulation of sewage treatment and disposal;
    (e) the protection of consumers of water supply and sewerage services.

(38) Buying, selling, leasing, and otherwise managing and disposing of the property of His Majesty's Government, or any Department or agency thereof, and managing any rents or proceeds therefrom.

(39) The imposition of punishment by fine, imprisonment, or other lawful penalty, for enforcing any law made in relation to any matter on this list.

(40) Subject to Chapter XIV –
(a) the institutions of the United Kingdom;
(b) laws applying to the Associated States, Crown Dependencies, or Overseas Territories;
(c) British citizenship.

(41) All other matters declared by this Constitution to be within the exclusive power of Parliament.

## Part II. List of Devolved Powers

(1) Agriculture and food within the County or City, in so far as it concerns –
(a) hunting and conservation;
(b) local irrigation, drainage, or improvement schemes;
(c) farmer markets and local producer cooperatives;
(d) horticulture, market gardening, smallholdings, and allotments;
(e) promotion of local and traditional foods.

(2) Betting, gaming, and lotteries (other than the National Lottery and online activities) and, subject to any Act of Parliament, the regulation and licensing of these activities within the County or City.

(3) Countryside and open spaces in the County or City (including the designation and regulation of parks, forests, nature reserves, and Areas of Outstanding Natural Beauty, but excluding National Parks and Sites of Special Scientific Interest).

(4) Culture and heritage within the County or City, including –
(a) archaeological remains, ancient monuments;
(b) buildings and places of historical or architectural interest;
(c) arts and crafts;
(d) theatres, cultural activities and projects, libraries, museums and art galleries (except those specified by Act of Parliament as being of national significance);
(e) archives and historical records (except the National Archives).

(5) Disaster relief and emergency response planning in the County or City.

(6) Economic development in the County or City, including –
(a) urban redevelopment and rural development;
(b) reclamation of derelict land;
(c) promotion of business and social enterprise;
(d) apprenticeships and work training schemes.

(7) Educational provision generally in the County or City, including –
(a) pre-school education;
(b) primary and secondary education;

    (c) further education, vocational education, and adult education;

    (d) education for persons with special educational needs –

(8) Environmental protection in the County or City, including –

    (a) control and removal of pollution, nuisances, and hazardous substances;

    (b) prevention, reduction, collection, management, treatment, and disposal of waste;

    (c) recycling facilities, dumps, and similar facilities;

    (d) control and removal of pests and hazardous or invasive species;

    (e) protection of natural habitats, including coastal protection;

    (f) biodiversity;

    (g) flood risk management;

    (h) local adaptations to climate change.

(9) Financial and non-financial support to charities, social enterprises, and non-profit organisations having social, educational, charitable, or similar purposes within the County or City.

(10) Fire and rescue services in the County or City, including mountain rescue services.

(11) Flag, anthem, coat-of-arms, and other symbols representing the County or City.

(12) Health promotion and public health within the County and City, subject to any national minimum standards or criteria, including –

    (a) ambulance and paramedic services;

    (b) first-aid training;

    (c) health promotion and health education;

    (d) local measures for the control of diseases;

    (e) family planning and sexual education; and

    (f) public and environmental health within the County or City.

(13) Housing generally within the County or City, including –

    (a) public or social housing for people on low incomes;

    (b) prevention of homelessness and aid to homeless people;

    (c) encouragement of home energy efficiency and conservation;

    (d) home improvement and home maintenance grants;

    (e) residential caravans, caravan sites, and mobile homes;

(14) Local government within the County or City, at parish, town, borough, and district levels.

(15) Policing generally within the County or City, including the maintenance of a County or City Police Service, but excluding matters specified on the Reserved List.

(16) Poor relief and any supplementary public assistance to people in poverty within the County or City, additional to, and without prejudice to, relief or assistance provided by national authorities.

(17) Public houses, inns, clubs; and the licensing and regulation of the sale and consumption of intoxicating liquor and beverages within the County or City.

(18) Social services generally in the County or City, including –
(a) protection and well-being of children (including adoption and fostering services) and of young adults, care of children, young adults, vulnerable people, and older people, and care standards;
(b) provision of facilities for people with a disability or people with learning difficulties;
(c) drug, alcohol, and addiction counselling and rehabilitation services.

(19) Tourism in the County or City, including –
(a) amenities for visitors;
(b) registration and licensing of tour guides;
(c) registration and licensing of hotels, guest houses, and other places for the accommodation of visitors;
(d) promotion of tourism generally.

(20) Transport and transport infrastructure in the County or City, including –
(a) highways (other than motorways), including associated bridges, tunnels, street works, and the management and regulation of traffic (but not including the Highway Code).
(b) regulation and licensing of taxi services;
(c) the development, construction, operation, management and integration of public transport facilities and services, including cycle-ways, bus services, tramways, light rail services, underground railways, and regional railways.

(21) Town and country planning in the County or City, including –
(a) listed buildings and conservation areas, spatial planning, and protection of visual amenities;
(b) new towns, industrial estates, and other planned developments;
(c) common land, town and village greens;
(d) land drainage and land improvement.

(22) Taxes (other than income or payroll taxes, corporation taxes, value added taxes, customs, and any other taxes excluded by Act of Parliament) in order to raise revenue for County or City purposes; and the imposition of charges and fees for any service or licence.

(23) Buying, selling, leasing, and otherwise managing and disposing of the property of the County or City, and managing any rents or proceeds therefrom.

(24) The imposition of punishment by fine, imprisonment, or other lawful penalty, for enforcing any Act of Assembly made in relation to any matter within the competence of the County or City.

# FOURTH SCHEDULE –
# ENTRENCHED PROVISIONS

**Part I. Entrenched Provisions**

Chapter I – The State and the Constitution

Chapter II – Fundamental Rights and Freedoms

Section 44 – His Majesty to be Head of State

Section 70 – Composition of the House of Commons

Section 101 – Amendment of the Constitution

Subsection (1) of Section 107 – Dissolution of Parliament

Section 108 – General Elections

Subsections (1) and (3) of section 114 – Tenure and Removal of Judges

Section 117 – Judicial Independence and Neutrality

Section 165 – The Church of England

Part I of this Schedule

**Part II. Specially Entrenched Provisions**

Chapter XIV – The United Kingdom

Part II of this Schedule

The Sixth Schedule

# FIFTH SCHEDULE –
# 'NOLAN' PRINCIPLES

(1) Selflessness: holders of public office should act solely in terms of the public interest. They should not do so in order to gain financial or other benefits for themselves, their family, or their friends.

(2) Integrity: holders of public office should not place themselves under any financial or other obligation to outside individuals or organisations that might seek to influence them in the performance of their official duties.

(3) Objectivity: in carrying out public business, including making public appointments, awarding contracts, or recommending individuals for rewards and benefits, holders of public office should make choices on merit.

(4) Accountability: holders of public office are accountable for their decisions and actions to the public and must submit themselves to whatever scrutiny is appropriate to their office.

(5) Openness: holders of public office should be as open as possible about all the decisions and actions that they take. They should give reasons for their decisions and restrict information only when the wider public interest clearly demands.

(6) Honesty: holders of public office have a duty to declare any private interests relating to their public duties and to take steps to resolve any conflicts arising in a way that protects the public interest.

(7) Leadership: holders of public office should promote and support these principles by leadership and example.

# SIXTH SCHEDULE –
# THE UNITED KINGDOM

(1) Associated States in Union with England –
   (a) Scotland;
   (b) Wales; and
   (c) Northern Ireland.

(2) Crown Dependencies –
   (a) the Bailiwick of Jersey;
   (b) the Bailiwick of Guernsey; and
   (c) the Isle of Man.

(3) Self-governing Overseas Territories –
   (a) Anguilla;
   (b) Bermuda;
   (c) British Virgin Islands;
   (d) Cayman Islands;
   (e) Falkland Islands;
   (f) Gibraltar;
   (g) Montserrat;
   (h) Saint Helena, Ascension, and Tristan da Cunha; and
   (i) Turks and Caicos Islands.

(4) Overseas Territories without self-governing status –
   (a) British Antarctic Territory;
   (b) Pitcairn Islands;
   (c) South Georgia and South Sandwich Islands; and
   (d) Akrotiri and Dhekelia.

(5) If any Associated State, Crown Dependency, or Overseas Territory, at any time becomes independent under the terms of section 181 (or, in the case of Northern Ireland, if it unites with the Republic of Ireland under section 180), it shall thereby be deemed not to appear in this Schedule.

# SEVENTH SCHEDULE –
# TRANSITIONAL PROVISIONS

(1) This Constitution shall come into effect on the appointed day.

(2) Subject to the provisions of this Constitution –
   (a) the existing law, in so far as it is not inconsistent with this Constitution, shall continue to be in force on and after the appointed day, until repealed or amended in accordance with this Constitution;
   (b) all rights, obligations, and liabilities arising under the existing law shall continue to exist on and after the appointed day and shall be recognised, exercised, and enforced accordingly, and
   (c) proceedings in respect of offences committed against the existing law before the appointed day may be instituted on and after the appointed day in the court having the appropriate jurisdiction, and offenders shall be liable to the punishments provided by the existing law at the time of the offence.

(3) The United Kingdom as hereby constituted is the continuing State to the United Kingdom of Great Britain and Northern Ireland in international law, and accepts all rights and obligations applying to the said United Kingdom under international law immediately before the appointed day.

(4) The Associated States, Crown Dependencies, and Overseas Territories are not independent countries, and, as parts of the United Kingdom, they shall continue to form, for the purposes of international law and international recognition, integral parts of His Majesty's Dominions under this Constitution.

(5) Where in the existing law reference is made to His Majesty the King in right of the United Kingdom of Great Britain and Northern Ireland, or to the Crown in right of the United Kingdom of Great Britain and Northern Ireland, that reference shall, unless the context otherwise requires, be construed as a reference to His Majesty the King, or to the Crown, in accordance with this Constitution.

(6) All property which immediately before the appointed day is vested in His Majesty the King in right of the United Kingdom of Great Britain and Northern Ireland, or to the Crown in right of the United Kingdom of Great Britain and Northern Ireland, or in the Government of the United Kingdom of Great Britain and Northern Ireland, or any

Minister or Department thereof, shall, to the extent that such property lies within England, be vested in His Majesty or in the Crown in right of England, or in the Government of England, or the equivalent Minister or Department thereof.

(7) Any person who immediately before the appointed day held ministerial office shall continue to hold the corresponding ministerial office as if he or she had been duly appointed thereto under this Constitution, and shall continue in that office until he or she ceases to hold it in accordance with this Constitution.

(8) Any person holding office as Prime Minister or other Minister by virtue of the preceding subsection who immediately before the appointed day was assigned responsibility for any business of the Government shall be deemed to have been assigned responsibility for such business under this Constitution.

(9) Subsections (7) and (8) shall not apply to any Minister holding office immediately before the appointed day whose departmental responsibility was solely concerned with any territory beyond England.

(10) Every person who immediately before the appointed day holds or is acting in a public office shall, as from the appointed day, hold or act in that office or the corresponding public office established by or under this Constitution as if he or she had been duly appointed to do so in accordance with the provisions of the Constitution and shall be deemed to have taken any oaths required upon such appointment by any existing law.

Provided that any person who under the existing law would have been required to vacate office at the expiration of any period or on the attainment of any age shall vacate his or her office under the Constitution upon the expiration of the period or upon the attainment of the age specified by this Constitution, and may be removed in accordance with this Constitution.

Further provided that every public officer whose normal place of duty immediately before the appointed day is in a territory that by virtue of this Constitution becomes an Associated State, shall have the right at their option either to retire with their earned pension rights, to continue in the Civil Service of that Associated State, or to be transferred to an equivalent position in England.

(11) Every person who immediately before the appointed day holds or is acting in any judicial office in England shall, as from the appointed day, hold or act in that office or the corresponding judicial office established by or under this Constitution as if he or she had been appointed to do so in accordance with the provisions of the Constitution and shall be deemed to have taken any oaths required upon such appointment by any existing law.

Provided that any person who under the existing law would have been required to vacate office at the expiration of any period or on the attainment of any age shall vacate his or her office under this Constitution upon the expiration of the period or upon the attainment of the age specified by this Constitution, and may be removed in accordance with this Constitution.

(12) Subject to this Constitution and until otherwise provided by Act of Parliament, the composition, jurisdiction, powers, and authority of all courts in England shall remain as they were immediately before the appointed day.

(13) Any power, function, duty, or right that, immediately before the appointed day, is vested in the Equality and Human Rights Commission, Electoral Commission, Boundaries Commission, Judicial Appointments Commission, Public Service Commission, or the offices of Ombudsman (Parliamentary and Health Service Ombudsman), Auditor-General, or Director of Public Prosecutions shall from the appointed day be vested, subject to this Constitution, in the corresponding commission or office established under this Constitution; and the members of those commissions, or the holders of those offices, except those appointed specifically to represent Scotland, Wales, or Northern Ireland, shall, subject to the provisions of this Constitution relating to their tenure, removal, and disqualification, continue in office until their successors are duly appointed in accordance with this Constitution.

(14) Members of the House of Commons in the Parliament of the United Kingdom sitting for English constituencies immediately before the appointed day shall continue to sit as members of the House of Commons of England, in accordance with this Constitution, until the next dissolution.

(15) The existing House of Commons shall be dissolved by His Majesty, on the advice of the Prime Minister, within twelve months after the appointed day, and the first general election under this Constitution shall then take place in accordance with section 108.

(16) It shall be the duty of the Boundaries Commission, before dissolution under subsection (15) takes place, to renew the electoral roll and to revise the boundaries of the electoral constituencies in accordance with the provisions of this Constitution. The *provisio* to subsection (9) of section 148 shall not apply to the first general election held under this Constitution.

(17) If the seat of a Member of Parliament becomes vacant before the date of the first general election held after the appointed day in accordance with subsection (15), that vacancy shall, unless contrary provision is made by Act of Parliament, remain vacant until the first general elections held after the appointed day.

(18) The Speaker and the Deputy Speaker of the House of Commons in office immediately before the appointed day, if they sit for an English seat, shall be deemed to have been duly elected as Speaker and Deputy Speaker, respectively, under this Constitution.

(19) Until provision under subsection (1) of section 87 is made, the salaries, allowances, and pensions of Members of Parliament and Peers shall be set at such rates and on such conditions as applied to Members of the House of Commons and Lords respectively immediately before the appointed day.

(20) Subject to this Constitution, and until other provision is made in accordance with this Constitution, the powers, privileges, and immunities of each House of Parliament, its members and committees, and the Standing Orders, as they were immediately before the appointed day, shall continue to apply.

(21) The first election of County and City Authorities shall take place on a date, being the same date throughout England, and no later than twelve months after the appointed day, proclaimed by His Majesty acting on the advice of the Electoral Commission.

(22) The powers of County or City Authorities under this Constitution shall be assumed by them upon the first meeting of the County or City Assembly after the elections held in accordance with subsection (21) of this Schedule.

(23) The members of the Greater London Assembly, the Mayor of London, and other Combined Authority Mayors, in office immediately before the appointed day shall continue to hold office under this Constitution until elections have been held in accordance with subsection (21) of this Schedule.

(24) Where any power or function has before the appointed day been vested in any Combined Authority, the City or County which is the successor to that Combined Authority (in accordance with the Second Schedule) shall continue to have that power or function after the appointed day, until otherwise provided, subject to this Constitution, by Act of Parliament.

(25) Until other provision is made according to law, the salaries, allowances, and pensions of members of County and City Assemblies shall be set uniformly at such rates and on such conditions as applied to members of the London Assembly immediately before the appointed say, and the salaries, allowance, and pensions of Mayors of Counties and Cities shall be set uniformly at such rates and on such conditions as applied to the Mayor of London immediately before the appointed day.

(26) The Lords Spiritual and Temporal being members of the House of Lords immediately before the appointed day shall, notwithstanding

subsection (1) of section 75, continue to sit as Parliamentary Peers under this Constitution, until such time as they cease to be members of that House in accordance with section 78; and a vacancy shall not be deemed to have arisen in the House of Lords for the purposes of section 79 until the number of Parliamentary Peers is less than four hundred.

Provided that any member of the House of Lords who was made a Peer in the Resignation Honours list of Elizabeth Truss shall cease to be a Parliamentary Peer upon the appointed day.

(27) The office of Police and Crime Commissioner (including Police, Fire, and Crime Commissioner) is abolished. All powers, functions, and duties vested in the Police and Crime Commissioners immediately before the appointed day, except as otherwise provided by this Constitution, or subsequently provided for by Act of Parliament, are hereby transferred to the Mayor of each County and City; and all powers, functions, and duties vested in the Police and Crime Panels (including Police, Fire, and Crime Panels) immediately before the appointed day, except as otherwise provided by this Constitution, or subsequently provided for by Act of Parliament, are hereby transferred to the respective County and City Assemblies.

(28) Lords Lieutenant, Vice Lieutenants and Deputy Lieutenants, and High Sheriffs and Deputy Sheriffs, in office immediately before the appointed day shall continue to serve under the terms of this Constitution in their existing Lieutenancy areas and Shrieval areas, but provision shall be made within twelve months to align the Lieutenancy and Shrieval areas with County and City boundaries in accordance with section 142.

(29) Coroners in office immediately before the appointed day shall be deemed to have been validly appointed under this Constitution and shall continue to serve as coroners under the terms of this Constitution; but existing coroners shall be reassigned to the coroner's areas specified in section 116 within twelve months of the appointed day.

(30) A person who immediately before the appointed day was a Privy Counsellor shall, if an English national, be deemed from the appointed day to have been lawfully appointed as member of the Privy Council of England under this Constitution; and a person who was a Privy Counsellor of the United Kingdom immediately before the appointed day, but who is not an English national under this Constitution, shall retain the style and title of a Privy Counsellor, but shall not be reckoned as a member of the Privy Council or England.

(31) Where any private person, company, or other for-profit enterprise, has, before the appointed day, been appointed as the Responsible Authority for any free zone under the Customs and Excise Management Act 1979 or any other law, that appointment is hereby revoked, and the County or City Authority in which that free zone wholly or principally lies shall

be the Responsible Authority for the free zone in accordance with the Customs and Excise Management Act 1979 or any other law regulating free zones.

(32) Nothing in this Constitution shall affect the Court of Chivalry, the office of the Earl Marshall, or the College of Arms, but the same shall continue as heretofore, unless otherwise provided by Act of Parliament.

Provided that appeals from the Court of Chivalry shall lie to the Supreme Court, not to the Judicial Committee of the Privy Council.

(33) This Constitution shall be directly enforceable as law.

(34) From the appointed day, existing law shall, to the extent possible, be interpreted and applied in ways that are compatible with this Constitution; but where there is any incompatibility between this Constitution and any other law, whether enacted before or after the appointed day, this Constitution shall prevail over the incompatible law.

(35) Until and unless otherwise provided by Act of Parliament, the royal style and title of His Majesty in right of England shall be 'Charles the Third, by the Grace of God, of England, the United Kingdom and His other Realms and Territories, King, Head of the Commonwealth, Defender of the Faith'.

(36) Until and unless otherwise provided by Act of Parliament, the City of Westminster shall be the capital city of England, the seat of Government, and the usual meeting place of Parliaments; but this shall not prevent Parliament from being summoned in any other place in England, according to section 105, if the Prime Minister, after consultation with the Speaker of the House of Commons and the Lord Speaker, reasonably considers the public interest to so require.

(37) For a period of twenty-four months immediately following the appointed day, it shall be lawful for His Majesty, on the advice of the Prime Minister or a responsible Minister, to make provision by Order-in-Council for the implementation of this Constitution, which may include the amendment or repeal of any Act of Parliament or other law enacted before the appointed day which is necessary to give effect to this Constitution or to bring existing laws into conformity with this Constitution.

(38) A territory which is not part of the United Kingdom may become an Associated State by means of a bilateral agreement between the Government of that territory and the Government of England, and by subsequent amendment of the Sixth Schedule to include that territory.

(39) The existing Constitutions of Overseas Territories shall remain in effect, subject to this Constitution, until amended or replaced under subsections (2) and (3) of section 177.

(40) The independence of any Associated State, Crown Dependency, or Overseas Territory shall not affect the continuance of the United Kingdom as a Union between England and the other Associated States, Crown Dependencies, and Overseas Territories.

# Index

EU authorised representative for GPSR:
Easy Access System Europe, Mustamäe tee 50,
10621 Tallinn, Estonia
gpsr.requests@easproject.com